EXTERNALITIES

EXTERNALITIES:

Theoretical Dimensions of Political Economy

Edited by
Robert J. Staaf
and
Francis X. Tannian

DUNELLEN

New York * London

© by the Dunellen Publishing Company, Inc.
386 Park Avenue South
New York, New York 10016
and
Kennikat Press, Inc.
Port Washington, New York

International Standard Book Number, hard cover: 0-8424-0063-x
                                      soft cover: 0-8424-0052-4
Library of Congress Catalog Card Number: 72-91991
Printed in the United States of America.

Contents

Part IV Political Economy and Externalities 177

Part V Collective Decision-making and Policy 235

SECTION A: THE TAX-SUBSIDY ALTERNATIVE 235

SECTION B: NEW DIMENSIONS IN COLLECTIVE DECISION-MAKING 273

INTRODUCTION

The concept of externalities in spite of some recent growth in importance has remained at the fringes of mainline economic theory. This is so even though the externality concept and its implications figure importantly in many traditional areas or subspecialties such as microeconomics and macroeconomics, welfare economics, public finance and urban-regional analysis. Indeed, most basic expositional textbooks and many model analyses in these subspecialties merely mention externalities or assume them away. The intent of this book and its selection is to bring together theoretical papers that treat the issue of externalities in a general way. While these articles emphasize theoretical arguments, the reason for troubling to put them together is not solely to honor the expansion of one parcel of economic theory. Instead, it is believed that the art of allocative decision making might be better handled by teachers, students, and practitioners if the theoretical dimensions of the externality notion were better understood.

Why are theoretical discussions of externalities significant? One reason lies in the nature of the real world. A second reason springs from what may be termed incompleteness in most standard presentations of economic theory.

In most countries of the world, population densities are rising in metropolitan areas. This means that supply (production) and demand (consumption) choices will increasingly be made by firms and individuals in ways that stand to affect other firms and individuals. Air pollution, water pollution, traffic congestion are examples of externality problems. Each is the outcome of actions of some parties (individuals) affecting the well-being (costs and benefits) of other parties (individuals). In countries like the United States, large amounts of private and public resources may be invested to cope with such spillovers. There are questions as to how much should be invested. If investments are made, what operational schemes should be followed? Should the agency operating be private, quasi-public, or public? Should taxes or charges be used to collect revenues? Exploration of externality concept formulatives may provide insights for decision-making policy, which policies may have higher probabilities of reaching standards of efficiency or equity.

Within the standard definition of economics as "the study of the allocation of scarce resources among alternative uses," micro theory has largely been concerned with "market" allocative mechanisms as the media for consumption and production choices. External to market allocative mechanisms such as congestion, blight, and pollution have normally not been explicitly integrated into the theoretical framework. Although some writers who place emphasis on choice situations might argue that the market versus nonmarket dichotomy is superficial, it is fair to say that much microeconomic writing seems to have been willing to assume that matters such as externalities lie across some conceptual demarcation line and that while externalities may merit mention and definition they are somehow outside the basic microeconomic body of knowledge.

Readings in Part I attempt to state the general terms and elements surrounding the externality scheme. Part II presents some early statements of the externality problem and is a series of papers that elaborate upon technical aspects of externalities from the production or supply side of the market. Parts III and IV encompass the contemporary controversy over the theoretical and operational methods of coping with externalities. A recurrent theme in this area is the role of information. Some writers have devoted attention to internalizing externalities to the market mechanism. Other analysts have attempted to elaborate upon a social welfare function, defining such a function not on the basis of individual choice calculus but emphasizing higher level goals such as the public interest.

Part V (A) is a series of articles covering several dimensions of the "classical" solution to externalities: tax-subsidy schemes. Part V (B) is a more general extension of V (A) encompassing other solutions, and more specifically, alternative organizational arrangements for coping with the externality problem. There is an array—a menu—of solutions to externality problems. Similarly an array of decision-making organizations can be established to implement these solutions. But as this section points out, both the solutions and the organizations set up to carry out solutions can themselves generate externalities. This section might be considered as an interrelated solution-organizational matrix. In selecting the articles, the major objective has been to use primarily pieces that deal with externalities in a general way. Many fine analytical pieces that deal with externalities in specific contexts such as pollution, housing, congestion, health, and development have been omitted. It was felt, however, that selection on the basis of general arguments would have wider appeal and serve better to place the externality concept on its own footing.

The introductory comments preceding each section should not be viewed as a critique of the articles, but rather as statements that seek to provide a cursory overview of the unifying (conflicting) themes, which from our perspective determined the classification of the articles in separate sections. In addition, these comments also seek to highlight the major points of the articles.

Many readers, as they proceed through this collection, may discover that many articles overlap. Others may feel that the classification by sections is somewhat arbitrary. Both kinds of reactions have legitimacy but this is both largely unavoidable and may not always produce harmful results. The order and grouping of articles presented is only one alternative among many we could think of. It is neither believed nor claimed that this set and order is necessarily the optimal arrangement. Rather, this is one arrangement, based on conceptual kinship between articles, that represents this literature. In any event it is felt that this collection brings together the main body of the theoretical externality literature in a single source. Perhaps some readers who through this collection have a chance to view the externality concept in a manner not previously possible will tend to agree with its editors that the externality concept is an emerging paradigm in economics and potentially a unifying concept for policy science.

PART I
EXTERNALITIES:
GENERAL DIMENSIONS

The two readings of Part I, taken as a section, are intended to orient readers to the general nature of the externality concept. Each author discusses the kinds of practical problems with which the externality concept is attempting to deal. These two papers are similar in that each explores the analytical heritage of earlier literature and surveys a range of theoretical and practical implications. Separately, the papers accomplish these goals by different modes of discussion. It is hoped that the perspectives of these two approaches, or modes, will serve to complement one another. One aim is to permit the reader to view the externality concept in different dimensions.

In "On the Nature and Significance of Social Costs," K. William Kapp states some reasons why social costs have grown in importance. He poses problems related to the nature of the social cost concept itself and to the policy relevance of microeconomic theory. Much attention is given to arguments attempting to establish a proper scope for the term "externalities." Kapp feels that narrow definitions of the concept (e.g., exclusion of pecuniary externalities) will affect policy analysis by economists and others on such problems as water pollution and development programs. The author concludes with an unspecified appeal for interdisciplinary analysis.

In the second reading, Sherman Krupp states that the externality concept is difficult and ambiguous. One way to see why this is so is to review some of the logical structures upon which microeconomic theory is built. In "Analytic Economics and the Logic of External Effects," Krupp explains some logic-based characteristics of microeconomics. He then goes on to relate certain analytical difficulties economists face with the externality concept to those considerations of logic which are built into the deductive framework of microeconomics.

For readers interested in an additional detailed survey of the externality issue beyond that offered here, the editors of this volume recommend an article by E. J. Mishan, published in the *Canadian Journal of Economics and Political Science* in 1965. In more than a survey, "Reflections on Recent developments in the Concept of External Effects," Mishan attempts to put order into the terminology and critically evaluates analysis of various writers. His survey paper opens with a list of 12 propositions or major analytical reference points surrounding the externality concept. The second part of Mishan's "Reflections" paper is a helpful but piecemeal critique of a list of conceptual contributions. Most of these contributions are presented in the following sections of this book.

On the Nature and Significance of Social Costs*

By K. WILLIAM KAPP

In a general way social costs considered as losses caused by productive activities and borne by third persons or as cost elements shifted to society as a whole have been a familiar topic in economic discussions ever since the early critics of classical political economy began to question the normative laissez-faire conclusions derived from this body of thought. Today air and water pollution are perhaps the most acute and the most generally recognized instances of social costs which arise in one form or another in connection with a variety of economic activities not only of private entrepreneurs but also of public authorities.

As a critical analytical instrument and as a possible stepping-stone for a reorientation of economic theory the analysis of social costs and their theoretical implications has a much shorter history. Thus it is only during the last 20 years that social costs have attracted increasing attention not only in connection with practical problems related to the formulation of policies designed to control or to minimize these costs but also with respect to their theoretical implications. This is perhaps not surprising if one considers that the concept of social costs refers to farreaching cumulative interdependencies which are assuming increasing significance not only in industrialized countries but also in less developed economies. Hand in hand with the empirical study of social costs goes the endeavour to define the concept with greater precision. This concern with precision is to be welcomed. Concepts which view and organize social phenomena from a new perspective are bound to prepare the way for new empirical explorations in the course of which they will lead not only to the discovery of hitherto neglected instances of social costs but are likely to disclose possible inconsistencies and indeterminacies of the original definition. Indeed, the systematic use of the concept of social costs as an instrument of empirical analysis has yielded new evidence of social losses and has reinforced the hypothesis that social costs are not minor exceptions to the rule but are typical phenomena. Their neglect either in theory or in practice can only have the effect of misleading us in our explanation of the economic process and of leading us astray in our policies of allocating resources.

*In the course of his discussion the Author reviews the following books: W. MICHALSKI, *Grundlegung ines operationalen Konzepts der Social Costs,* Tubingen 1965; K.H. STEINHOFLER, *Gesellschaftisschadigungen und Wohlfahrsokonomik,* Berlin 1966; C. UHLIG, *Das Problem der Social Costs in der Entwicklungspolitik–Eine theoretische und empirische Analyse,* Stuttgart 1966; and H. WOLOZIN (Ed.), *The Economics of Air Pollution,* New York 1966.

Reprinted by permission of the publisher: K. William Kapp, "On the Nature and Significance of Social Costs," *Kyklos,* Vol. XXII (Fasc. 2, 1969), pp. 334-347.

The theoretical evaluation of the phenomena of social costs has not followed a uniform pattern. Economists brought up in the neoclassical tradition of micro- and general equilibrium analysis have frequently chosen to protect the conventional system by introducing new or more explicit assumptions in an effort to strengthen the model against the obvious theoretical challenge raised by social costs. Thus, some analysts have taken the position that their neglect is the result of a lack of information or is due to an inadequate system of adjudication of damages caused and sustained. From this point of view all that may be necessary is to assume complete transparency of the situation and a perfect judicial system. Similarly, by juxtaposing social costs (viewed as so-called external diseconomies) to external economies and by assuming that the former tend to be annulled by the latter it is believed that the traditional model can be saved. Alternatively, the theorist may be tempted to redefine the unit of analysis (e.g. the firm) in such a fashion that 'social costs' external to a firm are borne by the unit (i.e. an industry, a region or a sector). Social costs are thus 'internalized' and made to disappear from the scheme of analysis. The aim of these and similar analytical techniques is always the same: to protect the traditional analytical model against empirical phenomena which contradict its basic assumptions and which stand in the way of the traditional interpretation of the economic process.

However, these analytical devices cannot satisfy those who disagree with traditional economic analysis. These dissenters, among whom socialists and institutionalists have played a major role, hold that social costs are normal and typical phenomena, and are moreover of such a character as to put in question the whole theoretical equilibrium theory including its practical conclusions. Indeed, the fact that part of the costs of production can be shifted to third persons or to society as a whole is merely another way of saying that costs and hence profits depend at least to some extent on the power of the individual firm to do so. In short what the conventional theory treats as given is in fact already the result of a constellation of market or non-market interdependencies between units of a heterogenous character and with different degrees of economic control and domination. A network of interdependencies connects the various producing and consuming units. Firms of unequal size and with unequal bargaining power and with more or less access to, and control of relevant information—including the possibility of manipulating such information in one's own favor—all these elements are integral parts of contemporary economic life from which economic theory can abstract only at the price of losing its relevance for the interpretation of economic processes.

In other words, theoretical representation of this network of relationships requires a framework of analysis which transcends the theoretical scope of neoclassical economics. Even the useful but relatively limited concept of externalities which ALFRED MARSHALL developed in connection with his concept of the representative firm (constant costs) and which has more recently

4

been enlarged to accommodate a great variety of interdependencies under dynamic conditions, has remained a more or less empty box particularly as far as the phenomena of social costs are concerned. The existence of social costs is always an indication of precisely those cumulative dynamic interdependencies between economic units which raise serious doubts as to the validity and purpose of some of the most essential assumptions of economic theory. For if economic units with unequal power are able to shift part of their costs to others—and moreover are able to play their sales and hence consumers' demand through sales promotional activities—market costs and prices must be regarded as more or less arbitrary and indeed unreliable measures of economic rationality. Hence it becomes necessary not only for the purpose of evaluating and measuring social costs but also for the determination of priorities to elaborate a theory of social value in the sense of value to society based upon objective, i.e. empirically ascertained criteria of what is necessary and essential for human life and survival.

The four books which provide the occasion for the preceding restatement of previously expressed views on the phenomena of social costs and their implications for economic theory[1] are concerned in varying degrees with some of these problems. W. MICHALSKI'S *Grundlegung eines operationalen Konzepts der Social Costs* starts with a survey of the history of the concept of social costs. While this survey contains the most complete bibliography on the topic to date one cannot help feeling that the author has been rather generous not to say indiscriminate in including authors in his list. As a result of this procedure MICHALSKI conveys the impression that the term 'social costs' is more indeterminate than is actually the case. Indeed, the greater the number of authors considered, the greater the danger that the term 'social costs' will be found to refer to different phenomena or, alternatively, that different terms are used in the literature to refer to the same phenomena. In this context MICHALSKI complains of a semantic confusion without taking sufficiently into account that many of the different terms used are essentially synonyms or represent merely clarifying adjectives (e.g. 'unpaid costs', 'uncompensated damages', 'uncharged disservices'). Moreover, there is the fact that social costs are being viewed by different authors from different perspectives. Had MICHALSKI considered these different perspectives he might have looked upon the variety of terms in a less critical light. Moreover, in the social sciences and particularly with respect to social costs, we are often faced with an inescapable residuum of indeterminacy, which has its basis partly in gaps in our knowledge, partly in actual conditions and complex interdependencies and partly also in a lack of homogenous generally accepted (human) evaluations of the relative importance of actual losses. It must be regarded as a sign of loose thinking and logical error—if not of hidden bias, all of which are detrimental to scientific analysis—if we try to overcome this indeterminacy by formulating concepts with greater precision than is justified by the nature of the conditions under study and by our knowledge. For this reason one should resist one's legitimate desire for precision in concept formation and not push beyond the point of diminishing returns. After all, what matters most is to avoid concepts which are empty, irrelevant and value-loaded[2].

At this point we cannot avoid raising the fundamental question of whether concept formation in the social sciences should be guided exclusively by our desire of arriving at quantitative statistically measurable definitions which lend themselves to a smooth incorporation into pre-established analytical systems or whether we should insist that our concepts maintain an actual relationship to observable empirical conditions. Indeed, in the social sciences concepts are not the byproduct of measurements as in the physical sciences: They are the result of a selective process of abstraction which is necessarily guided by the specific perspective of the theorist including his value premises and hidden bias. Different theorists invite the reader to abstract from different phenomena and to categorize observations in different ways. Hence the plethora of terms and concepts, many of which remain ambiguous particularly at the beginning and continuous effort is required to give them clarity and precision.

According to MICHALSKI the term social costs is being used first with reference to costs or cost elements which are not reflected in entrepreneurial or public accounts; second with reference to lost opportunities or benefits foregone as a result of the fact that the outcome of the process of production and distribution falls short of some notion of optimum; third with reference to public outlays made necessary by remedial action designed to eliminate or minimize social costs shifted to third persons or society as a whole and finally with reference to actual or total costs of production. Is this use of the term social costs with apparently four different connotations evidence of a semantic confusion? *Prima facie* it would appear so and would indeed be problematical if no attempt were made to state clearly the sense in which the term is being used in a particular context. If some authors appropriate the term social costs in order to refer to the total or actual cost of production in the sense of costs to society they give it an apparently more harmless meaning than those who prefer to use the term with reference to costs not reflected in conventional cost accounts. Nevertheless it is important to point out that these authors admit at least implicitly that private or public costs diverge from actual (total) costs. It is this divergence which is the essential point stressed by the concept and the theory of social costs. Similarly, the use of the term social costs with reference to costs of public investments designed to remedy or minimize the negative effects of productive activities constitute an extension of the original meaning of the term. If this extension is carried to the point where the term becomes synonymous with public outlays in general regardless of whether or not they serve the purpose of remedying negative effects of productive activities we would, indeed, use the term in a loose and undifferentiated manner. However, as long as the term social costs is used with reference to public outlays designed to remedy the meaning in the sense of 'unpaid' or 'unaccounted' costs to those losses and damages which society has considered to be of sufficient importance to warrant public impression that public outlays either effectively measure the full extent of social costs or that they actually eliminate them. For this reason it would be preferable to look upon public outlays for remedial action merely as an indicator, and, for that matter, a very incomplete one, of the relative magnitude of social costs not accounted for in conventional cost accounts.

More fundamental questions arise if we use the term social costs in the sense of social opportunity costs. For, in this case we not only widen its meaning considerably but are immediately confronted with the problem of defining in some meaningful way the notion of rational or efficient use of resources. We do not think that formal equilibrium economics provides adequate standards in this respect not only because its theoretical assumptions are obviously and deliberately fictitious but also because it considers as given a whole range of institutions whose social value is taken for granted but which may have the effect of preventing the use of resources in any other way. The theory of social costs has always regarded this positivistic acceptance of institutions as a severe self-imposed limitation of neoclassical analysis. The use of the concept of social costs in the sense of social opportunity costs provides a tool for the critical analysis and appraisal of the institutional *status quo*. In other words, anybody who is willing to use the term social costs in this broader and critical sense will have to make explicit that he departs from the traditional positivistic framework of analysis. This may be a source of annoyance to some theoreticians but does not constitute a source of semantic confusion.

Those who use the concept of social costs as an instrument of analysis in order to trace the possible negative effects of productive activities will not consider it essential to incorporate it in the theoretical framework of neoclassical analysis. It is true there are points of contact between the concept of social costs and MARSHALL's notion of 'externalities' and PIGOU's social marginal product. In both instances we discover divergencies between entrepreneurial outlays and total costs or between private and social net products. But what do we gain by an attempt to incorporate social costs into the framework of external economies and diseconomies or for that matter, into welfare theory? PIGOU developed his concept without reference to MARSHALL's notion of external economies, which, incidentally, was never intended to include social costs into the body of economic reasoning but served the rather specific purpose of introducing into an essentially static system of analysis the (theoretically) not necessarily compatible dynamic aspects of externalities.

Criticism of the concept of externalities and more recent refinements in welfare theory have led to a distinction between 'pecuniary' externalities which are the result of price and cost changes and are transmitted via the market and 'technological' and 'psychological' diseconomies which are transmitted directly i.e. outside the market. If we accept this distinction we prepare the way for a redefinition of the concept of social costs which in effect would seriously narrow its scope. This is precisely what MICHALSKI attempts when he proposes to confine the concept exclusively to those 'externalities' which are primarily of a technological origin[3]. With this definition MICHALSKI aims at the exclusion of virtually all pecuniary and monetary effects of innovations transmitted by the market in the form of higher costs including capital and human losses. As a justification for this narrower definition of social costs the author advances the twofold aim of analytical convenience ('analytische Zweckmässigkeit'), and of operational relevance for a policy of economic growth. By analytical convenience is meant in this context a seamless incorporation of the new concept into existing theory (Nahtlose Einfügung des neuen Konzepts in die bestehende ökonomische Theorie', S.80). The exclusive concentration on the goal of maximizing G.N.P. is justified by two explicit assumptions, namely that voluntary savings and planned investments are equal and that employment and income distribution are optimal. In other words, the annoying and disturbing conditions of economic instability, unemployment and income inequality which give rise to social costs of major proportions are excluded from the very beginning by assumption and are thus omitted from any further consideration. Is this a legitimate procedure for the formation of concepts? MICHALSKI is aware of the fact that his procedure and particularly the omission of market interdependencies resulting in pecuniary social losses rests entirely on an analytical technique which enables the analyst to regard disadvantages transmitted via markets (e.g. losses of purchasing power of one group) as being normally offset by corresponding advantages (gains of purchasing power) of another. In this way there appear to arise no net social losses from the point of view of society as a whole.

The exclusion of psychological effects which certain productive activities and distributional practices may have on the worker or the consumer is justified on the ground that we possess no generally agreed and objective criteria for their determination. Hence they are said to be 'uninteresting' and without relevance for policy formulation (pp. 95−6). This way of deciding issues of concept formation leaves much to be desired particularly if we consider the role which frustration, dissatisfaction and despair of disadvantaged minorities, untrained youths and of unemployables plays in the social life of some of our contemporary complex societies. To the extent that pure economic theory continues to ignore these psychological effects on the ground of analytical convenience the less relevant and the more misleading is it likely to become for public decision-making.

In the actual world of markets a wide variety of pecuniary negative effects continue to arise as a result of market relations. Their elimination from the concept of social costs will therefore distract attention from such important problems as the impairment of the human factor by occupational diseases and industrial accidents, the accelerated exhaustion of non-renewable resources, the negative effects of innovations on capital assets and labor income and employment. For, actual markets offer no guarantee that these negative effects are offset by corresponding benefits which in the pure model would be taken as evidence of 'zero' social costs. In fact, even if benefits and negative effects were equal and thus may be regarded as zero it would still be true that the monetary gains and advantages of one group are purchased by income reductions and disadvantages of an entirely different group—a fact which the global, aggregate approach has a tendency to conceal. In short, in the actual world of affairs which admittedly bears no resemblance to the assumed conditions of the analytical model, pecuniary negative effects continue to arise via market interdependencies. It is not important how we call these losses—terminological problems are never that crucial—but it is necessary precisely from the point of view of a workable and relevant theory that we do not exclude them from our empirical and theoretical explorations. In fact, by assuming them away we run the risk of reverting to the analytical optimism which has characterized the reasoning of economic liberalism in the past. This indeed seems to be the inevitable result of the intended seamless incorporation of the concept of social costs into the conventional wisdom. Analytical convenience, statistical measurability and alleged operationality of theory for policy purposes thus turn out to be doubtful criteria of concept formation, doubtful because their real effects not only narrow the concept but deprive it of many (although, indeed, not all)[4] of its critical implications for a methodical analysis of economic processes in modern industrial society and as we shall see in underdeveloped economies.

Among the many new insights which the study of underdevelopment has yielded is the realization that any simple association of social costs with modern technology and industrialization will not stand up under empirical scrutiny. Underdeveloped countries have their own ways of producing important social costs. The systematic use of the concept of social costs as an analytical instrument for the determination of causal interdependencies within the context of the development process is therefore an important research task likely to yield new knowledge relevant both for the definition of social costs and the formulation of development strategies and policies.

CHRISTIAN UHLIG[5] considers social costs as side-effects of human action. Following E. SPRANGER[6] he makes the interesting point that all action takes place within, and has repercussions on, a natural and social environment which has its own logic and is subject to specific regularities and laws. If these regularities are either not known, ignored or neglected the outcome of decisions is likely to differ from what one intended to achieve or, even if the original goals are attained, there may be unintended effects of a negative or harmful character. This is indeed a useful and more generalized way of looking upon the phenomena of social costs.

However, as far as the definition of social costs is concerned UHLIG follows MICHALSKI and wants to confine it to extra-market or technological interdependencies, although he has no illusion about the relevance of the competitive model for the interpretation of underdeveloped economies. This, it seems to us, underlines the weakness of the narrower concept of social costs. Indeed, neither labor nor land nor commodities nor money markets,† especially in the field of agriculture, are market mechanisms in the sense in which economic theory uses the term. They are 'squeezing mechanisms' to appropriate a useful term suggested by MYRDAL, particularly if we consider the powerful economic, politico-administrative position of landlords, money lenders and merchants on the one hand and the absence of economic alternatives for tenants and landless laborers and their lack of education and information on the other.

9

Under these circumstances, losses sustained by the dominated group may far exceed possible gains and advantages of politically stronger groups. To look upon such losses as being normally offset by the gains of the dominating group and hence disregard them as social costs appears to be a particularly unconvincing attempt to define a problem out of existence. Indeed, the whole procedure of balancing social costs by so-called quasi-rents can only be viewed as a misrepresentation. Here again it becomes evident that the formation of concepts in accordance with established theoretical systems which bear no

However, even the systematic use of the narrower concept as an analytical instrument yields, particularly with reference to underdeveloped countries, an impressive picture of their range and significance. For example, among the social costs in underdeveloped countries are the damages resulting from water pollution particularly the losses connected with development projects (salinization, water logging, greater incidence of malaria and other waterborne diseases). UHLIG analyzes also the social costs in agriculture and forestry such as soil depletion,erosion and deforestation. His summary of quantitative data indicates that these social costs are of considerable importance and are likely to assume increasing proportions if protective measures for their prevention or minimization are not made part of development planning and project design. The author makes it abundantly clear that rational development planning requires careful prior research in order to determine beforehand the relevant technological and social interdependencies with a view to exploring possible alternative courses of action and project design. His conclusions support the thesis that the line between the technological and the economic, between means and ends are not as clear and determinate as our traditional static theory likes to assume. The inner logic of technical (and social) interdependencies which we find in underdeveloped as well as highly industrialized economies can be ignored only at the peril of causing the failure of both the macro- and the micro-economic plan. As a matter of fact, this applies to any system of economic organization or indeed to any form of decisionmaking. No development strategy, indeed no economic policy whether formulated or carried out in New Delhi or Peking or for that matter in Washington, Moscow or Bonn can make a legitimate claim to rationality in a substantive sense of the word as long as it ignores the phenomena of social costs. In order to explore the relative costs and benefits of alternative designs especially of micro-economic projects rational planning demands in all cases prior research which—depending upon the complexity of the problems under consideration—must enlist the cooperation of scientists from both the social and the natural disciplines. The relevance of social costs for the formulation of development policies derives from the fact that they saddle third persons and public budgets with considerable expenditures for remedial measures and outlays thereby binding scarce resources which are thus not available for other uses. For this reason it must be regarded as rather unconvinging when UHLIG maintains with HIRSCHMAN—apparently because he deliberately excludes from his concept of social costs the negative effects

10

transmitted by market interdependencies—that the old 'capitalist trick' of shifting some costs to third persons or to society would lead to a more rapid rate of economic development. Certainly, whenever the impairment of the human factor interferes with the productivity of labor the avoidance of such costs through protective labor legislation and the maintenance of minimum standards of health and human efficiency would doubtless be more conducive to a higher rate of labor productivity and hence of economic development than the current more or less complete neglect of these losses. Nor can we agree with UHLIG'S qualified justification of shifting the social costs to the traditional sector because such shifting could be regarded as a form of forced saving or dishoarding. While we agree with the thesis that substantial (potential) surpluses are used for less essential non-productive purposes the deliberate shifting of social costs to the traditional sector is hardly a suitable measure for their mobilization—particularly if the mobilization takes the form of *ex-post* remedial action for damages caused (i.e. costs not fully borne) by the modern sector. The mobilization of the potential surplus would call rather for deliberate institutional changes—a problem which has to be faced openly instead of surreptitiously by the shifting of social costs in the futile hope that this action may channel available inputs and potential surpluses to more essential uses.

Despite these and other qualifications we feel that UHLIG'S systematic use of the concept of social costs as an analytical instrument for the determination of causal interdependencies and the tracing of social costs in the context of the development process is an important contribution to the literature dealing with the political economy of poverty and backward areas in general. The exploration and the *ex ante* avoidance of social costs in underdeveloped countries belongs to those tasks which must be solved if the development process is not to bog down under the destructive effects of social losses and a misallocation of resources.

In contrast to MICHALSKI and UHLIG K.H. STEINHÖFLER[7] aims at an incorporation of the concept of social costs into a theoretical system which is still to be developed. The author is convinced that both the old and the new welfare theory treat the problem of social costs rather as a side or marginal problem. STEINHÖFLER distinguishes between social costs resulting from an avoidable destruction or impairment of valuable capital assets or other positive values and social opportunity costs in the sense of missed opportunities or lost potential benefits. He rejects the principle of modern welfare economics as a sufficient and workable framework for the evaluation of relative gains and losses because it is based upon static individualistic estimates of utilities and disutilities—an evaluation which he regards as particularly inadequate in all cases where social costs take the form of social opportunity costs which, of necessity, extend into the future and possess a time dimension. The author favors an interpretation of economic and productive processes in terms of a system of balances of energy inputs and useful outputs expressed in terms of some unit of effective mechanical labor. He advocates the use of a coefficient designed to measure efficiency of energy transformation—a coeeficient which, while always smaller than 1 will be greater or smaller depending upon the relative size of

11

necessary (actual) inputs and avoidable social costs. This obviously technical efficiency concept is not intended to replace but rather to supplement the economic rationality concept which relates valued inputs and valued outputs. The author does not indicate how the two types of efficiency measures—the technical and the economic—are to be coordinated nor does he answer the question as to the relative weight one is to attribute to each of the two. He too seems to question the traditional sharp analytical distinction between the technical and the economic.

A concluding short part surveys in summary fashion the possible ways and means open for the control or minimization of social costs. The author makes the point that it would be much more difficult to induce public authorities and planners to minimize social costs than the planners of private concerns—a statement which in this general form may require some qualification with reference to the political structure of the society under discussion. For instance social costs could be controlled or minimized by a more adequate representation of all persons affected by innovation and investment decisions. Similarly a more liberal system of compensation by means of social and wage policies, the provision of facilities for retraining and adult education as well as subsidies to the costss of moving would doubtless reduce the residual elements of opposition which innovations may encounter. Probably the most effective way of minimizing social costs in public and private enterprises would be the systematic exploration of interdependencies and the elimination of negative effects of technological innovations by giving high priority to these objectives in any intermediate and long-term research and development plan[8].

The foregoing discussion has made it clear, we hope, that the problem of social costs presents challenging difficulties to economic analysis. It remains doubtful whether these difficulties can be coped with adequately within the traditional boundaries of economic science. Neither the theory of resource allocation nor applied economics seem to provide us with adequate categories for the theoretical treatment of social costs or practical guidelines for their control. This is precisely one of the important conclusions arrived at by some of the contributors to the Symposium entitled *The Economics of Air Pollution*[9]. Indeed, instead of abdicating to the techniques and perspectives and to the narrow categorical limits of individual disciplines in which our scientists, physicians and engineers—and one may add economists—are trained, we need to develop what L.A. CHAMBERS, a biologist, calls 'a technology of complexity' designed to analyze and cope with the problem arising from man's deliberate or inadvertent tinkering with ecological systems of a perplexing complexity. What is needed, according to this view, is nothing less than a review of national needs and costs within the broader scientific framework of a *system* of sciences of environmental health the purpose of which would be to survey and analyze the whole complex of interrelationships raised by air pollution, radiological fallout and milk and food sanitation. CHAMBERS[10] sees the main problem of social costs in the notable absence of acceptable indices of values other than dollars and of expressing costs only in units of commercial exchange; he makes the

12

point that a society whose several systems of ethics do not condone sacrifices of individual life and health to the common good or to economic growth is confronted with uneasy ethical paradoxes as soon as it begins to impute (monetary) values to contemporary life and human welfare. The cliché of a 'calculated risk' which accepts the impairment of some relatively 'unfit' persons in some indefinable numbers—unfit that is to survive in a polluted environment —is today a popular device of neglecting the task of controlling social costs. This perspective shows the impasse of an economic analysis which asserts that an adverse benefit-cost ratio must necessarily mean a vote against air pollution control measures or, for that matter, speak against the control of social costs. In this context, the economist WOLOZIN observes that 'the limitation of benefit-cost analysis, the unresolved debate on the goals and tools [...] of economic analysis in general—all of these stand in the way of obtaining objective criteria for expenditures of public funds on the control of air pollution'[11]. Instead of all attempts to pass from 'given' individual tastes and preferences to a pattern of social decision-making WOLOZIN favors an approach based upon MUSGRAVE'S concept of 'social wants' (which are in line with consumers' preferences) and 'merit wants' (which are not) and which, because of their importance (i.e. their 'meritorious' character), must be satisfied through the public budget if necessary against existing want patterns and consumers' preferences. In other words, the process of determining public expenditures required for the control of social costs (associated with air pollution) will have to be based upon socio-political and psychological considerations and factors which must be built into the theoretical framework if we are to take account of the complexities created by modern industrial technologies. WOLOZIN concludes this part of his discussion with a few pertinent questions: 'What is the nature of that rational choice which tolerates dangerous levels of air pollution? Are economic preferences immutable? How do they change over time?' To what extent has modern economics which lays claims to an empirical science been concealing phenomena rather than elucidating them?[12] While he does not answer these questions he is doubtless correct in suggesting that 'there are certain costs and benefits which either defy measurement or at best can only be measured in units which are not comparable'[13]. Indeed, the attempt of 'putting the decision-making tools within [the] market framework may have retarded the development of effective means to handle the economics of social policy'[14].

It would carry us too far afield to review the other papers in this volume in an equally detailed manner. Suffice it to call attention to a report of a study designed to measure the costs of air pollution damage which pleads for disaggregation, cross-section data rather than time series and criticizes existing data on social costs in general[15]. That our data on social costs are inadequate derives largely from the fact that our statistical data gathering systems were never designed to trace the social costs of productive activities. As a matter of fact our statistical data reflect the interests and preoccupations of most of our social scientists, and social costs, at least until recently, were not among them. RIDKER who, on the whole, is more confident about the prospects of measuring the social costs of air pollution suggests that instead of waiting for a complete set of evidence on damages before acting, we 'should perhaps use an incremental approach in which we try out alternative controls and simply observe whether the electorate appears to be satisfied with them or not'[16]. LESTER GOLDNER[17], in a sobering case study of public policy formulation related to air pollution control in Boston, raises the disturbing question of whether industrialized America can long afford its present system of decision-making. The current situation, is marked by widespread public apathy on the part of the disadvantaged, inarticulate groups on the one hand, and the existence of highly organized and articulate groups on the other. The latter are not only strategically located and have easy access to various administrative and legislative decision-making institutions but also tend to oppose effective control action because their economic interests are at stake. In the middle of this constellation we find the Federal, State and Municipal agencies of public health beset on both sides with sufferers—those who are burdened with the negative effects of present industrial practices and those who will have to bear the costs of enforced control of social costs. That is to say from the perspective of society 'the difficulty of being rational' in the substantive sense of the term economy lies in the unequal distribution of power and influence between those two groups—a distribution which economic theory has long ignored or considered as given. The result of this tacit acceptance of the *status quo* as regards the unequal distribution of influence and power can only have the effect of distorting the assessment of social costs—particularly if we continue to use overt behavior and declared preferences as relevant indicators and criteria of what is desirable and economically justified.

Conclusions: The concept of social costs was developed as an analytical instrument and as a critique of the method and scope of classical and neoclassical economic analysis. As such it stressed certain dynamic cumulative consequences and interdependencies within and beyond the narrow system of relationships which economic analysis selected as its subject of investigation. While concepts should be clearly defined and made as precise as possible this legitimate scientific desire for precision becomes a sign of loose thinking if concepts are given a purely fictitious precision which bears little or no relation to the nature of the problems under discussion. Social costs refer to consequences of productive activities and policy decisions which, for several reasons, carry an inevitable residuum of indeterminacy but which are nevertheless real and important—even though their approximate magnitude can be determined only after careful factual study and which in many instances call for an evaluation based upon criteria other than market values.

Any attempt to adjust the concept of social costs in such a manner as to incorporate it into the existing body of formal economic theory can only have the effect of narrowing and thereby neutralizing the critical implications of the concept by depriving it of its central content and aim: namely to call attention to highly relevant and potentially destructive side-effects of productive activities not recorded in traditional cost accounts. It is true such side-effects borne either by third persons or by society at large are not the only effects of economic activities or decision-making for there may be benefits equally diffused and unaccounted for in conventional cost accounts. Rather than assuming that these social benefits offset in a general way the social costs, the task of the social scientist interested in the analysis of actual causal sequences of events is to identify and to trace both the social costs and the social benefits with a view to ascertaining their significance and magnitude. In this attempt it will be necessary to accept at least initially a certain measure of indeterminacy—an indeterminacy which reflects as much our incomplete knowledge of causal relationships as the lack of uniform judgments as to the relative importance of the respective costs and benefits. In this endeavor to identify and to determine social costs and social benefits it would be futile to expect much help from formal economic theory because its logico-mathematical deductions are not concerned with actual causal sequences in the world of experience but rather with the elaboration of hypothetical sequences under chosen conditions ms pg. 346 of rationality one seeks to determine by means of these mathematical constructs are hypothetical and fictitious because they presuppose the absence of precisely those conditions which give rise to social costs and social benefits (e.g. the diffusion of costs and benefits throughout society, non-market interdependencies and circular cumulative causation, transparency of the situation, etc.).

Social costs and social benefits emphasize the limitations of our traditional concepts of economic rationality. Their occurrence supports the conclusion that the formal rationality of a sub-organization like that of a firm, of an industry or even of the economy as a whole in equilibrium can coincide with an over-all irrationality of the social system of which the economic process is a part. Admittedly the concept of social rationality is an elusive one which cannot be formulated simply in terms of market prices because many of the relevant social costs and social benefits have no market value and, even if they did or could be assigned such value for purposes of 'objective' cost-benefit calculations, we would still be faced with the problem of their political evaluation. Such an evaluation is possible only and hence presupposes careful and continuous *ex ante* exploration of the overall interdependencies and consequences of policies and investment decisions. Technical feasibility surveys and a systematic elaboration of objective criteria of human well-being as the basis for the determination of the essential restraints, aims and priorities will have to play a central role in this context. In short, the concept of social rationality must of necessity be a substantive concept which takes account of actual levels of satisfaction and requirements.

This will call for wider rather than narrower concepts of social costs and social benefits than those which emerge from any attempt to incorporate these notions into traditional economic theory. The concept of social costs will have to include, in addition to the so-called 'economic' consequences those destructive effects and human sacrifices which a modern industrial society and modern technology impose on the physical and psychological health of the individual on the one hand and his actual freedom of determining his choices, his action, his life and his leisure on the other[18]. Similarly social benefits will have to be defined, as already indicated, with reference to essential human needs, objectively determined and politically agreed upon, instead of positivistically taken as given particularly in a world which has increasingly resorted to their manipulation by advertising and sales promotional activities. Such a widening of the concept of social costs (and of social benefits) implies radically new modes of thinking. Indeed it calls for a type of analysis which incorporates the methods and results of other social disciplines. Economic analysis will have to tackle these tasks if it takes seriously its claims to remain an empirical science which intends to place human needs into the center of its analysis.

NOTES

1. Cf. K. WILLIAM KAPP, *Social Costs of Business Enterprise,* New York, Bombay 1963, pp. 281–301, and 'Nationalokonomie und rationaler Humanismus', *Kyklos,* vol. XXI, 1968, pp. 1–25.
2. GUNNAR MYRDAL, 'Value Loaded Concepts', in: H. HEGELAND (Ed.), *Money, Growth and Methodology,* Essays in Honor of J. Akerman, Lund 1961, pp. 273–5, and PAUL STREETEN, 'The Use and Abuse of Models in Development Planning', in: *The Teaching of Development Economics* (Eds. K. MARTIN and J. KNAPP), London 1967, pp. 60–5. See also GUNNAR MYRDAL, *Asian Drama,* Vol. III, New York 1968, particularly Appendix 1, 6 and 16, also pp. 1912–19.
3. 'Social costs im Sinne der vorliegenden Analyse sind nunmehr alle primar technologisch bedingten, durch Unternehmungen verursachten, externen Belastungen, welche von Dritten, namlich von Haushalten, von Unternehmungen oder von der Gesellschaft als ganzer, in Form von erhohten Aufwendungen bzw. Ausgaben oder in Form von realen Beeintrachtigungen oder Schaden getragen werden.' *Op.cit.,* p. 109.
4. In fact, by recognizing the occurrence of social costs in the form of primarily technological nonmarket interdependencies, MICHALSKI weakens none of the serious doubts regarding the rationality of the allocation and steering mechanism of the market.
5. *Das Problem der Social Costs in der Entwicklungspolitik–Eine theoretische und empirische Analyse,* Stuttgart 1966.
6. *Das Gesetz der ungewollten Nebenwirkungen in der Erziehung,* Heidelberg 1962.
7. *Gesellschaftschadigungen und Wolfahrtsokonomik,* Berlin 1966.
8. This is for example the case in the Czechoslovak Republic where the exploration of the effects of innovations and the positive planning of man's social and economic environment in harmony with human requirements is reported to be one of the priorities of the research and development plan. Cf. BEDRICH LEVCIK, 'Technischer Fortschritt in Osteuropa, *Atomzeitalter,* No. 3, March 1968, p. 128.
9. H. WOLOZIN (Ed.), New York 1966, cf. especially p. 13.
10. *Risks versus Costs in Environmental Health, Ibid.,* pp. 51–60.
11. *Ibid.,* p. 189.
12. *Ibid.,* p. 178
13. *Ibid.,* p. 182.
14. *Ibid.,* p. 179.
15. R.G. Ridker, *Strategies for measuring the Costs of Air Pollution, Ibid.,* pp. 87-101.
16. *Ibid.,* p. 100.
17. *Air-Pollution Control in the Metropolitan Boston Area: A Case Study in Economic Policy Formation, Ibid.,* pp. 127–61.
18. That there arise in modern industrial society a great variety of social costs such as the dramatic consequences of uncontrolled urban growth, the destruction of the natural and aesthetic environment and the degeneration of social values and social structure goes perhaps without saying. For a convincing survey of these new dimensions of social costs see ERICH EGNER, 'Die Konsumgesellschaft, Wirklichkeit oder Aufgabe?' (esp. pp. 523–35), *Jahrbucher fur Nationalokonomie und Statistik,* Bd. 181, Heft 6 (1968), as

well as ALAN MOOREHEAD, *The Fatal Impact,* London Penguin Books, 1968, and ALFRED BUHLER, 'Die messianischen Bewegungen der Naturvolker und ihre Bedeutung fur Probleme der Entwicklungslander', *Acta Tropica,* XXI, 4 (Basel), 1964, pp. 362—82.

Analytic Economics and the Logic Of External Effects*

By SHERMAN KRUPP

The complexity of subject matter in a science often creates difficulties. But difficulties arise from relationships between concepts as well as from the relationships between things. A problem of this kind is external effects or externalities in microeconomic price theory. Externalities involve statements about the properties of aggregates, when these properties are not wholly deductible from their atomic elements. It is a difficulty which lies at the boundaries of microeconomic price analysis and which concerns the scope of some familiar derivations in deductive economic theory. Therefore, I will discuss some logical limits of deduction in microeconomic theory. External effects seem to elude normal derivations of microeconomic theory as well as to receive less than their share of attention. I believe these difficulties may become more understandable through analysis of the logical ambiguities of the concept.

This paper consists of two parts. First, I will introduce a few ideas, familiar to philosophers, in order to explain the logical character of the problem of externalities—a type of problem common to many deductive theories. Second, I will try to relate the economic side of the problem to these logical and philosophical considerations.

COMPOSITION LAWS AND DISCONTINUOUS DEDUCTIVE CHAINS

Pure economic analysis is a deductive form of explanation. Ordinarily, deductive formulation of a science proceeds by postulating simple, primary units and simple laws of combination for these units. Gravitation for mechanical physics or maximization in economic analysis provide the basic concepts from which the laws are generated. The laws of mechanical physics follow from assumptions concerning mass-points and describe their relations to one another; maximizing units are the atomic elements of economic analysis. In deductive systems, combinations of units obey the same laws as individual units. Theorems governing the operation of

*For their critical review of this manuscript, the author wishes to thank Wells Keddie, Melvin Leiman, Fritz Machlup, Helen Raffel, Eli Schwartz, and Herbert Spitz.

Reprinted by permission of the publisher: Sherman Krupp, "Analytic Economics and the Logic of External Effects," *American Economic Review,* 53 (May 1963), pp. 220-226.

aggregates are deduced from laws operating in the smaller units and their combinations. The scope of a theory describes the range of application of its theorems. Thereby, theorems which apply to the more elementary units of the system are presumed to apply throughout all further deductions within the system. Ideally, the scope of a theory is coextensive with the range of its subject matter.

Among the axioms that determine theoretical scope are the composition laws. Composition laws govern the extension of relationships derived from the micro-units. In its simplest form a composition rule permits a theorist to say that the laws that apply to two units are also true for 200, or 2,000,000. Thus the axioms that apply to one or two individuals, along with composition rules, permit the extension of relationships derived from these axioms to larger sectors.

The type of composition rule which may be applied to units depends on the relationships assumed to hold between those units—in particular, their inter-dependence. An example of a composition rule is the law of constant returns to scale. According to this law if all input factors are added in the existing ratio, there will be proportionate increases in the volume of production. Because it is assumed that no other external factor affects the ratio of the inputs, the law implies that they are independent of such external factors. Moreover, the action of an input A on input B is assumed to have no significant feedback. In micro-economic theory the independence of the units within some designated range permits the same axioms to apply to all units of the system; that is, all units are subject to the same composition law. As I said before, theorems derived from units, with composition laws, may be applied to aggregates of these units. For example, the laws that apply to the firm and the theorems that derive from these laws are theoretically applicable to the industry and the economy.

But if one of the factors becomes lumpy, the law of constant returns to scale ceases to apply because the logical requirements of the law are no longer being fulfilled. The point at which a factor becomes lumpy is where the input factors influence one another in a way not accounted for by the composition law of constant returns to scale. Thus, composition laws may cease to apply at certain levels of complexity or aggregation. When this occurs, the implications that are deducted from the individual units (say, the firm) apply only with important reservations and conditions to the larger fields (say, the industry).

It is obvious, therefore, that the laws of composition may at some point stop yielding significant results. In physics, for example, theorems based on the independence of mass and velocity are no longer useful as velocities approach the speed of light. In economics, theorems based on the independence of firms are no longer useful when firms enter into collusion. Collusion, as a kind of interdependence, cannot be explained by equilibrium analysis which assumes the independence of the units. Interdependence arises which is not deducible from the initial postulates. The laws and relationships that apply at the new level of analysis are frequently undefined. When this occurs, the theorems may have reached their outer limits, their boundaries.

A theory may be extended beyond the limits created by its initial axioms by the addition of new variables. That is, the feedback of the new relationship may be interpreted as a new variable introduced into the initial situation. Marshall's "external economies" are such an addition (an addition by means of which the situation ceased to be held constant). His definition of external economies concerned "how far the full economies of division of labor can be obtained by the concentration of large numbers of small business of a similar kind in the same locality." External economies are present only when units are aggregated. Marshall described external economies as a characteristic of the industrial aggregate. He released new variables from his pound of *ceteris paribus* to account for interdependence due to external economies, thereby preserving the main theorems of his analysis. Increasing returns resulting from economies internal to the firm imply monopoly; if progress can be accounted for by increasing returns due to external economies, competition has no necessary restriction. Although Marshall described external economies, he did not deduce them from his micro-units. In fact, his use of the conceptual device, "the representative firm," enabled statements about properties of the firm to be derived from a description of the industry. The industry had been described by theorems deduced from the firm in combination with externalities. In turn, these relationships were then incorporated in the representative firm. He defines this as a firm which has normal access to the economies, external and internal, "which has normal access to the economies, external and internal, taken of . . . the economic environment generally."

Where composition rules are not entirely adequate, the addition of new variables is one solution. An alternative way of handling the theoretical problem posed by the emergence of new relationships is the modification of the composition rules. A new composition rule may be introduced when at some level, or for some range of problems, the assumption of independence is inadequate. Here, the modified theoretical system retains many of the elementary axioms and laws of the original theory, although the manner in which the units are combined is altered at the new level. Some axioms, however, may be abandoned and controversy usually arises regarding selection. A familiar illustration of this is the socialist model of Oscar Lange, in which many of the axioms of microequilibrium theory are retained, although crucial problems are submitted to collective rather than private criteria for judgment.

We have seen that there are limits to the scope of deductive theories. The introduction of new variables and the modification of composition laws are two methods of extending the scope of a deductive system. The question is one of bridging the gap at the outer limits of deductive explanation.

However, some problems cannot be handled adequately no matter how a theory is adjusted. While it may be true that some explanations are impossible within a given theory, it is also true that poor explanations occur when sound theories are pushed too far.

But how are these logical considerations relevant to external effects? Externalities are not simple observables; they are not things. They arise as a consequence of certain microeconomic concepts and they reflect conceptual difficulties at the boundaries of microeconomic theory.

EXTERNALITIES AND DEDUCTIONS

The problem of externalities concerns the interdependence that emerges when individual units are aggregated with consequences not predictable under theorems derived from the individual units. Externalities are introduced at the point in theory where deductive explanation becomes unsatisfactory. This point I have called a boundary. The failure of the main theorems to resolve important problems requires at a minimum either the introduction of new variables or the incorporation of new composition laws into the axioms of the theory. Where the failure is complete, the theory itself must be abandoned.

The problem in logical analysis may be illustrated by the following examples from the field of economics: externalities in relation to rising supply price; externalities in relation to the distinction between marginal private and marginal social cost; and externalities in relation to direct physical interdependence.

Rising supply price is defined as the increase in price that is necessary to bring forth an increase in the scale of output. The scale of output for the industry is external to the decisions of any one firm. The shape of the supply curve, therefore, may not be directly deducible from the production functions of individual firms. Its shape depends upon the relative elasticity of the supply of factors. A rising supply function is commonly attributed to diminishing returns or rising transfer payments. What is important in this familiar illustration is that the industry supply curve can be deduced only when the external diseconomies have been added to the sum of the cost curves. At this point a break has occurred in the deductive chain. The original axioms are not sufficient for predicting the new relationships. The theory has accounted for some complexities but not for others. New variables must be released from the pound of *ceteris paribus* to account for the influence on output of a large number of firms in an industry because the joint effect on output of a large number of firms is not the simple sum of their individual effects. Although implications deduced from the independently conceived micro-units are valid laws, the inclusion of external effects on the micro-units yields results different from those obtainable by Walrasian methods alone. Shifting the focus to the industry-wide situation thus requires refinements of logical procedure. The addition of a new variable may adequately comprehend this new situation—the relationship between the firm and society—or it may not. If not, a new level of theoretical complexity may be required. The possibility of such a level is one of the implications to be drawn from Pigou when he said that industries operating under increasing or decreasing returns make greater or lesser contributions to the social product.

The concept of externalities can act as a bridge between the private and social points of view. Because conditions external to an industry are internal to society, externalities focus on the relationship between the individual firm or industry and the whole of society. Allyn Young has used the concept of externalities to describe a crucial factor in economic progress. According to Young, industrial aggregates themselves facilitate the development of new products, new tools, and new industries: ". . . the progressive division and specialization of industries is an essential part of the process by which increasing returns are realized. What is required is that industrial operations be seen as an inter-related whole". The concept of externalities facilitates this vision of a unified economic field by acting as a bridge between microdeductions and inferences about the larger aggregates. It introduces a kind of interdependence which is not directly deducible from microtheory. Since microtheory develops from the private point of view, and since economic progress is a social concept, a term that will permit the transformation of one into another is extremely important. For Young, externalities provided such a concept.

The relation between marginal private product and marginal social product again brings the logical problem of composition rules to the fore. Marginal private product is the value of an incremental increase in output from the point of view of the producers of that product. Marginal social product is the value of the increase in total output from the point of view of society. This change in reference alters the structure of the problem. It may be handled by changing the composition laws. Such a change would be unnecessary if the derivations from the micro-units yielded theorems that applied equally to the aggregate. If the theorems do not apply equally, a change in the composition law may be necessary.

In microanalytic theory investment is assumed to flow to the sectors of highest private return. External effects may make the marginal private product of this investment diverge from the marginal social product. For example, marginal private gains from basic research seem to bear no necessary relation to marginal social product greater than the marginal private product. If there is no way of deducing consequences in the public sector from operations in the private sector, no single composition law can be said to apply. It may not be necessary, however, to reject altogether the assumption of independence and the composition laws dependent on it. Schumpeter's concept of progress, for example, derives from internal economies in the micro-units. The sum of the effects of the micro-units yield aggregate economies. The laws of the aggregate, for Schumpeter, could be deduced from the laws of the units. However, if for some ranges of theory deductions from the micro-units do not apply, new laws of composition may be required.

Where direct physical or social interdependence exists, the aggregate of firms produces effects other than those expressed by price: industrial smoke affects real estate values; ecological changes are introduced by pesticides; a hospital complex reduces absenteeism; education raises productivity beyond the increased efficiency of the recipient of education. In these examples, the activities of one sector contribute benefits or losses to third parties in the form of side effects which are not reflected in the price paid for the economic activity under consideration. Microeconomic theory fails to provide an adequate theory of the economic consequences of direct inter- dependence. New complexities are introduced by the combined effects of inter- dependence—complexities which the addition of single variables may not satisfac- torily explain. Whether these consequences are trivial or not, the failure of micro- economic theory to provide a theoretical basis for evaluating them virtually disregards their existence. Consequently, they are often neglected, sometimes by inattention and sometimes by intent. The theory does not force consideration of the economic consequences of physical or social interdependence. Might not adequate treatment of these relationships require abandoning the assumption of independence logically required by certain basic postulates of the system as its stands? The theoretical problem posed by the concept of external effects, which Scitovsky has called "one of the most elusive in economic literature," is most strongly presented by direct physical or social interdependence.

CONCLUSION

The application of microeconomic theory to instances of externality constitutes a challenge to the scope of existing theory. When theoretical development permits the adaptation of a theory to new extensions of scope, the range of the theory is increased and the validity of its premises is reinforced. The value of an explanatory system is demonstrated by the theory's capacity to grow in coherence and breadth, accounting for more phenomena more accurately. At present, the difficulty of adapting theorems drawn from axioms about independent units to permit handling phenomena of common interdependence must be recognized as a major structural problem in microtheory.

External effects derive from interdependence. As we have seen, microeconomic theory has adapted differently to diverse kinds of interdependence. In the case of rising supply price, theoretical scope can be extended by interpreting the externality as a variable and adding it to the main theorems of the system. Direct interdependence permits no such solution. Moreover, if interdependence becomes crucial for the analysis of marginal social product, the inability of microeconomic theory to deal with this aspect of economic behavior would be a severe limitation to the usefulness of the theory.

The use of the concept of marginal social product, it has been suggested, may require modification of the composition laws before certain kinds of externality can be included in the scope of microeconomic theory. Problems in deductive economic explanation arise when interdependence emerges which is not directly deducible from the initial postulates of the theory. The applications of microeconomic price analysis to larger fields is limited by these forms of interdependence. How to make direct application of unmodified microanalysis to larger fields is still an open question as the theory stands.

REFERENCES

1. Gustav Bergman, *Philosophy of Science* (Univ. of Wisconsin, 1957).
2. Richard Bevon Braithwaite, *Scientific Explanation* (New York, 1953).
3. D.C. Broad, *The Mind and Its Place in Nature* (London, 1925).
4. Arthur Danto and Sidney Morganbesser, eds., *Philosophy of Science* (New York, 1960).
5. Herbert Feigl and May Brodbeck, eds., *Readings in the Philosophy of Science* (New York, 1953).
6. Sherman Krupp, *Pattern in Organization Analysis* (Philadelphia, 1961).
7. Henry Margenau, *The Nature of Physical Reality* (New York, 1950).
8. Alfred Marshall, *Principles of Economics*, 8th ed. (London, 1947).
9. Ernest Nagel, *The Structure of Science* (New York, 1961).
10. A. C. Pigou, *The Economics of Welfare*, 4th ed. (London, 1948).
11. Gilbert Ryle, *Dilemmas* (London, 1956).
12. Joseph Schumpeter, *The Theory of Economic Development* (Harvard Univ. Press, 1934).
13. Tibor Scitovsky, "Two Concepts of External Economies," *J.P.E.*, Apr., 1954, pp. 143-151.
14. P. Wiener, ed., *Readings in the Philosophy of Science* (New York, 1953).
15. Allyn Young, "Increasing Returns and Economic Process," *Econ. J.*, Dec., 1928, pp. 527-42.

PART II
EXTERNALITIES: PRODUCTION
AND MARKET STRUCTURE

The main issues in the readings of Part II are the relationships of externalities to production theory and to market structure. Such analysis has been called the "technical" side of externality discussions. If external costs and benefits of a firm's technical processes of using resources and generating output occur, what are the possible impacts on market structure and welfare?

As the literature developed, controversy arose over the adequacy of the purely competitive model to take "external" to market factors into account. Corrective policy devices to accommodate for divergencies between so-called ideal outputs which included externalities and the result of the competitive market model were advanced. These policy correctives amount to an array of tax-subsidy schemes. Following Adam Smith's theorem that "the division of labour is limited by the extent of the market," the notion of externality as we know it today was submerged and became an implicit argument in production theory. It was not until Alfred Marshall that "external" and "internal" economies and diseconomies became explicit. Marshall's tax-bounty scheme, as a welfare proposition to handle diseconomies and economies, became a classic solution which was later elaborated upon by Pigou. Piero Sraffa, in his article "The Laws of Returns under Competitive Conditions," took exception to Alfred Marshall's methodological treatment of externalities in a partial equilibrium framework.[1]

The writings of J. M. Clark on "Social Overhead Capital" from the production side and Thorstein Veblen on "Conspicuous Consumption," further developed by Duesenberry, are related classics, but have been excluded from the readings presented here for lack of space and because they are readily available elsewhere.

Part II, developed as a separate section, is not intended to give the impression that the role externalities play in affecting production is not also treated in subsequent parts of this book. Rather, the papers of Part II are presented as a section to give emphasis to the fact that externalities have a purely technical side which may affect market structure. Further, it was felt that by introducing the reader to the technical side of externalities and other concepts such as pecuniary versus technical externalities, a way would be paved for more comprehensive analysis, as when consumption and production externalities are brought together.

The first article, by Howard S. Ellis and William Fellner, is concerned with Pigou's analysis of the divergence between ideal and competitive outputs with the presence of externalities. Distinctions are made with respect to reversible and irreversible economies. This article is primarily concerned with pecuniary externalities, that is, interdependence through the market mechanism versus what the authors call "real" externalities. The second article, by Dean A. Worcester, extends beyond the first and uses neoclassical analysis to analyze pecuniary and technological (e.g., real) externalities under various market models. Worcester reduces various types of externalities into eight categories and states that "any technological economy or diseconomy can be converted into a pecuniary one by appropriate pricing of inputs."

Articles three and four are primarily concerned with technical externalities or interdependence which does not flow through the market mechanism. J. E. Meade's article distinguishes externalities into "unpaid factors of production" and "creation of atmosphere." Returns to scale for industry versus society and a tax-subsidy scheme are discussed. Tibor Scitovsky's article explores the concept of externalities at two levels: (1) Equilibrium theory and (2) the theory of industrialization in underdeveloped countries. The analytical distinction between technical versus pecuniary externalities is also made.

NOTES

1. Robert V. Ayres and Allen V. Kneese in "Production, Consumption, and Externalities," *American Economic Review* (June 1969) deal with this issue in perhaps a more comprehensive way and at a different level than Sraffa envisioned.

External Economies and Diseconomies

By HOWARD S. ELLIS AND WILLIAM FELLNER

I. INTRODUCTION

Along with its answer to the principal problem which it set for itself as to how competition allocates resources amongst various uses, neo-classical economics bequeathed to the present generation the much debated proposition that competition causes output under "diminishing returns" to exceed, and under "increasing returns" to fall short of, an output corresponding to the social optimum. Since this issue involves only negligibly any disagreement as to the economic facts, since it is indeed almost a purely quantitative problem not complicated by ethical or other preconceptions, one may find difficulty in understanding how theorists such as Marshall, Pigou, Viner, Graham, Hicks, and Lange could be ranged squarely against Allyn Young, Knight, and Stigler. The answer seems to be that apparently simple technical concepts are often fraught with confusing ambiguities; and the extensive discussion of this subject over a period of years[1] reveals that these ambiguities have already become perennial.

The effort to resolve the issues disputed amongst such distinguished protagonists is in itself an interesting undertaking in the development of theoretical ideas, but there is also no lack of pragmatic justification. The interpretation of certain commonly employed cost functions, of opportunity cost, and of marginal *versus* average cost can not be purely "academic" matters. Furthermore, the Marshall-Pigou proposals of taxes upon "industries of diminishing returns" and bounties upon those of "increasing return," and the Pigou-Graham proposals of a protective tariff in certain instances upon much the same theoretical argument, lead directly to important questions of fiscal and commercial

Reprinted by permission of the publishers and authors: Howard S. Ellis and William Fellner, "External Economies and Diseconomies," *American Economic Review*, 33 (September 1943), pp. 493-511.

policy. Finally the recent descriptions of price systems under socialism show that the present issues intimately affect not only the formulation of policies in a private enterprise economy but the very concept of the socially optimum employment of resources under (a more or less ideal form of) socialism.

Throughout the period of classical political economy it was a settled but vaguely supported conviction that the price of agricultural produce tends to increase under the influence of diminishing returns, but that "it is the natural effect of improvements to diminish gradually the real price of almost all manufactures."[2] This bad mixture of a dubious "law" of economic history on the one hand, and a truncated part of the static principle of combining proportions on the other may have been engendered originally out of resentment against the Corn Laws and the landed gentry; but it seems to have been perpetuated to the present day through simple confusion. Marshall attempted to give quantitative precision to the notion that "diminishing returns" somehow represent a less favorable application of economic resources than "increasing returns."[3] His demonstration, which ran in terms of the effect of taxes and bounties upon consumers' surpluses in the two cases, is sorely limited by the author's admission that it requires quite special elasticities of demand and supply and that it assumes that marginal utility of money to be constant; and it is entirely destroyed by the failure of the author to include producers' surpluses into the social surplus to be maximized.[4]

The advocates of the tax-bounty thesis have mostly referred to Pigou rather than to the original Marshallian version of the thesis. We turn first to Pigou's analysis so far as it pertains to "diminishing returns" (in his own terminology), which includes also rising transfer costs, leaving until later the case of "increasing returns" (in his terminology), which actually means external economies.

II. DIMINISHING RETURNS AND RISING TRANSFER COSTS ("EXTERNAL DISECONOMIES"), WITHOUT EXTERNAL ECONOMIES

In *Wealth and Welfare*,[5] the first edition of the work later to be more widely known as *The Economics of Welfare*, Pigou draws two positively inclined cost functions (as in Fig. 1), the lower of which, labeled S_1, he calls "a supply curve of the ordinary type," and the upper, labeled S_2, "a curve of marginal supply prices." The function S_1 is further described as showing at each point the cost or price at which the corresponding output on the abscissa can be maintained in the long run, and function S_2 as showing at each point "the difference made to *aggregate* expenses"[6] by the production of one more unit. With austere brevity, Pigou concludes directly from the description of the two functions that the intersection of S_1 with the demand schedule at C corresponds to output and price under competition, whereas the intersection of S_2 with the demand schedule at I represents the correct output[7] under an ideal allocation of social resources.

In the universe of discourse of Pigou's problem, economic theory now operates with a number of cost functions presently to be de-

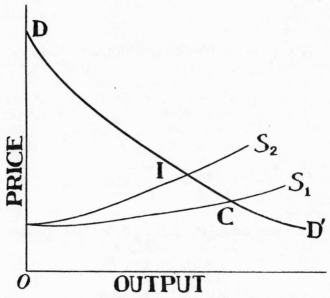

Fig. 1—Pigou's Cost Functions.

scribed; but from the exposition of *Wealth and Welfare* it is impossible to discover which of three mathematical functions Pigou intended to employ. Retrospectively, in answer to criticisms, Pigou acknowledged one possible interpretation but denied that he had intended to draw his conclusions on this basis, proposed another interpretation, and finally, even upon this interpretation, limited his thesis to a special argument concerning international trade.

In a review of *Wealth and Welfare* appearing about a year after the publication of the book, Allyn Young hailed Pigou's S_2 curve as a "new and powerful instrument of economic analysis" especially as applied to monopoly, but denied that it proved a divergence of competitive from the ideal output.[8] Young's criticism also did not distinguish the three interpretations we shall point out. In fact it did not need to do so, as it is equally valid upon any of them; but Pigou did not believe this to be the case, and so we must examine the merits of each separately.

The three possible interpretations of Pigou's functions arise from the fact that increasing costs in an industry may come from (1) diminishing returns due to the presence of a factor which is fixed in supply for the industry; (2) rising transfer costs due to the presence of a factor which can be drawn in greater amounts from other industries only by a rise in its price; or (3) a combination of (1) and (2). In 1920 Pigou focused attention upon the *first* interpretation by admitting it as a legitimate reading of his cost curves but not what he had intended.[9] This interpretation permits us to give unambiguous definitions to the S_1 and S_2 curves of Figure 1 and to trace out the reasoning on this basis. The "supply curve of the ordinary type," S_1, in Pigou's language is the usual "marginal cost curve," that is, the curve indicating the cost of production of the marginal unit of output; and S_2 a function which adds to S_1 at each point the *aggregate* increment of costs on all intramarginal units of output.[10] Thus, if an expansion of output from 50,000 to 51,000 units involves a rise of cost at the margin from $1.00 to $1.01, the ordinate of S_1 at 51,000 units is $1.01, and the ordinate of S_2 is the difference between 50,000 times $1.00 and 51,000 times $1.01, or $1,510, divided by 1000, or $1.51.

On the present interpretation of Pigou (which he acknowledged as a possibility) increasing costs arise solely from rising transfer costs; and to make this interpretation explicit, in Figure 2 we give to S_1 and S_2, respectively, the distinctive labels of ε and γ. Pigou's S_1 (our ε) shows the cost of the marginal unit in isolation, or more explicitly: marginal cost excluding all increments of transfer cost; alternatively ε shows also *average cost* per unit of output, including transfer rent. Pigou's S_2 (our γ) shows "marginal costs" also but in a different sense—marginal cost including the *total* increment to transfer costs *on all units*.

Pigou originally maintained that the intersection at C represents competitive equilibrium, but that the ideal allocation of resources would be given by reducing output through appropriate taxation to a magnitude given by the intersection at I. Allyn Young accepted this description of competitive equilibrium (as do all parties to the dispute) but denied that the *total* increment of cost to the industry could be regarded as a cost to society. In Pigou's excellent paraphrase, "In other words, according to Professor Young's view, the excess of marginal supply prices [our γ] in industries of diminishing returns [read: 'increasing costs'] over the corresponding supply prices [our ε] is merely a nominal excess of money paid, and not a real excess representing resources employed."[11]

If Young had spoken the magical word "rent," it seems probable that Pigou would have capitulated completely. For Young could have put his proposition in these words: "If the expansion of an industry gives a factor a higher per unit remuneration, whether or not that

30

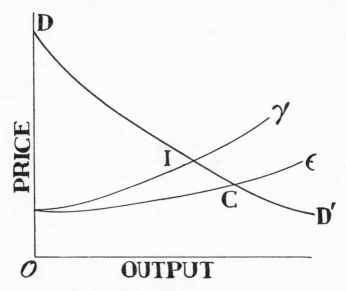

Fig. 2—Rising Transfer Costs.

higher price induces a greater aggregate [social] supply of the factor, the units already being supplied earn producers' rents [or increase the previous rent]; and rent is not a cost in social resources." Consequently if the output of a commodity expands, the rise in transfer costs (*i.e.*, in the value) of the intramarginal units of the transferred resource is not part of the marginal social cost of producing the commodity under consideration. The marginal social (opportunity) cost of transferring resources yielding n units is merely the cost of transferring the resources required for the production of the n-th unit. This cost is expressed by ϵ not by γ. The γ function is not a social cost curve because it includes increments to rent.

Pigou accepted this criticism without reservation so far as concerns transfer costs; and, we may add, he accepted it gracefully and without seeing, at that time, its full import. For he proceeded to argue in the sentences immediately following that his conclusions are valid for diminishing returns, although not for rising transfer costs:

The reason why diminishing returns in terms of money [read: "increasing costs"] appear when they do appear is, in general, not that the money price of factors employed is increased, but that that proportionate combination of different factors, which it is most economical to employ when $(x + \Delta x)$ units of commodities are being produced is a less efficient proportionate combination than that which it is most economical to employ when x units are being produced; and the extra cost involved in this fact is real, not merely nominal. For these reasons Professor Young's objection, as a general objection, fails.[12]

31

Employing a useful notation introduced by Mrs. Joan Robinson,[13] we show in Figure 3 the functions germane to diminishing returns, transfer costs assumed constant.

Mathematically the definitions of α and β, respectively, are precisely the same as for γ and ε, since both α and γ satisfy the requirements of Pigou's S_2, and β and ε the requirements of S_1. Only the economic implication is changed: α refers to marginal cost including the total increment of Ricardian rent, and β to marginal cost excluding Ricardian rent or average cost including average Ricardian rent. The function δ, to which there is no counterpart in the case of rising transfer costs, is the familiar curve of average cost excluding rent. According to the first edition of *The Economics of Welfare,* the intersection at C shows the competitive solution, as before; and the intersection at I again is held to represent the socially ideal output, though this time on the grounds that less efficient combinations of factors signify a social "extra cost."[14]

However real the "extra cost" from these grounds, the application of Young's reasoning proves it to be adequately included in β, the cost *at the margin, i.e.,* the incremental cost in the variable factor. Unless rent is a social cost, it is erroneous to envisage the social marginal cost as including the increment to rent as in the function α.

To maximize the aggregate of producers' and consumers' surpluses, the relevant magnitude is *DCA,* not *DIA,* if the marginal utility of

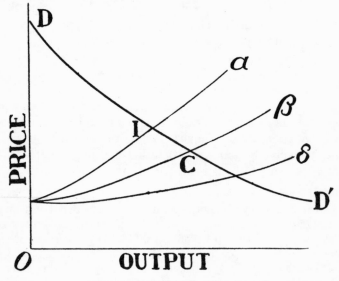

Fig. 3—Diminishing Returns.

money is assumed to be constant. Dropping the assumption of constant marginal utility for money renders it impossible to express the aggregate surplus of consumers and producers by areas lying between demand and supply curves. It still remains true, however, that the optimum output will be reached at the intersection of the demand curve with β, not α. The price will still express for each consumer the value of the change in total utility occasioned by the marginal unit of the commodity, although it will express this change in terms of the variable marginal utility of money rather in a constant unit of measurement.

If marginal social cost equals price, it also equals the value of the marginal addition to the utility of each consumer as expressed in terms of the marginal utility of the money stock actually owned by him. This, however, implies that, given the distribution of wealth and income, the β intersection is optimal. If resources were to be shifted out of the industry in question, each consumer would lose more utility, as expressed in terms of money, than the saving in social cost; and if further resources were to be shifted into the industry, the addition to social cost would outweigh the gain in utility.

That his reply to Young was inadequate, Pigou admitted four years later in the *Economic Journal*,[15] adumbrating a revised statement in the second edition of *The Economics of Welfare*. The revision consisted in the abandonment of the general thesis that, under increasing cost, output under competition exceeds the ideal, and the adoption of the very limited proposition that a divergence occurs only from the viewpoint of one nation against another when it pays agricultural rents to foreign owners in the price of imports.[16]

This limited version of the proposition, retained in the later editions of *The Economics of Welfare*, requires the use of functions which express the effects of rising transfer costs as well as those of Ricardian diminishing returns. In Figure 4, average costs as affected by diminishing returns but not by rising transfer costs[17] are shown by β; average costs as affected by rising transfer costs but not by diminishing returns[18] are shown by ε; and average costs as affected by both forces in conjunction are shown by φ. The function φ may be described further as marginal cost excluding all Ricardian rent and all increments to transfer rent, or as average cost including average Ricardian and average transfer rent. To this magnitude, at each point, θ adds the *total* increment of transfer rent on the intramarginal transferred units, and the *total* increment of Ricardian rent.[19] Pigou's argument with respect to foreign trade would then mean that rents transferred abroad, whether those rents originated in diminishing returns or rising transfer costs, are costs to the domestic economy; the competitive purchases of such imports would run to the foreign output as determined by φ, whereas ideally the importing country should buy only the foreign output as determined by θ.

33

But even the foreign trade argument, which had been adumbrated by Graham a year[20] previous to Pigou's decision to restrict the argument to rents disbursed to foreign owners, is subject to rather severe

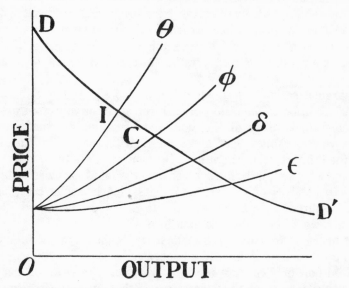

Fig. 4—Diminishing Returns and Rising Transfer Costs.

limitation if not complete rejection. After all, the doctrine of optimum allocation in all of the versions here considered is a "cosmopolitan" doctrine in that it does not distinguish between surpluses accruing to domestic owners *and consumers* on the one hand and surpluses accruing to foreigners on the other. The qualifications required to allow for policies distinguishing between the interests of domestic economic subjects and foreigners are much more extensive than would be suggested by the limitation of Pigou's argument to such increases in rents as are included in the value of commodity imports. One would have to exclude from the aggregate to be maximized all consumers' surpluses accruing to foreigners; and also all producers' surpluses accruing to foreign stockholders or other foreign owners of domestic enterprise.

The Pigou doctrine in the latest and narrowest version would lead one to believe that in a competitive world the "national"—as opposed to the "cosmopolitan"—aggregate of surpluses is increased by a tax reducing the output of industries which, by importing raw materials, increase the value of foreign resources. The cosmopolitan net surplus is surely reduced by such a tax; whether the "national" net surplus is increased or reduced depends on how the aggregate of consumers' and producers' rents accruing to domestic economic subjects changes when other industrial activities are partly substituted for those connected with raw material imports.

To replace the "cosmopolitan" approach with the "national" would require a reinterpretation of the entire doctrine no less fundamental than that which would be required if the distribution of wealth within the economy were not to be accepted as "given." In both cases the "votes" of the consumers and of the producers whose behavior determines the allocation of resources is held to be weighted incorrectly. The important qualifications arising from this consideration must either be disregarded, which means accepting the cosmopolitan point of view and taking the distribution of wealth and income as given; or they must be dealt with in the framework of a broad sociological approach extending to questions such as reprisals in international relations, the potential stability of different patterns of distribution within social communities, etc. In no event does it seem satisfactory to confine the reinterpretation of the "cosmopolitan" doctrine to industries which, by importing raw materials, give rise to foreign producers' rents.

The preceding analysis is not concerned with the genuine diseconomies arising from phenomena such as the smoke nuisance, the wasteful exploitation of natural resources, etc.

So far as concerns the present heading—diminishing returns and rising transfer costs—we have found: (1) There is no divergence between the ideal and competitive outputs. (2) Pigou originally believed that output under competition is excessive because the total increment to rent is not included as cost. (3) Under the force of Allyn Young's criticism that rents are not social costs, Pigou gradually attenuated his thesis to the case of imports produced under rising supply price. (4) Writers who invoked the authority of Pigou after 1924 on what had once been his *general* thesis did so unjustifiably.[21] (5) Even the restricted foreign trade thesis has little or no validity as a single qualification because the entire problem would have to be reformulated if this qualification, in conjunction with more important ones, were to become valid. (6) Since rents are not social costs, the relevant cost function—one which maximizes the total of consumers' and producers' surpluses—is marginal cost in the sense of costs of the marginal unit of output alone ($=$ average cost including average rent), that is, ε or β, and *not* marginal cost including the total increment of rent, that is, γ or α. (7) The atomistic single seller notices and acts correctly upon the costs of ε or β; he does not notice and should ignore the additional costs incorporated in γ or α.

III. EXTERNAL ECONOMIES

Economists upholding the special tax in the diminishing returns case also maintain the necessity of a bounty for the realization of external economies. One of the most debated issues in the entire discussion of the tax-bounty thesis has always been the reality of external economies.[22] Many supposed examples have proved to be spurious or far-fetched; but we do not propose to begin upon the painstaking inquiries into techniques and economic history which would be necessary to appraise the possibilities. Among the many difficulties and complexities, however, there are a few certainties.

One is that if an "external economy" is an internal economy to another *industry,* the outcome is either monopoly in the second industry, or else the complete exploitation of the internal and hence the disappearance of the external economies.[23] If the outcome is monopoly in the second industry, costs are very unlikely to decline in the first, since a monopolist will respond to a rise in demand with a reduction of price only (1) in case he is operating in the downward range of his *marginal* cost curve (and the elasticity of the new demand curve is not *sufficiently smaller* than was that of the old one to offset the downward slope of the marginal cost curve); or (2) if the new demand curve is *more* elastic than was the old one (and the upward slope of the marginal cost curve in the relevant range is insufficient to offset this circumstance).

Usually the monopolist will raise his price if demand increases, in which case such economies as are internal economies in the "second"

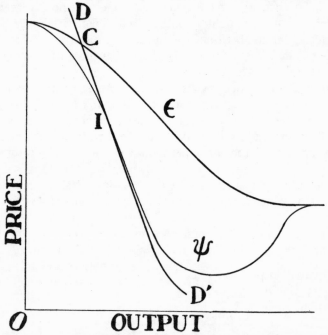

FIG. 5.—External Economies in the Absence of Diminishing Returns and Rising Transfer Costs.

industry will not lead to the realization of economies in the "first" industry. As Mr. Sraffa has suggested, the concept of external economies may, however, be rescued by illustrations not depending upon lowering the price of a commodity supplied by another *industry,* but upon the better rendering of *services.*[24] The development of a skilled labor force, the migration of suitable labor, the appearance and progress of professional and trade associations and journals, and the like, are not to be dismissed as unrelated to output in every case.

When and if external economies exist, they must be incorporated into the structure of economic theory; but it must be confessed that the theoretical treatment of this subject still leaves much to be desired. The first step in reconstruction is a clear description of the cost functions and of competitive equilibrium.

In Figure 5 we assume that there is no "scarce" factor for this particular industry, and that its demand for factors is atomistic so that an extension of output does not cause rising transfer costs. The function ε signifies, as in earlier contexts, average cost, or marginal cost in the sense of costs for the marginal output in contrast to smaller outputs.[25] The function ψ is defined somewhat analogously to γ and α as the total cost difference on *all* units (marginal and intramarginal). If there are no external economies (or none unexploited), ε and ψ coincide in a horizontal line; if there are, ψ lies below ε. Thus without economies the per unit cost might be \$4.00 for all outputs. With economies the first "unit" costs \$4.00 if only one unit is produced; if "two units" are produced the second unit costs \$3.00 and the costs of the first unit also decline to \$3.00. At an output of two units $\varepsilon = \$3.00$, $\psi = \$2.00$.

We employ the symbol ε because external economies have exactly the opposite significance *to the industry* as rising transfer costs. One must be on guard against an extension of the meaning of ε from the behavior of *output* costs to the price of the variable factor; if ε declines because of external economies, factor price almost necessarily rises. This probable rise, however, is disregarded in the graphic representation and in the foregoing example, where the industry in question is assumed to be atomistic and consequently constant factor prices are assumed.

The equilibrium to be expected from competition is determined by the intersection of DD' and ε. The costs of production at the margin will be equated to price. The circumstance that further expansion of the industry would reduce intramarginal costs will not produce such an expansion, since to the right of C costs at the margin fall short of price. Now it has been argued that optimum allocation in these circumstances requires subsidizing the industry under consideration in such a manner as to make its output expand to I, corresponding to the intersection of DD' with ψ (instead of ε).

This argument was presented by Pigou at the time when he first attempted to establish the proposition that increasing cost industries tend to overexpand in free competition. But while the proposition relating to increasing cost industries was gradually limited to the foreign trade proposition previously discussed, the thesis that decreasing cost industries do not expand sufficiently was and is maintained by him and other authors.[26] It is worth pointing out that shifting resources into decreasing cost industries is not the same thing as shifting resources out of competitive increasing cost industries, since competitive industries may also operate under constant costs, not to speak of industries operating under monopoly and monopolistic competition. Besides, the proposition that the social optimum output of increasing cost industries is determined by S_2 functions (rather than S_1 functions)[27] would be basically different from the proposition that the social optimum output of decreasing cost industries is determined by S_2 functions (rather than S_1 functions), even if subsidizing decreasing-cost industries could be carried out only by taxing increasing-cost industries. We shall now be concerned with the second of these two propositions.

The reasoning by which it can be shown that the argument relating to increasing cost industries is faulty does not affect the validity of the argument relating to decreasing cost industries. The crucial point here is that, while in conditions of increasing supply price, the *rise* in intramarginal costs is rent rather than social cost, the *decline* in intramarginal costs attending the expansion of decreasing cost industries is a social economy, *i.e.*, social cost with a negative sign. One might therefore conclude that in conditions of decreasing supply price the ψ function expresses marginal social cost; and that the social optimum output is I instead of C.[28] The competitive output, one might conclude, is determined by the socially "incorrect" cost function ε, which fails to express the marginal saving in intramarginal social cost, that is, the saving in social cost on intramarginal units of the resource attending the increase in total output by a marginal unit. The ψ function contains the necessary correction; and a permanent bounty inducing the production of I is required to achieve optimum allocation. It would have to be added that a two-dimensional presentation, like that in Figure 5, overstates the deviation from the optimum in case the industry is not atomistic. In this event the ψ curve shifts upward as output expands, since opportunity costs rise as resources are shifted away from other employments.

This conclusion is correct if the external economies are "reversible": the ψ function actually expresses marginal social cost in case the economies appear with an expansion of output, but *disappear* if and when output subsequently contracts.[29] In the event of irreversibility

38

the problem acquires different characteristics, however. It may be suggested that irreversible external economies are much more significant than are reversible ones. Certain industries must usually reach some stage of growth before a geographical region starts to develop significantly and also before human and material resources become more specialized. But it is rarely true in these cases that a contraction of the output of any one industry would lead to a loss of the economies in question.

If irreversible external economies are potentially present, competi-

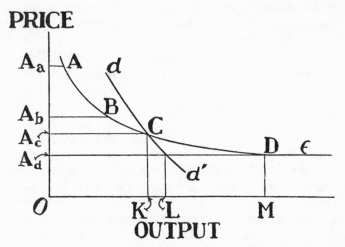

Fig. 6—Irreversible External Economies in the Absence of Diminishing Returns and Rising Transfer Costs.

tive equilibrium fails to achieve optimum allocation; at the same time I ceases to be the optimum output and the bounty required to achieve optimum allocation is temporary.

In the circumstances now considered the ψ function loses its significance. What happens in conditions like these can best be expressed by the statement that the ε function shifts permanently as we move downward along the curve.

Assuming that transfer costs remain unaffected by the output of the industry in question and that the industry does not give rise to Ricardian rents, there will be a point (D) on the ε curve to which an output (OM) corresponds that exhausts all potential external economies. Once that output is reached, the ε curve will intersect with the ordinates at Ad and it will be horizontal throughout its course. Before any output whatsoever is produced, the path of the function is marked by the points A, B, C, D; the curve is horizontal only to the right of D. If a point lying along the curve (such as A or B) has already been realized, a movement backward, toward the ordinate, occurs along a horizontal line (such as AA_a or BA_b); whereas a movement forward, toward D occurs along the still unused portion of the original function (such as $ACBD$ or BCD).

To say that external economies are mostly of this kind, instead of being "reversible," may be interpreted to mean that they are typically *dynamic* phenomena. Whether shifts like these should be excluded from equilibrium analysis as Knight suggests and then relegated to "dynamic theory" is clearly a matter of convenience. The opinion may be expressed, however, that, so long as certain shifts of functions are on the same level of predictability as are movements along the functions, it is not very fruitful to distinguish between two types of theory dealing with these two kinds of changes respectively. The shifts reflecting irreversible external economies surely are not always on the same level of predictability as movements along given supply curves. But the difference may in some cases be insufficient to warrant the exclusion of the phenomenon from the type of theory we are concerned with at present.

Returning now to Figure 6, we observe that the conditions sketched there would, in the first approximation, justify a temporary bounty raising the output of the industry from OK to OM and thereby producing the lowest obtainable social cost curve for the commodity. After the discontinuation of the bounty the output of the industry drops to OL and social net output is higher than it was prior to the interference and higher than it would be if the bounty were continued. We said this conclusion was justified only "in the first approximation" because it disregards the waste involved in moving temporarily an excessive stock of resources into the industry under consideration. The perpetual income stream yielded by the capital value of the temporary excess of resources is a loss to be counted against the decline in social cost if the excess of resources (corresponding to the temporary excess output OM minus OL) is completely immobile. The more mobile the excess is, the smaller does the loss become.

Moreover, by directly subsidizing certain processes, such as migration or the specialization of resources, it may be possible to induce, at the "permanent" output level OL, the economies that would develop automatically at the output level OM, and thus to avoid the detour over the excessive output OM. Such temporary subsidies, raising the output of the industry from OK directly to OL, might in certain circumstances achieve the maximum obtainable saving in social cost, with no sinking of an excessive stock of specialized resources into the subsidized industry. The detour over OM does involve costs of this character. If the costs of a detour are unavoidable the true optimum output which takes account of these costs may be different from OL since the temporary excess of output is not the same for the different potential final outputs.[30]

40

In the preceding pages we considered external economies in isolation, disregarding diminishing returns and rising transfer costs. If, as seems plausible to assume, external economies occur in conjunction with the two cost-raising forces functionally related to industry output, the fundamentals of the preceding analysis are not altered. For a comparison of competitive output with social optimum output it is not necessary to divorce the two *cost-raising* forces from one another, since neither of them upsets the identity of the two outputs in question. But it is necessary to divorce the *cost-diminishing* forces from those *raising* cost, because the divergence of social optimum output from competitive output is determined by the *cost-diminishing* forces, regardless of whether the interaction of all forces makes for increasing, constant or declining supply price.

It should be repeated in this connection that statements like the foregoing one imply that it is fruitful to include in equilibrium theory the analysis of certain phenomena that in a sense are "dynamic," *i.e.,* that reflect themselves in shifts of the curves used in traditional equilibrium theory. Reversible external economies, not implying shifts of the curves, are in all probability unimportant. Whether it is fruitful to take account of "dynamic"—that is, irreversible—external economies in this type of approach depends on the degree of predictability, or, as it may be expressed alternatively, on the "regularity" of the phenomenon called external economies. Inclusion into the body of equilibrium theory may be warranted in some cases, but certainly not in all cases in which costs are declining "historically."

IV. SUMMARY

We have found that diminishing returns and external diseconomies (rising transfer costs) do not result in a divergence between social and competitive costs. Social cost equals resource (opportunity) cost, *i.e.,* the cost of production of additional or marginal units. If this cost advances because of diminishing returns or rising transfer costs, the higher cost to society is completely exhausted by a price covering the increment to costs on marginal units. The increment to rents on intramarginal units are not social costs; they do not enter into competitive supply prices and they should not. The statement made by certain writers[31] that an ideal allocation of resources requires that production be guided by "marginal cost," and not by "average cost" as it is under competition is either meaningless or erroneous. It is meaningless because cost *including* the total increment to rent on intramarginal units (γ, α, and θ) is "marginal cost" in one sense; and cost on the marginal units excluding these rents (ϵ, β, and ϕ) are also "marginal costs" in another sense; and because the second set of functions, forming the supply curves under competition, are both "marginal" and "average," according as the cost is computed incrementally without rent, or aver-

41

aged including *average* rent. The statement is wrong if it means that functions such as γ, α, and θ represent social costs.

When unexploited external economies exist, competitive output falls short of the optimum. But again this can not be expressed for all cases as a divergence of "average" and "marginal" cost, the former being represented as the correct guide. In the case of "reversible" external economies—those which disappear when the subsidy is terminated—a marginal function such as ψ, which subtracts from the increment to costs attributable to the marginal unit in isolation the decrement to costs on intramarginal units occasioned by the external economies, should be regarded as the true social costs function.[32] But in the case of "irreversible" economies, the contrast of average and marginal costs can not be used to indicate the divergence of competitive from social costs, inasmuch as the economies simply cause a downward shift of average costs as a horizontal function up to each realized output; "marginal," as anything distinct from this successive lowering of average costs, has no meaning.

Retrospectively, it is also worth remarking that the "atomistic" character of one producer's output under competition, frequently thought to be crucial in the external economies—diseconomies context, is not decisive of itself. In the "diseconomies" case, as we have seen, the private calculus of the single competitive producer results in no divergence of competitive and ideal output, for rents are not social costs. Where there are *genuine* diseconomies ignored by the competitive producer—smoke nuisance, wasteful exploitation of resources, etc.—these results follow not from the atomistic character of production, but from technical or institutional circumstances as a consequence of which scarce goods are treated as though they were free; and the divorce of scarcity from effective ownership may be equally complete for atomistic, oligopolistic, and monopolistic private enterprise.

The divergence of competitive from ideal output under external economies is more closely related to the atomistic position of the single competitor because, to the monopolist, ψ functions are the marginal cost functions if the economies are reversible; and he may take account of the downward shift of the ε functions if the economies are irreversible but predictable. It must not be overlooked, however, that, on the demand side, precisely the same circumstance—the non-atomistic position of the single producer—leads to the determination of output by marginal revenue which falls short of demand price. This in and of itself always tends to reduce output below the competitive level.

We have found theoretical possibilities of achieving by state interference more external economies than are given by competition; but it is, to say the least, doubtful whether frequent or extensive interference would be justified in practice upon this basis. Where economies are such as to be permanent (irreversible) once the requisite output is developed, we have an almost perfect analogy with the infant industry argument for tariffs, and little more need be said to emphasize the pitfalls.

The departure of the economist's *free* competition from the ideal of social costs is in fact negligible for external economies and non-existent for the cost-increasing forces. The departures of *actual* competition and the manifold other market forces from free competition are striking, just as the departures of actual forms of the corporate state, socialism, and planning from more or less ideal prototypes might also be striking.

NOTES

[1] The footnotes, including n. 22, p. 503, supply a fairly complete bibliography on the subject.

[2] Adam Smith, *The Wealth of Nations,* Cannan ed., (New York, 1937) Bk. I, chap. 9, p. 242 *et passim; cf.* also J. S. Mill, *Principles of Political Economy,* Gonner ed., (London, 1909), Bk. I, chap. 12, p. 184 *et passim.*

[3] Alfred Marshall, *Principles of Economics,* 3rd ed. (London, 1895), pp. 518-531; and in the corresponding chapter (Bk. V, chap. 12) in later editions.

[4] *Cf.* J. R. Hicks, "The Rehabilitation of Consumers' Surplus," *Rev. of Econ. Stud.,* Vol. 8 (Feb., 1941), pp. 112-15.

[5] A. C. Pigou, *Wealth and Welfare* (London, 1912), pp. 172-79.

[6] Our italics.

[7] By implication also the ideal price, but Pigou does not stress this.

[8] Allyn A. Young, "Pigou's Wealth and Welfare," *Quart. Jour. of Econ.,* Vol. 27 (Aug., 1913), pp. 672-86. Edgeworth also called the function "the marginal increment of cost from the viewpoint of a monopolist"; *cf.* F. Y. Edgeworth, "Contributions to the Theory of Railroad Rates, IV: A Digression on Professor Pigou's Thesis," *Econ. Jour.,* Vol. 23 (June, 1913), p. 211.

[9] A. C. Pigou, *The Economics of Welfare,* 1st ed. (London, 1920), pp. 934-36.

[10] If the n-th unit of the output is produced at a cost of $f(n)$, then $S_1 = f(n)$, and
$$S_2 = \frac{d[nf(n)]}{dn} = f(n) + nf'(n)$$

[11] Pigou, *op. cit.,* p. 935.

[12] Pigou, *op. cit.,* p. 936.

[13] Joan Robinson, *The Economics of Imperfect Competition* (London, 1933), chap. 10, "A Digression on the Four Cost Curves." While her chapter fails to distinguish ε and restricts the concept of rent to "Ricardian" surplus on the fixed factor, it is in general accurate and illuminating, and has contributed indirectly very much toward the present analysis.

[14] Pigou's contention (*cf.* 1st ed., p. 194) that of two roads connecting the same two points the one, assumed to be superior but narrow and therefore subject to diminishing returns, is overexploited in competition unless taxed differentially, seems to have rested on the notion that competitive output is determined by the δ function. The contention was proven to be fallacious by Professor Knight, who has shown that the owner of the good road will charge a toll that will raise costs to users to the β level. *Cf.* F. H. Knight, "Fallacies in the Interpretation of Social Cost," *Quart. Jour. of Econ.,* Vol. 38 (Aug., 1924), pp. 582-606, reprinted as chap. VIII in *idem, The Ethics of Competition* (New York, 1935), pp. 217-36. Pigou omitted the "two roads" example from the second edition

of his book which happened to appear almost simultaneously with Knight's criticism, and does not refer to the latter. No special significance should be attributed to Pigou's recantation of the "two roads" proposition because it was inconsistent with his own position and should have been dropped even if his position had not been modified.

[15] A. C. Pigou, "Comment," *Econ. Jour.*, Vol. 34 (Mar., 1924), p. 31.

[16] A. C. Pigou, *The Economics of Welfare*, 2nd ed. (London, 1924), pp. 194-95. The third edition (London, 1929), p. 225, made no change. F. Y. Edgeworth, "The Revised Doctrine of Marginal Social Product," *Econ. Jour.*, Vol. 35 (Mar., 1925), p. 35, agreed with this version of Pigou.

[17] *I.e.*, calculated at constant transfer costs.

[18] *I.e.*, calculated as though constant returns prevailed.

[19] Mrs. Robinson makes α do double duty as a designation for marginal cost including only the total increment of Ricardian rent and as a designation for our θ. This is an undesirable ambiguity. Furthermore, since she omitted to distinguish ϵ, she has no function corresponding to our ϕ, which adds ϵ and β.
The functions α, lying between θ and β, and γ, lying between θ and ϵ have been omitted in Fig. 4; δ has likewise not been drawn.

[20] F. D. Graham, "Some Aspects of Protection Further Considered," *Quart. Jour. of Econ.*, Vol. 37 (Feb., 1923), pp. 199-227; "The Theory of International Values Reexamined," *ibid.*, Vol. 38 (Nov., 1923), pp. 54-86; "Some Fallacies in the Interpretation of Social Costs; a Reply" (to F. H. Knight), *ibid.*, Vol. 39 (Feb., 1925), pp. 324-30.

[21] Oscar Lange (and F. M. Taylor), *On the Economic Theory of Socialism* (Minneapolis, 1938), pp. 98-99; Jacob Viner, "Cost Curves and Supply Curves," *Zeitschrift für Nationalokonomie*, Vol. 3 (Sept., 1931), p. 42.

[22] In addition to the literature elsewhere cited in these pages, see the following: J. H. Clapham, "Of Empty Economic Boxes," *Econ. Jour.*, Vol. 32 (Sept., 1922), pp. 305-14; A. C. Pigou, "Empty Economic Boxes: A Reply," *ibid.*, Vol. 34 (Dec., 1922), pp. 458-65; *idem* and D. H. Robertson, "Those Empty Boxes," *ibid.*, Vol. 34 (Mar., 1924) pp. 16-31; G. J. Stigler, *The Theory of Competitive Price* (New York, 1942) pp. 106, 142-44; K. E. Boulding, *Economic Analysis* (New York, 1941), p. 194; Joan Robinson, *op. cit.*, Appendix, pp. 337-43.

[23] Thus Knight, *op. cit.*, p. 229, and "On Decreasing Cost and Comparative Costs," *Quart. Jour. of Econ.*, Vol. 39 (Feb., 1925), pp. 331-33; and Joan Robinson, *op. cit.*, p. 340.

[24] Piero Sraffa, "Laws of Returns under Competitive Conditions," *Econ. Jour.*, Vol. 37 (Dec., 1926), pp. 535-50.

[25] On the assumption of free competition, costs to all firms are the same for their equilibrium outputs.

[26] A recent exposition of the thesis is found in Hicks, *op. cit.*

[27] *Cf.* Figure 1.

[28] We mean, of course, the corresponding distances along the abscissa. In the event of more than one intersection the optimum is reached at the intersection maximizing the expression $\int [D(x)-\Psi(x)]dx$, where $D(x)$ is the demand curve.

[29] As was pointed out in the preceding paragraph, the function ceases to be a *curve* if the industry is not atomistic. In this event Ψ is a function of more than one variable. The "curve" shifts upward when output expands, and downward when it contracts.

[30] If the distance between the demand curve and the original curve increases monotonously to the right of OK, then the temporary excess will be smaller for final outputs smaller than OL.

[31] Lange, *op. cit.*, pp. 98-99, n. 2; A. P. Lerner, "Statics and Dynamics in Socialist Economies," *Econ. Jour.*, Vol. 47 (June, 1937), pp. 253-70.

[32] Ψ, as was shown, is a function of more than one variable, and hence not a curve, if the industry in question is not atomistic.

Pecuniary and Technological Externality, Factor Rents, and Social Cost

By DEAN A. WORCESTER, JR.*

Analysis of external effects in production has turned during the last 15 years from analysis of pecuniary and technological economies and diseconomies of well defined industries (and a belief that the effects are minor),[1] to analysis of interdependence among very few, often only two, individual utility or production functions (and the belief that the effects may be important).[2] This shift seems to have been inspired by Ronald Coase [4]. He is the first to have shown that firms in competitive industries which have interdependent production functions will find negotiations that properly adjust for the externality to be profitable. He also shows that merger of the two firms will result in optimal resource allocation.

No one has argued recently that all of the externalities in even a small enterprise economy can be overcome by negotiation, merger of the interdependent firms, or by wholesale merger of all firms into an administratively planned economy. On the contrary, recent work has emphasized the difficulties that make even conceptual solutions appear virtually impossible for a wide range of cases.

Neoclassical analysis, which rests on the relationships between firms and industries, is utilized in this paper for five reasons. (1) It is adequate to reveal the basic source of externalities. (2) It provides a logical progression of steps for the extension of the analysis. (3) It is more readily applicable to feasible social controls that can, in many cases, reduce the considerable distortions due to the presence of externalities. (4) It lends itself to an analysis of the welfare effects of alternative market structures in the presence of externalities. (5) It is appropriate for both separable and nonseparable cost functions as defined by Otto Davis and

*Department of economics, University of Washington. He wishes to thank José Encarnacion and J. Timothy Peterson for their helpful comments on an earlier draft and the anonymous reader for many helpful suggestions and especially for skillful excisions which sharpened this paper and provided much grist for additional work.

Reprinted by permission of the publishers and author: Dean A. Worcester, Jr., "Pecuniary and Technological Externality Factor Rents, and Social Costs," *American Economic Review*, 59 (December 1969), pp. 873-885.

Andrew Whinston.

The principal points to be made here are: (1) Technological economies and diseconomies occur when the firms comprising the industry are not able to equalize the ratios of marginal products to factor price ratios which reflect alternative costs, because one or more of the factor costs to the firm do not equal opportunity cost to the industry (or to society). This is often the case, arising when the technical production function of an industry is not accommodated properly by the prevailing system of ownership, legal rights and the like. Technological diseconomies exist when, in addition to discrepancies between the ratios of marginal products to opportunity costs, the firms' average and marginal cost curves shift upwards as the total demand for some resource rises thus generating a rising industry supply price.[3] Technological economies exist when the firms' curves fall under these circumstances. Pecuniary economies (diseconomies) exist when the industry average cost is falling (rising) but the marginal equalities between factor prices which reflect alternative social costs and their marginal products prevail. (2) The size of the welfare loss associated with economies and diseconomies (henceforth referred to simply as economies unless otherwise specified) is very much affected by the particular type of externality present and the structure of the industry in question. The types of externalities considered are pecuniary or technological and the types of industry structures are competition, simple and first degree discriminating monopoly, and simple and first degree discriminating monopsony. (3) It is useful to distinguish economies that are internal to an industry from those that are external to it because some industry structures offset technological externalities when they are internal to a specific industry, but cannot when they are external.

The plan for this paper is as follows: (1) A linear homogeneous production function is described which will provide the basis for theoretical analysis. (2) The analysis relevant to a competitive industry experiencing technological diseconomies is examined in detail so as to provide a solid basis for the treatment of other industry structures and for economies. (3) The advantages and disafvantages of a few of the alternative ways of harmonizing private and social costs are examined. Analysis of specific cases, however, is left to another occasion.

I. THE PRODUCTION FUNCTION

The following analysis is illustrated by examples based upon a production function homogeneous of degree one, which displays ridge lines in the positive quadrant and which is considered to be relevant to a whole industry whether organized competitively or otherwise. This simple, comparatively well known function is chosen to emphasize the fact that neither technological nor pecuniary economies or diseconomies rest fundamentally upon the nature of the returns to the industry, but rather rest upon violation of the equality of the ratios of marginal products to their factor prices at equilibrium positions.[4]

Figure 1 consists of four panels which describe the production function, the costs and revenues, and the demand for factors of production by an industry

46

that will alternately be considered to represent each of five industry structures. Panel A illustrates a production function of the postulated type with two inputs, labor (L), and lant (T). Since proportionate increases in inputs yield proportionate increases in output, all outputs are readily determined if the output index is taken as 1.0 where isoquant Q_0 crosses ridge line OL. Land represents some input whose supply is fixed and which is useful only in the industry under consideration. Fixity of supply is not essential to the argument but is a useful simplifying assumption relevant to a number of important industries. Usefulness to but one industry, while not essential to the principal conclusion, is not only relevant to important industries but involves significant theoretical and practical distinctions. Removal of this restriction generates pecuniary externalities, which I wish to ignore. Panel B shows the relationship between output and total cost. It also provides a money scale that permits one to show alternative total revenue functions which correspond to alternative prices. The usual geometric relationships are used to find the industry marginal and average money cost curves shown in Panel C. They are drawn on the assumption that the price of land, W_T is zero, and the price of labor, W_L, is positive at the level illustrated in Panel D. Rising factor costs to the industry are considered later when pecuniary economies are analyzed.

The lines on Panel D reveal the marginal products of both labor and land, calculated in principle for land as a shadow marginal product implied by the marginal rates of substitution at the intersections of the various isoproduct curves with the expansion path TT^1. The input axis of Panel D shows the proportion between the variable factor (labor) and the fixed factor (land) associated with each level of output. If price is a constant at P_0 (see Panel C), these curves also depict the value of the various marginal and average products, and provide a scale upon which money wages and rents can be shown.

No panel shows the position of an individual firm when the industry is viewed as being competitive. The average cost for the industry (AC_I) is identical to the conventional long-run supply curve (referred to henceforth as $LRSP$) traced out by the loci of the average cost associated with the intersections of the long-run marginal cost and short-run marginal cost as the number of firms fluctuates in response to changed industry demand.[5] Whatever the industry structure, this curve is considered to represent minimum cost of production for each output when factor prices are fixed at W_L and W_T (Panel D).

The $LRSP$ of a competitive industry as shown by the $LRSP$ in Panel C may be said to reflect technological economies from zero output up to Q_E, and technological diseconomies beyond that point, because with constant factor prices the U-shape depends solely upon the production function for the industry. A corresponding function with the same shape reflects pecuniary economies where an optimal rent is charged. The size of the rent must vary as the industry price and optimal output varies. It will be a charge sufficient to make the private factor cost equal to its social cost.

II. COMPETITIVE EQUILIBRIUM FOR A SUB-INDUSTRY

To facilitate a clear distinction between rents and profits, consider first a sub-industry, catching a particular kind of fish from a particular fishing ground. It is assumed to comprise so small a part of the market for that species that its

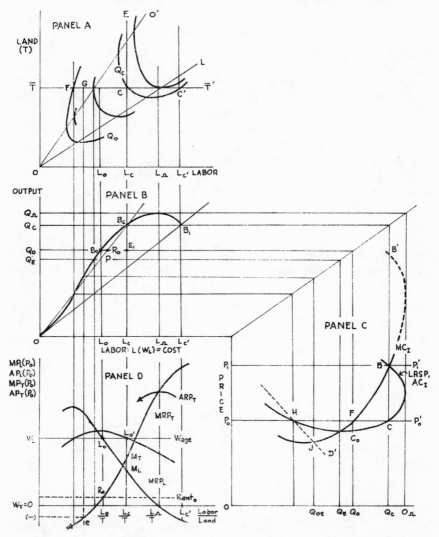

FIGURE 1. PRODUCTION FUNCTION, COST AND REVENUE AND RELATED FUNCTIONS FOR AN INDUSTRY

price is affected overwhelmingly by the demand for fish in general and only imperceptibly by its own output. Two of these narrowly defined industry demand curves are shown in Panel C, namely $P^0 P^0$, and $P^1 P^1$, and in Panel B by the corresponding total revenue curves, OBc and OB^1. Such a sub-industry will expand output until profits fall to a level just sufficient to hold the firms in the

48

industry, their summed outputs equalling the quantity demanded. The equilibrium output is in this case the same for both of these demand functions as is shown by Qc (Panels B and C) and points c and c' on isoquant Qc in Panel A. Where labor inputs exceed #Ω (Panels A, B, and D), this competitive industry exhibits a true backward bending supply curve. Such have been observed in certain fisheries and oil fields with multiple owners, and probably exist for other common property resources and publicly supplied goods.[6] This happens because in the absence of a charge for land, the average value product of labor for each firm is equal to the wage rate at equilibrium, although the marginal factor cost to the industry is much higher. In this instance, all costs are labor costs, and the industry expands or contracts until abnormal profits are eliminated. This occurs where price = $LRSP$ in the product market (point C in Panel C), although marginal cost to the industry is at point B.

At the higher price, P^1, valuable resources with positive opportunity costs are employed, specifically additional labor in the amount of $LcLc$ (Panels A and B), with no net addition to total production, the marginal product of labor being positive at first but negative beyond $L\Omega$. Lesser, but still substantial waste occurs if price is P_0, output Qc, and inputs Lc/T. Attention is henceforth confined to the analysis of this lesser amount of waste.

It is immediately evident from Panel D that, where inputs are Lc/T, the marginal product of labor to the industry point M_L is a bit less than 50 percent of the wage rate, and that the marginal product of land, M_T, is far above the (zero) price at which it enters the firms' cost functions. This relationship is also shown in Panel A by the negative slope of the industry isoquant at point C where isoquant Qc is not tangential to the isocost line $LcCE$. The latter is vertical because the price of land is zero. The inevitable conclusion follows (however paradoxical it might have seemed to Ricardo or Marx). Although labor gets the whole return, social output is much reduced because labor is being wasted for want of price on land. Labor is being wasted because its alternative marginal contribution to other industries exceeds its marginal value product here. Output should, of course, be contracted until labor's marginal productivity to the industry (rather than its average productivity) equals its wage. This occurs at point L_0/T in Panel D and corresponds to an optimal output of Q_0 in Panels B and C. At that point, a positive rent exists since the marginal product of land is R_0 (Panel D). This is equivalent to the difference between the average and marginal products of labor (Panel D), the gap between total revenue and total cost, B_0R_0, shown in Panel B, and the difference between $LRSP$ and price times the output, C_0F (P_0F) in Panel C.

Ownership of the land will tend strongly to produce an optimal level of production. In this case, where output of the sub-industry does not affect the output price, it does not matter whether ownership of land is concentrated or dispersed.

This treatment seems one-sided since the classical remedy via taxation is ignored. In the case under discussion, taxation, either of inputs or outputs is, in principle, an effective means for optimizing output. An optimal license type tax on inputs is equivalent to rents. A tax on the output sufficient to reduce the net price to suppliers to C_0 (Panel C) would also result in optimal output. Taxation is widely regarded as superior to rents because the tax revenues supposedly have more desirable income effects than do rents. There are disadvantages in administration, however, for it is also true that the tax rate, whether levied against inputs or outputs, must be optimally adjusted for every change of product price, factor costs, and technology that affects factor proportions. One can believe that the adjustment process via changing rents will be more finely tuned than via tax adjustment.

III. WELFARE LOSS DUE TO FAILURE TO CHARGE RENTS

The welfare loss resulting from a failure to charge the optimum rent in the case illustrated by Figure 1 can be shown by either of two areas in Panel C, or by a comparison of cost and revenue in Panel B. If price is P_0 and if no rents are charged, equilibrium output is Qc and both total revenue and total cost for the industry are $QcBc$ (Panel B), or $QcCP_0O$ in Panel C.[7] Yet, marginal social cost, which is equal to MCI in Panel C, is QcB, about 60 percent higher than P_0. If maximum rents are charged, output drops to Q_0 and unit costs to Q_0C_0 (Panel C) where the social optimum is indicated by the intersection of MC_I with P_0 at point F. Total costs (excluding rents) and revenues are equal to Q_0B_0 and Q_0R_0 respectively on Panel B.

Comparison with the competitive equilibrium shows that consumers lose satisfaction for which they would have paid R_0E^1 (Panel B), while resources valued at B_0E^1 are saved and presumably used to produce an equivalent value of goods and services in other industries. The net gain, which is the largest attainable, is B_0R_0; precisely equal to the maximum rent.

The same result is illustrated, perhaps more persuasively, in Panel C where the rent and the welfare gain appear as different areas. The maximum rent is shown by the rectangle with sides P_0F and FC_0. The welfare gain resulting from the imposition of the rent is shown by the approximately triangular area FCB. The fact that these two areas must be equal appears obvious from Panel B, but it holds only when price is equal to marginal revenue for the industry. Otherwise the rectangular area includes a combined maximum of rent and profit, which occurs when output is restricted below the optimum level and the demand curve is sloping. The profit plus rent rectangle is augmented, but the welfare gain is reduced. This situation is analyzed below.

IV. "TECHNOLOGICAL" DISECONOMIES
COMPETITION, NORMAL INDUSTRY DEMAND

Now that the flat sub-industry demand curve has enabled us to define the narginal social cost function and to relate it to rents, it is time to admit that even sub-industries typically confront demand curves that slope downward and toward the right as illustrated in Figure 2, which is otherwise the equivalent of Panel C. The relationships among physical inputs and outputs, and the prices of the factors remain the same as in Figure 1, and the now sloping demand curve is

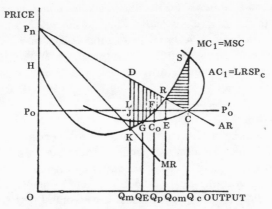

FIGURE 2. OPTIMA: TECHNOLOGICAL DISECONOMIES

drawn to leave the no rent competitive price P_0 *and output* Q_0 unchanged. The money demand for factors as a whole would (if shown) be rotated clockwise around their former equilibrium positions.

The principal modification of the analysis is the reduction in the size of the welfare gain incident to the imposition of an optimal rent to the shaded area *CBPr* and an increase of optimal rent to *PrE* per unit of output. In this case, optimal rents are approximately doubled while the potential welfare gain is lessened. Each of these modifications follows from the fact that a smaller adjustment of output below the competitive level suffices to achieve the optimal result, since price rises as output is reduced so that optimum output and price occur at Q_0M and *Pr*.

SIMPLE AND DISCRIMINATING MONOPSONY

The same situation illustrated by Figure 2 can also be viewed as a monopsony. Suppose that the freely competing fishermen must sell to a single cannery (perhaps a local government monopoly). The cannery may be completely devoid of monopoly power, selling its products in distant markets in competition with hundreds of rivals. In this case the appropriate demand curve for the fish is the horizontal line, P_0P_0. A maximizing simple monopsonist will buy quantity Q_0 at price C_0 which it resells at price OP_0 plus its value added per unit. His profit is equal to FC_0 per unit of output, exactly the maximum rent under competition. Output is induced to the optimal level because his profits are maximized where MC_I (the marginal social cost in this case) equals price. The price paid to the fishermen, C_0, is on the *LRSP* for the industry, so only the correct number of firms and levels of output are induced. If the demand curve is *PnC*, the competitive optimum (with rents) is attained at output Q_0M, and fishermen's price E.

A discriminating monopsonist, on the other hand, will overproduce. This is illustrated by the extreme case of the perfectly discriminating monopsonist who drives all or nothing bargains with each fisherman, or pays a minimum price for each unit purchased thus making the discriminating monopsonist's marginal cost curve equal to his average cost curve which is the *LRSP* for the industry as shown in Figures 1 and 2. A discriminating monopolist maximizes profit when output is carried to the competitive no rent level, *Qc*. Welfare loss (FCB) is the same as under competition; profits exceed optimal rent slightly more than FC_0C.[8]

SIMPLE MONOPOLY[9]

Consider again the effect of the sloping industry demand curve *PnC*. Should the firms in this industry form a perfectly efficient cartel such that the control over output becomes absolute and the industry cost function is not raised above that for competition, the cartel would, if a simple monopolist, maximize its profit at Q_M. Price is then $Q_M D$. Because it has control over entry, it will not overuse the resource (which we have assumed thus far to be useful only in this industry), and it will consider the effect of its output on price. Thus marginal revenue will be made equal to marginal social cost.

All of the factors (the price of which we continue to hold constant) including the natural resources are underused by monopolists. Compared to the competitive result when an optimal rent is paid, value of output to the consumers is reduced by the area under *DPr* while costs are reduced only by the area under *KPr*. There is a welfare loss of the shaded area *DPr*K to be set against the welfare gain of *PrBC*, the other shaded area, as compared to competitive equilibrium when no rent is paid. Simple monopoly may be either better or worse than competition if no rents are charged depending upon the relative elasticities of the industry demand and of the long-run average cost curve of the monopolist, assuming the latter to be identical to the long-run supply price for the industry when organized competitively.

In this example, rent per unit of output falls to *JL*, but profit per unit of output is *LD*. In either case, the gains, if any, to the consumer are small compared to the gains in profits plus rents to the cartelizers, when both are measured in money. One must imagine brutish consumers and epicurean businessmen to be willing to urge the merits of increased efficiency by monopolization even in those cases where there is a clear welfare gain. A government monopoly might find approbation if the industry is thought to be essential and if the profits plus rents were utilized to accelerate economic growth, but it is not a welfare optimum.

A sophisticated combination of subsidies that effect marginal costs and induce larger output and a license type tax to capture pure profits or rents can, in principle, produce an optimum result under simple monopoly. The relevant curves must be accurately known, and prompt adjustments made when they shift if an optimum is to be attained.

PERFECTLY DISCRIMINATING MONOPOLY

A perfectly discriminating monopolist, whose long-run average cost is identical to the competitive long-run supply curve, would carry output to the socially optimal level (Q_0M in Figure 2) provided that variable inputs' wages are determined independently of industry output and that fixed inputs are specific to the industry, as is the case here.

Implicit rent is restored to the maximum level (EPr per unit of output) and profit plus rent is maximized ($PnPrKH$). The reason for the good allocation result is that all social costs are internalized by the decision making unit when such an industry is monopolized, and the demand curve is also the industry marginal revenue curve. This is true with perfect discrimination since the firm need not cut the price on any unit of sales in order to extend its sales further by means of lower prices to otherwise excluded buyers. The transfer to the monopolist is enormous and may be more objectionable to many social critics than the misallocation that is overcome, but this is a different problem.

V. PECUNIARY DISECONOMIES

Virtually all of the conclusions which relate differing industry structure to optimal allocation in the presence of technological diseconomies must be reversed when pecuniary diseconomies cause cost changes as an industry expands or contracts. Optimal allocation of resources occurs under competition and perfectly discriminating monopsony; restricted production and welfare loss is a consequence of simple monopoly, perfectly discriminating monopoly, and of simple monopsony.

The textbook distinction between technological and pecuniary diseconomies is that the latter is accounted for by rising factor costs per unit of output, not the nature of the production function. The preceding analysis has shown this distinction to be but a special case of a more fundamental difference. Technological diseconomies occur when the cost of output is rising and the cost of some input to the firms is less than its opportunity costs to its industry without reference to the shape of the factor supply curves. Hence any rise in output cost is pecuniary if the marginal equalities are maintained between the prices of factors which reflect opportunity costs and their respective marginal products. Whenever this is true, the *LRSP* is the curve of marginal social costs (*MSC*), and optimal output is found where *LRSP = P*. *This is true because any* increase in the marginal cost of output per unit reflects either (1) a rise in the opportunity cost of the factors due to expansion of this industry which thereby raises their opportunity costs in each of their uses, or (2) because of lower marginal productivity, or both.

This may be illustrated with Figures 1 and 2 when optimum rents are charged. The *LRSP* for a competitive industry becomes identical to the *MSC* (which, it will be recalled, coincides with the former MC_I). These are shown in Figure 3 as $LRSP_{pec}$ and MC_{tech}. The *MSC* curve, of course, does not shift.

A new marginal cost to the industry arises which is marginal to the new *LRSP*. It is denoted MC_{pec} *in Figure 3, and is relevant to pecuniary* externalities.

The welfare effects relevant to the five alternative market structures are readily compared using the standard definitions of equilibrium. Optimal output

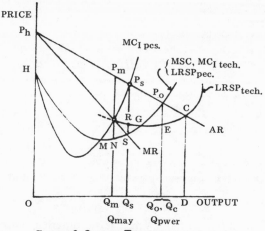

FIGURE 3. OPTIMA: TECHNOLOGICAL AND
PECUNIARY DISECONOMIES

occurs at Q_0 where MSC = Demand. This is also the competitive equilibrium because $LRSP_{pec} \equiv MSC$. Simple monopoly operates at Q_M where $MR = MC_{pec}$ and produces a welfare loss of $P_M P_0 N$. Unlike the situation where the diseconomies are technological and monopolistic restriction tends to offset competitive overexpansion, this is an unmitigated, even a multiplied, loss because the firm's marginal cost lies above marginal social cost and its marginal revenue lies below the demand curve in the relevant ranges. A perfectly discriminating monopolist maximizes where MC_{pec} = Price. A welfare loss of $P_3 P_0 S$ results since MC_{pec} lies above MSC.

Viewed as a simple monopsony, the supply curve to a single buyer in this competitive market is $LRSP_{pec} = MSC$. The buyer's marginal cost is, therefore, MC_{pec} which he will set equal to his demand curve, and buy Q_{msy} at price S.[10] Again the welfare loss is $P_3 S_0 S$. A perfectly discriminating monopsonist will find his marginal factor cost to be equal to the $LRSP_{pec}$. Profit maximization occurs at Q_0 which is the same as the competitive output and is a welfare optimum according to the usual definitions. Profits, however, are not normal, being equal to $P_H P_0 MH$.

All of the noncompetitive structures garner profits, but the relationship between the size of the profits and the size of the welfare loss is highly irregular.

VI. EXTERNAL ECONOMIES

Figure 1 illustrates too, the welfare results of alternative structures for external technological and pecuniary economies. The dashed line in Panel C is interpreted as the industry demand curve. The cost curves of Panel C up to Q_E, and the corresponding portions of the associated curves in the other panels in Figure 1, relate the alternative equilibria to the basic technological and factor price constraints where external economies accompany the expansion of the industry. Market demand is such that with the most efficient organization of

54

production, competitive equilibrium must occur at point H (with zero price of land) at which point $LRSP$ is still falling. Tracing this equilibrium back to Panel A, we find point F which is outside of the economic sector because the slope of the isoquant denotes a negative marginal product for land. Tracing this combination to Panel D, we discover not only that the marginal product of land is well below its (zero) price to the firms in the industry, but that the marginal product of labor is correspondingly far above its wage rate. Labor is being wasted by insufficiently intensive use. Yet profits are only normal.

Point J (Panel C) represents optimal allocation where demand = MSC. If its associated output, $Q_0 e$, is traced back to Panel A, we find a smaller but still negative marginal product of land implied by the interpolated slope of the isoquant at point G. The corresponding points in Panel D seem to suggest a continued failure to bring the marginal cost of labor into equality with its wage rate, but this is an illusion. The price of the product is about one-fourth lower at J, as compared to H, so that the value of the marginal product in Panel D should be altered proportionately. This produces the desired equality.

The value of the marginal product of land requires a similar adjustment, but it must remain negative at the optimal output and combination of inputs. Thus, the optimal marginal product of land must be negative, and a competitive industry can produce at the optimal rate only if a negative rent (a subsidy) of optimal size be paid for the use of the unpriced resource.

The need for a subsidy to competitive industries to induce optimal levels of operation in the presence of technological economies has long been known. The very similar argument favoring subsidization of regulated monopolies when economies of scale are internal to the firm is based on the same analytical conclusion, that profitable operation is impossible at the socially optimal rate of output.

The equilibrium positions for other industry structures where external technological or pecuniary economies exist are illustrated in Figure 4 which reproduces Panel C and also includes the cost curves relevant to pecuniary economies. Subscripts t and p are used to designate points relevant, respectively, to technological and pecuniary externalities. The analysis of all four conditions, technological and pecuniary diseconomies and economies, is summarized in Table 1.

It is evident that a given structure yeilds the same general welfare effect whether such external effects are diseconomies or economies, and that a structure that optimizes when economies are pecuniary will fail to do so when they are technological and vice versa.

VII. EXTERNALITIES EXTERNAL TO THE INDUSTRY

One important limitation has been retained thus far, the industry concept and the implication that externalities exist only among firms producing a homogeneous product. When this limitation is removed, choice among means for correcting for externalities is reduced in principle and virtually eliminated as a practical matter. One can argue persuasively that optimization by simple

Structure	Equilibrium Condition (all cases)	Diseconomies (See Fig. 3)		Economies (See Fig. 4)	
		Price Quantity	Welfare Loss	Price Quantity	Welfare Loss
Competition					
Technological	$LRSP_t=P$	C, D	P_0CE	Pe, Qe	$PePoE$
Pecuniary	$LRSP_p=P$	P_0, Q_0	optimum	P_0, Q_0	optimum
Simple Monopoly					
Technological	$MC_t=MR$	Pa, Qa	PaP_0S	P_{MT}, Q_{MT}	$P_{MT}P_0K$
Pecuniary	$MC_p=MR$	Pm, Qm	PmP_0N	P_{MP}, Q_{MP}	$P_{MP}P_0K'$
Discriminating Monopoly					
Technological	$MC_t=P$	P_0, Q_0	optimum	P_0, Q_0	optimum
Pecuniary	$MC_p=P$	Pe, Qa	PaP_0S*	Pa, Qa	PaP_0E'
Simple monopsony (where demand is seen as marginal value product and $LRSP$ as the supply function)					
Techno-logical†	$MC_t=MFC=P$	E, Q_0	optimum	W, Q_0	optimum
Pecuniary	$MC_p=MFC=P$	S, Qa	$PaP_0 S*$	E', Qa	PaP_0E'
Discriminating Monopsony					
Technological	$LRSP_t=P$	C, D	P_0CE	} same as simple monopsony**	
Pecuniary	$LRSP_p=P$		optimum		

† Note that the wage lies on the supply curve, $LRSP$ even when the supply curve lies above the demand curve.
*This is equal to the loss for a simple monopolist under technological economies only by coincidence.
** Discriminating monopsony yields lower profits than simple monopsony when the supply curve is downward sloping because discrimination raises the average price of the factor. Hence a firm with power to discriminate will not utilize it.

monopsony or by organizing perfect monopolistic discrimination is entirely impractical in any case even if income effects should be ignored. If the economies or diseconomies are external not only to the firms in an industry, but also to any given industry, i.e., among firms that are not producing homogeneous products, the structural options are lost even in principle. An optimizing policy must attempt to achieve competitive equilibrium with inputs priced according to their alternative costs. This is true because it is virtually certain that the factor proportions of different users will differ so that the improperly priced factor will not be properly allocated by discrimination or regulation among competing users. The foregoing analysis assumes that the improperly priced factor has but one use and will be given an optimal implied value by a monopolist who treats it as a residual. This implied price is the rent. If the improperly priced factor is used in two or more industries, its allocation among them needs to be such that its implicit marginal value to each industry is the same.[11]

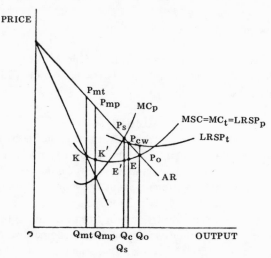

FIGURE 4. OPTIMA: TECHNOLOGICAL AND PECUNIARY ECONOMIES

VIII. ARE ANY BOXES EMPTY?

It is now possible to list the various types of external economies. They fall conveniently into eight categories. Each is listed below with an illustrative example. This classification should not obscure the more basic fact that any technological economy or diseconomy can be converted into a pecuniary one by appropriate pricing of inputs. The listing reflects the author's judgment of the typical pricing practices in the United States. These should be examined more carefully after alternative methods of adjusting for technological economies and diseconomies have been surveyed and refined.

A. Externalities which are internal to a specific industry:

1. Technological diseconomy: common property resources; fisheries, and oil formations used by competing firms.
2. Technological economy: public utilities; especially electric power, water supply, sewage disposal where a single price covers all costs.
3. Pecuniary diseconomy: the most common case, where expansion encounters rising factor prices and/or declining marginal productivity.
4. Pecuniary economy: increased specialization via purchased inputs or subcontracting with expansion of industry output; clothing, aircraft.

B. Externalities which are external to a particular industry:

5. Technological diseconomy: most public services which are supplied without a charge to the user according to use; city streets, air.

57

6. Technological economy: basic research, exploration, law and order, provision of information service.
7. Pecuniary diseconomy: There are many of these; high cost of living, and wages in the larger cities as city size increases.
8. Pecuniary economies: General specialization.

The same industry will often appear in both type A and type B. Thus, the internal technological economy for electric power production (#2) can also be cited for external pecuniary economy (#8).

IX. SUMMARY

All external effects are found in principle to be reducible by correct input pricing to economies or diseconomies. This holds for separable and nonseparable externalities in production and for externalities viewed either in terms of specific firms or among industries. Different industry structures produce optimal allocation either for technological or for pecuniary externalities if the externalities are internal to an industry and the firms therein use the same factor proportions. When these conditions do not hold, only competitive structures and pecuniary externalities suffice to produce an optimum in the absence of very complicated combinations of taxes and subsidies which require a wealth of accurate detailed data utilized with consummate insight and speed.

NOTES

1. The traditional literature came of age with Pigou's [15] *Economics of Welfare,* which extended Marshall's treatment [11] and Young's [23] constructive review of Pigou's earlier *Wealth and Welfare* before the first World War. It reached its first plateau in the 1920's with the controversy among Clapham [5], Robertson [17], and Pigou [14] over "Those Empty Economic Boxes" and Knight's article [9]. Viner [21] systematized the literature in the early 1930's. Ellis and Fellner [8] and Lerner [10] made contributions during the 1940's. The first satisfactory statement distinguishing between technological and pecuniary economies, Samuelson notwithstanding [18, p. 209], seems to have been made by Baumol [1], although he does not claim originality.
2. The recent analysis seems to have begun with Weade [12] and has been continued by Scitovsky [19], Buchanan and Stubblebine [3], Davis and Whinston [6]. Jirveu [20], and Wellisz [22]. It is well summarized up to 1965 by Mishan [13], but continues, in the work of Plott [16], Buchanan [2], Dolbear [7], and others.
3. "Industry supply curve" refers to the locus of minimum average cost for a group of one or more firms producing a homogeneous product where the quantity of all factors (which are assumed to be homogeneous) and the numbers of firms are freely variable as industry output expands except that the total supply of some input or inputs may be fixed to the industry. It may be defined alternatively as the summed output of all firms in the industry at each price where the long-run and the short-run marginal cost are both equal to each alternative price. This is often referred to as the long-run supply price (*LRSP*) curve. "Industry marginal cost" (MC_1) is similarly construed, and is marginal to the industry average cost. Under competitive conditions, MC_1 is a decision variable for no firm although it denotes marginal social cost (*MSC*) when a technological externality is present.
4. This point seems to have been made first by Abba P. Lerner in 1943 [10, Ch. 15, 16, 17] but, so far as I know, has not become part of the literature. Lerner did not thus distinguish between technological and pecuniary (dis)economies because his "Rule" is

58

carefully designed to price indivisible and fixed factors according to what might now be termed their shadow marginal products. The present analysis attempts to show that this procedure converts technological into pecuniary diseconomies and thereby supports Lerner's conclusion that misallocation under these circumstances is nothing more than a failure to adhere to the equality of the ratios of factor prices to their respective marginal products. Lerner's handling of technological economies is just as advanced (virtually the 1968 level), if not so satisfactory. Acceptance of Lerner's procedure may have suffered because it directs attention to his proposed social control devices rather than his analysis, but fundamentally it seems simply to have been too neat.

5. Point B is marginal to $LRSP$ at point C The marginal cost to $LRSP$ at point B is far higher and is shown inexactly as B'.

6. An example of publicly supplied goods is streets, especially freeways that are so overloaded at peak hours as to suffer a reduction of traffic flow. If possible, rents should be charged during these periods without further impeding traffic flow. Such a system apparently is technically feasible. I have been told that the Netherland's traffic police use electronic devices which photograph speeding cars on certain freeways. Fines are charged against their owners, the photographed license plate providing the needed information for sending the bill. If such a system exists, it could be expanded to photograph all cars at rush periods; those choosing to use the freeway at that time would be billed for the rent.

7. It should be kept in mind that each firm is in zero pure profit equilibrium with $MC = AC = P$ when the industry operates at Q_0, or indeed at any other output where $LRSP = P$.

8. The appropriate profit calculation is somewhat troublesome because external economies are shown up to Q_E and external diseconomies thereafter. In a later section, we find the direction of adjustments reversed for external economies. In the present instance, it seems most reasonable to assume that the discriminating monopsonist will use his power to hold purchase prices to the minimum average cost, G, for supplies up to quantity Q_E. The addition to profit (in addition to the rent equivalent) resulting from perfect discrimination is that shown by FC_0C, plus the difference between buying prices G and C_0 for every unit up to Q_E plus a diminishing sliver of profit between Q_E and Q_0.

9. The nature of costs under monopoly and monopsony are often insufficiently defined. If long-run monopoly and competitive equilibria are to be contrasted on the assumption of long-lived barriers to entry, then full adjustment to alternative output levels must be permitted. This includes alteration of number of establishments, centralized and decentralized control systems, and the like. When this is done, the average cost curve of the monopolist comes from the same family as the $LRSP$ of the competitive industry. The U-shapes which are universally drawn for monopolists are questionable generalizations.

It seems much more likely that they are like the $LRSP$ under competition plus an additional cost per unit to cover the additional costs of coordination and preservation of the barriers to entry. Yet, some economies may also be forthcoming. Here the $LRSP$ under competition and the LAC under monopoly are treated as identical, and analysis is confined to the effect of structure on the conditions for equilibrium and their effect on optimal resource allocation. A U-shaped $LRSP$ is used only for illustrative purposes and to reduce the number of figures, since that shape contains all three types of returns.

10. The reader may note an anomaly here. $LRSP_{pec}$ is taken as the supply price even to the left of point G where the optimum rent is zero. This implies an optimum negative rent where $LRSP_{pec} < LRSP_{tech}$. This is indeed the correct implication. In this range, technological economies exist which involve negative shadow marginal products for the unpriced fixed factor. This case is discussed in the next section.

11. This point is also valid within an industry when the various firms utilize different processes and have different implied values for the input fixed to the industry.

REFERENCES

1. W. J. Baumol, *Welfare Economics and the Theory of the State*, Cambridge 1952.

2. J. M. Buchanan, "Joint Supply, Externality and Optimality," *Economica*, Nov. 1966, *33*, 404-15.

3. _____, and W. C. Stubblebine, "Externality," *Economica*, Nov. 1962, *29*, 371-84.

4. R. Coase, "The Problem of Social Cost," *J. Law Econ.*, Oct. 1961, *3*, 1-44.

5. J. H. Clapham, "Of Empty Economic Boxes," *Econ. J.*, Sept. 1922, *32*, 305-14; reprinted in K. E. Boulding and G. J. Stigler, *AEA Readings in Economic Theory*, Vol. 6, Homewood 1952; and Clapham, "Rejoinder," *Econ. J.* Dec. 1922, *32*, 560-63.

6. O. A. Davis and A. Whinston, "Externalities, Welfare and the Theory of Games," *J. Polit. Econ.*, June 1962, *70*, 241-62.

7. F. T. Dolbear, Jr., "On the Theory of Optimal Externality," *Amer. Econ. Rev.*, Mar. 1967, *57*, 90-103.

8. H. Ellis and W. Fellner, "External Economies and Diseconomies," *Amer. Econ. Rev.*, Sept. 1943, *33*, 493-511; reprinted in *Readings* [5].

9. F. H. Knight, "Fallacies in the Interpretation of Social Cost,' *Quart. J. Econ.* Aug. 1924, *38*, 582-606; reprinted in *Readings* [5].

10. A. P. Lerner, *The Economics of Control*, New York 1943.

11. A. Marshall, *Principles of Economics*, 8th ed. London 1920.

12. J. E. Meade, "External Economies and Diseconomies in a Competitive Situation," *Econ. J.*, Mar. 1952, *67*, 54-67.

13. E. J. Mishan, "Reflections on Recent Developments in the Concept of External Effects," *Can. J. Econ.*, Feb. 1965, *31*, 1-34.

14. A. C. Pigou, "Empty Economic Boxes: A Reply," *Econ. J.*, Dec. 1922, *32*, 458-65; reprinted in *Readings* [5].

15. *J. A. Bouheuel*, The Economics of Welfare, *4th ed., London 1952.*

16. C. R. Plott, "Externalities and Corrective Taxes," *Economica,* Feb. 1966, *33*, 84-87.

17. D. H. Robertson, "Those Empty Boxes," *Econ. J.*, March 1924, *24*, 16-30; reprinted in *Readings* [5].

18. P. A. Samuelson, *Foundations of Economic Analysis*, Atheneum ed. New York 1965.

19. T. Scitovsky, "Two Concepts of External Economies," *J. Polit. Econ.*, Apr. 1954, *57*, 143-51.

20. Ralph Turvey, "On Divergencies Between Social Cost and Private Cost," *Economica*, Aug. 1963, *30*, 309-13.

21. J. Viner, "Cost Curves and Supply Curves," *Z. Nationalo*kon., *1931*, 3, 23-46; reprinted in the *Readings* [5].

22. S. Wellisz, "On External Diseconomies and the Government Assisted Invisible Hand," *Economica*, Nov. 1964, *31*, 345-62.

23. A. Young, "Pigou's Wealth and Welfare Review," *Quart. J. Econ.*, Aug. 1913, *27*, 672-86.

External Economies and Diseconomies in a Competitive Situation[1]

By J. E. MEADE

I. THE SCOPE OF THE PAPER

THE purpose of this note is to distinguish between certain types of external economies and diseconomies which are connected with marginal adjustments in purely competitive situations. We shall not be dealing with divergences between private and social interests due to monopolistic or monopsonistic situations, nor with any of the problems which arise from indivisibilities such as the lumpiness of investment in particular forms, nor with any questions about large structural changes such as whether a particular industry should exist at all or not. We shall be concerned only with small adjustments to existing competitive situations.

II. THE COMPETITIVE SITUATION WITH NO EXTERNAL ECONOMIES OR DISECONOMIES

Let us consider two industries. These " industries " may or may not in fact produce identically the same product and so in reality constitute a single industry. That is immaterial to our general theory. But we assume that within each " industry " there are a large number of independent competing firms, so that to each individual entrepreneur the price of the product and of the factors is given. In the absence of any external economies or diseconomies, each entrepreneur will hire each factor up to the point at which the additional product of the factor multiplied by its price is equal to the price of the factor. Moreover, there will be constant returns to scale. If every factor in either of our two industries were increased by 10%, including the number of

---

Reprinted by permission of the publishers and author: J. E. Meade, "External Economies and Diseconomies in a Competitive Situation," *Economic Journal*, 62 (March 1952), pp. 54-67.

entrepreneurs, then the product also would be increased by 10%.
Let us write x_1 and x_2 for the products of industry 1 and
industry 2 respectively. We assume that there are two factors,
l and c, or labour and capital, employed in both industries, so
that $l_1 + l_2 = l$ and $c_1 + c_2 = c$. We will write $\bar{x}_1$, $\bar{l}_1$, $\bar{c}_1$, etc.,
for the market prices of the products and factors; and $X_1 =
x_1\bar{x}_1$, $L_1 = l_1\bar{l}_1$, $C_1 = c_1\bar{c}_1$, etc., for the total value of the output of
x_1 or for the total income earned by l_1, etc. Finally, we shall
write $\bar{L}_1$, $\bar{C}_1$, etc., for the amounts which the factors would have
to be paid if they received the value of their marginal social
net products. In our model capital is always the hiring factor, and
its reward is, therefore, always equal in each industry to the total
output of that industry minus the wages paid to labour in that
industry, so that $C_1 = X_1 - L_1$ and $C_2 = X_2 - L_2$.

In the case in which there are no divergences between private
and social net products we can write

$$\begin{aligned} x_1 &= H_1(l_1,\, c_1) \\ x_2 &= H_2(l_2,\, c_2) \end{aligned} \right\} \quad \dots \quad (1)$$

where H_1 and H_2 are homogeneous functions of the first degree,
expressing the fact that there are constant returns to scale in
both industries. Now

$$x_1 = \frac{\partial x_1}{\partial l_1} l_1 + \frac{\partial x_1}{\partial c_1} c_1$$

or

$$1 = \frac{l_1}{x_1}\frac{\partial x_1}{\partial l_1} + \frac{c_1}{x_1} \cdot \frac{\partial x_1}{\partial c_1}$$

We shall write $\epsilon_{l_1}^{x_1}$ for $\dfrac{l_1}{x_1} \cdot \dfrac{\partial x_1}{\partial l_1}$ and so on, so that we have

$$\epsilon_{l_1}^{x_1} + \epsilon_{c_1}^{x_1} = \epsilon_{l_2}^{x_2} + \epsilon_{c_2}^{x_2} = 1 \quad \dots \quad (2)$$

These expressions describe the fact that if, for example, a 10%
increase in labour alone causes a 3% increase in output, then a
10% increase in capital alone must cause a 7% increase in output,
because a 10% increase in both factors will cause a 10% increase
in output.

In this situation l_1 will be paid a money wage (L_1) equal to
$\frac{\partial x_1}{\partial l_1} l_1\bar{x}_1$ or $\epsilon_{l_1}^{x_1}X_1$, and this will also be equal to the value of its
marginal social net product. Capital in industry 1 will receive
$X_1 - L_1$ which from equation (2) equals $\epsilon_{c_1}^{x_1}X_1$, which is also equal
to the value of capital's marginal social net product, so that in
this case we have

$$L_1 = \bar{L}_1 = \epsilon_{l_1}^{x_1} X_1 \qquad\qquad L_2 = \bar{L}_2 = \epsilon_{l_2}^{x_2} X_2$$
$$C_1 = \bar{C}_1 = \epsilon_{c_1}^{x_1} X_1 \qquad\qquad C_2 = \bar{C}_2 = \epsilon_{l_2}^{x_2} X_2$$

Moreover, since $\epsilon_{l_1}^{x_1} = \dfrac{L_1}{X_1}$, we can measure $\epsilon_{l_1}^{x_1}$ from the proportion of the total product in industry, which goes to labour. And similarly for the measurement of $\epsilon_{c_1}^{x_1}$, $\epsilon_{l_2}^{x_2}$ and $\epsilon_{c_2}^{x_2}$.

III. TWO TYPES OF EXTERNAL ECONOMY AND DISECONOMY

Such is the simplest competitive model. We intend now to consider cases where what is done in one industry reacts upon the conditions of production in the other industry in some way other than through the possible effect upon the prices of the product or of the factors in that other industry. All such reactions we shall describe as constituting external economies or diseconomies, because the individual entrepreneur in the first industry will take account of the effect of his actions only upon what happens inside the first industry (the internal effect), but will leave out of account the effect of his actions upon the output of the second industry, in which it may improve production (an external economy) or diminish production (an external diseconomy).

But the purpose of this note is to distinguish between two types of such external economies or diseconomies. The first type we shall call " unpaid factors of production," and the second the " creation of atmosphere." The essential difference between these two types of external economy or diseconomy is that in the first case there are still constant returns to scale for society as a whole, though not for the individual industry, whereas in the second case there are still constant returns to scale for each individual industry but not for society as a whole.

IV. UNPAID FACTORS

Suppose that in a given region there is a certain amount of apple-growing and a certain amount of bee-keeping and that the bees feed on the apple-blossom. If the apple-farmers apply 10% more labour, land and capital to apple-farming they will increase the output of apples by 10% ; but they will also provide more food for the bees. On the other hand, the bee-keepers will not increase the output of honey by 10% by increasing the amount of land, labour and capital applied to bee-keeping by 10% unless at the same time the apple-farmers also increase their output and so the food of the bees by 10%. Thus there are constant returns to scale for both industries taken together : if the amount of labour and of capital employed both in apple-farming and bee-keeping are doubled, the output of both apples and honey will be doubled. But if the amount of labour and capital are doubled in beé-keeping alone, the output of honey will be less than doubled; whereas, if the amounts of labour and capital in apple-farming are doubled, the output of apples will be doubled and, in addition, some contribution will be made to the output of honey.

We call this a case of an unpaid factor, because the situation is due simply and solely to the fact that the apple-farmer cannot charge the bee-keeper for the bees' food, which the former produces for the latter. If social-accounting institutions were such that this charge could be made, then every factor would, as in other competitive situations, earn the value of its marginal social net product. But as it is, the apple-farmer provides to the bee-keeper some of his factors free of charge. The apple-farmer is paid less than the value of his marginal social net product, and the bee-keeper receives more than the value of his marginal social net product.

This situation is shown if industry 1 represents bee-keeping and industry 2 apple-farming and if we replace equations (1) and (2) with

$$\left. \begin{array}{l} x_1 = H_1(l_1,\, c_1,\, x_2) \\ x_2 = H_2(l_2,\, c_2) \end{array} \right\} \quad . \quad . \quad . \quad (4)$$

so that $\qquad \epsilon_{l_1}^{x_1} + \epsilon_{c_1}^{x_1} + \epsilon_{x_2}^{x_1} = \epsilon_{l_2}^{x_2} + \epsilon_{c_2}^{x_2} = 1$

In this case l_1 will be paid the value of its marginal social net product, and we have $L_1 = \bar{L}_1 = \epsilon_{l_1}^{x_1} X_1$. c_1 will be paid $X_1 - L_1$ or $\epsilon_{c_1}^{x_1} X_1 + \epsilon_{x_2}^{x_1} X_2$; but $\epsilon_{c_1}^{x_1} X_1$ is the value of c_1's marginal social net product, so that we have $C_1 = \bar{C}_1 + \epsilon_{c_1}^{x_1} X_1$. In other words, c_1 will have to have its earnings taxed at an *ad valorem* rate of $\dfrac{X_1}{C_1} \epsilon_{x_2}^{x_1}$ in order to be paid a net reward equal to the value of its marginal social net product.

But, on the other hand, l_2 and c_2 will be paid just so much less than the value of their marginal social net products.

$$\bar{L}_2 = l_2 \left(\bar{x}_2 \frac{\partial x_2}{\partial l_2} + \bar{x}_1 \frac{\partial x_1}{\partial x_2} \cdot \frac{\partial x_2}{\partial l_2} \right)$$

$$= \epsilon_{l_2}^{x_2} X_2 \left(1 + \frac{X_1}{X_2} \epsilon_{x_2}^{x_1} \right)$$

But l_2 will receive only $\epsilon_{l_2}^{x_2} X_2$, so that $\bar{L}_2 = L_2 \left(1 + \frac{X_1}{X_2} \epsilon_{x_2}^{x_1} \right)$

and the wages of labour in apple-farming will need to be subsidised at an *ad valorem* rate of $\dfrac{X_1}{X_2}\epsilon_{x_2}^{x_1}$ in order to equate rewards to the value of the factor's marginal social net product. Similarly, $\bar{C}_2 = C_2(1 + \dfrac{X_1}{X_2}\epsilon_{x_2}^{x_1})$, and the same *ad valorem* rate of subsidy should be paid to the earnings of capital in apple-farming. Since $C_2 + L_2 = X_2$, the total tax revenue of $X_1\epsilon_{x_2}^{x_1}$ raised on C_1 will be equal to the two subsidies of $C_2\dfrac{X_1}{X_2}\epsilon_{x_2}^{x_1}$ and $L_2\dfrac{X_1}{X_2}\epsilon_{x_2}^{x_1}$.[2] In order to discover the appropriate rates of tax and subsidy the essential factor which will need to be estimated is $\epsilon_{x_2}^{x_1}$, the percentage effect on the output of honey which a 1% increase in the output of apples would exercise.

Now the relationship which we have just examined might be a reciprocal one. While the apples may provide the food of the bees, the bees may fertilise the apples.[3] Once again we may have constant returns to scale for society as a whole; a 10% increase in all factors in both industries would cause a 10% increase in the output of both products. In this case instead of equations (4) we should have

$$
\left.
\begin{aligned}
x_1 &= H_1(l_1,\, c_1,\, x_2) \\
x_2 &= H_2(l_2, c_2, x_1) \\
\epsilon_{l_1}^{x_1} + \epsilon_{c_1}^{x_1} + \epsilon_{x_2}^{x_1} &= \epsilon_{l_2}^{x_2} + \epsilon_{c_2}^{x_2} + \epsilon_{x_1}^{x_2} = 1
\end{aligned}
\right\} \quad . \quad . \quad (5)
$$

By a process similar to that adopted in the previous case we can obtain formulæ to show what subsidies and taxes must be imposed in order to equate each factor's income in each industry to the value of its marginal social net product.

We can obtain the actual rewards of the factors in exactly the same way as in the previous example. Labour in industry 1 will obtain a wage equal to the value of its marginal private net product or $\bar{x}_1\dfrac{\partial x_1}{\partial l_1}$, so that $L_1 = \epsilon_{l_1}^{x_1}X_1$. Capital in industry 1 will receive the remainder, or $X_1 - L_1$, so that from equations (5) $C_1 = X_1(\epsilon_{c_1}^{x_1} + \epsilon_{x_2}^{x_1})$. Similarly, $L_2 = \epsilon_{l_2}^{x_2}X_2$ and $C_2 = X_2(\epsilon_{c_2}^{x_2} + \epsilon_{x_1}^{x_2})$.

To obtain expressions for the value of each factor's marginal social net product we have now to allow for the repercussions of each industry upon the other. Thus the value of the marginal social net product of labour in apple-farming includes not only the increased output of apples directly produced but also the increased output of honey caused by this increase in apple-output plus the further increase in apple-output due to this increase in honey-output plus the still further increase in honey-output due to this increase in apple-output and so on in an infinite progression. The final result can be obtained in the following manner. Differentiating the main equations in equations (5), we have

$$dx_1 = \frac{\partial x_1}{\partial l_1} dl_1 + \frac{\partial x_1}{\partial c_1} dc_1 + \frac{\partial x_1}{\partial x_2} dx_2$$

$$dx_2 = \frac{\partial x_2}{\partial l_2} dl_2 + \frac{\partial x_2}{\partial c_2} dc_2 + \frac{\partial x_2}{\partial x_1} dx_1$$

If we keep c_1, l_2 and c_2 constant $(dc_1 = dl_2 = dc_2 = 0)$ but allow l_1 to vary $(dl_1 \neq 0)$, dx_1 and dx_2 will give the marginal social net products of l_1 in the two commodities. We obtain

$$\frac{dx_1}{dl_1} = \frac{\dfrac{\partial x_1}{\partial l_1}}{1 - \dfrac{\partial x_1}{\partial x_2} \cdot \dfrac{\partial x_2}{\partial x_1}} \quad \text{and} \quad \frac{dx_2}{dl_1} = \frac{\dfrac{\partial x_2}{\partial x_1} \cdot \dfrac{\partial x_1}{\partial l_1}}{1 - \dfrac{\partial x_1}{\partial x_2} \cdot \dfrac{\partial x_2}{\partial x_1}}$$

But

$$\bar{L}_1 = l_1 \bar{x}_1 \frac{dx_1}{dl_1} + l_1 \bar{x}_2 \frac{dx_2}{dl_1}$$

$$= l_1 \frac{\partial x_1}{\partial l_1} \frac{\bar{x}_1 + \bar{x}_2 \dfrac{\partial x_2}{\partial x_1}}{1 - \dfrac{\partial x_1}{\partial x_2} \cdot \dfrac{\partial x_2}{\partial x_1}}$$

$$= L_1 \frac{1 + \dfrac{X_2}{X_1} \cdot \epsilon_{x_1}^{x_2}}{1 - \epsilon_{x_2}^{x_1} \epsilon_{x_1}^{x_2}}$$

Similarly, we get the following expressions for the values of the marginal social net products of the other factors.

$$\bar{L}_2 = L_2 \frac{1 + \dfrac{X_1}{X_2} \epsilon_{x_2}^{x_1}}{1 - \epsilon_{x_2}^{x_1} \epsilon_{x_1}^{x_2}}$$

$$\bar{C}_1 = \epsilon_{c_1}^{x_1} X_1 \frac{1 + \dfrac{X_2}{X_1} \epsilon_{x_1}^{x_2}}{1 - \epsilon_{x_2}^{x_1} \epsilon_{x_1}^{x_2}} = (C_1 - \epsilon_{x_2}^{x_1} X_1) \frac{1 + \dfrac{X_2}{X_1} \epsilon_{x_1}^{x_2}}{1 - \epsilon_{x_2}^{x_1} \epsilon_{x_1}^{x_2}}$$

$$\bar{C}_2 = (C_2 - \epsilon_{x_1}^{x_2} X_2) \frac{1 + \dfrac{X_1}{X_2} \epsilon_{x_2}^{x_1}}{1 - \epsilon_{x_2}^{x_1} \epsilon_{x_1}^{x_2}}$$

On these expressions we can make the following three comments:

First, remembering that $L_1 + C_1 = X_1$ and $L_2 + C_2 = X_2$, we can see from the above expressions that $\bar{L}_1 + \bar{L}_2 + \bar{C}_1 + \bar{C}_2 = X_1 + X_2$. In other words, if the factors were all paid rewards equal to the value of their marginal social net products, this would absorb the whole of the product, neither more nor less. This is due, of course, to the essential constant-returns nature of the production functions at equations (5), from which it can be seen that if l_1, l_2, c_1 and c_2 were to increase by 10%, then the production conditions would be satisfied if both outputs also increased by 10%. In other words, we are still dealing with a pure unpaid-factor case; there is no adding-up problem for society; every factor can be given a reward equal to the value of its marginal social net product if the revenue from the taxes levied on those which ought to be taxed is used to subsidise the earnings of those which ought to be subsidised.

Secondly, $\bar{L}_1$, $\bar{L}_2$, $\bar{C}_1$ and $\bar{C}_2$ are all seen to be positive finite quantities, provided that $\epsilon_{x_2}^{x_1}\epsilon_{x_1}^{x_2} < 1$. From the last of equations (5) it can be seen that $\epsilon_{x_2}^{x_1}$ and $\epsilon_{x_1}^{x_2}$ are both < 1; it requires a 10% increase of land, labour and apple-blossom to increase the output of honey by 10%, so that a 10% increase in the supply of apple-blossom alone will increase the output of honey by less than 10%. But $\epsilon_{x_2}^{x_1}$ and $\epsilon_{x_1}^{x_2}$ are both positive, since we are dealing with external economies and not diseconomies. It follows, therefore, that $0 < \epsilon_{x_2}^{x_1}\epsilon_{x_1}^{x_2} < 1$, so that $\bar{L}_1$, $\bar{L}_2$, $\bar{C}_1$ and $\bar{C}_2$ are all positive finite quantities. It is because $\epsilon_{x_2}^{x_1}$ and $\epsilon_{x_1}^{x_2}$ are both positive fractions that the infinite progression of an increase in apple-output causing an increase in honey-output, causing an increase in apple-output and so on, adds up only to a finite sum. For example, if both $\epsilon_{x_2}^{x_1}$ and $\epsilon_{x_1}^{x_2}$ are one-half, a 10% increase in apple-output causes a 5% increase in honey-output, but this 5% increase in honey-output causes only a $2\frac{1}{2}$% increase in apple-output; which causes only a $1\frac{1}{4}$% increase in honey-output and so on in a diminishing geometric progression.

Thirdly, from the above expressions for L_1 and $\bar{L}_1$, we obtain

$$\frac{\bar{L}_1 - L_1}{L_1} = \frac{\dfrac{X_2}{X_1}\epsilon_{x_1}^{x_2} + \epsilon_{x_2}^{x_1}\epsilon_{x_1}^{x_2}}{1 - \epsilon_{x_2}^{x_1}\epsilon_{x_1}^{x_2}}$$

which shows the *ad valorem* rate of subsidy which must be paid to l_1 to bring its earnings up to the value of its marginal social net product. We can obtain a similar expression for the rates of tax levyable upon C_1.

$$\frac{C_1 - \bar{C}_1}{C_1} = \frac{\epsilon_{x_2}^{x_1}\dfrac{X_1}{C_1} - \dfrac{X_2}{X_1}\epsilon_{x_1}^{x_2} + \dfrac{X_2 - C_1}{C_1}\epsilon_{x_2}^{x_1}\epsilon_{x_1}^{x_2}}{1 - \epsilon_{x_2}^{x_1}\epsilon_{x_1}^{x_2}}$$

Corresponding expressions for $\dfrac{\bar{L}_2 - L_2}{L_2}$ and $\dfrac{C_2 - \bar{C}_2}{C_2}$ can be obtained by interchanging the subscripts 1 and 2. It can be seen from adding $C_1 - \bar{C}_1$ and $C_2 - \bar{C}_2$ that there will be a positive tax revenue raised from capital as a whole. But either $C_1 - \bar{C}_1$

or $C_2 - \overline{C}_2$ might be negative, *i.e.*, a subsidy might be payable on the earnings of capital in one of the two industries as well as upon the earnings of labour in both of the industries. For example, $C_2 - \overline{C}_2$ would be < 0 if $\epsilon_{x_1}^{x_1}$ were very large relatively to $\epsilon_{x_1}^{x_2}$. This would mean, for example, that the production of honey (industry 1) did very little to help the production of apples (industry 2), while the production of apples did much to help the production of bees. Capitalists in apple-farming should be subsidised because the unpaid benefits which they confer upon the bee-keepers more than outweigh the unpaid benefits which they receive from labour and capital employed in bee-keeping. Indeed, all the results obtained from equations (4) can be obtained from the expressions derived from equations (5) by writing $\epsilon_x^{x_1} = 0$.

V. THE CREATION OF ATOMOSPHERE

A distinction must be drawn between a " factor of production " and a physical or social " atmosphere " affecting production. We may take the rainfall in a district as a typical example of atmosphere. The rainfall may be deficient in the sense that a higher rainfall would increase the farmers' output, but nevertheless what rainfall there is will be available to all farms in the district regardless of their number. Thus if in the district in question the amount of land, labour and capital devoted to, say, wheat-farming were to be increased by 10%, the output of wheat would also be increased by 10% even if the rainfall were to remain constant. This is quite different from the case of a factor of production for which no payment is made ; in our previous example, a 10% increase in the output of apples (and so in the supply of apple-blossom) would be necessary, in addition to a 10% increase in the amount of land, labour and capital devoted to bee-keeping, if the output of honey is to be increased by 10%. In these examples, rainfall is an " atmosphere " for wheat-farming; but the output of apples is an "unpaid factor of production" for bee-keeping.

The distinction should now be clear. Both a factor of production and an atmosphere are conditions which affect the output of a certain industry. But the atmosphere is a fixed condition of production which remains unchanged for all producers in the industry in question without anyone else doing anything about it, however large or small—within limits—is the scale of operations of the industry. On the other hand, the factor of production is an aid to production which is fixed in amount, and which is therefore available on a smaller scale to each producer in the industry if the number of producers increases, unless someone does something to increase the total supply of the factor.

The external economies which we have examined in the last section are concerned with factors of production for which the individual producer pays nothing. We must turn now to external economies and diseconomies which are due to the fact that the activities of one group of producers may provide an atmosphere which is favourable or unfavourable to the activities of another group of producers. For example, suppose that afforestation schemes in one locality increase the rainfall in that district and that this is favourable to the production of wheat in that district. In this case the production of timber creates an atmosphere favourable to the production of wheat.

In these cases there is an adding-up problem for society as a whole. There may be constant returns to the factors of production employed in either industry alone. That is to say, a 10% increase in the amounts of land, labour and capital employed in producing wheat might, in any given atmosphere, result in a 10% increase in the output of wheat. And a 10% increase in the amount of land, labour and capital employed in producing timber might, apart from its effect in changing the atmosphere for wheat-farmers, cause a 10% increase in the output of timber. It follows that a 10% increase in the amount of land, labour and capital employed both in the timber industry and in wheat-farming will increase the output of timber by 10% and the output of wheat by more than 10% (because of the improvement in the atmosphere for wheat producers). To society as a whole there are now increasing returns to scale; to pay every factor a reward equal to the value of its marginal social net product will account for more than the total output of the two industries; revenue will have to be raised from outside sources by general taxation if subsidies are to be paid on a scale to bring every factor's reward up to the value of its marginal social net product.

We can express this sort of situation by the following equations :

$$x_1 = H_1(l_1, c_1)A_1(x_2)$$
$$x_2 = H_2(l_2, c_2)$$

where once more

$$\epsilon_{l_1}^{x_1} + \epsilon_{c_1}^{x_1} = \epsilon_{l_2}^{x_2} + \epsilon_{c_2}^{x_2} = 1.\ [1]$$

. . . (6)

---

[1] Since $l_1 \dfrac{\partial H_1}{\partial l_1} = \dfrac{l_1}{H_1 A_1} \cdot \dfrac{A_1 \partial H_1}{\partial l_1} H_1 = \dfrac{l_1}{x_1} \cdot \dfrac{\partial x_1}{\partial l_1} H_1 = \epsilon_{l_1}^{x_1} H_1$, we have $H_1 = \epsilon_{l_1}^{x_1} H_1 + \epsilon_{c_1}^{x_1} H_1$, so that $1 = \epsilon_{l_1}^{x_1} + \epsilon_{c_1}^{x_1}$.

$x_2 = H_2(l_2, c_2)$ is the ordinary competitive constant-returns production function for the timber industry. There is the same type of production function for the wheat industry; but in this case the output due to the use of labour and land $(H_1[c_1, l_1])$ is subject to an atmosphere (A_1). If the atmosphere is favourable then $H_1(l_1, c_1)$ is multiplied up by a large factor to give the actual output (x_1). In the case which we are examining the atmosphere for the wheat industry (A_1) is made to depend upon the output of the timber industry $(A_1 = A_1[x_2])$.

The atmosphere factor (A_1) is thus subject to the following conditions. $A_1(0) = 1$, i.e., we define our terms in such a way that $H_1(l_1, c_1)$ is equal to what the output of wheat would be if there were no timber output. A_1 is always >0, i.e., there cannot be so powerful an external diseconomy that the output of the industry affected becomes negative. When $A_1(x_2) > 1$, then there is an average external economy, i.e., the output of wheat is greater than it would have been had there been a zero output of timber instead of a positive output (x_2); and similarly, when $A_1(x_2) < 1$, there is an average external diseconomy. When $A_1'(x_2)$ is >0, then there is a marginal external economy, i.e., the output of wheat would be improved by a further increase in the output of timber; and when $A_1'(x_2)$ is <0, there is a marginal external diseconomy.

The actual rewards of the factors of production are easily seen to be $L_1 = \epsilon_{l_1}^{x_1} X_1$, $C_1 = X_1 - L_1 = \epsilon_{c_1}^{x_1} X_1, L_2 = \epsilon_{l_2}^{x_2}\ X_2$ and $C_2 = X_2 - L_2 = \epsilon_{c_2}^{x_2} X_2$. In the case of the factors employed in wheat-farming (industry 1) there will be no divergence between the reward paid and the value of the marginal social net product; and $L_1 = \bar{L}_1$ and $C_1 = \bar{C}_1$.

But the rewards actually paid to the factors of production in the timber industry (industry 2) will be lower than the value of their marginal social net products because they will not be paid for the favourable atmosphere which they create for wheat farmers. Thus

$$\bar{L}_2 = \epsilon_{l_2}^{x_2} X_2 + l_2 \bar{x}_1 \frac{\partial x_1}{\partial x_2} \cdot \frac{\partial x_2}{\partial l_2}$$

$$= L_2 \left(1 + \frac{X_1}{X_2} \cdot \epsilon_{x_2}^{x_1}\right)$$

where $\epsilon_{x_2}^{x_1} = \dfrac{x_2}{x_1} \cdot \dfrac{\partial x_1}{\partial x_2}$ or $\dfrac{x_2}{A_1} \cdot \dfrac{\partial A_1}{\partial x_2}$, the percentage increase in the output of wheat which would be brought about by a 1% increase in the output of timber through the improvement in the atmosphere for wheat production. And similarly, it can be shown that $\bar{C}_2 = C\left(1 + \dfrac{X_1}{X_2}\epsilon_{x_2}^{x_1}\right)$. In other words, the earnings of both l_2 and c_2 or, alternatively, the price of the product x_2 must be subsidised from general revenue at the *ad valorem* rate of $\dfrac{X_1}{X_2}\epsilon_{x_2}^{x_1}$ if all factors are to receive rewards equal to the value of their marginal social net products.

As in the case of unpaid factors, these reactions of one industry upon the other may be reciprocal. Industry 1 may create a favourable or unfavourable atmosphere for industry 2, as well as industry 2 for industry 1. In this case we have

$$
\left.
\begin{aligned}
x_1 &= H_1(l_1, c_1)A_1(x_2) \\
x_2 &= H_2(l_2, c_2)A_2(x_1)
\end{aligned}
\right\} \qquad \cdots \quad (7)
$$

where

$$\epsilon_{l_1}^{x_1} + \epsilon_{c_1}^{x_1} = \epsilon_{l_2}^{x_2} + \epsilon_{c_2}^{x_2} = 1$$

Here again $L_1 = \epsilon_{l_1}^{x_1}X_1$, $C_1 = X_1 - L_1 = \epsilon_{c_1}^{x_1}X_1$, $L_2 = \epsilon_{l_2}^{x_2}X_2$ and $C_2 = X_2 - L_2 = \epsilon_{c_2}^{x_2}X_2$.

But when we come to consider the marginal social net product, we have to take into account the infinite chain of action and reaction of the one industry upon the other, as in the case of apple-growing and bee-keeping examined above. The marginal social net product of l_1, for example, is obtained by differentiating the first two of equations (7), keeping l_2, c_1 and c_2 all constant. We obtain

$$
\frac{dx_1}{dl_1} = \frac{\epsilon_{l_1}^{x_1} \cdot \dfrac{x_1}{l_1}}{1 - \epsilon_{x_2}^{x_1}\epsilon_{x_1}^{x_2}}
\qquad \text{and} \qquad
\frac{dx_2}{dl_1} = \frac{\epsilon_{l_1}^{x_1}\epsilon_{x_1}^{x_2} \cdot \dfrac{x_2}{l_1}}{1 - \epsilon_{x_2}^{x_1}\epsilon_{x_1}^{x_2}}
$$

Now $\bar{L}_1 = l_1\bar{x}_1\dfrac{dx_1}{dl_1} + l_1\bar{x}_2\dfrac{dx_2}{dl_1}$, so that $\dfrac{\bar{L}_1}{L_1} = \dfrac{1 + \dfrac{X_2}{X_1}\epsilon_{x_1}^{x_2}}{1 - \epsilon_{x_2}^{x_1}\epsilon_{x_1}^{x_2}}$

Similarly, we can show that $\dfrac{\bar{C}_1}{C_1} = \dfrac{\bar{L}_1}{L}$ and that

$$
\frac{\bar{L}_2}{L_2} = \frac{\bar{C}_2}{C_2} = \frac{1 + \dfrac{X_1}{X_2}\epsilon_{x_2}^{x_1}}{1 - \epsilon_{x_1}^{x_2}\epsilon_{x_2}^{x_1}}
$$

In other words, in order that each factor should obtain a reward equal to the value of its marginal social net product both labour and capital in industry 1, or alternatively, the price of the product of industry 1, should be subsidised at the, *ad valorem* rate of $\epsilon^{x_1}_{x_2}\dfrac{\dfrac{X_2}{X_1} + \epsilon^{x_1}_{x_2}}{1 - \epsilon^{x_2}_{x_1}\epsilon^{x_1}_{x_2}}$; and similarly, in industry 2 a rate of subsidy of $\epsilon^{x_1}_{x_2}\dfrac{\dfrac{X_1}{X_2} + \epsilon^{x_2}_{x_1}}{1 - \epsilon^{x_2}_{x_1}\epsilon^{x_1}_{x_2}}$ should be paid.

So far throughout this note we have assumed that in all external economies or diseconomies, whether of the unpaid-factor or of the atmosphere-creating kind, it is the *output* of one industry which affects production in the other. But this is, of course, not necessarily the case. It may be the employment of one *factor* in one industry which confers an indirect benefit or the reverse upon producers in the other industry.[4] Moreover, in the case in which atmosphere is created, the output of industry 2 may create an atmosphere for industry 1 which increases the efficiency of a particular *factor* in industry 1 rather than the general level of *output*.[5] Or the employment of a particular *factor* in industry 2 might create conditions which improved the efficiency of a particular factor in industry 1.[6] And any combination of these indirect effects of industry 2 upon industry 1 might be combined with any other combination of such effects of industry 1 on industry 2. Clearly, we cannot consider in detail all the very many possibilities.

But consider the following particular case :

$$\left.\begin{aligned}
x_1 &= H_1(\lambda_1, c_1)\\
x_2 &= H_2(\lambda_2, c_2)\\
\lambda_1 &= l_1 A(l)\\
\lambda_2 &= l_2 A(l)\\
l &= l_1 + l_2
\end{aligned}\right\} \quad . \quad . \quad . \quad . \quad . \quad (8)$$

where $l_1 = $ the number of workers employed in industry 1 and $\lambda_1 = $ the equivalent number of workers of an efficiency which an individual worker would have if the total labour force were very small ($l \to 0$, so that $A \to 1$.)

This is the case where the total labour force in the two industries (l) affects the general efficiency of labour. We may suppose that, up to a certain point, a growth in the absolute size of the labour force employed in these two industries causes a general atmosphere favourable to the efficiency of labour by enabling workers to communicate to each other a certain know-how about, and interest in, the mechanical processes which are common to the two industries.

Now the individual employer in any one firm in either industry will regard A as being unaffected by his own actions, because the indirect effect which an increase in the number of workers employed by him alone will have upon the general efficiency of his own labour will be a negligible quantity. He will go on taking on labour of any given level of efficiency until the wage paid to a unit of labour is equal to the price paid for its marginal product at that level of efficiency. In other words,

$$L_1 = \lambda_1 \bar{x}_1 \frac{\partial x_1}{\partial \lambda_1} = \epsilon_{\lambda_1}^{x_1} X_1$$

The reward paid to c_1 will be $C_1 = X_1 - L_1 = \epsilon_{c_1}^{x_1} X_1$.
Similarly, $L_2 = \epsilon_{\lambda_2}^{x_2} X_2$ and $C_2 = \epsilon_{c_2}^{x_2} X_2$.

In this case $\bar{C}_1 = \epsilon_{c_1}^{x_1} X_1$ and $\bar{C}_2 = \epsilon_{c_2}^{x_2} X_2$ because there are no external economies or diseconomies involved in decisions to apply more capital in either industry, so that $C_1 = \bar{C}_1$ and $C_2 = \bar{C}_2$.

But in evaluating the value of the marginal social net product of labour we have to take into account the effect which the employment of more labour by one particular employer may have upon the efficiency of labour for all other employers in industry 1 and for all other employers in industry 2. The value of the marginal social net product exceeds the wage which will be offered for it by these two sums, so that

$$\bar{L}_1 = L_1 + l_1 \bar{x}_1 \frac{\partial x_1}{\partial \lambda_1} \cdot \frac{\partial \lambda_1}{\partial l} \cdot \frac{\partial l}{\partial l_1} + l_1 \bar{x}_2 \frac{\partial x_2}{\partial \lambda_2} \cdot \frac{\partial \lambda_2}{\partial l} \cdot \frac{\partial l}{\partial l_1}.$$

Since $\quad \frac{\partial l}{\partial l_1} = 1, \quad \frac{\partial \lambda_1}{\partial l} = \frac{\lambda_1}{A} \cdot \frac{\partial A}{\partial l}, \quad$ and $\quad \frac{\partial \lambda_2}{\partial l} = \frac{\lambda_2}{A} \cdot \frac{\partial A}{\partial l},$

we have $\quad \bar{L}_1 = L_1 + (L_1 + L_2) \frac{l_1}{l} \epsilon_l^A, \quad$ where $\quad \epsilon_l^A = \frac{l}{A} \cdot \frac{dA}{dl}.$

Similarly, $\bar{L}_2 = L_2 + (L_1 + L_2) \frac{l_2}{l} \epsilon_l^A.$ Now if the wage-rate is the

same in both industries so that $\frac{l_1}{l} = \frac{L_1}{L_1 + L_2}$ and $\frac{l_2}{l} = \frac{L_2}{L_1 + L_2},$

we have $\frac{\bar{L}_1}{L_1} = \frac{\bar{L}_2}{L_2} = 1 + \epsilon_l^A.$ The employment of labour in

both industries must be subsidised at the *ad valorem* rate of ϵ_l^A, if rewards are to be raised to the value of marginal social net products.

73

VI. CONCLUSION

It is not claimed that this division of external economies and diseconomies into unpaid factors and the creation of atmosphere is logically complete. External economies exist whenever we have production functions of the form

$$x_1 = F_1(l_1, c_1, l_2, c_2, x_2)$$
$$x_2 = F_2(l_2, c_2, l_1, c_1, x_1)$$

where F_1 and F_2 are not necessarily homogeneous of the first degree. But it is claimed that it may clarify thought on different types of external economy and diseconomy to distinguish thus between : (1) those cases in which there are constant returns for society, but not necessarily constant returns in each industry to the factors which each industry employs and pays for, and (2) those cases in which there are constant returns in each industry to those factors which it controls and pays for, but in which there are not constant returns for the two industries taken together, the scale of operations being important in the one industry because of the atmosphere which it creates for the other. One of the most important conclusions to be drawn is that in the case of type (1)—the unpaid-factor case—there is no adding-up problem for society as a whole; in order to pay every factor a reward equal to the value of its marginal social net product some factors must be taxed and others subsidised, and the revenue from the appropriate taxes will just finance the expenditure upon the appropriate subsidies. But in the case of the creation of atmosphere (type (2)) the subsidies (or taxes) required to promote (or discourage) the creation of favourable (or unfavourable) atmosphere are net additions to (or subtractions from) society's general fiscal burden. But, in fact, of course, external economies or diseconomies may not fall into either of these precise divisions and may contain features of both of them.

NOTES

[1] This note has arisen, out of a consideration of the problems of the economic development of under-developed territories, in the preparation of Volume II of my *Theory of International Economic Policy* for the Royal Institute of International Affairs.

[2] In this case it would, of course, have exactly the same effect if the subsidy were paid not on the wages of labour and profits of capital in apple-farming but at the same *ad valorem* rate on the value of the apple-output, X_2.

[3] If the bees had a bad effect upon the apples, then we should have an external diseconomy, which may be regarded as an unpaid negative factor of production. The bee-keepers, in addition to getting the bee-food free of charge, are also not charged for some damage which they do to the apple-farmers. In what follows

$\epsilon_{x_1}^{x_2}$ would be < 0, so that $\epsilon_{l_2}^{z_2} + \epsilon_{c_2}^{z_2} > 1$.

[4] In this case we should have equations of the type of $x_1 = H_1(l_1, c_1, l_2)$ in the case of unpaid factors, and of the type of $x_1 = H_1(l_1, c_1)A_1(l_2)$ in the case of atmosphere-creation.

[5] In this case the equations would be of the type $x_1 = H_1\{l_1 A_1(x_2), c_1\}$.

[6] For example, $x_1 = H_1\{l_1 A(c_2), c_1\}$.

No. 245—VOL. LXII.   F

Two Concepts of External Economies[1]

By TIBOR SCITOVSKY

The concept of external economies is one of the most elusive in economic literature. Our understanding of it has been greatly enhanced by the active controversy of the twenties over the nature of the "empty economic boxes"; but full clarity has never been achieved. Definitions of external economies are few and unsatisfactory. It is agreed that they mean services (and disservices) rendered free (without compensation) by one producer to another; but there is no agreement on the nature and form of these services or on the reasons for their being free. It is also agreed that external economies are a cause for divergence between private profit and social benefit and thus for the failure of perfect competition to lead to an optimum situation; but for this there are many reasons, and it is nowhere made clear how many and which of these reasons are subsumed under the heading of "external economies." Nor do examples help to clarify the concept. The literature contains many examples of external economies; but they are as varied and dissimilar as are discussions of the subject. Some give the impression that external economies are exceptional and unimportant; others suggest that they are important and ubiquitous. Indeed, one might be tempted to explain this strange dichotomy by ideological differences between the different authors; but such an explanation would be both unwarranted and unnecessary. For, with the increasing rigor of economic thinking and separation of the different branches of economic theory, it is becoming increasingly clear that the concept of external economies does duty in two entirely different contexts. One of these is equilibrium theory, the other is the theory of industrialization in underdeveloped countries. It is customary to discuss these two subjects at different levels of abstraction and on the basis of very different sets of assumptions: no wonder that "external economies" stand for very different things in the two contexts. Indeed, I shall argue that there are two entirely different definitions of external economies, one much wider than the other; and that external economies as defined in the theory of industrialization include, but go far beyond, the external economies of equilibrium theory. The latter have been discussed and rogorously defined in Professor Meade's "External Economies and Diseconomies in a Competitive Situation",[2] but, since they form part

---

Reprinted by permission of the publishers and author: Tibor Scitovsky, "Two Concepts of External Economies," *Journal of Political Economy,* 62 (April 1954), pp. 143-151.

of external economies as defined in the theory of industrialization, we shall deal with them briefly here.

I

Equilibrium theory, in both its general and its partial form, is a static theory, concerned with the characteristics of the economic system when it is in equilibrium. Most of its conclusions are based on the assumptions of (1) perfect competition on both sides of every market and (2) perfect divisibility of all resources and products. These assumptions underlie the main conclusion of general equilibrium theory, viz., that the market economy leads to a situation of economic optimum (in Pareto's sense), provided that every economic influence of one person's (or firm's) behavior on another person's well-being (or firm's profit) is transmitted through its impact on market prices. Expressed differently, equilibrium in a perfectly competitive economy is a situation of Paretian optimum, except when there is interdependence among the members of the economy that is direct, in the sense that it does not operate through the market mechanism. In general equilibrium theory, then, direct interdependence is the villain of the piece and the cause for conflict between private profit and social benefit.

One can distinguish four types of direct (i.e., nonmarket) interdependence (and one of these—the last one in the following enumeration—is known as "external economies"): (1) The individual person's satisfaction may depend not only on the quantities of products he consumes and services he renders but also on the satisfaction of other persons. In particular, the high income or consumption of others may give a person pain or pleasure; and so may his knowledge that some others are less well off than he is. This is known as the "interdependence of consumers' satisfaction." (2) A person's satisfaction may be influenced by the activities of producers not only through their demand for his services and supply of the products he buys but also in ways that do not operate through the market mechanism. These may be called the producer's "direct" (i.e., nonmarket) influence on personal satisfaction and are best known by the example of the factory that inconveniences the neighborhood with the fumes or noise that emanate from it. (3) The producer's output may be influenced by the action of persons more directly and in other ways than through their offer of services used and demand for products produced by the firm. This is a counterpart of the previous case, and its main instance is inventions that facilitate production and become available to producers without charge. (4) The output of the individual producer may depend not only on his input of productive resources but also on the activities of other firms. This is a counterpart of case 1 and may be called "direct interdependence among producers" but is better known under the name of "external economies and diseconomies."[3]

Of these four cases of direct interdependence, the first, interdependence among consumers, is undoubtedly important. It is (together with the case mentioned in n. 3) among the main reasons for the current controversy in welfare economics and the reluctance of economists to make any welfare statements concerning the consumer. Nowadays, welfare statements are usually confined to the field of production, where the main conclusion of general equilibrium theory seems to stand on firmer ground, primarily because the remaining three cases of direct interdependence (all of which involve the producer) seem exceptional and unimportant. The second case seems exceptional, because most instances of it can be and usually are eliminated by zoning ordinances and industrial regulation concerned with public health and safety. The third case is unimportant, because patent laws have eliminated the main instance of this form of direct interdependence and transformed it into a case of interdependence through the market mechanism.[4] The fourth case seems unimportant, simply because examples of it seem to be few and exceptional.

The last statement appears at first to be contradicted by the many examples of external economies and diseconomies quoted in the literature; but most of these are *not* examples of direct interdependence among producers, which is the only meaning that can be attributed to the term "external economies" within the context of equilibrium theory. It will be useful in this connection to have a rigorous definition of direct interdependence among producers. Meade gave such a definition when he defined external economies; and I can do no better than to reproduce it. According to him, external economies exist whenever the output (x_1) of a firm depends not only on the factors of production $(l_1, c_1, \ldots)$ utilized by this firm but also on the output (x_2) and factor utilization l_2, $c_2, \ldots)$ of another firm or group of firms.[5] In symbols,

$$x_1 = F(l_1, c_1, \ldots ; \quad x_2, l_2, \ldots),$$

where the existence of external economies is indicated by the presence of the variables to the right of the semicolon. Since $F(*)$ is a production function, external economies as here defined are a peculiarity of the production function. For this reason it is convenient to call them "technological external economies."[6] While this will distinguish them from another category of external economies to be introduced presently, we must bear in mind that technological external economies are the only external economies that can arise, because of direct interdependence among producers and within the framework of general equilibrium theory.

The examples of external economies given by Meade are somewhat bucolic in nature, having to do with bees, orchards, and woods. This, however, is no accident: it is not easy to find examples from industry. Going through the many examples of external economies quoted in the literature, I found only two that fit the above definition: the case in which a firm benefits from the labor market created by the establishment of other firms and that in which several firms use a resource which is free but limited in supply.[7] For a more detailed discussion the reader is referred to Meade's article, which will, I think, convince him of the scarcity of technological external economies.

The other field in which the concept of external economies occurs frequently is the theory of industrialization of underdeveloped countries, where the concept is used in connection with the special problem of allocating savings among alternative investment opportunities. This last is one of the many practical problems to which economists are wont to apply the conclusions of general equilibrium theory. Most of them realize, of course, that general equilibrium theory is limited in its assumptions and applicability; but the only limitation taken seriously by most economists is that imposed by the assumption of perfect competition; and this—as is well known—is not always a necessary condition for the conclusions of equilibrium theory to hold good. In particular, many economists regard a uniform degree of monopoly as all that is necessary for market forces to bring about an optimum allocation of investment funds; and this weaker condition is held to be more nearly fulfilled in our society. Whether for this reason or for some other, the private profitability of investment is usually considered a good index of its social desirability, at least as a general rule.

To this rule, however,, the exceptions are too great and obvious to be ignored, especially in underdeveloped countries; and it is customary to impute most of them to external economies. While the nature of these external economies is often discussed, I have been unable to find a definition of the concept in the literature dealing with underdeveloped countries. It is possible, however, to infer a definition from the many examples, discussions, and obiter dicta. It seems that external economies are invoked whenever the profits of one producer are affected by the actions of other producers. To facilitate comparison with Meade's definition, we can express this in symbols by the function

$$P_1 = G(x_1, l_1, c_1, \ldots ; x_2, l_2, c_2, \ldots),$$

which shows that the profits of the firm depend not only on its own output and factor inputs but also on the output and factor inputs of other firms; and we shall say that in the context of underdeveloped countries external economies are said to exist whenever the variables to the right of the semicolon are present.

This definition of external economies obviously includes direct or nonmarket interdependence among producers, as discussed above and defined by Meade. It is much broader, however, than his definition, because, in addition to direct interdependence among producers, it also includes interdependence among producers through the market mechanism. This latter type of interdependence may be called "pecuniary external economies" to distinguish it from the technological external economies of direct interdependence.[8]

Interdependence through the market mechanism is all-pervading, and this explains the contrast between the exceptional and often awkward examples of external economies cited in discussions of equilibrium theory and the impression one gains from the literature on underdeveloped countries that the entrepreneur creates external economies and diseconomies with his every move.

What is puzzling, however, is that interdependence through the market mechanism should be held to account for the failure of the market economy to lead to the socially desirable optimum, when equilibrium theory comes to the opposite conclusion and *relies* on market interdependence to bring about an optimum situation. Pecuniary external economies clearly have no place in equilibrium theory. The question is whether the concept is meaningful elsewhere. To answer this question we must first investigate the nature of the pecuniary external economics, to which interdependence through the market mechanism gives rise.

Investment in an industry leads to an expansion of its capacity and may thus lower the prices of its products and raise the prices of the factors used by it. The lowering of product prices benefits the users of these products; the raising of factor prices benefits the suppliers of the factors. When these benefits accrue to firms, in the form of profits, they are pecuniary external economies—Marshall called, or would have called, them (together with the benefits accuring to persons) consumers' and producers' surplus, respectively. According to the theory of industrialization, these benefits, being genuine benefits, should be explicitly taken into account when investment decisions are made; and it is usually suggested that this should be done by taking as the maximand not profits alone but the sum of the profits yielded and the pecuniary external economies created by the investment.

This prescription seems to be in direct conflict with the results of equilibrium theory. For, according to the latter and subject to its usual assumptions and limitations, market interdependence in the competitive system insures that the maximization of profit by each firm and of satisfaction by each person brings about an optimum situation, which, as is well known, is sometimes described as a situation in which consumers' and producers' surpluses are maximized. In other words, equilibrium theory tells us that in equilibrium the sum of consumers' and producers' surpluses will be maximized, although they do not enter explicitly, as part of the maximand, the economic decisions of any producer.[9] Assuming that these conflicting views are both right, the conflict can be resolved only if we should find that the limitations of general equilibrium theory render it inapplicable to the problems of investment. This, indeed, must often be so; but in the following we shall single out three special cases, which seem especially important and in which the above conflict is resolved.

a) One reason why the conclusions of general equilibrium theory may be inapplicable to the practical problem of investment is that the former's assumption of perfect divisibility is not always fulfilled. Perfect competition leads to a position of economic optimum, because under perfect competition the marginal conditions of economic optimum are contained (in the absence of direct interdependence) in the marginal conditions of profit maximization by producers and satisfaction maximization by householders. Indivisibilities, however, may prevent the producer from fulfilling these marginal conditions. For example, he may find himself unable to equate marginal costs to price and, instead, face the choice of producing either less or more than the output that would equate these two quantities. In such a case one of the available alternatives will still yield him a higher profit than all others; but this need no longer be the one that is also the

81

best from society's point of view. Hence the need, in such cases, to take society's point of view explicitly into consideration.

This fact was recognized as early as 1844 by Dupuit.[10] He was looking for a criterion of the social desirability of investment in such public utilities as canals, roads, bridges, and railways—the typical examples of indivisibilities in economics—and he found this criterion not in the actual profitability of such investments but in what their profitability would be in the hypothetical case in which the operator of the utility practiced price discrimination and thus appropriated to himself the consumers' surplus that would normally (i.e., in the absence of price discrimination) accrue to the users of the public utility. In other words, Dupuit's test of social desirability is whether the sum of profit and consumers' surplus is positive.[11] Dupuit's text and his use of the consumers' surplus concept underlying it were vindicated by Professor Hicks;[12] but neither Hicks nor Dupuit makes clear the role of indivisibilities in rendering the above test necessary. For this last point, as well as for an excellent statement of the entire argument, the reader should consult chapter xvi of Professor Lerner's *Economics of Control.*[13]

b) The second reason for the inapplicability of general equilibrium theory to the problems of investment is that the former is a static or equilibrium theory, whereas the allocation of investment funds is not a static problem at all. According to equilibrium theory, the producer's profit-maximizing behavior brings about a socially desirable situation *when the system is in equilibrium;* or, to give this result a more dynamic, if not entirely correct, interpretation, profit-maximizing behavior brings closer the socially desirable optimum if it also brings closer equilibrium. Investment, however, need not bring the system closer to equilibrium; and, when it does not, the results of equilibrium theory may not apply.

Profits are a sign of disequilibrium; and the magnitude of profits, under free competition, may be regarded as a rough index of the degree of disequilibrium.[14] Profits in a freely competitive industry lead to investment in that industry; and the investment, in turn, tends to eliminate the profits that have called it forth. This far, then, investment tends to bring equilibrium nearer. The same investment, however, may raise or give rise to profits in other industries; and to this extent it leads away from equilibrium. For example, investment in industry A will cheapen its product; and if this is used as a factor in industry B, the latter's profits will rise. This, then, is a case where the price reduction creates, not a consumers' surplus proper, accruing to persons, but pecuniary external economies, benefiting firms. Is this difference sufficient to render the conclusions of general equilibrium theory inapplicable?

To answer this question, we must pursue the argument a little further. The profits of industry B, created by the lower price of factor A, call for investment and expansion in industry B, one result of which will be an increase in industry B's demand for industry A's product. This in its turn will give rise to profits and call for further investment and expansion in industry A; and equilibrium is reached only when successive doses of investment and expansion in the two industries have led to the simultaneous elimination of profits in both. It is only at this stage, where equilibrium has been established, that the concluisons of equilibrium theory become applicable and we can say (on the usual assumptions and in the absence of direct interdependence) that the amount of investment profitable in industry A is also the socially desirable amount. This amount is clearly greater than that which is profitable at the first stage, before industry B has made adjustment. We can conclude, therefore, that when an investment gives rise to pecuniary external economies, its private profitability understates its social desirability.

Unfortunately, however, the test of social desirability applicable in the previous case is not applicable here, although it would probably give a better result than a simple calculation of profitability. This can easily be seen by comparing the situation under consideration with that which would obtain if industries A and B were integrated (although in such a way as to preserve the free competition assumed so far). In this case the pecuniary external economies created by investment in industry A would become "internal" and part of the profits of the investors themselves. Investment in A would be more profitable and pushed further than in the absence of integration; but, *without investment and expansion also in industry B,* it would not be pushed far enough. For what inhibits investment in A is the limitation on the demand for industry A's product imposed by the limited capacity of industry B, the consumer of this product; just as investment in industry B is inhibited by the limited capacity of industry A, the supplier of one of industry B's factors of production. These limitations can be fully removed only by a simultaneous expansion of both industries. We conclude, therefore, that only if expansion in the two industries were integrated and planned together would the profitability of investment in each one of them be a reliable index of its social desirability.

It hardly needs adding that the relation between industries A and B discussed above illustrates only one of the many possible instances of pecuniary external economies that belong in this category. Expansion in industry A may also give rise to profits (i) in an industry that produces a factor used in industry A, (ii) in an industry whose product is complementary in use to the product of industry A, (iii) in an industry whose product is a substitute for a factor used in industry A, or (iv) in an industry whose product is consumed by persons whose incomes are raised by the expansion of industry A—and this list does not include the cases in which the expansion causes external *dis*economies. It is apparent from this list that vertical integration alone would not be enough and that complete integration of all industries would be necessary to eliminate all divergence between private profit and public benefit. This was fully realized by Dr. Rosenstein-Rodan, who, in dealing with the "Problems of Industrialisation of Eastern and South-Eastern Europe,"[15] considered most instances of pecuniary external economies listed above and advocated that "the whole of the industry to be created is to be treated and planned like one huge firm or trust."[16] To put this conclusion differently, profits in a market economy are a bad guide to economic optimum as far as investment and industrial expansion are concerned; and they are worse, the more decentralized and differentiated the economy.

This entire argument can be restated in somewhat different terms. In an economy in which economic decisions are decentralized, a system of communications is needed to enable each person who makes economic decisions to learn about the economic decisions of others and coordinate his decisions with theirs. In the market economy, prices are the signaling device that informs each person of other people's economic decisions; and the merit of perfect competition is that it would cause prices to transmit information reliably and people to respond to this information properly. Market prices, however, reflect the economic situation as it is and not as it will be. For this reason, they are more useful for co-ordinating current production decisions, which are immediately effective and guided by short-run considerations, than they are for co-ordinating investment decisions, which have a delayed effect and—looking ahead to a long future period—should be governed not by what the present economic situation is but by what the future economic situation is expected to be. The proper co-ordination of investment decisions, therefore, would require a signaling device to transmit information about present plans and future conditions as they are determined by present plans; and the pricing system fails to provide this.[17] Hence the belief that there is need either for centralized investment planning or for some additional communication system to supplement the pricing system as a signaling device.

It must be added that the argument of this section applies with especial force to underdeveloped countries. The plant capacity most economical to build and operate is not very different in different countries; but, as a percentage of an industry's total capacity, it is very much greater in underdeveloped than in fully industrialized economies. In underdeveloped countries, therefore, investment is likely to have a greater impact on prices, give rise to greater pecuniary external economies, and thus cause a greater divergence between private profit and social benefit.

c) I propose to consider yet another reason for divergence between the profitability of an investment and its desirability from the community's point of view; but this is very different from those discussed in the last two sections and has to do with the difference between the national and international points of view. In appraising the social desirability of an economic action from the international point of view, all repercussions of that action must be fully taken into account, whereas, from the national point of view, the welfare of domestic nationals alone is relevant and the losses suffered and benefits gained by foreigners are ignored. The two points of view need not necessarily lead to different appraisals; but they usually do when the economic action considered is the allocation of investment funds among purely domestic, import-competing, and export industries. From the international point of view, all external economies and diseconomies must be taken into consideration; from the national point of view, one must count only the external economies and diseconomies that accrue to domestic nationals and leave out of account the pecuniary

84

external economies accruing to foreign buyers from the expansion of export industries and the diseconomies inflicted on foreign competitors by the expansion of import-competing industries. Accordingly, investment in export industries is always less, and that in import-competing industries is always more, desirable from the national, than from the international, point of view.

In discussions on investment policy this difference between the national and international points of view usually appears in the guise of a difference between the criteria of social benefit and private profit. For social benefit, when considered explicitly, is usually identified with national benefit in our society, whereas private profit, although an imperfect index of social desirability, accounts or fails to account for external economies and diseconomies without national bias and therefore probably comes closer to registering the social welfare of the world as a whole than that of a single nation. Hence investment tends to be more profitable in export industries and less profitable in import-competing industries than would be desirable from a narrow nationalistic point of view.

It is worth noting that this argument is in some respects the reverse of the argument of Section II*b* above. There it was the failure of profit calculations to take into account pecuniary external economies that caused the divergence between private profit and social benefit; here the divergence is caused by the entry into the profit criterion of pecuniary external economies and diseconomies that accrue to foreigners and should therefore be excluded from social accounting concerned with national, rather than world, welfare. The argument is well known as the "terms-of-trade argument" and has been used to explain the failure of foreign investments in colonial areas to benefit fully the borrowing countries.[18] The divergence between national welfare and private profit depends on the foreigners' import-demand and export-supply elasticities; and it can be offset by an appropriate set of import and export duties. This has been shown by Mr. J. de V. Graaff, in his "Optimum Tariff Structures."[19] De Graaff presents his optimum tariff structure as one that will bring about that flow of goods and services which optimizes[20] the nation's welfare; but the same tariff structure will also bring about the allocation of investment funds that is optimal from the national point of view.

NOTES

1. I am indebted to Professor Bernard Haley and Mr. Ralph Turvey for many helpful suggestions. The responsibility for errors, however, is entirely mine.

2. *Economic Journal,* LXII (1952), 54-67.

3. A fifth and important case, which, however does not quit fit into the above classification, is that where society provides social services through communal action and makes them available free of charge to all persons and firms.

4. I.e., patent laws have created a market and a market price for the inventor's services, which in the absence of such laws would often be free goods. The case where the results of government-sponsored research into industrial and agricultural methods are made gratuitously available to industrialists and farmers belongs in the category mentioned on n. 3 above.

5. *Op. cit.*

6. The term is used in Jacob Viner's "Cost Curves and Supply Curves," *Zeitschrift für Nationalökonomie,* III (1931), 23-46.

7. Instances of this are the oil well whose output depends on the number and operation of other wells on the same oil field; the fisherman whose catch depends on the operations of other fishermen in the same waters; and the firm that uses a public road (or other publicly owned utility) and is partly crowded out of it by other firms using the same road.

8. Cf. Viner, *op. cit.*

9. Cf. J. R. Hicks, "The Rehabilitation of Consumers' Surplus," *Review of Economic Studies, VIII (1941), 108-16. We need not enter here the debate on the usefulness of this terminology. Nor is it necessary to stress that this way of stating the results of perfect* competition is characteristic of partial equilibrium analysis.

10. Cf. Jules Dupuit, "De la mesure de l'utilité des travaux publics," *Annales des ponts et chaussées,* 2d ser., Vol. VIII (1844); reprinted in *International Economic Papers,* No. 2 (1952), pp. 83-110.

11. This is so whether the consumers' surplus accrues to persons or represents external economies accruing to firms.

12. Cf. J. R. Hicks, "L'Economie de bien-être et la théorie des surplus du consummateur," and "Quelques applications de la théorie des surplus du consommateur," both in *Economie appliquée,* No. 4 (1948), pp. 432-57.

13. A. P. Lerner, *Economics of Control* (New York: Macmillan Co., 1944). Lerner's solution is slightly different and, I believe, more correct than Dupuit's, in that he takes account also of producers' surplus. It might be added in passing that the type of indivisibility considered by Dupuit establishes a relation among the users of the public utility that is similar in all essentials to direct interdependence among consumers.

14. However, the absence of profits is not a sufficient condition of equilibrium.

15. *Economic Journal,* LIII (1943), 202-11.

16. *Ibid.,* p. 204.

17. Professor Kenneth Arrow pointed out to me, however, that, in a formal sense, futures markets and futures prices could provide exactly such a signaling device.

18. Cf. H. W. Singer, "The Distribution of Gains between Investing and Borrowing Countries," *American Economic Review (Proceedings),* XL (1950), 473-85.

19. *Review of Economic Studies,* XVII (1949-50), 47-59.

20. In Pareto's sense.

PART III
EXTERNALITIES: THE PUBLIC
SECTOR AND EXTERNALITIES

The group of articles in Part III serves to provide what can be called a modern and general framework for considering externalities. One theme that unites these papers is an attempt to construct more explicit ways of admitting externalities into economic analysis. A second theme is the general relationship to externalities of governmental allocation of goods and distribution of these costs, and of legal definition by the courts of property rights. While the first three articles get at the externality issue by way of considering aspects of public and private goods, the fourth and fifth articles emphasize the role property rights play in guiding decisions, when these decisions involve harmful or beneficial side effects to other parties or to persons other than the decision makers themselves.

"Aspects of Public Expenditure Theories" and "The Pure Theory of Public Expenditure" are two parts of what might loosely be called a series (1954 to 1958) of three directly related statements by Paul A. Samuelson which bear on externalities and fiscal theory.[1] So long as public collective services exist, analysis of their nature is needed. If, among other features, some public goods have external effects on the consumption side, adjustment or abandonment of earlier theory seems called for. It will pay rational men to mask individual preferences for many collective goods in order to avoid payment. In any event, a complete theory requires that all direct and indirect benefits and costs of social decisions be accounted for. Complex policy questions about just or equitable taxing or pricing for public goods with external effects remain.

Otto Davis and Andrew Whinston restate the elements of Samuelson's central arguments, then go on to discuss some policy implications of "market failure." Conditions for distributing Samuelsonian public goods and the act of paying for such goods are reviewed. The important role of property rights is briefly treated. The authors maintain that the nature of individual public goods, supply conditions, or technological considerations will help determine feasible institutional arrangements for provision of various public goods. Social costs will tend to vary with the institutional arrangements. The role of government policy in subscription television is used as a theoretical case study; but Davis and Whinston go further. They survey implications attending the provision of a wide range of other goods of the type normally left to public regulation: for example, bridges, where there are negligible marginal costs and extreme decreasing average costs. Their analysis leads them to conclude it is perhaps "a shame that public goods are called 'public'."

87

Just as the series of articles by Samuelson has tended to become an analytical reference point in modern public goods theory, so has the work by Ronald Coase, "The Problem of Social Cost." In this article Coase reviews a series of externality situations and the potential for exchange given legal rulings to overcome side effect results. The externality case examples presented in the article are deceptively simple. Through these examples Coase explores how far the government can effectively go to offset externalities through legal actions. He then contrasts expected governmental performance to what might happen if market-type adjustments were allowed to be negotiated between the parties benefiting or being damaged. If remedial steps are to be taken, both costs and benefits to private parties must be considered. In any event, the remedies themselves, whether market or governmental, have costs and benefits of their own and can affect the ways in which resources are used.

Pigovian welfare economics concepts as relating to externalities are critically reviewed. Finally, Coase argues that all factors of production should be thought of as rights. In choosing social arrangements within which people exercise these rights, adequate analysis must attempt to take into account the total effect.

"Toward a Theory of Property Rights," by Harold Demsetz, builds directly upon this matter of rights and the way it has generally been treated by economists. Demsetz reasons that a primary function of property rights is to guide choices of individuals so that there is "a greater internalization of externalities." The right of ownership and right of sale are discussed in terms of the military draft.

It is argued, and supported with examples, that property rights evolve with the technical emergence of costs and benefits from changes in resource use activities. In order to show what role private property rights play, Demsetz reviews a series of resource-use situations that can arise with a communal, rather than private, land property right system. Central to his discussion is the impact various rights arrangements can have upon individual initiatives. In conclusion he states, "All problems of externalities are closely analogous to those which arise in the land ownership example. The relevant variables are identical." The ideas developed in this article should be useful to analysts grappling with social policy problems ranging from natural resource use to ownership structures of universities.

Readers who want to follow up or explore further this property rights idea are urged to look at two other papers by Harold Demsetz which appeared in *The Journal of Law and Economics:* "The Exchange and Enforcement of Property Rights" (1964) and "Some Aspects of Property Rights" (1966).

NOTE

1. Space limitations in this book of readings forced the deletion of Samuelson's other article, "Diagrammatic Exposition of a Theory of Public Expenditure," *Review of Economics and Statistics* (November 1955).

The Pure Theory of Public Expenditure*

By PAUL A. SAMUELSON

1. ASSUMPTIONS

Except for Sax, Wicksell, Lindahl, Musgrave, and Bowen, economists have rather neglected the theory of optimal public expenditure, spending most of their energy on the theory of taxation. Therefore, I explicitly assume two categories of goods: ordinary *private consumption goods* $(X_1, \ldots, X_n)$, which can be parcelled out among different individuals $(1, 2, \ldots, i, \ldots, s)$ according to the relations

$$\bar{X}_j = \sum_{i=1}^{s} X_j^i;$$

and *collective consumption goods* $(X_{n+1}, \ldots, X_{n+m})$, which all enjoy in common in the sense that each individual's consumption of such a good leads to no subtraction from any other individual's consumption of that good, so $X_{n+j} = X_{n+j}^i$ simultaneously for each and every ith individual and each collective consumptive good. I assume no mystical collective mind that enjoys collective consumption goods; instead I assume each individual has a consistent set of *ordinal preferences* with respect to his consumption of all goods (collective as well as private), which can be summarized by a regularly smooth and convex utility index $u^i = u^i(X_1^i, \ldots, X_{n+m}^i)$ (any monotonic stretching of the utility index is of course also an admissible cardinal index of preference). I shall throughout follow the convention of writing the partial derivative of any function with respect to its jth argument by a j subscript, so $u_j^i = \partial u^i / \partial X_j^i$, etc. Provided economic quantities can be divided into two groups, (1) *outputs* or goods which everyone always wants to maximize and (2) inputs or factors which everyone always wants to minimize, we are free to change the algebraic signs of the latter category and from then on to

---

* *The Review of Economics and Statistics*, 36(1954): pp. 387–89. Reprinted by courtesy of the author and *The Review of Economics and Statistics*.

Reprinted by permission of the publishers and author: Paul A. Samuelson, "The Pure Theory of Public Expenditure," *The Review of Economics and Statistics*, 36 (1954), pp. 387-389.

work only with "goods," knowing that the case of factor inputs is covered as well. Hence by this convention we are sure that $u_j^i > 0$ always.

To keep production assumptions at the minimum level of simplicity, I assume a regularly convex and smooth production-possibility schedule relating totals of all outputs, private and collective; or $F(X_1, \ldots, X_{n+m}) = 0$, with $F_j > 0$ and ratios F_j/F_n determinate and subject to the generalized laws of diminishing returns.

Feasibility considerations disregarded, there is a *maximal* (ordinal) *utility frontier* representing the Pareto-optimal points—of which there are an $(s - 1)$-fold infinity—with the property that from such a frontier point you can make one person better off only by making some other person worse off. If we wish to make normative judgments concerning the relative ethical desirability of different configurations involving some individuals being on a higher level of indifference and some on a lower, we must be presented with a set of ordinal interpersonal norms or with a *social welfare function* representing a consistent set of ethical preferences among all the possible states of the system. It is not a "scientific" task of the economist to "deduce" the form of this function; this can have as many forms as there are possible ethical views; for the present purpose, the only restriction placed on the social welfare function is that it shall always increase or decrease when any one person's ordinal preference increases or decreases, all others staying on their same indifference levels: mathematically, we narrow it to the class that any one of its indexes can be written $U = U(u^1, \ldots, u^s)$ with $U_j > 0$.

2. OPTIMAL CONDITIONS

In terms of these norms, there is a "best state of the world" which is defined mathematically in simple regular cases by the marginal conditions

$$\frac{u_j^i}{u_r^i} = \frac{F_j}{F_r} \qquad \begin{array}{l} (i = 1, 2, \ldots, s; r, j = 1, \ldots, n) \text{ or} \\ (i = 1, 2, \ldots, s; r = 1; j = 2, \ldots, n), \end{array} \tag{1}$$

$$\sum_{i=1}^{s} \frac{u_{n+j}^i}{u_r^i} = \frac{F_{n+j}}{F_r} \qquad \begin{array}{l} (j = 1, \ldots, m; r = 1, \ldots, n) \text{ or} \\ (j = 1, \ldots, m; r = 1), \end{array} \tag{2}$$

$$\frac{U_i u_k^i}{U_q u_k^q} = 1 \qquad \begin{array}{l} (i, q = 1, \ldots, s; k = 1, \ldots, n) \text{ or} \\ (q = 1; i = 2, \ldots, s; k = 1). \end{array} \tag{3}$$

Equations (1) and (3) are essentially those given in the chapter on welfare economics in my *Foundations of Economic Analysis*. They constitute my version of the "new welfare economics." Alone (1) represents that subset of relations which defines the Pareto-optimal utility frontier and which by itself represents what I regard as the unnecessarily narrow version of what once was called the "new welfare economics."

The new element added here is the set (2), which constitutes a pure theory of government expenditure on collective consumption goods. By themselves (1) and (2) define the $(s - 1)$fold infinity of utility frontier points; only when a set of interpersonal normative conditions equivalent to (3) is supplied are we able to define an unambiguously "best" state.

Since formulating the conditions (2) some years ago, I have learned from the published and unpublished writings of Richard Musgrave that their essential logic is contained in the "voluntary-exchange" theories of public finance of the Sax-Wicksell-Lindahl-Musgrave type, and I have also noted Howard Bowen's independent discovery of them in Bowen's writings of a decade ago. A graphical interpretation of these conditions in terms of *vertical* rather than *horizontal* addition of different individuals' marginal-rate-of-substitution schedules can be given; but what I must emphasize is that there is a different such schedule for each individual at each of the $(s - 1)$fold infinity of different distributions of relative welfare along the utility frontier.

3. IMPOSSIBILITY OF DECENTRALIZED SPONTANEOUS SLOUTION

So much for the involved optimizing equations that an omniscient calculating machine could theoretically solve if fed the postulated functions. No such machine now exists. But it is well known that an "analogue calculating machine" can be provided by competitive market pricing, (a) so long as the production functions satisfy the neoclassical assumptions of constant returns to scale and generalized diminishing returns and (b) so long as the individuals' indifference contours have regular convexity and, we may add, (c) so long as all goods are private. We can then insert between the right- and left-hand sides of (1) the equality with uniform market prices p_j/p_r, and adjoin the budget equations for each individual

$$p_1 X_1^i + p_2 X_2^i + \cdots + p_n X_n^i = L^i \qquad (i = 1, 2, \ldots, s), \qquad (1')$$

where L^i is a lump-sum tax for each individual so selected in algebraic value as to lead to the "best" state of the world. Now note, if there were no collective consumption goods, then (1) and (1') can have their solution enormously simplified. Why? Because on the one hand perfect competition among productive enterprises would ensure that goods are produced at minimum costs and are sold at proper marginal costs, with all factors receiving their proper marginal productivities; and on the other hand, each individual, in seeking as a competitive buyer to get to the highest level of indifference subject to given prices and tax, would be led as if by an Invisible Hand to the grand solution of the social maximum position. Of course the institutional framework of competition would have to be maintained, and political decision making would still be necessary, but of a computationally minimum type: namely, algebraic taxes and transfers $(L^1, \ldots, L^s)$ would have to be varied until society is swung to the ethical observer's optimum. The servant of the ethical observer would not have to make explicit decisions about each person's detailed consumption and work; he need only decide about generalized purchasing power, knowing that each person can be counted on to allocate it optimally. In terms of communication theory and game terminology, each person is motivated to do the signalling of his tastes needed to define and reach the attainable-bliss point.

Now all of the above remains valid even if collective consumption is not zero but is instead *explicitly set* at its optimum values as determined by (1), (2), and (3). *However no decentralized pricing system can serve to determine optimally these levels of collective consumption.* Other kinds of "voting" or "signalling" would have to be tried. But, and this is the point sensed by Wicksell but perhaps not fully appreciated by Lindahl, now it is in the selfish interest of each person to give *false* signals, to pretend to have less interest in a given collective consumption activity than he really has, etc. I must emphasize this: taxing according to a benefit theory of taxation can not at all solve the computational problem in the decentralized manner possible for the first category of "private" goods to which the ordinary market pricing applies and which do not have the "external effects" basic to the very notion of collective consumption goods. Of course, utopian voting and signalling schemes can be imagined. ("Scandinavian consensus," Kant's "categorical imperative," and other devices meaningful only under conditions of "symmetry," etc.) The failure of market catallactics in no way denies the following truth: given sufficient knowledge the optimal decisions can always be found by scanning over all the attainable states of the world and selecting the one which according to the postulated ethical welfare function is best. The solution "exists"; the problem is how to "find" it.

One could imagine every person in the community being indoctrinated to behave like a "parametric decentralized bureaucrat" who *reveals* his preferences by signalling in response to price parameters or Lagrangean multipliers, to questionnaires, or to other devices. But there is still this fundamental technical difference going to the heart of the whole problem of *social* economy: by departing from his indoctrinated rules, any one person can hope to snatch some selfish benefit in a way not possible under the self-policing competitive pricing of private goods; and the "external economies" or "jointness of demand" intrinsic to the very concept of collective goods and governmental activities makes it impossible for the grand ensemble of optimizing equations to have that special pattern of zeros which makes *laissez-faire* competition even *theoretically* possible as an analogue computer.

4. CONCLUSION

To explore further the problem raised by public expenditure would take us into the mathematical domain of "sociology" or "welfare politics," which Arrow, Duncan Black, and others have just begun to investigate. Political economy can be regarded as one special sector of this general domain, and it may turn out to be pure luck that within the general domain there happened to be a subsector with the "simple" properties of traditional economics.

Aspects Of Public Expeniture Theories *

By PAUL A. SAMUELSON

Economic theorists have done work of high quality and great quantity in the field of taxation. Public expenditure seems to have been relatively neglected. To illustrate this, let me turn to Professor Pigou. I do so with some diffidence, remembering what Ralph Waldo Emerson said to Oliver Wendell Holmes when Holmes showed him a youthful criticism of Plato. "When you strike at a King," Emerson said, "be sure you kill him."

I have no wish to assassinate Professor Pigou. Nor even to criticize him. But immortality does have its price: if one writes an outstanding treatise such as Pigou's *A Study in Public Finance,* one must expect other men to swarm about it, picking a nugget here and probing for a weakness there.

Of a book of some 285 pages, Pigou devotes most attention to taxes. At least 200 pages to taxes; of the rest, most are concerned with fiscal policy and its impact on the business cycle. What about the pure theory of public expenditure? I can find barely half a dozen pages devoted to the heart of this matter—specifically, pages 30-34. And even if we widen the category—to include Pigou's definitions of transfer and exhaustive expenditure and his discussion of pricing of state-operated public utilities—we still cannot bring the total of pages much beyond twenty.

Now it may be that this ratio of 200 on taxes to 20 on expenditure is the proper one. Perhaps there is really nothing much to say about expenditure, and so heavily overbalanced a page budget may be truly optimal. On the other hand, we must admit that fashion has a great influence in economics, which suggests that we ought periodically to survey the neglected areas of theory to make sure that they do deserve to be left in their underdeveloped and backward states.

I have previously published (this Review, XXXVI, November 1954, 387-89) some thoughts on public expenditure theory; and in order to widen the discussion among economic theorists, I later gave a non-mathematical exposition

*This is a slight revision of a paper delivered at the December 1955 meetings of the Econometric Society and the American Economic Association. Acknowledgment to the Ford Foundation for research aid is gratefully made.

Reprinted by permission of the publishers and author: Paul A. Samuelson, "Aspects of Public Expenditure Theories," *The Review of Economics and Statistics,* 40 (November 1958), pp. 332-336.

(ibid.,, XXXVII, November 1955, 350-56). I do not propose here to give a detailed review of these theories. Rather, I'd like to think aloud about some of the difficulties with expenditure theory and with political decision-making. On these subjects, Richard Musgrave and Julius Margolis have done outstanding research and I must confess my obligation to them for much friendly counsel.

I

Let me first take a fresh look at the nature of government and of public finance from a purely analytical viewpoint. I must give warning: the result will be rather like a New Yorker's map of the United States, in which vast areas of the country are compressed into almost nothing and certain places—like Hollywood, Cape Cod, and Times Square—are blown up far beyond their true proportions.

Similarly, I shall commit all the sins of those bad historians and anthropologists who recreate the history of the human race according to their *a priori* conception of the moment. To keep from getting caught, I'll imagine a planet rather like the earth.

Once upon a time men on this planet were all alike and very scarce. Each family hunted and fished its symmetrical acres; and each ended with the same production and real income.

Then men turned to cultivating the soil and domesticating animals. This left even more of the globe vacant, but did not disturb the symmetry of family incomes.

But finally population grew so big that the best free land was all occupied. Now there was a struggle for elbow room. According to the scenario as I choose to write it, the struggle was a gentlemanly one. But men did have to face the fact that recognizing squatter's rights and respecting *laissez-faire* did result in differences of real incomes among families.

Optimal transfer expenditure. Here then for the first time, government was introduced on this planet. A comprehensive program of redistributing income so as to achieve a maximum of the community's social welfare function was introduced. The budget was balanced at a non-zero level: taxes were raised in a non-distorting lump-sum fashion, and transfer expenditure was allocated among families so as to achieve the marginal conditions necessary to maximize the defined social welfare function.

Now here on earth, things don't seem to have worked out exactly according to such a time-table. In fact, look at Adam Smith's 1776 discussion of the three duties of government—protection against external aggressors, maintenance of order at home, and erecting those public institutions and works "which though they may be in the highest degree advantageous to a great society, could never repay the expense to any individual." We could interpret the last of these in so broad and tautological a way as to be compatible with anything. But if we stick to a narrower non-empty interpretation, it would appear that our planet began with redistributional governmental functions that Smith had not even dreamed of and which would most surprise him if he were to come to life and revisit any modern nation.

Now why do I describe so bizarre a model? It is to underline this theoretical point: Given a social welfare function, and given the absence of all technological and taste externalities, and given universal constant returns to scale, there would be needed only one type of public policy—redistributive transfers. (Under some ethical assumptions, these might be from poor to rich rather than rich to poor; but only by chance alone would zero redistributions maximize a specified social welfare function that depends solely on real incomes.)

Minimal collective expenditure. But what about the neglected exhaustive elements of public expenditure that even the most thoroughgoing *laissez-faire* economy will want to make—e.g., courts of justice to enforce contracts or any of the other items under Smith's first two duties? Later I shall review a possible theory of such expenditure. But first let me mention why the problem of financing such expenditures is, so long as they remain small, secondary to that of transfers.

Even on other planets, perfectionist lump-sum taxes are rarely feasible. We tax the objects that we can feasibly tax. And this must introduce deadweight-theoretically-avoidable tax burdens in addition to the unavoidable real burden involved in having to use resources for public purposes. (This doesn't mean the public services aren't worth their costs; on well-run planets, they are.)

Years ago, when studying this problem, I encountered what was to me a surprising fact. It turns out that, so long as exhaustive expenditure is "small," the deadweight burden is "negligible" no matter what system of taxation is used. Only in the second approximation, so to speak, does it matter what tax structure we use to "cover" the needed program. At least this would be the case if incomes were already distributed optimally. *If,* as is more likely, *incomes are distributed prior to taxation in a non-optimal manner* (not as determined by me but as determined by the relevant social welfare function), *then the manner of taxing is very important even at the first level of approximation; and it is the interpersonal distributive elements that are all important in defining an optimal tax structure.*

It is because of this conclusion that my planet had to start out with transfer taxation. As I have said, this result seemed odd to me at first; but having been led there by the invisible hand of mathematical logic, I was forced to draw my map in this way.

Sizable exhaustive public expenditure. Once we admit the possibility of public collective services on our planet, we have to face the possibility that they will be large rather than small; and in any case they will be finite rather than zero or infinitesimal. So we do need an analysis of their logical nature.

We can approach this indirectly. What is our theory of *non*-public expenditure? So long as goods are producible at constant returns to scale and so long as each person's consumption of a good is measurably distinct from any other person's, the perfect-competition model of markets can be used as *an* optimal social computing device. If we deny constant returns to scale—and technology on this or any other planet may make this denial mandatory in many areas—an opening wedge for an alternative kind of social allocation arises. And if we deny that every good's consumption is purely individualistic, instead insisting on strong "external effects," we will have still another reason why the ordinary private marketing calculus must be non-optimal.[1]

To handle one difficulty at a time, let's keep to a strict assumption of constant returns to scale in all production. But let's introduce important externalities ("neighborhood" effects, etc.) into the consumption sphere. Thus, the battleship that protects your rights and investments also protects mine.

I don't suppose that anyone, upon reflection, would try to build up a theory of public expenditure without bringing in some kind of externality. Yet it is surprising that Pigou, who above all welfare economists has reminded us of external diseconomies of the smoke nuisance type, should in his brief discussion of expenditure theory have left this externality element almost completely implicit.

Now remembering that we theorists like to work with extreme polar cases, what is the natural model to formulate so as to give strongest emphasis to external effects? I have long thought that this is best brought out by the following model.

Assume that some goods, like bread, are privately consumed: this means that the total of bread can be written as the sum of the bread consumptions of each separate individual. But along with such purely private goods, assume public goods—like national defense—which *simultaneously* enter into many persons' indifference curves. Then assuming no transcendental group mind, but only a set of individual tastes and an ethical social welfare function dependent upon these tastes and ranking them in order of deservingness, we can prove that the perfect-competition market model will not work optimally. We can prove that there exists an inefficient configuration from which all men can be made better off, and a frontier of efficient points from which no universally advantageous movements are possible; of all the infinity of such efficient points, a socially best one is definable in terms of a specified normative welfare function.

It is this model that I explored in the two cited papers. And it is also this model that Sax, Wicksell, Lindahl, Musgrave, Bowen, and other economists of the last 75 years had considered under the "voluntary exchange theory of public finance" name or some other. The principle conclusions of this analysis seem to be the following:

1. Efficient, inefficient, and socially optimal configurations can be theoretically defined: a point on the efficiency frontier requires equality between the vertically-added marginal rates of substitution of all men for the public and private goods; and the best of such points requires lump-sum redistributions of the transferable private goods until they have equal marginal social significance.

2. Although the optimum is definable, rational people will not, if left to themselves, be led by an invisible hand to the bliss point. On the contrary, it will

pay for each rational man to dissemble, trying to mask his preference for the public goods and to engage in other game-strategy maneuvers which, when all do them, will necessarily involve deadweight loss to society.

Having called attention to the nature of the difficulty, I do not wish to be too pessimistic. After all, the world's work does somehow get done. And to say that market mechanisms are non-optimal, and that there are difficulties with most political decision processes, does not imply that we can never find new mechanisms of a better sort. (Example: skillful use of the symmetry that prevails between individuals may enable us to find optimal computing algorithms. Example: Interrogate people for their tastes with respect to public goods in such large homogeneous groups as to give each respondent the feeling that his answer can be a "true" one without costing him anything extra.)

Decreasing-cost phenomena. Once people have understood the above model, they are likely to object to its unrealism. Thus, Drs. Stephen Enke and Julius Margolis have both pointed out that many, if not all, government expenditures can be qualitatively varied so as to confer more benefit on one man at the expense of another man. This raises the question whether we cannot bring back to the market pricing mechanism, charging fees for public services and letting their quantity and quality be determined by money voting of the supply and demand type.

Certainly, it should be possible for the theorist to go beyond the polar cases of (1) pure private goods and (2) pure public goods to (3) some kind of a mixed model which takes account of all external, indirect, joint-consumption effects. I shall not write down such a mathematical model. But if I did do so, would we not find—as Pigou and Sidgwick so long ago warned us is true of all external economies and diseconomies—that the social optimum could not be achieved without somebody's taking into account all direct and indirect utilities and costs in all social decisions?

Now in connection with running a particular railroad, highway, or concert, we might find just the right conditions of scarcity of space and of independence of consumptions so that ordinary market pricing could lead to the optimum. In such a case, we can really reduce matters to our first category of purely private goods, and self-policing perfect competition might be an optimal social signalling and computing device.

However, generally, a mixed model that refuses to fall in my polar case of a pure public good will not thereby obligingly go into the other polar case of a pure private good. The mixed case has elements of both in it. And while we cannot by pure logic alone deduce that the intermediate case must qualitatively be a blend of the properties of the two poles, we can by logic know that ordinary pricing will be non-optimal unless it happens to be able to pick up each indirect external marginal utility.

Here is a contemporary instance. The Federal Communications Commission is now trying to make up its mind about permitting subscription television. You might think that the case where a program comes over the air and is available for any set owner to tune in on is a perfect example of my public good. And in a way it is. But you would be wrong to think that the essence of the phenomenon is inherent in the fact that the broadcaster is not able to refuse the service to whatever individuals he pleases. For in this case, by use of unscramblers, it is technically possible to limit the consumptions of a particular broadcast to any specified group of individuals. You might, therefore, be tempted to say: A descrambler enables us to convert a public good into a private good; and by permitting its use, we can sidestep the vexing problems of collective expenditure, instead relying on the free pricing mechanism.

Such an argument would be wrong. Being able to limit a public good's consumption does not make it a true-blue private good. For what, after all, are the true marginal costs of having one extra family tune in on the program? They are literally zero. Why then prevent any family which would receive positive pleasure from tuning in on the program from doing so?

Upon reflection, you will realize that our well known optimum principle that goods should be priced at their marginal costs would not be realized in the case of subscription broadcasting. Why not? In the deepest sense because this is, by its nature, not a case of constant returns to scale. It is a case of general decreasing costs. So long as increasing returns prevail in the actual range of consumption, we know that perfect competition will not be self-preserving and market behavior is unlikely to be optimal.

The case of decreasing costs may be empirically very important. Certainly, when you try to analyze why public utilities are public utilities and why certain activities (like railroads, water supply, electricity, and postoffices) may fall into either the category of public or private enterprise,, you will usually find that some significant deviation from strict constant returns to scale is involved. I cannot then be completely satisfied with Pigou's statement:

> These are not problems of Public Finance, as I understand that term. I do not propose, therefore, to discuss at all the question over what classes of enterprise it is desirable that public operation should be extended, but to proceed on the assumption that this is already determined. (Page 24.)
> Considerations concerning waste thus enable us to say, with regard to several classes of goods and services [primarily those which do not have an inelastic demand], that, if the government decides to provide them, it should finance their provision by fees. (Pages 27-28.)

It is precisely in such cases that uniform average cost pricing will sin against the rule that prices should equal marginal costs. As Hotelling has insisted, there is here a *prima facie* case for government subsidy. To argue, as some economists have done, that the government budget is already so loaded with necessary expenditure as to make it undersirable for it to have to take on such subsidy expenditures, is to miss the point I am trying to make. This *is* one of the needed functions of government, and in making compromises because of fiscal necessities, there is no *a priori* reason why this function should be particularly neglected.

There is a related significant point that needs stressing. It is not enough in the decreasing cost case to come closer to marginal cost pricing in the Lerner-Lange manner, making up the deficits by general taxation. As soon as decreasing cost and diversity of product appear, we have the difficult non-local "total conditions" to determine what finite mix of product is optimal. This involves a terrible social computation problem: we must scan the almot infinite number of possible products and select the best configuration; we cannot feel our way to the optimum but must make judgment at a distance to determine the *optimum optimorum*.

All this is familiar. But what I have to point out are the complications that arise when there are two or more people on the planet. I like my cider sour; you like it sweet. With constant returns we could both get what we want, or at least what we deserve. But with initial indivisibilities or other forms of increasing returns, what I get will depend on what you get. (This is true even if we pay in the form of fees the marginal costs of our separate consumption.)

Now, how can society decide on the product mix which will maximize a specified social welfare function? It must weigh in all the different individuals' utilities from each decision. And *this is a problem that is analytically almost exactly like my model of public expenditure.*

Given the individual indifference curves and the social welfare function compromising them, one could define the theoretical optimum. (In practice, finding the solution might be very tedious.) But now try to devise a system of "benefit taxation" that will in some sense make people pay for what they get—either because justice or equity requires this, or, more subtly, because the necessity of having to make such payments is thought to be a way of helping to determine the proper place for society to arrive in the end. Instantly, you will discover that the same game-theory reasons that compel rational men to hide their desires for public goods will be motivating them to hide their consumers' surpluses from different product configurations.

II

Once again, in contemplating the dilemmas that most forms of political voting involve, we are reminded of the beautiful and special simplicities of the *laissez-faire* model. But, alas, the difficulties are those of the real world. And it would be quite illogical to conclude from all this that men and technology should be different, should be such as to make the competitive game all-sufficient. That would be as silly as to say that we should all love sawdust because its production is so beautiful.

CONCLUSION

Unfortunately, I have only gotten my planet started. Time hasn't permitted me to do more than describe its transfer expenditures, to relate them to the financing of small public services, and to formulate some of the analytic difficulties with a theory of public services. Though my model of pure public goods has turned out to be an unrealistic polar case, it turns out that almost all deviations from constant returns to scale and almost all externalities must inevitably involve some of the same analytic properties and dilemmas of my polar case.

We must leave to other times and other stars the exploration of those momentous coalitions of decision-making that are part of the essence of the political process. To the theorist, the theory of public finance is but part of the general theory of government. And at this frontier, the easy formulas of classical economics no longer light our way.

Appendix: *Strotz and Tiebout Discussions*

1. *Distributional aspects of public goods.* I should like to comment briefly on two papers that have grown out of the earlier discussion. In the present issue Professor Robert H. Strotz has pointed out a formal implication of my original equations (1) and (2): they define a Pareto optimality frontier[2]

$$u^1 = f(u^2, u^3, ..., u^5);$$ (A)

and each point on that frontier will generally determine a set of all public goods

$$X_{n+j} = g^j(u^2, u^3, ..., u^5) \ (j = 1, 2, ..., m).$$ (B)

Now under what conditions can the left-hand variables in (B) be regarded as independent variables? If $s - 1 = m$ and the Jacobian matrix $[g^i{}_j]$ is well-behaved, (B) can be inverted. Or if $s - 1 > m$ and the Jacobian $[g^i{}_j]$ is of rank m, m of (B)'s right-hand u's can be solved for in terms of the public goods $(X_n{}^{+1}, -, X_n{}^1{}_m)$ and the remaining right-hand u's. So the Strotz conclusion follows: Any public good configuration is optimal if only the "distribution of income" is such as to get us to a point on the Pareto-frontier compatible with that public good configuration.[3]

In view of the modern trend to regard mere Pareto-optimality or efficiency as incomplete necessary conditions, what follows from the above conclusion? To me, this.

It is wrong to make, as some have made, a sharp separation between correct public-good decisions and correct redistributional-taxation decisions. Changing public goods *does* materially affect the distribution of income and all decisions have to be made *simultaneously*.

As Professor Strotz says, there is no disagreement between our analyses.

2. *Local Finance and the mathematics of marriage.* A second paper of interest in the present connection is that of Professor Charles M. Tiebout.[4] He argues that the public expenditure theory simplifies itself at the local level—as people spontaneously join in forming homogeneous communities which will legislate what each (and all) want in the way of collective goods.

This attempted solution fits in under one or another of the "symmetry" principles that I had referred to. That it goes some way toward solving the problem, few would doubt. As a solution, though, it raises a number of serious questions.

Thus, when you study in detail a supposedly homogeneous suburb, you find it riddled with conflicting desires. The old, with grown-up children, oppose the desire of the young for more school expenditure. And so it goes. It avails little for one group to say to another: "If you don't like it here, go back where you came from." Ours is a fluid society, with little respect paid to hard-to-identify charter members. People want to "improve" their community, not abdicate from it.

Secondly, people often take heterogeneity even though it involves conflict. The old don't want to live in homogeneous ghettos with their own kind, and the same goes for many other groups. In an interdependent world, one man's privacy is another man's condemnation to loneliness.

Thirdly, there is the political and ethical question whether groups of like-minded individuals shall be "free" to "run out" on their social responsibilities and go off by themselves. At the national level, society respects no such freedom: e.g., migration control. compulsory taxation, etc.

A simple mathematical model will illustrate a few of the intricacies of the problem. If a group of men and women have each a preference rating for members of the opposite sex, who will end up marrying whom? This assignment problem—which is stated in biological terms only for concreteness—is also faced by colleges and students choosing each other, by clubs and fraternities, etc. In real life, it is solved by dynamic reconnoiter, contact, proposal, refusal or acceptance—in short, by general trial and error, which is not guaranteed to represent any optimum.

Consider the trivial case of 2 boys A and B and two girls 1 and 2. Each boy has an ordinal preference rating of the girls, which in this simple case must be either the permutations $(1, 2)$ or $(2, 1)$. Each girl's rating of the boys must be (A, B) or (B, A).

Now what are the possible preference configurations? In this simple case they are essentially only the following (where the first row lists people, with their choices shown in the columns below them):

1	2					A	B
A	B					1	2
B	A					2	1

or

1	2					A	B
A	A					1	2
b	B					2	1

or   or

1	2					A	B
A	B					2	1
B	A					1	2

or

1	2		A	B
A	A		1	1
B	B		2	2

Of these four cases, the first fits Tiebout's attempt best. All the guinea pigs are in agreement: 1 and A want to marry; so do 2 and B; all get their first choices. The solution (1, A; 2, B) is Pareto-optimal; being the only Pareto-optimal solution, it is also Bergson-optimal, maximizing *any* social welfare function that respects individual's tastes.

But now turn to the last case. A and 1 are preferred by all of the other sex. If we give persons the "property right" to form bilateral compacts, the favored ones will presumably marry each other with (1, A; 2, B) the resulting equilibrium.

However, given a social welfare function which respects tastes, this outcome is not necessarily optimal. The other possible outcome (2, A; 1, B) might be "ethically better" (e.g., where 2 has a "great" preference in favor of A but 1 is "almost" indifferent, and 2 is "ethically deserving" of great social respect). Or we can put the matter a little differently: (2, A; 1, B) is just as Pareto-optimal as is (1, A; 2, B). When you leave the former and go to the latter, you make two people happier and two people unhappier.

In the second case, there is likewise no unique Pareto-optimal point. Left to themselves with certain "freedoms" and "property rights" to make bilateral conclusions, probably 1 and A will marry, ignoring 2 and B. And B will be glad. But 2 will not be glad, showing that the configuration (2, A; 1, B) is also Pareto-optimal. Of course, if you used a crude majority vote rule, (1, A; 2, B) would be the winning position. But—as Arrow, Black, and others have shown—majority-rule devices are subject to many intransitivities and drawbacks.

Finally, the third case is like the last in that both outcomes are Pareto-optimal and in going from one to the other you sadden two people and gladden two. Whether the girls or boys are to be made glad cannot be decided except in terms of a given determinate social welfare function.

I conclude from all this that there remain many important analytical problems of public-good determination that still need investigation at every level of government.

NOTES

1. There are still other basic reasons for governmental action or interferences: e.g., "paternalistic" dissatisfaction by the electorate with the effective tastes that they will all display in their day-to-day market preference acts—leading to public policies in the field of education, capital formation, etc.; exercise of economic entrepreneurship and decision-making by public officials; and many more.

2. I use my original notation, which is related to Strotz's by $X\,\overset{+}{n} = S\,j$, $s = I$, $m = K$, $L' = st$, etc.

3. When you reflect that the degrees of freedom to *completely specify* a single post office exceed the number of people in the United States, the case where $s-1 < m$ may seem most realistic. In such a case, or in case people's preferences for public goods are so alike as

to lead to ill-behaved Jacobians, an arbitrary choice of $(Xn\,l\,j)$ will be compatible with no Pareto-optimal point.

4. Charles M. Tiebout, "A Pure Theory of Local Expenditures," *Journal of Political Economy*, LXIV (October 1956), 416-24.

On the Distinction Between Public and Private Goods*

By OTTO A. DAVIS
and ANDREW B. WHINSTON

I. INTRODUCTION

Some years ago, in a now classic series of articles [13] [14] [15], Professor Paul A. Samuelson made an admittedly polar distinction between public and private goods. Briefly, private consumption goods, like bread, must be parceled out among persons with one man getting a loaf more if another gets a loaf less. Thus, if x_{ij} represents the ith person's consumption of the jth private good and X_j represents the quantity available, then $\sum_i x_{ij} = X_j$. A public consumption good, on the other hand, differs in that one man's consumption does not diminish the quantity available for another. Thus, if y_{ik} represents the ith person's consumption of the kth public good and Y_k represents the quantity available, $y_{ik} = Y_k$ for all men. Prime examples are supposed to be outdoor circuses, national defense, and, some may have thought, radio waves and TV signals.

Recently, responding to Minasian's argument [10] that market allocation (via subscription) of television might be a more desirable arrangement, Professor Samuelson [16] claimed that the possession by television of the characteristics of a public good did not constitute evidence either for or against a market arrangement via subscription. There is no doubt but that Samuelson's claim (or admission?) is correct. Aside from television and radio signals, there are many examples of goods which are allocated in the market place and yet which exhibit various degrees of "Samuelsonian publicness." The products of the researcher's efforts, the outpuring of the jukebox and the record player, under-

* This research was supported by grants from Resources for the Future and the National Science Foundation to the Graduate School of Industrial Administration, Carnegie Institute of Technology, and by a Ford Foundation Fellowship to one ⸀ the authors. The authors are greatly indebted to Professor James M. Buchanan, University of Virginia, who provided important support in the form of both stimulation and encouragement. We are also indebted to our colleagues G. Graves, M. Intriligator, and R. Wagner. Of course, only the authors bear responsibility for errors.

Reprinted by permission of the publishers and authors: Otto A. Davis and Andrew B. Whinston, "On the Distinction Between Public and Private Goods," *American Economic Review*, 57 (May 1967), pp. 360-373.

capacity indoor (why be restricted to the outdoors?) circuses and performances of movies and various forms of entertainment, the unhurried and uncrowded viewing of old masters which are owned by a private art collector, etc.—all exhibit aspects of publicness. Olsen [12] claims that the concept can be applied to all large organizations.[1]

When one is faced with such examples, it is only natural to wonder if it is possible to determine in any objective fashion whether a good should be governmentally or privately produced. Samuelson's classic articles seem to provide few clues to an answer. Yet, the problem appears to merit consideration.

II. INSTITUTIONAL ARRANGEMENTS AND SAMUELSON'S MODEL

It is important to understand that, despite the title, Samuelson's model is not directly concerned with public expenditures. Rather, it is a model of market failure. What is shown is that in a system incorporating his "public" consumption goods, the market "fails" in the sense that the necessary conditions for the attainment of Pareto optimality are not automatically satisfied. One should observe two facts here. First, despite the name given to the public goods, the failure of the pricing mechanism to satisfy the necessary conditions for Pareto optimality does not constitute a prima facie case for public ownership, or even public regulation, of the relevant facilities for either production or distribution. Second, the institutional arrangements under which a good, even a public consumption good, is distributed in a market perform an important role in determining the characteristics of the performance of the pricing mechanism.

Recall the definition of Samuelson's public good. One of the implicit notions is that whatever is produced is available to all. Obviously, even if the appropriate maximization problem yields the necessary optimality conditions with the associated Lagrange multipliers, it is difficult to even imagine real prices performing the role indicated by the multipliers. Behaviorally, the problem appears to be much more complicated and rich than is indicated by the simple mathematics. At issue is the fact that paying the price does not give one control of the good. Instead, the act of paying the price is somehow separated from the act of consumption. Consider the following example in order to clarify the behavioral implications of this point.

Imagine that the government decided to alter the institutional arrangements or organization of the market for bread, which is certainly a private good. Suppose that the government decided to separate the act of paying from the act of obtaining the bread. Accordingly, imagine that payments for the desired quantity of bread were made by consumers to the government in the early morning at the "revenue center." Later in the day, bread could be obtained at the "distribution center." However, suppose that there is no communication between the revenue and distribution centers so that the acts of paying and obtaining are truly separated. The bread is distributed on a first come, first served basis. One might observe that this institutional arrangement would certainly affect the functioning of the market mechanism. Consumers could not be counted upon to reveal their preferences at the revenue center. Nor would the distribution center fare much better since consumers could simply take the bread they wanted, if it happened to be available, no matter what their payment at the revenue center. Price could not perform its traditional functions. The institutional arrangements cause market failure.

Observe that, at least under one interpretation, there are certain similarities between the above example and the Samuelsonian model of public consumption goods. By definition, a public good in Samuelson's model is available to all consumers no matter whether a consumer chooses to pay or not. From the standpoint of an individual consumer, a payment could not give one control over the public good in the sense of deciding the precise quantity to be consumed. The act of paying is separated from the act of consuming. It is not surprising that the market fails. For a consumer actually to make a payment would be nothing more or less than an act of pure charity.

III. SOME CONDITIONS NEEDED FOR THE OPERATION OF A MARKET

Since he was interested in the problem of attaining an efficient or Pareto optimal allocation, Samuelson did not discuss the possibility of making a market for public goods operate much as if it were allocating private goods. Nevertheless, such a possibility is often available as an alternative to the collective provision of the public good if the appropriate institutional arrangements can be accomplished. Accordingly, a brief and informal discussion of some of the conditions which seem to be needed if a market is to operate in a reasonable manner appears to be merited.

It is obvious that the first requirement is a provision for some type of ownership or property rights. Without ownership, at least in some form, there would seem to be no basis for exchange. Of course, there are complex issues involved in the definition of property rights. The very definition can affect the manner in which exchange takes place and the way in which a market operates.[2] The definition of property rights can sometimes determine whether externalities are allowed to exist in the market. Zoning ordinances, for example, can be interpreted as an effort to remove the influence of externalities in the urban property market.[3] It might be noted that in a sense a good may be characterized by the control an owner may exercise, so that the same piece of property is in effect a different good once the zoning ordinance is changed.

The second requirement, which is related to the issues of ownership and property rights, concerns "control" over the good or service. The act of buying or paying for the good or service must be related to the use or consumption of it. Even in the case of public good, purchase can sometimes be made to give some control and establish a connection between the act of paying and consumption as the example of television signals with scramblers illustrates.

The third requirement, which is related to both of the previous ones, concerns the possibility of exclusion. While perfect exclusion need not be required for markets to function reasonably well, as numerous examples of the presence of externalities amply illustrates, it is easily seen that exclusion does provide basic motivation for exchange.[4]

IV. THE MARKET ALLOCATION OF SAMUELSONIAN PUBLIC GOODS

In part, the question of whether the above requirements can be satisfied for some particular good depends upon the technological characteristics of the good. In order to illustrate this point, consider the case of television. In the age of electronic scramblers, exclusion is possible. The signals can be "owned" and their services sold. Thus it is possible to establish a direct relationship between the consumption of the service and the payment for it. The above requirements for a market can be satisfied. Since the issue does not seem to have been considered fully, it appears appropriate to discuss briefly the operation of such a market on the basis of an excessively simple model.

Consider a society composed of people deciding upon viewing a pay television program. For simplicity, let the capital or fixed costs of producing the program be ignored. Assume that there is no advertising. Consider the following definitions:

$$x_i = \begin{cases} 0 \text{ if the } i\text{th person does not watch the program} \\ 1 \text{ if that person does watch the program} \end{cases}$$

$$y = \begin{cases} 0 \text{ if the program is not produced} \\ 1 \text{ if the program is produced} \end{cases}$$

$u_i(x_i)$: The value or "utility" to the ith person from watching the program.

$g(y)$: A function indicating the amount of some homogeneous (for simplicity) resource used to produce the program.

M: An arbitrarily large number.

K: The "minimal" amount of the homogeneous resource used to produce the program; i.e., $9(1) = K$.

Given these definitions, and assuming that the objective is to attain a Pareto optimum in television viewing, consider the following vector maximization problem:

(1.1) $\quad \max\ [u_1(x_1),\ u_2(x_2),\ \cdots,\ u_n(x_n)]$

$\quad\quad\quad$ subject to

(1)

$\quad$ (1.2) $\quad \sum_i x_i - My \le 0$

$\quad$ (1.3) $\quad g(y) \le K$

$\quad$ (1.4) $\quad x_i = 0, 1;\ y = 0, 1 \quad\quad i = 1, \cdots, n$

It is convenient to replace the vector (1.1). Following the procedure introduced in [8], let α_i represent the reciprocal of the ith individual's marginal utility of income. Define $d_i = u_i(1)$ and $c_i = \alpha_i d_i$. Assuming for simplicity that the α_i are not affected by the decision to watch or not watch the program, one can replace the vector (1.1) by

$$(2) \quad\quad \sum_i \alpha_i u_i(x_i) = \sum_i \alpha_i d_i x_i = \sum_i c_i x_i$$

and maximize (2) subject to the same constraints so that the problem is reduced to one of integer maximization. Note that the use of M in (1.2) means that once $y = 1$ the constraint is never binding. The program must be available if someone watches it.

Let p represent the price of the homogeneous resource and assume that p is given by a perfect market. Define $k = p \cdot g(1)$ so that $p \cdot g(y) = ky$. Problem (1) can now be replaced by the following equivalent problem:

$$\max \sum_i c_i x_i - ky$$

(3) $\quad\quad\quad\quad$ subject to

$$\sum_i x_i - My \le 0$$

and the solution to (3) is obvious. If $\sum_i c_i \ge k$ for $c_i \ge 0$, then the program should be presented and all x_i corresponding to $c_i \ge 0$ should be set equal to one. If there is an i such that $c_i < 0$, then that $x_i = 0$. All persons who enjoy the program should be able to view it.

Consider whether the above solution could be achieved by a non-discriminatory pricing device. Let λ denote the price of being able to view the program. Obviously, if no one who wishes to see the program is to be excluded, then the best that the television network can do is to set

$$(4) \quad\quad\quad\quad \lambda = \min c_i \ge 0$$

so that the total revenue to the network is $\lambda \sum_i x_i$ where the sum is over all i whose $c_i \ge 0$. Two issues are relevant here. First, $\lambda \sum x_i < k$ is a likely outcome so that a subsidy may be required to pay for the costs of the program. The fact that total revenue is less than variable costs (recall that fixed costs are ignored here) does not necessarily indicate that the program is unwarranted. Second, there seems to be no feasible way for the network to determine the appropriate value of λ as indicated in (4). Obviously, the network cannot ask potential viewers to reveal the value of their c_i. One might think of starting with a zero price and raising it by successive increments until some viewer turned off his set; but surely viewers would catch on to this little game and bluff by turning off their set at any positive price so that it would be driven back down to zero. Therefore, it does not appear that pricing, with or without subsidization, can result in the achievement of the solution to (3).

Since the presence of market failure does not imply the existence of a superior nonmarket alternative, consider the "second-best" type of problem where the television program is priced, there is no subsidy and costs must be covered. It seems obvious in these circumstances that the "best of the second best" possibilities is one which allows costs to be covered exactly. In other words, values of both λ and the x_i must be determined such that

(5)
$$\lambda \sum_i x_i - k = 0$$

and the other conditions are also satisfied. It is not always true that such a solution exists or that it is unique. Assuming existence, presumably one could find such a solution by starting with an extremely low price and then raising it by increments until (5) was satisfied. Note that the existence of (5) removes the incentive for bluffing. In other words, in this second-best type of allocation by pricing, there is no problem of individuals emitting false signals or not revealing true preferences. Observe, however, that this second-best solution does impose costs of exclusion upon the society. This cost is given by $\sum c_i$ where the sum is taken over those c_i satisfying the relation $0 \leq c_i \leq \lambda$ where here λ represents the particular value of λ which was selected to satisfy (5).

Note that no motivational premise, such as profit maximization, was introduced as the basis for the selection of the second-best constraint (5). However, it can be argued that in an expanded model where alternate networks compete for viewers of their programs, the very competition will cause the "no profit" condition (5) to be satisfied so that this analysis does provide a basis (at least as a first approximation) for the assessment of the costs of the private provision of television services by the pricing mechanism.

Observe again that the particular pricing arrangement analyzed above depended upon the technological feasibility of scrambling (and descrambling) devices. However, even if these devices were not available, market allocations are still possible if certain institutional actions are taken. Law might require that television sets be made in such a manner that a special device is required to tune into any given channel. The purchase of one of these special devices would give the owner of the set the right to view the specified channel as often as desired. Such an arrangement would not markedly differ from the practice of many private swimming clubs, for example, of selling a season pass instead of charging for each trip to the pool. Similarly, channels might be assigned to the networks who might "rent" the right to make sets capable of tuning into the specified channels to the various manufacturers. Obviously, various arrangements are possible. Each possibility has its own operating characteristics and corresponding social cost.

The point here is that technological considerations can determine partially which institutional arrangements are feasible. The feasibility of various institutional arrangements certainly has an influence in the determination of which particular one is to be selected as the most appropriate. Since technology changes over time, one can expect that institutions should be modified accordingly.

V. INSTITUTIONAL CHOICE FOR SAMUELSONIAN PUBLIC GOODS

The recent exchange between Minasian and Samuelson, which was concerned with the issue of subscription television, illustrates the fact that the optimality conditions are only of limited value in making an institutional choice.[5] Samuelson [16] emphasizes that there is no presumption that the particular arrangement which does satisfy the necessary conditions is one which produces a Pareto optimal allocation. Sufficient conditions must also be considered. Even more important, one must determine whether there are feasible institutional arrangements which could result in the satisfaction of both sets of conditions. It is obviously a fact that there is nothing inherent in the derivation of either necessary or sufficient conditions for a Pareto optimum which suggests that feasible arrangements for satisfying these conditions exist. It is interesting to note that Samuelson stressed this very point in the first of his series of papers on this topic.[6]

The consequence of a lack of feasible institutional arrangements for satisfying both necessary and sufficient conditions for Pareto optimality in systems which include public goods is the realization that institutional choice involves the comparison of alternative arrangements which are necessarily nonoptimal in the sense of Pareto. The problem is not to choose from the Pareto optimum positions that one considered ethically desirable. Rather, the problem is to choose from a feasible set of institutional arrangements that particular one which gives the most suitable or "best" allocation of the good under consideration.

It is obvious that in choosing between alternative institutional arrangements the actual operating characteristics of these various arrangements are factors of great importance. As Buchanan has argued so eloquently, it makes little sense to compare operating characteristics of unobtainably ideal arrangements in making an institutional choice.[7] Consequently, if one is choosing, for example, between the alternative institutional arrangements of subscription television, zero pricing and financing by advertising, or zero pricing without advertising with governmental provision of the service, it is not sufficient to argue that subscription television should be ruled out because a nonzero price violates the necessary condition for efficiency, that financing by advertising results in programs appealing to mass taste so that cultural and educational values are overlooked, and that these reasons indicate governmental provision. One cannot simply assume (and be correct) that governmental provision will be "ideal" simply because the other two arrangements are not. One must consider the actual operating characteristics of all alternative arrangements. The problem of institutional choice often involves the comparison of alternative problems of second best which characterize the available possibilities.

For a Samuelsonian public good, there are certain costs associated with private provision and exclusion. When the requirements for a market are satisfied, at the expense of those costs imposed upon the system by exclusion and the operation of a pricing system, one obtains those advantages provided only by markets.[8] Information concerning desires is provided and can be incorporated into decisions concerning supply, quality of the good, etc. It is worthwhile noting that the relative intensity of desires can be at least partially revealed in even an imperfect market system while this kind of information is much more difficult to obtain under any other arrangement. Nevertheless, the costs of exclusion are not to be taken lightly.

Governmental provision of a public good at, say, a zero price, on the other hand, also has problems associated with it. How are the decisionmakers to decide, for example, the quantity which should be provided? One can give the easy answer to this question by saying that the political process makes the decision. However, such an answer only evades the issue. How does the policitican get information which would lead to the proper decision? One must realize that politicians make decisions at least in part upon the basis of political costs which might be approximated in terms of votes. There does not appear to be any reason to suspect that votes are superior indicators of desires in a system where there are many issues and few elections, so that a vote may enjoy alternative interpretations.

There are obvious difficulties in analyzing those problems of second best where the institutional arrangement is governmental provision, or governmental regulation, of the good under consideration. One does not yet know the appropriate behavioral characteristics which should determine the form of the second-best constraints in the models. What are the behavioral rules which guide the decisions and the actions of governmental agencies? It appears that this question must be answered in a satisfactory and useful manner before there will be a very reasonable basis for analyses capable of adequately determining whether given "public" goods should be governmentally produced and distributed or left to the private sector, with or without regulation.

Finally, it should be noted that ethical considerations cannot completely be ignored in institutional choice. Strotz [17] emphasizes the fact that public goods have important distributional implications. Similarly, alternative institutional arrangements for the allocation of public goods have distributional implications.

VI. THE ALLOCATION OF NON-SAMUELSONIAN PUBLIC GOODS

It has long been recognized that Samuelson's admittedly polar definition of public goods omits much of governmental activity. It can be argued that another class of goods which should be either governmentally provided or regulated is characterized by extreme decreasing costs. This class of goods involves a high, fixed, and negligible marginal cost coupled with the presence of a capacity constraint. Roads and bridges are prime examples. Leaving aside the question of whether these goods "should" be governmentally produced and distributed, and also leaving the question of how the government actually would do it, let us consider the problem of how such a good "should" be produced and its services allocated over time. One needs to have the benchmark of ideal performance in order to either access or influence actual performance.

Consider a good (say a bridge or a road) which must be constructed in an initial period and whose services must be allocated in that period and also T periods in the future. Supposedly this good becomes obsolete and disintegrates at the end of the Tth period. One incurs the high fixed cost in the initial period and only negligible costs thereafter. Two interrelated questions appear. One must choose the capacity (or decide "how much to consume") in the initial period and also determine an allocation over time.

In order to answer the above questions, let us consider a very simple model in which there are only two goods. One good (say bread) is produced and consumed during each period. It is an ordinary private good. The other good is the one discussed above. In our system it is often (but not necessarily always) a governmental good and for convenience will be termed such here. Consider the following definitions:

$x^i_1(t)$: The amount of the private good consumed by the ith person during period t.

$x^i_2(t)$: The amount of the governmental good consumed by the ith person during period t.

$y_1(t)$: The quantity of the private good produced and available for consumption during period t. For simplicity, assume no storage or carryover between periods.

$y_2(1)$: The quantity of the governmental good produced during the initial period and available for consumption during each of the T periods.

$g(y_1(t))$: An implicit "production possibility" function relating available resources (assumed to be one) to $y_1(t)$ during periods $t = 2, \cdots, T$.

$H(y_1(1), y_2(1))$: An implicit "production possibility" function relating available resources (assumed to be one) to the quantities $y_1(1)$, $y_2(1)$ of the two goods which are produced during the initial period.

U_t^i: The assumed concave utility function of the ith individual during period t.

It is convenient to simplify the problem by ignoring side issues and assuming that there are no externalities in the system. Consequently, it is assumed that in the initial period the productions of the two goods are not functionally interrelated so that H is separable and can be written in the form

(6) $$H(y_1(1), y_2(1)) = h_1(y_1(1)) + h_2(y_2(1))$$

and that the decisions of the initial period do not affect the production possibilities of the following periods so that g can be given as indicated. It is also assumed that utility depends only upon consumption in the given period so that there are no functional interdependencies over time. In addition, it is convenient to assume that utility functions can be written in the separable form

(7) $$U_t^i(x_1^i(t), x_2^i(t)) = u_{1t}^i(x_1^i(t)) + u_{2t}^i(x_2^i(t))$$

so that there is no interaction. The utility from bread does not influence the utility from crossing the bridge and vice versa.

Since interest here is centered upon deriving the conditions for Pareto optimality, it is obvious that the problem is one of vector maximization. It is convenient, however, to apply the Kuhn-Tucker equivalence theorem and follow the procedure outlined in [8] in order to state the criterion function in a more appropriate form. Accordingly, and as before, let α_i represent the (unspecified but assumed positive) reciprocal of the ith consumer's marginal utility of income. The maximization problem can be written as follows:

(8.1) $$\max \sum_i \sum_t \alpha_i u_{1t}^i(x_1^i(t)) + \sum_i \sum_t \alpha_i u_{2t}^i(x_2^i(t))$$

subject to

(8)

(8.2) $$\sum_i x_1^i(t) \leq y_1(t) \qquad t = 1, \cdots, T$$

114

$$(8.3) \quad \sum_i x_2^i(t) \leq y_2(1) \qquad t = 1, \cdots, T$$

$$(8.4) \quad h_1(y_1(1)) + h_2(y_2(1)) \leq 0$$

$$(8.5) \quad g(y_1(t)) \leq 0 \qquad t = 2, \cdots, T$$

$$(8.6) \quad x_1^i(t) \geq 0,\ x_2^i(t) \geq 0,\ y_1(t) \geq 0,\ y_2(1) \geq 0 \qquad \begin{matrix} t = 1, \cdots, T \\ i = 1, \cdots, n \end{matrix}$$

Note that (8.1) is the criterion (social welfare) function which is stated in a form useful for determining the conditions for Pareto optimality. Constraint (8.2) states that no more of the private good can be consumed than is available in any given period. Constraint (8.3) indicates that no more of the governmental good can be consumed in any period than is made available in the first period. Note that the quantity available of the governmental good is measured in terms of capacity. Constraints (8.4) and (8.5) indicate that no more of the goods can be produced than is allowed by the available resources. Finally, (8.5) indicates the nonnegativity conditions.

It is obvious from the very structure of problem (8) that the usual and familiar conditions apply for the private good. Accordingly, these Pareto conditions are not presented here. Competitive markets are fully capable of satisfying these conditions and performing the desirable allocation. Attention is centered on the conditions for the production and allocation of the governmental good. Let $\lambda(t)$ represent the multiplier associated with constraint (8.3). Recall that this multiplier can be interpreted as a shadow price. Then the conditions on the demand side are

$$(9.1) \quad \alpha_i \frac{\partial u_{2t}^i}{\partial x_2^i(t)} - \lambda(t) \begin{Bmatrix} \leq \\ = \end{Bmatrix} 0 \quad \text{if} \quad x_2^i(t) \begin{Bmatrix} = \\ > \end{Bmatrix} 0, \qquad \begin{matrix} i = 1, \cdots, n \\ t = 1, \cdots, T \end{matrix}$$

which are also the conventional and familiar Pareto conditions. If the governmental good is chosen, then an individual should consume that amount in each period which equates his weighted marginal utility to the price of the good during the period. Let β represent the multiplier associated with (8.4). Then on the supply side the condition is

$$(9.2) \quad \sum_t \lambda(t) - \beta \frac{\partial h_2}{\partial y_2(1)} \begin{Bmatrix} \leq \\ = \end{Bmatrix} 0 \quad \text{if} \quad y_2(1) \begin{Bmatrix} = \\ > \end{Bmatrix} 0$$

which has an interesting interpretation. Note that if one were to determine the quantity (or capacity) of the governmental good to be made available according to a profit maximization criterion with the prices taken as given, then one would consider the problem

$$(10) \quad \max_{y_2(1) \geq 0} \left\{ \sum_t \lambda(t) y_2(1) - \beta h_2(y_2(1)) \right\}$$

115

and the conditions for the solution to this problem are given by (9.2). Note that condition (9.2) can be interpreted as saying that if the governmental good is to be supplied, then that quantity (capacity) should be chosen in the initial period which will equate the sum of the prices to the marginal cost of supplying the selected quantity. The solution is that given by profit maximization.

Under the usual assumptions, the conditions derived from (8) are both necessary and sufficient for Pareto optimality. Observe that, in regard to the governmental good, one obtains as a solution to (8) a vector of consumption quantities $(x_2^i(1), \cdots, x_2^i(T))$ for each i, a number $y_2(1)$ which is the quantity made available in each period (the capacity), and a vector of prices or charges $(\lambda(1), \cdots, \lambda(T))$. This solution is Pareto optimal. Note, however, that it cannot be decentralized period by period.

There are some interesting aspects to the solution to this problem which have important implications for the planning for the provision of the class of goods (such as bridges and roads) under consideration. Note that if demand is at all variable, it is likely that the charge $\lambda(t)$ which rations the available supply $y_2(1)$ is likely to be zero for some periods. From the point of view of planning, the zero charge does not imply no exclusion. It merely means that a person does not have to pay to obtain the right to use the bridge, but he must still obtain that right. Also note the implication of (9.2). The capacity (quantity supplied) should not be selected to be so large that the corresponding constraint (8.3) never becomes binding. The constraint must become binding during some periods so that the charge becomes positive. If demand is such that the charge can never become positive, the facility is not justified.[9] The implication for planning for this class of goods is that one should make a forecast of possible usage over the life of the facility. This forecast should be conditional upon the use of the appropriate charges during each period. Given that revenues can cover costs, one selects the appropriate capacity accordingly.[10] Once the facility is constructed, actual prices (as opposed to the forecasted ones) should be simply adjusted by the conventional rule to ration the available supply.

In terms of practical planning of bridges and roads, where it is usually assumed to be not feasible to use direct charges as a rationing device, the implications of the above analysis would seem to indicate that facilities should not be constructed so as to eliminate congestion during all periods. The constraint (8.3) must be binding during some periods in order to have a rational allocation of resources. Since congestion costs serve (imperfectly) as prices, the construction of facilities which never became congested during their useful life should serve as a clear indication of a misallocation of resources.[11] Rational action should not eliminate congestion but merely obtain a (here undefined) appropriate amount of it.

116

VII. CONCLUDING COMMENTS

This paper has not included a discussion of whether the so-called "governmental goods" should really be produced and distributed by the public sector. The issues here are much the same as those discussed for the so-called "public goods." All that is indicated in the previous section is a benchmark analysis against which the behaviors of private, regulated or public actors could be measured. It is true that analytic models of public actors are needed before institutional choices can be made on anything approaching a reasonable basis. Nevertheless, it does appear to be a shame that public goods are called "public."

REFERENCES

1. James M. Buchanan, "Politics, Policy, and the Pigovian Margins," *Economica*, Feb., 1962, pp. 17–28.
2. ———, "An Economic Theory of Clubs," *Economica*, Feb., 1965, pp. 1–14.
3. James M. Buchanan and W. Craig Stubblebine, "Externality," *Economica*, Nov., 1962, pp. 371–84.
4. Ronald H. Coase, "The Federal Communications Commission," *J. of Law and Econ.*, Oct., 1959, pp. 1–40.
5. ———, "The Problem of Social Cost," *J. of Law and Econ.*, Oct., 1960, pp. 1–44.
6. Otto A. Davis, "Economic Elements in Municipal Zoning Decisions," *Land Econ.*, Nov., 1963, pp. 375–86.
7. Otto A. Davis and Andrew B. Whinston, "Some Notes on Equating Private and Social Cost," *S. Econ. J.*, Oct., 1965, pp. 113–26.
8. ———, "Welfare-Economics and the Theory of Second Best," *Rev. of Econ. Studies*, Jan., 1965, pp. 1–14.
9. Harold Demsetz, "The Exchange and Enforcement of Property Rights," *J. of Law and Econ.*, Oct., 1964, pp. 11–26.
10. Jora R. Minasian, "Television Pricing and the Theory of Public Goods," *J. of Law and Econ.*, Oct., 1964, pp. 71–80.
11. Richard A. Musgrave, *The Theory of Public Finance* (McGraw-Hill, 1959).
12. Mancur Olson, *The Logic of Collective Action* (Harvard Univ. Press, 1965).
13. Paul A. Samuelson, "The Pure Theory of Public Expenditure," *Rev. of Econ. and Statis.*, Nov., 1954, pp. 387–89.
14. ———, "Diagrammatic Exposition of a Theory of Public Expenditure," *Rev. of Econ. and Statis.*, Nov., 1955, pp. 350–56.
15. ———, "Aspects of Public Expenditure Theories," *Rev. of Econ. and Statis.*, Nov., 1958, pp. 332–38.
16. ———, "Public Goods and·Subscription TV: Correction of the Record," *J. of Law and Econ.*, Oct., 1964, pp. 81–84.
17. Robert H. Strotz, "Two Propositions Related to Public Goods," *Rev. of Econ. and Statis.*, Nov., 1958, pp. 329–31.
18. Richard E. Wagner, "Pressure Groups and Political Entrepreneurs: A Review Article," G. Tullock, ed., *Papers on Non-Market Decision Making* (Charlottesville: Thomas Jefferson Center, Univ. of Virginia, 1966), pp. 161–70.

NOTES

[1] But see Wagner's review [18] of Olsen's theme.
[2] This basic point seems to have been first pointed out by Coase [4] [5]. See also Buchanan and Stubblebine [3] and Davis and Whinston [7].
[3] See Davis [6].
[4] Musgrave [11] emphasizes the notion of exclusion.
[5] See Minasian [10] and Samuelson [16].
[6] See Samuelson [13], pp. 388–89.
[7] See Buchanan [1].
[8] The point that markets are costly to operate has been emphasized by Coase [5]. Demsetz [9] also makes this point but with a greater emphasis upon the costs associated with policing the property rights.
[9] Note, however, that supply is assumed to be infinitely divisible.
[10] Recall, however, the convenient assumption of no externalities. If there are externalities,

then one has to make an adjustment in this rule to take them into account.

[11] One must make an exception here for the very real problem caused by indivisibility in urral areas. Recall the convenient assumption that the size of the facility was continuously divisible.

The Problem Of Social Cost

By R. H. COASE

I. THE PROBLEM TO BE EXAMINED[1]

This paper is concerned with those actions of business firms which have harmful effects on others. The standard example is that of a factory the smoke from which has harmful effects on those occupying neighbouring properties. The economic analysis of such a situation has usually proceeded in terms of a divergence between the private and social product of the far`.ory, in which economists have largely followed the treatment of Pigou in *The Economics of Welfare*. The conclusions to which this kind of analy`ris seems to have led most economists is that it would be desirable to make the owner of the factory liable for the damage caused to those injured by the smoke, or alternatively, to place a tax on the factory owner varying with the amount of smoke produced and equivalent in money terms to the damage it would cause, or finally, to exclude the factory from residential districts (and presumably from other areas in which the emission of smoke would have harmful effects on others). It is my contention that the suggested courses of action are inappropriate, in that they lead to results which are not necessarily, or even usually, desirable.

II. THE RECIPROCAL NATURE OF THE PROBLEM

The traditional approach has tended to obscure the nature of the choice that has to be made. The question is commonly thought of as one in which A inflicts harm on B and what has to be decided is: how should we restrain A? But this is wrong. We are dealing with a problem of a reciprocal nature. To avoid the harm to B would inflict harm on A. The real question that has to be decided is: should A be allowed to harm B or should B be allowed to harm A? The problem is to avoid the more serious harm. I instanced in my previous article[2] the case of a confectioner the noise and vibrations from whose machinery disturbed a doctor in his work. To avoid harming the doctor would inflict harm on the confectioner. The problem posed by this case was essential-

---

Reprinted by permission of the publishers and author: R. H. Coase, "The Problem of Social Cost," *Journal of Law and Economics, 3 (1960), pp. 1-44.*

ly whether it was worth while, as a result of restricting the methods of production which could be used by the confectioner, to secure more doctoring at the cost of a reduced supply of confectionery products. Another example is afforded by the problem of straying cattle which destroy crops on neighbouring land. If it is inevitable that some cattle will stray, an increase in the supply of meat can only be obtained at the expense of a decrease in the supply of crops. The nature of the choice is clear: meat or crops. What answer should be given is, of course, not clear unless we know the value of what is obtained as well as the value of what is sacrificed to obtain it. To give another example, Professor George J. Stigler instances the contamination of a stream.[3] If we assume that the harmful effect of the pollution is that it kills the fish, the question to be decided is: is the value of the fish lost greater or less than the value of the product which the contamination of the stream makes possible. It goes almost without saying that this problem has to be looked at in total *and* at the margin.

III. THE PRICING SYSTEM WITH LIABILITY FOR DAMAGE

I propose to start my analysis by examining a case in which most economists would presumably agree that the problem would be solved in a completely satisfactory manner: when the damaging business has to pay for all damage caused *and* the pricing system works smoothly (strictly this means that the operation of a pricing system is without cost).

A good example of the problem under discussion is afforded by the case of straying cattle which destroy crops growing on neighbouring land. Let us suppose that a farmer and a cattle-raiser are operating on neighbouring properties. Let us further suppose that, without any fencing between the properties, an increase in the size of the cattle-raiser's herd increases the total damage to the farmer's crops. What happens to the marginal damage as the size of the herd increases is another matter. This depends on whether the cattle tend to follow one another or to roam side by side, on whether they tend to be more or less restless as the size of the herd increases and on other similar factors. For my immediate purpose, it is immaterial what assumption is made about marginal damage as the size of the herd increases.

To simplify the argument, I propose to use an arithmetical example. I shall assume that the annual cost of fencing the farmer's property is $9 and that the price of the crop is $1 per ton. Also, I assume that the relation between the number of cattle in the herd and the annual crop loss is as follows:

Number in Herd (Steers)	Annual Crop Loss (Tons)	Crop Loss per Additional Steer (Tons)
1	1	1
2	3	2
3	6	3
4	10	4

Given that the cattle-raiser is liable for the damage caused, the additional annual cost imposed on the cattle-raiser if he increased his herd from, say, 2 to 3 steers is $3 and in deciding on the size of the herd, he will take this into account along with his other costs. That is, he will not increase the size of the herd unless the value of the additional meat produced (assuming that the cattle-raiser slaughters the cattle), is greater than the additional costs that this will entail, including the value of the additional crops destroyed. Of course, if, by the employment of dogs, herdsmen, aeroplanes, mobile radio and other means, the amount of damage can be reduced, these means will be adopted when their cost is less than the value of the crop which they prevent being lost. Given that the annual cost of fencing is $9, the cattle-raiser who wished to have a herd with 4 steers or more would pay for fencing to be erected and maintained, assuming that other means of attaining the same end would not do so more cheaply. When the fence is erected, the marginal cost due to the liability for damage becomes zero, except to the extent that an increase in the size of the herd necessitates a stronger and therefore more expensive fence because more steers are liable to lean against it at the same time. But, of course, it may be cheaper for the cattle-raiser not to fence and to pay for the damaged crops, as in my arithmetical example, with 3 or fewer steers.

It might be thought that the fact that the cattle-raiser would pay for all crops damaged would lead the farmer to increase his planting if a cattle-raiser came to occupy the neighbouring property. But this is not so. If the crop was previously sold in conditions of perfect competition, marginal cost was equal to price for the amount of planting undertaken and any expansion would have reduced the profits of the farmer. In the new situation, the existence of crop damage would mean that the farmer would sell less on the open market but his receipts for a given production would remain the same, since the cattle-raiser would pay the market price for any crop damaged. Of course, if cattle-raising commonly involved the destruction of crops, the coming into existence of a cattle-raising industry might raise the price of the crops involved and farmers would then extend their planting. But I wish to confine my attention to the individual farmer.

I have said that the occupation of a neighbouring property by a cattle-raiser would not cause the amount of production, or perhaps more exactly the amount of planting, by the farmer to increase. In fact, if the cattle-raising has any effect, it will be to decrease the amount of planting. The reason for this is that, for any given tract of land, if the value of the crop damaged is so great that the receipts from the sale of the undamaged crop are less than the total costs of cultivating that tract of land, it will be profitable for the farmer and the cattle-raiser to make a bargain whereby that tract of land is left uncultivated. This can be made clear by means of an arithmetical example. Assume initially that the value of the crop obtained from cultivating a given tract of land is $12 and that the cost incurred in cultivating this tract of land is $10, the net gain from cultivating the land being $2. I assume for purposes of simplicity that the farmer owns the land. Now assume that the cattle-raiser starts operations on the neighbouring property and that the value of the crops damaged is $1. In this case $11 is obtained by the farmer from sale on the market and $1 is obtained from the cattle-raiser for damage suffered and the net gain remains $2. Now suppose that the cattle-raiser finds it profitable to increase the size of his herd, even though the amount of damage rises to $3; which means that the value of the additional meat production is greater than the additional costs, including the additional $2 payment for damage. But the total payment for damage is now $3. The net gain to the farmer from cultivating the land is still $2. The cattle-raiser would be better off if the farmer would agree not to cultivate his land for any payment less than $3. The farmer would be agreeable to not cultivating the land for any payment greater than $2. There is clearly room for a mutually satisfactory bargain which would lead to the abandonment of cultivation.[4] But the same argument applies not only to the whole tract cultivated by the farmer but also to any subdivision of it. Suppose, for example, that the cattle have a well-defined route, say, to a brook or to a shady area. In these circumstances, the amount of damage to the crop along the route may well be great and if so, it could be that the farmer and the cattle-raiser would find it profitable to make a bargain whereby the farmer would agree not to cultivate this strip of land.

But this raises a further possibility. Suppose that there is such a well-defined route. Suppose further that the value of the crop that would be obtained by cultivating this strip of land is $10 but that the cost of cultivation is $11. In the absence of the cattle-raiser, the land would not be cultivated. However, given the presence of the cattle-raiser, it could well be that if the strip was cultivated, the whole crop would be destroyed by the cattle. In which case, the cattle-raiser would be forced to pay $10 to the farmer. It is true that the farmer would lose $1. But the cattle-raiser would lose $10. Clearly this is a situation which is not likely to last indefinitely since neither party would want this to happen. The aim of the farmer would be to induce the cattle-raiser to make a payment in return for an agreement to leave this land uncultivated. The farmer would not be able to obtain a payment greater than the cost of fencing off this piece of land nor so high as to lead the cattle-raiser to abandon the use of the neighbouring property. What payment would in fact be made would depend on the shrewdness of the farmer and the cattle-raiser as bargainers. But as the payment would not be so high as to cause the cattle-raiser to abandon this location and as it would not vary with the size of the herd, such an agreement would not affect the allocation of resources but would merely alter the distribution of income and wealth as between the cattle-raiser and the farmer.

I think it is clear that if the cattle-raiser is liable for damage caused and the pricing system works smoothly, the reduction in the value of production elsewhere will be taken into account in computing the additional cost involved in increasing the size of the herd. This cost will be weighed against the value of the additional meat production and, given perfect competition in the cattle industry, the allocation of resources in cattle-raising will be optimal. What needs to be emphasized is that the fall in the value of production elsewhere which would be taken into account in the costs of the cattle-raiser may well be less than the damage which the cattle would cause to the crops in the ordinary course of events. This is because it is possible, as a result of market transactions, to discontinue cultivation of the land. This is desirable in all cases in which the damage that the cattle would cause, and for which the cattle-raiser would be willing to pay, exceeds the amount which the farmer would pay for use of the land. In conditions of perfect competition, the amount which the farmer would pay for the use of the land is equal to the difference between the value of the total production when the factors are employed on this land and the value of the additional product yielded in their next best use (which would be what the farmer would have to pay for the factors). If damage exceeds the amount the farmer would pay for the use of the land, the value of the additional product of the factors employed elsewhere would exceed the value of the total product in this use after damage is taken into account. It follows that it would be desirable to abandon cultivation of the land and to release the factors employed for production elsewhere. A procedure which merely provided for payment for damage to the crop caused by the cattle but which did not allow for the possibility of cultivation being discontinued would result in too small an employment of factors of production in cattle-raising and too large an employment of factors in cultivation of the crop. But given the possibility of market transactions, a situation in which damage to crops exceeded the rent of the land would not endure. Whether the cattle-raiser pays the farmer to leave the land uncultivated or himself rents the land by paying the land-owner an amount slightly greater than the farmer would pay (if the farmer was himself renting the land), the final result would be the same and would maximise the value of production. Even when the farmer is induced to plant crops which it would not be profitable to cultivate for sale on the market, this will be a purely short-term phenomenon and may be expected to lead to an agreement under which the planting will cease. The cattle-raiser will remain in that location and the marginal cost of meat production will be the same as before, thus having no long-run effect on the allocation of resources.

IV. THE PRICING SYSTEM WITH NO LIABILITY FOR DAMAGE

I now turn to the case in which, although the pricing system is assumed to work smoothly (that is, costlessly), the damaging business is not liable for any of the damage which it causes. This business does not have to make a payment to those damaged by its actions. I propose to show that the allocation of resources will be the same in this case as it was when the damaging business was liable for damage caused. As I showed in the previous case that the allocation of resources was optimal, it will not be necessary to repeat this part of the argument.

I return to the case of the farmer and the cattle-raiser. The farmer would suffer increased damage to his crop as the size of the herd increased. Suppose that the size of the cattle-raiser's herd is 3 steers (and that this is the size of the herd that would be maintained if crop damage was not taken into account). Then the farmer would be willing to pay up to $3 if the cattle-raiser would reduce his herd to 2 steers, up to $5 if the herd were reduced to 1 steer and would pay up to $6 if cattle-raising was abandoned. The cattle-raiser would therefore receive $3 from the farmer if he kept 2 steers instead of 3. This $3 foregone is therefore part of the cost incurred in keeping the third steer. Whether the $3 is a payment which the cattle-raiser has to make if he adds the third steer to his herd (which it would be if the cattle-raiser was liable to the farmer for damage caused to the crop) or whether it is a sum of money which he would have received if he did not keep a third steer (which it would be if the cattle-raiser was not liable to the farmer for damage caused to the crop) does not affect the final result. In both cases $3 is part of the cost of adding a third steer, to be included along with the other costs. If the increase in the value of production in cattle-raising through increasing the size of the herd from 2 to 3 is greater than the additional costs that have to be incurred (including the $3 damage to crops), the size of the herd will be increased. Otherwise, it will not. The size of the herd will be the same whether the cattle-raiser is liable for damage caused to the crop or not.

It may be argued that the assumed starting point—a herd of 3 steers—was arbitrary. And this is true. But the farmer would not wish to pay to avoid crop damage which the cattle-raiser would not be able to cause. For example, the maximum annual payment which the farmer could be induced to pay could not exceed $9, the annual cost of fencing. And the farmer would only be willing to pay this sum if it did not reduce his earnings to a level that would cause him to abandon cultivation of this particular tract of land. Furthermore, the farmer would only be willing to pay this amount if he believed that, in the absence of any payment by him, the size of the herd maintained by the cattle raiser would be 4 or more steers. Let us assume that this is the case. Then the farmer would be willing to pay up to $3 if the cattle raiser would reduce his herd to 3 steers, up to $6 if the herd were reduced to 2 steers, up to $8 if one steer only were kept and up to $9 if cattle-raising were abandoned. It will be noticed that the change in the starting point has not altered the amount which would accrue to the cattle-raiser if he reduced the size of his herd by any given amount. It is still true that the cattle-raiser could receive an additional $3 from the farmer if he agreed to reduce his herd from 3 steers to 2 and that the $3 represents the value of the crop that would be destroyed by adding the third steer to the herd. Although a different belief on the part of the farmer (whether justified or not) about the size of the herd that the cattle-raiser would maintain in the absence of payments from him may affect the total payment he can be induced to pay, it is not true that this different belief would have any effect on the size of the herd that the cattle-raiser will actually keep. This will be the same as it would be if the cattle-raiser had to pay for damage caused by his cattle, since a receipt foregone of a given amount is the equivalent of a payment of the same amount.

It might be thought that it would pay the cattle-raiser to increase his herd above the size that he would wish to maintain once a bargain had been made, in order to induce the farmer to make a larger total payment. And this may be true. It is similar in nature to the action of the farmer (when the cattle-raiser was liable for damage) in cultivating land on which, as a result of an agreement with the cattle-raiser, planting would subsequently be abandoned (including land which would not be cultivated at all in the absence of cattle-raising). But such manoeuvres are preliminaries to an agreement and do not affect the long-run equilibrium position, which is the same whether or not the cattle-raiser is held responsible for the crop damage brought about by his cattle.

It is necessary to know whether the damaging business is liable or not for damage caused since without the establishment of this initial delimitation of rights there can be no market transactions to transfer and recombine them. But the ultimate result (which maximises the value of production) is independent of the legal position if the pricing system is assumed to work without cost.

V. THE PROBLEM ILLUSTRATED ANEW

The harmful effects of the activities of a business can assume a wide variety of forms. An early English case concerned a building which, by obstructing currents of air, hindered the operation of a windmill.[5] A recent case in Florida concerned a building which cast a shadow on the cabana, swimming pool and sunbathing areas of a neighbouring hotel.[6] The problem of straying cattle and the damaging of crops which was the subject of detailed examination in the two preceding sections, although it may have appeared to be rather a special case, is in fact but one example of a problem which arises in many different guises. To clarify the nature of my argument and to demonstrate its general applicability, I propose to illustrate it anew by reference to four actual cases.

Let us first reconsider the case of *Sturges v. Bridgman*[7] which I used as an illustration of the general problem in my article on "The Federal Communications Commission." In this case, a confectioner (in Wigmore Street) used two mortars and pestles in connection with his business (one had been in operation in the same position for more than 60 years and the other for more than 26 years). A doctor then came to occupy neighbouring premises (in Wimpole Street). The confectioner's machinery caused the doctor no harm until, eight years after he had first occupied the premises, he built a consulting room at the end of his garden right against the confectioner's kitchen. It was then found that the noise and vibration caused by the confectioner's machinery made it difficult for the doctor to use his new consulting room. "In particular . . . the noise prevented him from examining his patients by auscultation[8] for diseases of the chest. He also found it impossible to engage with effect in any occupation which required thought and attention." The doctor therefore brought a legal action to force the confectioner to stop using his machinery. The courts had little difficulty in granting the doctor the injunction he sought. "Individual cases of hardship may occur in the strict carrying out of the principle upon which we found our judgment, but the negation of the principle would lead even more to individual hardship, and would at the same time produce a prejudicial effect upon the development of land for residential purposes."

The court's decision established that the doctor had the right to prevent the confectioner from using his machinery. But, of course, it would have been possible to modify the arrangements envisaged in the legal ruling by means of a bargain between the parties. The doctor would have been willing to waive his right and allow the machinery to continue in operation if the confectioner would have paid him a sum of money which was greater than the loss of income which he would suffer from having to move to a more costly or less convenient location or from having to curtail his activities at this location or, as was suggested as a possibility, from having to build a separate wall which would deaden the noise and vibration. The confectioner would have been willing to do this if the amount he would have to pay the doctor was less than the fall in income he would suffer if he had to change his mode of operation at this location, abandon his operation or move his confectionery business to some other location. The solution of the problem depends essentially on whether the continued use of the machinery adds more to the confectioner's income than it subtracts from the doctor's.[9] But now consider the situation if the confectioner had won the case. The confectioner would then have had the right to continue operating his noise and vibration-generating machinery without having to pay anything to the doctor. The boot would have been on the other foot: the doctor would have had to pay the confectioner to induce him to stop using the machinery. If the doctor's income would have fallen more through continuance of the use of this machinery than it added to the income of the confectioner, there would clearly be room for a bargain whereby the doctor paid the confectioner to stop using the machinery. That is to say, the circumstances in which it would not pay the confectioner to continue to use the machinery and to compensate the doctor for the losses that this would bring (if the doctor had the right to prevent the confectioner's using his

126

machinery) would be those in which it would be in the interest of the doctor to make a payment to the confectioner which would induce him to discontinue the use of the machinery (if the confectioner had the right to operate the machinery). The basic conditions are exactly the same in this case as they were in the example of the cattle which destroyed crops. With costless market transactions, the decision of the courts concerning liability for damage would be without effect on the allocation of resources. It was of course the view of the judges that they were affecting the working of the economic system—and in a desirable direction. Any other decision would have had "a prejudicial effect upon the development of land for residential purposes," an argument which was elaborated by examining the example of a forge operating on a barren moor, which was later developed for residual purposes. The judges' view that they were settling how the land was to be used would be true only in the case in which the costs of carrying out the necessary market transactions exceeded the gain which might be achieved by any rearrangement of rights. And it would be desirable to preserve the areas (Wimpole Street or the moor) for residential or professional use (by giving non-industrial users the right to stop the noise, vibration, smoke, etc., by injunction) only if the value of the additional residential facilities obtained was greater than the value of cakes or iron lost. But of this the judges seem to have been unaware.

Another example of the same problem is furnished by the case of *Cooke v. Forbes*.[10] One process in the weaving of cocoa-nut fibre matting was to immerse it in bleaching liquids after which it was hung out to dry. Fumes from a manufacturer of sulphate of ammonia had the effect of turning the matting from a bright to a dull and blackish colour. The reason for this was that the bleaching liquid contained chloride of tin, which, when affected by sulphuretted hydrogen, is turned to a darker colour. An injunction was sought to stop the manufacturer from emitting the fumes. The lawyers for the defendant argued that if the plaintiff "were not to use . . . a particular bleaching liquid, their fibre would not be affected; that their process is unusual, not according to the custom of the trade, and even damaging to their own fabrics." The judge commented: ". . . it appears to me quite plain that a person has a right to carry on upon his own property a manufacturing process in which he uses chloride of tin, or any sort of metallic dye, and that his neighbour is not at liberty to pour in gas which will interfere with his manufacture. If it can be traced to the neighbour, then, I apprehend, clearly he will have a right to come here and ask for relief." But in view of the fact that the damage was accidental and occasional, that careful precautions were taken and that there was no exceptional risk, an injunction was refused, leaving the plaintiff to bring an action for damages if he wished. What the subsequent developments were I do not know. But it is clear that the situation is essentially the same as that found in *Sturges v. Bridgman*, except that the cocoa-nut fibre matting manufacturer could not secure an injunction but would have to seek damages from the sulphate of ammonia manufacturer. The economic analysis of the situation is exactly the same as with the cattle which destroyed crops. To avoid the damage, the sulphate of ammonia manufacturer could increase his precautions or move to another location. Either course would presumably increase his costs. Alternatively he could pay for the damage. This he would do if the payments for damage were less than the additional costs that would have to be incurred to avoid the damage. The payments for damage would then become part of the cost of production of sulphate of ammonia. Of course, if, as was suggested in the legal proceedings, the amount of damage could be eliminated by changing the bleaching agent (which would presumably increase the costs of the matting manufacturer) and if the additional cost was less than the damage that would otherwise occur, it should be possible for the two manufacturers to make a mutually satisfactory bargain whereby the new bleaching agent was used. Had the court decided against the matting manufacturer, as a consequence of which he would have had to suffer the damage without compensation, the allocation of resources would not have been affected. It would pay the matting manufacturer to change his bleaching agent if the additional cost involved was less than the reduction in damage. And since the matting manufacturer would be willing to pay the sulphate of ammonia manufacturer an amount up to his loss of income (the increase in costs or the damage suffered) if he would cease his activities, this loss of income would remain a cost of production for the manufacturer of sulphate of ammonia. This case is indeed analytically exactly the same as the cattle example.

Bryant v. Lefever[11] raised the problem of the smoke nuisance in a novel form. The plaintiff and the defendants were occupiers of adjoining houses, which were of about the same height.

Before 1876 the plaintiff was able to light a fire in any room of his house without the chimneys smoking; the two houses had remained in the same condition some thirty or forty years. In 1876 the defendants took down their house, and began to rebuild it. They carried up a wall by the side of the plaintiff's chimneys much beyond its original height, and stacked timber on the roof of their house, and thereby caused the plaintiff's chimneys to smoke whenever he lighted fires.

The reason, of course, why the chimneys smoked was that the erection of the wall and the stacking of the timber prevented the free circulation of air. In a trial before a jury, the plaintiff was awarded damages of £40. The case then went to the Court of Appeals where the judgment was reversed. Bramwell, L.J., argued:

. . . it is said, and the jury have found, that the defendants have done that which caused a nuisance to the plaintiff's house. We think there is no evidence of this. No doubt there is a nuisance, but it is not of the defendant's causing. They have done nothing in causing the nuisance. Their house and their timber are harmless enough.

128

It is the plaintiff who causes the nuisance by lighting a coal fire in a place the chimney of which is placed so near the defendants' wall, that the smoke does not escape, but comes into the house. Let the plaintiff cease to light his fire, let him move his chimney, let him carry it higher, and there would be no nuisance. Who then, causes it? It would be very clear that the plaintiff did, if he had built his house or chimney after the defendants had put up the timber on theirs, and it is really the same though he did so before the timber was there. But (what is in truth the same answer), if the defendants cause the nuisance, they have a right to do so. If the plaintiff has not the right to the passage of air, except subject to the defendants' right to build or put timber on their house, then his right is subject to their right, and though a nuisance follows from the exercise of their right, they are not liable.

And Cotton, L.J., said:

Here it is found that the erection of the defendants' wall has sensibly and materially interfered with the comfort of human existence in the plaintiff's house, and it is said this is a nuisance for which the defendants are liable. Ordinarily this is so, but the defendants have done so, not by sending on to the plaintiff's property any smoke or noxious vapour, but by interrupting the egress of smoke from the plaintiff's house in a way to which . . . the plaintiff has no legal right. The plaintiff creates the smoke, which interferes with his comfort. Unless he has . . . a right to get rid of this in a particular way which has been interfered with by the defendants, he cannot sue the defendants, because the smoke made by himself, for which he has not provided any effectual means of escape, causes him annoyance. It is as if a man tried to get rid of liquid filth arising on his own land by a drain into his neighbour's land. Until a right had been acquired by user, the neighbour might stop the drain without incurring liability by so doing. No doubt great inconvenience would be caused to the owner of the property on which the liquid filth arises. But the act of his neighbour would be a lawful act, and he would not be liable for the consequences attributable to the fact that the man had accumulated filth without providing any effectual means of getting rid of it.

I do not propose to show that any subsequent modification of the situation, as a result of bargains between the parties (conditioned by the cost of stacking the timber elsewhere, the cost of extending the chimney higher, etc.), would have exactly the same result whatever decision the courts had come to since this point has already been adequately dealt with in the discussion of the cattle example and the two previous cases. What I shall discuss is the argument of the judges in the Court of Appeals that the smoke nuisance was not caused by the man who erected the wall but by the man who lit the fires. The novelty of the situation is that the smoke nuisance was suffered by the man who lit the fires and not by some third person. The question is not a trivial one since it lies at the heart of the problem under discussion. Who caused the smoke nuisance? The answer seems fairly clear. The smoke nuisance was caused both by the man who built the wall *and* by the man who lit the fires. Given the fires, there would have been no smoke nuisance without the wall; given the wall, there would have been no smoke nuisance without the fires.

Eliminate the wall *or* the fires and the smoke nuisance would disappear. On the marginal principle it is clear that *both* were responsible and *both* should be forced to include the loss of amenity due to the smoke as a cost in deciding whether to continue the activity which gives rise to the smoke. And given the possibility of market transactions, this is what would in fact happen. Although the wall-builder was not liable legally for the nuisance, as the man with the smoking chimneys would presumably be willing to pay a sum equal to the monetary worth to him of eliminating the smoke, this sum would therefore become for the wall-builder, a cost of continuing to have the high wall with the timber stacked on the roof.

The judges' contention that it was the man who lit the fires who alone caused the smoke nuisance is true only if we assume that the wall is the given factor. This is what the judges did by deciding that the man who erected the higher wall had a legal right to do so. The case would have been even more interesting if the smoke from the chimneys had injured the timber. Then it would have been the wall-builder who suffered the damage. The case would then have closely paralleled *Sturges v. Bridgman* and there can be little doubt that the man who lit the fires would have been liable for the ensuing damage to the timber, in spite of the fact that no damage had occurred until the high wall was built by the man who owned the timber.

Judges have to decide on legal liability but this should not confuse economists about the nature of the economic problem involved. In the case of the cattle and the crops, it is true that there would be no crop damage without the cattle. It is equally true that there would be no crop damage without the crops. The doctor's work would not have been disturbed if the confectioner had not worked his machinery; but the machinery would have disturbed no one if the doctor had not set up his consulting room in that particular place. The matting was blackened by the fumes from the sulphate of ammonia manufacturer; but no damage would have occurred if the matting manufacturer had not chosen to hang out his matting in a particular place and to use a particular bleaching agent. If we are to discuss the problem in terms of causation, both parties cause the damage. If we are to attain an optimum allocation of resources, it is therefore desirable that both parties should take the harmful effect (the nuisance) into account in deciding on their course of action. It is one of the beauties of a smoothly operating pricing system that, as has already been explained, the fall in the value of production due to the harmful effect would be a cost for both parties.

Bass v. Gregory[12] will serve as an excellent final illustration of the problem. The plaintiffs were the owners and tenant of a public house called the Jolly Anglers. The defendant was the owner of some cottages and a yard adjoining the Jolly Anglers. Under the public house was a cellar excavated in the rock. From the cellar, a hole or shaft had been cut into an old well situated in the defendant's yard. The well therefore became the ventilating shaft for the cellar. The cellar "had been used for a particular purpose in the process of brewing, which, without ventilation, could not be carried on." The cause of the action was that the defendant removed a grating from the mouth of the well, "so as to stop or prevent the free passage of air from [the] cellar upwards through the well. . . ." What caused the defendant to take this step is not clear from the report of the case. Perhaps "the air . . . impregnated by the brewing operations" which "passed up the well and out into the open air" was offensive to him. At any rate, he preferred to have the well in his yard stopped up. The court had first to determine whether the owners of the public house could have a legal right to a current of air. If they were to have such a right, this case would have to be distinguished from *Bryant v. Lefever* (already considered). This, however, presented no difficulty. In this case, the current of air was confined to "a strictly defined channel." In the case of *Bryant v. Lefever,* what was involved was "the general current of air common to all mankind." The judge therefore held that the owners of the public house could have the right to a current of air whereas the owner of the private house in *Bryant v. Lefever* could not. An economist might be tempted to add "but the air moved all the same." However, all that had been decided at this stage of the argument was that there could be a legal right, not that the owners of the public house possessed it. But evidence showed that the shaft from the cellar to the well had existed for over forty years and that the use of the well as a ventilating shaft must have been known to the owners of the yard since the air, when it emerged, smelt of the brewing operations. The judge therefore held that the public house had such a right by the "doctrine of lost grant." This doctrine states "that if a legal right is proved to have existed and been exercised for a number of years the law ought to presume that it had a legal origin."[13] So the owner of the cottages and yard had to unstop the well and endure the smell.

The reasoning employed by the courts in determining legal rights will often seem strange to an economist because many of the factors on which the decision turns are, to an economist, irrelevant. Because of this, situations which are, from an economic point of view, identical will be treated quite differently by the courts. The economic problem in all cases of harmful effects is how to maximise the value of production. In the case of *Bass v. Gregory* fresh air was drawn in through the well which facilitated the production of beer but foul air was expelled through the well which made life in the adjoining houses less pleasant. The economic problem was to decide which to choose: a lower cost of beer and worsened amenities in adjoining houses or a higher cost of beer and improved amenities. In deciding this question, the "doctrine of lost grant" is about as relevant as the colour of the judge's eyes. But it has to be remembered that the immediate question faced by the courts is *not* what shall be done by whom *but* who has the legal right to do what. It is always possible to modify by transactions on the market the initial legal delimitation of rights. And, of course, if such market transactions are costless, such a rearrangement of rights will always take place if it would lead to an increase in the value of production.

VI. THE COST OF MARKET TRANSACTIONS TAKEN INTO ACCOUNT

The argument has proceeded up to this point on the assumption (explicit in Sections III and IV and tacit in Section V) that there were no costs involved in carrying out market transactions. This is, of course, a very unrealistic assumption. In order to carry out a market transaction it is necessary to discover who it is that one wishes to deal with, to inform people that one wishes to deal and on what terms, to conduct negotiations leading up to a bargain, to draw up the contract, to undertake the inspection needed to make sure that the terms of the contract are being observed, and so on. These operations are often extremely costly, sufficiently costly at any rate to prevent many transactions that would be carried out in a world in which the pricing system worked without cost.

In earlier sections, when dealing with the problem of the rearrangement of legal rights through the market, it was argued that such a rearrangement would be made through the market whenever this would lead to an increase in the value of production. But this assumed costless market transactions. Once the costs of carrying out market transactions are taken into account it is clear that such a rearrangement of rights will only be undertaken when the increase in the value of production consequent upon the rearrangement is greater than the costs which would be involved in bringing it about. When it is less, the granting of an injunction (or the knowledge that it would be granted) or the liability to pay damages may result in an activity being discontinued (or may prevent its being started) which would be undertaken if market transactions were costless. In these conditions the initial delimitation of legal rights does have an effect on the efficiency with which the economic system operates. One arrangement of rights may bring about a greater value of production than any other. But unless this is the arrangement of rights established by the legal system, the costs of reaching the same result by altering and combining rights through the market may be so great that this optimal arrangement of rights, and the greater value of production which it would bring, may never be achieved. The part played by economic considerations in the process of delimiting legal rights will be discussed in the next section. In this section, I will take the initial delimitation of rights and the costs of carrying out market transactions as given.

It is clear that an alternative form of economic organisation which could achieve the same result at less cost than would be incurred by using the market would enable the value of production to be raised. As I explained many years ago, the firm represents such an alternative to organising production through market transactions.[14] Within the firm individual bargains between the various cooperating factors of production are eliminated and for a market transaction is substituted an administrative decision. The rearrangement of production then takes place without the need for bargains between the owners of the factors of production. A landowner who has control of a large tract of land may devote his land to various uses taking into account the effect that the interrelations of the various activities will have on the net return of the land, thus rendering unnecessary bargains between those undertaking the various activities. Owners of a large building or of several adjoining properties in a given area may act in much the same way. In effect, using our earlier terminology, the firm would acquire the legal rights of all the parties and the rearrangement of activities would not follow on a rearrangement of rights by contract, but as a result of an administrative decision as to how the rights should be used.

It does not, of course, follow that the administrative costs of organising a transaction through a firm are inevitably less than the costs of the market transactions which are superseded. But where contracts are peculiarly difficult to draw up and an attempt to describe what the parties have agreed to do or not to do (e.g. the amount and kind of a smell or noise that they may make or will not make) would necessitate a lengthy and highly involved document, and, where, as is probable, a long-term contract would be desirable;[15] it would be hardly surprising if the emergence of a firm or the extension of the activities of an existing firm was not the solution adopted on many occasions to deal with the problem of harmful effects. This solution would be adopted whenever the administrative costs of the firm were less than the costs of the market transactions that it supersedes and the gains which would result from the rearrangement of activities greater than the firm's costs of organising them. I do not need to examine in great detail the character of this solution since I have explained what is involved in my earlier article.

But the firm is not the only possible answer to this problem. The administrative costs of organising transactions within the firm may also be high, and particularly so when many diverse activities are brought within the control of a single organisation. In the standard case of a smoke nuisance, which may affect a vast number of people engaged in a wide variety of activities, the administrative costs might well be so high as to make any attempt to deal with the problem within the confines of a single firm impossible. An alternative solution is direct Government regulation. Instead of instituting a legal system of rights which can be modified by transactions on the market, the government may impose regulations which state what people must or must not do and which have to be obeyed. Thus, the government (by statute or perhaps more likely through an administrative agency) may, to deal with the problem of smoke nuisance, decree that certain methods of production should or should not be used (e.g. that smoke preventing devices should be installed or that coal or oil should not be burned) or may confine certain types of business to certain districts (zoning regulations).

The government is, in a sense, a super-firm (but of a very special kind) since it is able to influence the use of factors of production by administrative decision. But the ordinary firm is subject to checks in its operations because of the competition of other firms, which might administer the same activities at lower cost and also because there is always the alternative of market transactions as against organisation within the firm if the administrative costs become too great. The government is able, if it wishes, to avoid the market altogether, which a firm can never do. The firm has to make market agreements with the owners of the factors of production that it uses. Just as the government can conscript or seize property, so it can decree that factors of production should only be used in such-and-such a way. Such authoritarian methods save a lot of trouble (for those doing the organising). Furthermore, the government has at its disposal the police and the other law enforcement agencies to make sure that its regulations are carried out.

It is clear that the government has powers which might enable it to get some things done at a lower cost than could a private organisation (or at any rate one without special governmental powers). But the governmental administrative machine is not itself costless. It can, in fact, on occasion be extremely costly. Furthermore, there is no reason to suppose that the restrictive and zoning regulations, made by a fallible administration subject to political pressures and operating without any competitive check, will necessarily always be those which increase the efficiency with which the economic system operates. Furthermore, such general regulations which must apply to a wide variety of cases will be enforced in some cases in which they are clearly inappropriate. From these considerations it follows that direct governmental regulation will not necessarily give better results than leaving the problem to be solved by the market or the firm. But equally there is no reason why, on occasion, such governmental administrative regulation should not lead to an improvement in economic efficiency. This would seem particularly likely when, as is normally the case with the smoke nuisance, a large number of people are involved and in which therefore the costs of handling the problem through the market or the firm may be high.

There is, of course, a further alternative, which is to do nothing about the problem at all. And given that the costs involved in solving the problem by regulations issued by the governmental administrative machine will often be heavy (particularly if the costs are interpreted to include all the consequences which follow from the Government engaging in this kind of activity), it will no doubt be commonly the case that the gain which would come from regulating the actions which give rise to the harmful effects will be less than the costs involved in Government regulation.

The discussion of the problem of harmful effects in this section (when the costs of market transactions are taken into account) is extremely inadequate. But at least it has made clear that the problem is one of choosing the appropriate social arrangement for dealing with the harmful effects. All solutions have costs and there is no reason to suppose that government regulation is called for simply because the problem is not well handled by the market or the firm. Satisfactory views on policy can only come from a patient study of how, in practice, the market, firms and governments handle the problem of harmful effects. Economists need to study the work of the broker in bringing parties together, the effectiveness of restrictive covenants, the problems of the large-scale real-estate development company, the operation of Government zoning and other regulating activities. It is my belief that economists, and policy-makers generally, have tended to over-estimate the advantages which come from governmental regulation. But this belief, even if justified, does not do more than suggest that government regulation should be curtailed. It does not tell us where the boundary line should be drawn. This, it seems to me, has to come from a detailed investigation of the actual results of handling the problem in different ways. But it would be unfortunate if this investigation were undertaken with the aid of a faulty economic analysis. The aim of this article is to indicate what the economic approach to the problem should be.

VII. THE LEGAL DELIMITATION OF RIGHTS AND THE ECONOMIC PROBLEM

The discussion in Section V not only served to illustrate the argument but also afforded a glimpse at the legal approach to the problem of harmful effects. The cases considered were all English but a similar selection of American cases could easily be made and the character of the reasoning would have been the same. Of course, if market transactions were costless, all that matters (questions of equity apart) is that the rights of the various parties should be well-defined and the results of legal actions easy to forecast. But as we have seen, the situation is quite different when market transactions are so costly as to make it difficult to change the arrangement of rights established by the law. In such cases, the courts directly influence economic activity. It would therefore seem desirable that the courts should understand the economic consequences of their decisions and should, insofar as this is possible without creating too much uncertainty about the legal position itself, take these consequences into account when making their decisions. Even when it is possible to change the legal delimitation of rights through market transactions, it is obviously desirable to reduce the need for such transactions and thus reduce the employment of resources in carrying them out.

A thorough examination of the presuppositions of the courts in trying such cases would be of great interest but I have not been able to attempt it.

Nevertheless it is clear from a cursory study that the courts have often recognized the economic implications of their decisions and are aware (as many economists are not) of the reciprocal nature of the problem. Furthermore, from time to time, they take these economic implications into account, along with other factors, in arriving at their decisions. The American writers on this subject refer to the question in a more explicit fashion than do the British. Thus, to quote Prosser on Torts, a person may

make use of his own property or . . . conduct his own affairs at the expense of some harm to his neighbors. He may operate a factory whose noise and smoke cause some discomfort to others, so long as he keeps within reasonable bounds. It is only when his conduct is unreasonable, *in the light of its utility and the harm which results* [italics added], that it becomes a nuisance. . . . . As it was said in an ancient case in regard to candle-making in a town, "Le utility del chose excusera le noisomeness del stink."

The world must have factories, smelters, oil refineries, noisy machinery and blasting, even at the expense of some inconvenience to those in the vicinity and the plaintiff may be required to accept some not unreasonable discomfort for the general good.[16]

The standard British writers do not state as explicitly as this that a comparison between the utility and harm produced is an element in deciding whether a harmful effect should be considered a nuisance. But similar views, if less strongly expressed, are to be found.[17] The doctrine that the harmful effect must be substantial before the court will act is, no doubt, in part a reflection of the fact that there will almost always be some gain to offset the harm. And in the reports of individual cases, it is clear that the judges have had in mind what would be lost as well as what would be gained in deciding whether to grant an injunction or award damages. Thus, in refusing to prevent the destruction of a prospect by a new building, the judge stated:

I know no general rule of common law, which . . . says, that building so as to stop another's prospect is a nuisance. Was that the case, there could be no great towns; and I must grant injunctions to all the new buildings in this town. . . .[18]

In *Webb v. Bird*[19] it was decided that it was not a nuisance to build a schoolhouse so near a windmill as to obstruct currents of air and hinder the working of the mill. An early case seems to have been decided in an opposite direction. Gale commented:

In old maps of London a row of windmills appears on the heights to the north of London. Probably in the time of King James it was thought an alarming circumstance, as affecting the supply of food to the city, that anyone should build so near them as to take the wind out from their sails.[20]

In one of the cases discussed in section V, *Sturges v. Bridgman,* it seems clear that the judges were thinking of the economic consequences of alternative decisions. To the argument that if the principle that they seemed to be following

were carried out to its logical consequences, it would result in the most serious practical inconveniences, for a man might go—say into the midst of the tanneries of *Bermondsey,* or into any other locality devoted to any particular trade or manufacture of a noisy or unsavoury character, and by building a private residence upon a vacant piece of land put a stop to such trade or manufacture altogether,

the judges answered that

whether anything is a nuisance or not is a question to be determined, not merely by an abstract consideration of the thing itself, but in reference to its circumstances; What would be a nuisance in *Belgrave Square* would not necessarily be so in *Bermondsey;* and where a locality is devoted to a particular trade or manufacture carried on by the traders or manufacturers in a particular and established manner not constituting a public nuisance, Judges and juries would be justified in finding, and may be trusted to find, that the trade or manufacture so carried on in that locality is not a private or actionable wrong.[21]

That the character of the neighborhood is relevant in deciding whether something is, or is not, a nuisance, is definitely established.

He who dislikes the noise of traffic must not set up his abode in the heart of a great city. He who loves peace and quiet must not live in a locality devoted to the business of making boilers or steamships.[22]

What has emerged has been described as "planning and zoning by the judiciary."[23] Of course there are sometimes considerable difficulties in applying the criteria.[24]

An interesting example of the problem is found in *Adams v. Ursell*[25] in which a fried fish shop in a predominantly working-class district was set up near houses of "a much better character." England without fish-and-chips is a contradiction in terms and the case was clearly one of high importance. The judge commented:

It was urged that an injunction would cause great hardship to the defendant and to the poor people who get food at his shop. The answer to that is that it does not follow that the defendant cannot carry on his business in another more suitable place somewhere in the neighbourhood. It by no means follows that because a fried fish shop is a nuisance in one place it is a nuisance in another.

In fact, the injunction which restrained Mr. Ursell from running his shop did not even extend to the whole street. So he was presumably able to move to other premises near houses of "a much worse character," the inhabitants of which would no doubt consider the availability of fish-and-chips to outweigh the pervading odour and "fog or mist" so graphically described by the plaintiff. Had there been no other "more suitable place in the neighbourhood," the case would have been more difficult and the decision might have been different. What would "the poor people" have had for food? No English judge would have said: "Let them eat cake."

137

The courts do not always refer very clearly to the economic problem posed by the cases brought before them but it seems probable that in the interpretation of words and phrases like "reasonable" or "common or ordinary use" there is some recognition, perhaps largely unconscious and certainly not very explicit, of the economic aspects of the questions at issue. A good example of this would seem to be the judgment in the Court of Appeals in *Andreae v. Selfridge and Company Ltd.*[26] In this case, a hotel (in Wigmore Street) was situated on part of an island site. The remainder of the site was acquired by Selfridges which demolished the existing buildings in order to erect another in their place. The hotel suffered a loss of custom in consequence of the noise and dust caused by the demolition. The owner of the hotel brought an action against Selfridges for damages. In the lower court, the hotel was awarded £4,500 damages. The case was then taken on appeal.

The judge who had found for the hotel proprietor in the lower court said:

I cannot regard what the defendants did on the site of the first operation as having been commonly done in the ordinary use and occupation of land or houses. It is neither usual nor common, in this country, for people to excavate a site to a depth of 60 feet and then to erect upon that site a steel framework and fasten the steel frames together with rivets. . . . Nor is it, I think, a common or ordinary use of land, in this country, to act as the defendants did when they were dealing with the site of their second operation—namely, to demolish all the houses that they had to demolish, five or six of them I think, if not more, and to use for the purpose of demolishing them pneumatic hammers.

Sir Wilfred Greene, M.R., speaking for the Court of Appeals, first noted

that when one is dealing with temporary operations, such as demolition and re-building, everybody has to put up with a certain amount of discomfort, because operations of that kind cannot be carried on at all without a certain amount of noise and a certain amount of dust. Therefore, the rule with regard to interference must be read subject to this qualification. . . .

He then referred to the previous judgment:

With great respect to the learned judge, I take the view that he has not approached this matter from the correct angle. It seems to me that it is not possible to say . . . that the type of demolition, excavation and construction in which the defendant company was engaged in the course of these operations was of such an abnormal and unusual nature as to prevent the qualification to which I have referred coming into operation. It seems to me that, when the rule speaks of the common or ordinary use of land, it does not mean that the methods of using land and building on it are in some way to be stabilised for ever. As time goes on new inventions or new methods enable land to be more profitably used, either by digging down into the earth or by mounting up into the skies. Whether, from other points of view, that is a matter which is desirable for humanity is neither here nor there; but it is part of the normal use of land, to make use upon your land, in the matter of construction, of what particular type and what particular depth of foundations and particular height of building may be reasonable, in the circumstances, and in view of the developments of the day. . . . Guests at hotels are very easily upset. People coming to this hotel, who were accustomed to a quiet outlook at the back, coming back and finding demolition and building going on, may very well have taken the view that the particular merit of this hotel no longer existed. That would be a misfortune for the plaintiff; but assuming that there was nothing wrong in the defendant company's works, assuming the defendant company was carrying on the demolition and its building, productive of noise though it might be, with all reasonable skill, and taking all reasonable precautions not to cause annoyance to its neighbors, then the planitiff might lose all her clients in the hotel because they have lost the amenities of an open and quiet place behind, but she would have no cause of complaint. . . . [But those] who say that their interference with the comfort of their neighbors is justified because their operations are normal and usual and conducted with proper care and skill are under a specific duty . . . to use that reasonable and proper care and skill. It is not a correct attitude to take to say: 'We will go on and do what we like until somebody complains!' . . . Their duty is to take proper precautions and to see that the nuisance is reduced to a minimum. It is no answer for them to say: 'But this would mean that we should have to do the work more slowly than we would like to do it, or it would involve putting us to some extra expense.' All these questions are matters of common sense and degree, and quite clearly it would be unreasonable to expect people to conduct their work so slowly or so expensively, for the purpose of preventing a transient inconvenience, that the cost and trouble would be prohibitive. . . . In this case, the defendant company's attitude seems to have been to go on until somebody complained, and, further, that its desire to hurry its work and conduct it according to its own ideas and its own convenience was to prevail if there was a real conflict between it and the comfort of its neighbors. That . . . is not carrying out the obligation of using reasonable care and skill. . . . The effect comes to this . . . the plaintiff suffered an actionable nuisance; . . . she is entitled, not to a nominal sum, but to a substantial sum, based upon those principles . . . but in arriving at the sum . . . I have discounted any loss of custom . . . which might be due to the general loss of amenities owing to what was going on at the back. . . .

The upshot was that the damages awarded were reduced from £4,500 to £1,000.

The discussion in this section has, up to this point, been concerned with court decisions arising out of the common law relating to nuisance. Delimitation of rights in this area also comes about because of statutory enactments. Most economists would appear to assume that the aim of governmental action in this field is to extend the scope of the law of nuisance by designating as nuisances activities which would not be recognized as such by the common law. And there can be no doubt that some statutes, for example, the Public Health Acts, have had this effect. But not all Government enactments are of this kind. The effect of much of the legislation in this area is to protect businesses from the claims of those they have harmed by their actions. There is a long list of legalized nuisances.

The position has been summarized in *Halsbury's Laws of England* as follows:

139

Where the legislature directs that a thing shall in all events be done or authorises certain works at a particular place for a specific purposes or grants powers with the intention that they shall be exercised, although leaving some discretion as to the mode of exercise, no action will lie at common law for nuisance or damage which is the inevitable result of carrying out the statutory powers so conferred. This is so whether the act causing the damage is authorised for public purposes or private profit. Acts done under powers granted by persons to whom Parliament has delegated authority to grant such powers, for example, under provisional orders of the Board of Trade, are regarded as having been done under statutory authority. In the absence of negligence it seems that a body exercising statutory powers will not be liable to an action merely because it might, by acting in a different way, have minimised an injury.

Instances are next given of freedom from liability for acts authorized:

An action has been held not to be against a body exercising its statutory powers without negligence in respect of the flooding of land by water escaping from watercourses, from water pipes, from drains, or from a canal; the escape of fumes from sewers; the escape of sewage: the subsidence of a road over a sewer; vibration or noise caused by a railway; fires caused by authorised acts; the pollution of a stream where statutory requirements to use the best known method of purifying before discharging the effluent have been satisfied; interference with a telephone or tele-graph system by an elctric tramway; the insertion of poles for tramways in the sub-soil; annoyance caused by things reasonably necessary for the excavation of authorised works; accidental damage caused by the placing of a grating in a roadway; the escape of tar acid; or interference with the access of a frontager by a street shelter or safety railings on the edge of a pavement.[27]

The legal position in the United States would seem to be essentially the same as in England, except that the power of the legislatures to authorize what would otherwise be nuisances under the common law, at least without giving compensation to the person harmed, is somewhat more limited, as it is subject to constitutional restrictions.[28] Nonetheless, the power is there and cases more or less identical with the English cases can be found. The question has arisen in an acute form in connection with airports and the operation of aeroplanes. The case of *Delta Air Corporation v. Kersey, Kersey v. City of Atlanta*[29] is a good example. Mr. Kersey bought land and built a house on it. Some years later the City of Atlanta constructed an airport on land immediately adjoining that of Mr. Kersey. It was explained that his property was "a quiet, peaceful and proper location for a home before the airport was built, but dust, noises and low flying of airplanes caused by the operation of the airport have rendered his property unsuitable as a home," a state of affairs which was described in the report of the case with a wealth of distressing detail. The judge first referred to an earlier case, *Thrasher v. City of Atlanta*[30] in which it was noted that the City of Atlanta had been expressly authorized to operate an airport.

By this franchise aviation was recognised as a lawful business and also as an enterprise affected with a public interest . . . all persons using [the airport] in the manner contemplated by law are within the protection and immunity of the franchise granted by the municipality. An airport is not a nuisance per se, although it might become such from the manner of its construction or operation.

Since aviation was a lawful business affected with a public interest and the construction of the airport was autorized by statute, the judge next referred to *Georgia Railroad and Banking Co. v. Maddox*[31] in which it was said:

Where a railroad terminal yard is located and its construction authorized, under statutory powers, if it be constructed and operated in a proper manner, it cannot be adjudged a nuisance. Accordingly, injuries and inconveniences to persons residing near such a yard, from noises of locomotives, rumbling of cars, vibrations produced thereby, and smoke, cinders, soot and the like, which result from the ordinary and necessary, therefore proper, use and operation of such a yard, are not nuisances, but are the necessary concomitants of the franchise granted.

In view of this, the judge decided that the noise and dust complained of by Mr. Kersey "may be deemed to be incidental to the proper operation of an airport, and as such they cannot be said to constitute a nuisance." But the complaint against low flying was different:

. . . can it be said that flights . . . at such a low height [25 to 50 feet above Mr. Kersey's house] as to be imminently dangerous to . . . life and health . . . are a necessary concomitant of an airport? We do not think this question can be answered in the affirmative. No reason appears why the city could not obtain lands of an area [sufficiently large] . . . as not to require such low flights. . . . For the sake of public convenience adjoining-property owners must suffer such inconvenience from noise and dust as result from the usual and proper operation of an airport, but their private rights are entitled to preference in the eyes of the law where the inconvenience is not one demanded by a properly constructed and operated airport.

Of course this assumed that the City of Atlanta could prevent the low flying and continue to operate the airport. The judge therefore added:

From all that appears, the conditions causing the low flying may be remedied; but if on the trial it should appear that it is indispensable to the public interest that the airport should continue to be operated in its present condition, it may be said that the petitioner should be denied injunctive relief.

In the course of another aviation case, *Smith v. New England Aircraft Co.*,[32] the court surveyed the law in the United States regarding the legalizing of nuisances and it is apparent that, in the broad, it is very similar to that found in England:

It is the proper function of the legislative department of government in the exercise of the police power to consider the problems and risks that arise from the use of new inventions and endeavor to adjust private rights and harmonize conflicting interests by comprehensive statutes for the public welfare. . . . There are . . . analogies where the invasion of the airspace over underlying land by noise, smoke, vibration, dust and disagreeable odors, having been authorized by the legislative department of government and not being in effect a condemnation of the property although in some measure depreciating its market value, must be borne by the land-owner without compensation or remedy. Legislative sanction makes that lawful which otherwise might be a nuisance. Examples of this are damages to adjacent land arising from smoke, vibration and noise in the operation of a railroad . . . , the noise of ringing factory bells . . . ; the abatement of nuisances . . . ; the erection of steam engines and furnaces . . . ; unpleasant odors connected with sewers, oil refining and storage of naphtha. . . .

Most economists seem to be unaware of all this. When they are prevented from sleeping at night by the roar of jet planes overhead (publicly authorized and perhaps publicly operated), are unable to think (or rest) in the day because of the noise and vibration from passing trains (publicly authorized and perhaps publicly operated), find it difficult to breathe because of the odour from a local sewage farm (publicly authorized and perhaps publicly operated) and are unable to escape because their driveways are blocked by a road obstruction (without any doubt, publicly devised), their nerves frayed and mental balance disturbed, they proceed to declaim about the disadvantages of private enterprise and the need for Government regulation.

While most economists seem to be under a misapprehension concerning the character of the situation with which they are dealing, it is also the case that the activities which they would like to see stopped or curtailed may well be socially justified. It is all a question of weighing up the gains that would accrue from eliminating these harmful effects against the gains that accrue from allowing them to continue. Of course, it is likely that an extension of Government economic activity will often lead to this protection against action for nuisance being pushed further than is desirable. For one thing, the Government is likely to look with a benevolent eye on enterprises which it is itself promoting. For another, it is possible to describe the committing of a nuisance by public enterprise in a much more pleasant way than when the same thing is done by private enterprise. In the words of Lord Justice Sir Alfred Denning:

. . . the significance of the social revolution of today is that, whereas in the past the balance was much too heavily in favor of the rights of property and freedom of contract, Parliament has repeatedly intervened so as to give the public good its proper place.[33]

There can be little doubt that the Welfare State is likely to bring an extension of that immunity from liability for damage, which economists have been in the habit of condemning (although they have tended to assume that this immunity was a sign of too little Government intervention in the economic system). For example, in Britain, the powers of local authorities are regarded as being either absolute or conditional. In the first category, the local authority has no discretion in exercising the power conferred on it. "The absolute power may be said to cover all the necessary consequences of its direct operation even if such consequences amount to nuisance." On the

142

other hand, a conditional power may only be exercised in such a way that the consequences do not constitute a nuisance.

It is the intention of the legislature which determines whether a power is absolute or conditional. . . . [As] there is the possibility that the social policy of the legislature may change from time to time, a power which in one era would be construed as being conditional, might in another era be interpreted as being absolute in order to further the policy of the Welfare State. This point is one which should be borne in mind when considering some of the older cases upon this aspect of the law of nuisance.[84]

It would seem desirable to summarize the burden of this long section. The problem which we face in dealing with actions which have harmful effects is not simply one of restraining those responsible for them. What has to be decided is whether the gain from preventing the harm is greater than the loss which would be suffered elsewhere as a result of stopping the action which produces the harm. In a world in which there are costs of rearranging the rights established by the legal system, the courts, in cases relating to nuisance, are, in effect, making a decision on the economic problem and determining how resources are to be employed. It was argued that the courts are conscious of this and that they often make, although not always in a very explicit fashion, a comparison between what would be gained and what lost by preventing actions which have harmful effects. But the delimitation of rights is also the result of statutory enactments. Here we also find evidence of an appreciation of the reciprocal nature of the problem. While statutory enactments add to the list of nuisances, action is also taken to legalize what would otherwise be nuisances under the common law. The kind of situation which economists are prone to consider as requiring corrective Government action is, in fact, often the result of Government action. Such action is not necessarily unwise. But there is a real danger that extensive Government intervention in the economic system may lead to the protection of those responsible for harmful effects being carried too far.

VIII. PIGOU'S TREATMENT IN "THE ECONOMICS OF WELFARE"

The fountainhead for the modern economic analysis of the problem discussed in this article is Pigou's *Economics of Welfare* and, in particular, that section of Part II which deals with divergences between social and private net products which come about because

one person A, in the course of rendering some service, for which payment is made, to a second person B, incidentally also renders services or disservices to other persons (not producers of like services), of such a sort that payment cannot be exacted from the benefited parties or compensation enforced on behalf of the injured parties.[35]

Pigou tells us that his aim in Part II of *The Economics of Welfare* is

to ascertain how far the free play of self-interest, acting under the existing legal

143

system, tends to distribute the country's resources in the way most favorable to the production of a large national dividend, and how far it is feasible for State action to improve upon 'natural' tendencies.[36]

To judge from the first part of this statement, Pigou's purpose is to discover whether any improvements could be made in the existing arrangements which determine the use of resources. Since Pigou's conclusion is that improvements could be made, one might have expected him to continue by saying that he proposed to set out the changes required to bring them about. Instead, Pigou adds a phrase which contrasts "natural" tendencies with State action, which seems in some sense to equate the present arrangements with "natural" tendencies and to imply that what is required to bring about these improvements is State action (if feasible). That this is more or less Pigou's position is evident from Chapter I of Part II.[37] Pigou starts by referring to "optimistic followers of the classical economists"[38] who have argued that the value of production would be maximised if the Government refrained from any interference in the economic system and the economic arrangements were those which came about "naturally." Pigou goes on to say that if self-interest does promote economic welfare, it is because human institutions have been devised to make it so. (This part of Pigou's argument, which he develops with the aid of a quotation from Cannan, seems to me to be essentially correct.) Pigou concludes:

But even in the most advanced States there are failures and imperfections. . . . there are many obstacles that prevent a community's resources from being distributed . . . in the most efficient way. The study of these constitutes our present problem. . . . its purposes is essentially practical. It seeks to bring into clearer light some of the ways in which it now is, or eventually may become, feasible for governments to control the play of economic forces in such wise as to promote the economic welfare, and through that, the total welfare, of their citizens as a whole.[39]

Pigou's underlying thought would appear to be: Some have argued that no State action is needed. But the system has performed as well as it has because of State action. Nonetheless, there are still imperfections. What additional State action is required?

If this is a correct summary of Pigou's position, its inadequacy can be demonstrated by examining the first example he gives of a divergence between private and social products.

It might happen . . . that costs are thrown upon people not directly concerned, through, say, uncompensated damage done to surrounding woods by sparks from railway engines. All such effects must be included—some of them will be positive, others negative elements—in reckoning up the social net product of the marginal increment of any volume of resources turned into any use or place.[40]

The example used by Pigou refers to a real situation. In Britain, a railway does not normally have to compensate those who suffer damage by fire caused by sparks from an engine. Taken in conjunction with what he says in Chapter 9 of Part II, I take Pigou's policy recommendations to be, first, that there should be State action to correct this "natural" situation and, second, that the railways should be forced to compensate those whose woods are burnt. If this is a correct interpretation of Pigou's position, I would argue that the first recommendation is based on a misapprehension of the facts and that the second is not necessarily desirable.

Let us consider the legal position. Under the heading "Sparks from engines," we find the following in Halsbury's Laws of England:

If railway undertakers use steam engines on their railway without express statutory authority to do so, they are liable, irrespective of any negligence on their part, for fires caused by sparks from engines. Railway undertakers are, however, generally given statutory authority to use steam engines on their railway; accordingly, if an engine is constructed with the precautions which science suggests against fire and is used without negligence, they are not responsible at common law for any damage which may be done by sparks. . . . In the construction of an engine the undertaker is bound to use all the discoveries which science has put within its reach in order to avoid doing harm, provided they are such as it is reasonable to require the company to adopt, having proper regard to the likelihood of the damage and to the cost and convenience of the remedy; but it is not negligence on the part of an undertaker if it refuses to use an apparatus the efficiency of which is open to bona fide doubt.

To this general rule, there is a statutory exception arising from the Railway (Fires) Act, 1905, as amended in 1923. This concerns agricultural land or agricultural crops.

In such a case the fact that the engine was used under statutory powers does not affect the liability of the company in an action for the damage. . . . These provisions, however, only apply where the claim for damage . . . does not exceed £ 200, [£ 100 in the 1905 Act] and where written notice of the occurrence of the fire and the intention to claim has been sent to the company within seven days of the occurrence of the damage and particulars of the damage in writing showing the amount of the claim in money not exceeding £ 200 have been sent to the company within twenty-one days.

Agricultural land does not include moorland or buildings and agricultural crops do not include those led away or stacked.[41] I have not made a close study of the parliamentary history of this statutory exception, but to judge from debates in the House of Commons in 1922 and 1923, this exception was probably designed to help the smallholder.[42]

Let us return to Pigou's example of uncompensated damage to surrounding woods caused by sparks from railway engines. This is presumably intended to show how it is possible "for State action to improve on 'natural' tendencies." If we treat Pigou's example as referring to the position before 1905, or as being an arbitrary example (in that he might just as well have written "surrounding buildings" instead of "surrounding woods"), then it is clear that the reason why compensation was not paid must have been that the railway had statutory authority to run steam engines (which relieved it of liability for fires caused by sparks). That this was the legal position was established in 1860, in a case, oddly enough, which concerned the burning of surrounding woods by a railway,[43] and the law on this point has not been changed (apart from the one exception) by a century of railway legislation, including nationalisation. If we treat Pigou's example of "uncompensated damage done to surrounding woods by sparks from railway engines" literally, and assume that it refers to the period after 1905, then it is clear that the reason why compensation was not paid must have been that the damage was more than £100 (in the first edition of *The Economics of Welfare*) or more than £200 (in later editions) or that the owner of the wood failed to notify the railway in writing within seven days of the fire or did not send particulars of the damage, in writing, within twenty-one days. In the real world, Pigou's example could only exist as a result of a deliberate choice of the legislature. It is not, of course, easy to imagine the construction of a railway in a state of nature. The nearest one can get to this is presumably a railway which uses steam engines "without express statutory authority." However, in this case the railway would be obliged to compensate those whose woods it burnt down. That is to say, compensation would be paid in the absence of Government action. The only circumstances in which compensation would not be paid would be those in which there had been Government action. It is strange that Pigou, who clearly thought it desirable that compensation should be paid, should have chosen this particular example to demonstrate how it is possible "for State action to improve on 'natural' tendencies."

Pigou seems to have had a faulty view of the facts of the situation. But it also seems likely that he was mistaken in his economic analysis. It is not necessarily desirable that the railway should be required to compensate those who suffer damage by fires caused by railway engines. I need not show here that, if the railway could make a bargain with everyone having property adjoining the railway line and there were no costs involved in making such bargains, it would not matter whether the railway was liable for damage caused by fires or not. This question has been treated at length in earlier sections. The problem is whether it would be desirable to make the railway liable in conditions in which it is too expensive for such bargains to be made. Pigou clearly thought it was desirable to force the railway to pay compensation and it is easy to see the kind of argument that would have led him to this conclusion. Suppose a railway is considering whether to run an additional train or to increase the speed of an existing train or to install spark-preventing devices on its engines. If the railway were not liable for fire damage, then, when making these decisions, it would not take into account as a cost the increase in damage resulting from the additional train or the faster train or the failure to install spark-preventing devices. This is the source of the divergence between private and social net products. It results in the railway performing acts which will lower the value of total production—and which

146

it would not do if it were liable for the damage. This can be shown by means of an arithmetical example.

Consider a railway, which is *not* liable for damage by fires caused by sparks from its engines, which runs two trains per day on a certain line. Suppose that running one train per day would enable the railway to perform services worth $150 per annum and running two trains a day would enable the railway to perform services worth $250 per annum. Suppose further that the cost of running one train is $50 per annum and two trains $100 per annum. Assuming perfect competition, the cost equals the fall in the value of production elsewhere due to the employment of additional factors of production by the railway. Clearly the railway would find it profitable to run two trains per day. But suppose that running one train per day would destroy by fire crops worth (on an average over the year) $60 and two trains a day would result in the destruction of crops worth $120. In these circumstances running one train per day would raise the value of total production but the running of a second train would reduce the value of total production. The second train would enable additional railway services worth $100 per annum to be performed. But the fall in the value of production elsewhere would be $110 per annum; $50 as a result of the employment of additional factors of production and $60 as a result of the destruction of crops. Since it would be better if the second train were not run and since it would not run if the railway were liable for damage caused to crops, the conclusion that the railway should be made liable for the damage seems irresistible. Undoubtedly it is this kind of reasoning which underlies the Pigovian position.

The conclusion that it would be better if the second train did not run is correct. The conclusion that it is desirable that the railway should be made liable for the damage it causes is wrong. Let us change our assumption concerning the rule of liability. Suppose that the railway is liable for damage from fires caused by sparks from the engine. A farmer on lands adjoining the railway is then in the position that, if his crop is destroyed by fires caused by the railway, he will receive the market price from the railway; but if his crop is not damaged, he will receive the market price by sale. It therefore becomes a matter of indifference to him whether his crop is damaged by fire or not. The position is very different when the railway is *not* liable. Any crop destruction through railway-caused fires would then reduce the receipts of the farmer. He would therefore take out of cultivation any land for which the damage is likely to be greater than the net return of the land (for reasons explained at length in Section III). A change from a regime in which the railway is *not* liable for damage to one in which it *is* liable is likely therefore to lead to an increase in the amount of cultivation on lands adjoining the railway. It will also, of course, lead to an increase in the amount of crop destruction due to railway-caused fires.

Let us return to our arithmetical example. Assume that, with the changed rule of liability, there is a doubling in the amount of crop destruction due to railway-caused fires. With one train per day, crops worth $120 would be destroyed each year and two trains per day would lead to the destruction of crops worth $240. We saw previously that it would not be profitable to run the second train if the railway had to pay $60 per annum as compensation for damage. With damage at $120 per annum the loss from running the second train would be $60 greater. But now let us consider the first train. The value of the transport services furnished by the first train is $150. The cost of running the train is $50. The amount that the railway would have to pay out as compensation for damage is $120. It follows that it would not be profitable to run any trains. With the figures in our example we reach the following result: if the railway is not liable for fire-damage, two trains per day would be run; if the railway is liable for fire-damage, it would cease operations altogether. Does this mean that it is better that there should be no railway? This question can be resolved by considering what would happen to the value of total production if it were decided to exempt the railway from liability for fire-damage, thus bringing it into operation (with two trains per day).

The operation of the railway would enable transport services worth $250 to be performed. It would also mean the employment of factors of production which would reduce the value of production elsewhere by $100. Furthermore it would mean the destruction of crops worth $120. The coming of the railway will also have led to the abandonment of cultivation of some land. Since we know that, had this land been cultivated, the value of the crops destroyed by fire would have been $120, and since it is unlikely that the total crop on this land would have been destroyed, it seems reasonable to suppose that the value of the crop yield on this land would have been higher than this. Assume it would have been $160. But the abandonment of cultivation would have released factors of production for employment elsewhere. All we know is that the amount by which the value of production elsewhere will increase will be less than $160. Suppose that it is $150. Then the gain from operating the railway would be $250 (the value of the transport services) minus $100 (the cost of the factors of production) minus $120 (the value of crops destroyed by fire) minus $160 (the fall in the value of crop production due to the abandonment of cultivation) plus $150 (the value of production elsewhere of the released factors of production). Overall, operating the railway will increase the value of total production by $20. With these figures it is clear that it is better that the railway should not be liable for the damage it causes, thus enabling it to operate profitably. Of course, by altering the figures, it could be shown that there are other cases in which it would be desirable that the railway should be liable for the damage it causes. It is enough for my purpose to show that, from an economic point of view, a situation in which there is "uncompensated damage done to surrounding woods by sparks from railway engines" is not necessarily undesirable. Whether it is desirable or not depends on the particular circumstances.

How is it that the Pigovian analysis seems to give the wrong answer? The reason is that Pigou does not seem to have noticed that his analysis is dealing with an entirely different question. The analysis as such is correct. But it is quite illegitimate for Pigou to draw the particular conclusion he does. The question at issue is not whether it is desirable to run an additional train or a faster train or to install smoke-preventing devices; the question at issue is whether it is desirable to have a system in which the railway has to compensate those who suffer damage from the fires which it causes or one in which the railway does not have to compensate them. When an economist is comparing alternative social arrangements, the proper procedure is to compare the total social product yielded by these different arrangements. The comparison of private and social products is neither here nor there. A simple example will demonstrate this. Imagine a town in which there are traffic lights. A motorist approaches an intersection and stops because the light is red. There are no cars approaching the intersection on the other street. If the motorist ignored the red signal, no accident would occur and the total product would increase because the motorist would arrive earlier at his destination. Why does he not do this? The reason is that if he ignored the light he would be fined. The private product from crossing the street is less than the social product. Should we conclude from this that the total product would be greater if there were no fines for failing to obey traffic signals? The Pigovian analysis shows us that it is possible to conceive of better worlds than the one in which we live. But the problem is to devise practical arrangements which will correct defects in one part of the system without causing more serious harm in other parts.

I have examined in considerable detail one example of a divergence between private and social products and I do not propose to make any further examination of Pigou's analytical system. But the main discussion of the problem considered in this article is to be found in that part of Chapter 9 in Part II which deals with Pigou's second class of divergence and it is of interest to see how Pigou develops his argument. Pigou's own description of this second class of divergence was quoted at the beginning of this section. Pigou distinguishes between the case in which a person renders services for which he receives no payment and the case in which a person renders disservices and compensation is not given to the injured parties. Our main attention has, of course, centred on this second case. It is therefore rather astonishing to find, as was pointed out to me by Professor Francesco Forte, that the problem of the smoking chimney—the "stock instance"[44] or "classroom example"[45] of the second case—is used by Pigou as an example of the first case (services rendered without payment) and is never mentioned, at any rate explicitly, in connection with the second case.[46] Pigou points out that factory owners who devote resources to preventing their chimneys from smoking render services for which they receive no payment. The implication, in the light of Pigou's discussion later in the chapter, is that a factory owner with a smokey chimney should be given a bounty to induce him to install smoke-preventing devices. Most modern economists would suggest that the owner of the factory with the smokey chimney should be taxed. It seems a pity that economists (apart from Professor Forte) do not seem to have noticed this feature of Pigou's treatment since a realisation that the problem could be tackled in either of these two ways would probably have led to an explicit recognition of its reciprocal nature.

In discussing the second case (disservices without compensation to those damaged), Pigou says that they are rendered "when the owner of a site in a residential quarter of a city builds a factory there and so destroys a great part of the amenities of neighbouring sites; or, in a less degree, when he uses his site in such a way as to spoil the lighting of the house opposite; or when he invests resources in erecting buildings in a crowded centre, which by contracting the air-space and the playing room of the neighbourhood, tend to injure the health and efficiency of the families living there."[47] Pigou is, of course, quite right to describe such actions as "uncharged disservices." But he is wrong when he describes these actions as "anti-social."[48] They may or may not be. It is necessary to weigh the harm against the good that will result. Nothing could be more "anti-social" than to oppose any action which causes any harm to anyone.

The example with which Pigou opens his discussion of "uncharged dis-services" is not, as I have indicated, the case of the smokey chimney but the case of the overrunning rabbits: ". . . incidental uncharged disservices are rendered to third parties when the game-preserving activities of one occupier involve the overrunning of a neighbouring occupier's land by rabbits. . . ." This example is of extraordinary interest, not so much because the economic analysis of the case is essentially any different from that of the other examples, but because of the peculiarities of the legal position and the light it throws on the part which economics can play in what is apparently the purely legal question of the delimitation of rights.

The problem of legal liability for the actions of rabbits is part of the general subject of liability for animals.[49] I will, although with reluctance, confine my discussion to rabbits. The early cases relating to rabbits concerned the relations between the lord of the manor and commoners, since, from the thirteenth century on, it became usual for the lord of the manor to stock the commons with conies (rabbits), both for the sake of the meat and the fur. But in 1597, in *Boulston*'s case, an action was brought by one landowner against a neighbouring landowner, alleging that the defendant had made coney-burrows and that the conies had increased and had destroyed the plaintiff's corn. The action failed for the reason that

. . . so soon as the coneys come on his neighbor's land he may kill them, for they are ferae naturae, and he who makes the coney-boroughs has no property in them, and he shall not be punished for the damage which the coneys do in which he has no property, and which the other may lawfully kill.[50]

As *Boulston*'s case has been treated as binding—Bray, J., in 1919, said that he was not aware that *Boulston*'s case has ever been overruled or questioned[51]—Pigou's rabbit example undoubtedly represented the legal position at the time *The Economics of Welfare* was written.[52] And in this case, it is not far from the truth to say that the state of affairs which Pigou describes came about because of an absence of Government action (at any rate in the form of statutory enactments) and was the result of "natural" tendencies.

Nonetheless, *Boulston*'s case is something of a legal curiosity and Professor Williams makes no secret of his distaste for this decision:

The conception of liability in nuisance as being based upon ownership is the result, apparently, of a confusion with the action of cattle-trespass, and runs counter both to principle and to the medieval authorities on the escape of water, smoke and filth. . . . The prerequisite of any satisfactory treatment of the subject is the final abandonment of the pernicious doctrine in *Boulston*'s case. . . . Once *Boulston*'s case disappears, the way will be clear for a rational restatement of the whole subject, on lines that will harmonize with the principles prevailing in the rest of the law of nuisance.[53]

The judges in *Boulston*'s case were, of course, aware that their view of the matter depended on distinguishing this case from one involving nuisance:

This cause is not like to the cases put, on the other side, of erecting a lime-kiln, dye-house, or the like; for there the annoyance is by the act of the parties who make them; but it is not so here, for the conies of themselves went into the plaintiff's land, and he might take them when they came upon his land, and make profit of them.[54]

Professor Williams comments:

Once more the atavistic idea is emerging that the animals are guilty and not the landowner. It is not, of course, a satisfactory principle to introduce into a modern law of nuisance. If A. erects a house or plants a tree so that the rain runs or drips from it on to B.'s land, this is A.'s act for which he is liable; but if A. introduces rabbits into his land so that they escape from it into B.'s, this is the act of the rabbits for which A. is not liable—such is the specious distinction resulting from *Boulston*'s case.[55]

It has to be admitted that the decision in *Boulston*'s case seems a little odd. A man may be liable for damage caused by smoke or unpleasant smells, without it being necessary to determine whether he owns the smoke or the smell. And the rule in *Boulston*'s case has not always been followed in cases dealing with other animals. For example, in *Bland v. Yates*,[56] it was decided that an injunction could be granted to prevent someone from keeping an *unusual and excessive* collection of manure in which flies bred and which infested a neighbour's house. The question of who owned the flies was not raised. An economist would not wish to object because legal reasoning sometimes appears a little odd. But there is a sound economic reason for supporting Professor Williams' view that the problem of liability for animals (and particularly rabbits) should be brought within the ordinary law of nuisance. The reason is not that the man who harbours rabbits is solely responsible for the damage; the man whose crops are eaten is equally responsible. And given that the costs of market transactions make a rearrangement of rights impossible, unless we know the particular circumstances, we cannot say whether it is desirable or not to make the man who harbours rabbits responsible for the damage committed by the rabbits on neighbouring properties. The objection to the rule in *Boulston's* case is that, under it, the harbourer of rabbits can *never* be liable. It fixes the rule of liability at one pole: and this is as undesirable, from an economic point of view, as fixing the rule at the other pole and making the harbourer of rabbits always liable. But, as we saw in Section VII, the law of nuisance, as it is in fact handled by the courts, is flexible and allows for a comparison of the utility of an act with the harm it produces. As Professor Williams says: "The whole law of nuisance is an attempt to reconcile and compromise between conflicting interests. . . ."[57] To bring the problem of rabbits within the ordinary law of nuisance would not mean *inevitably* making the harbourer of rabbits liable for damage committed by the rabbits. This is not to say that the sole task of the courts in such cases is to make a comparison between the harm and the utility of an act. Nor is it to be expected that the courts will always decide correctly after making such a comparison. But unless the courts act very foolishly, the ordinary law of nuisance would seem likely to give economically more satisfactory results than adopting a rigid rule. Pigou's case of the overrunning rabbits affords an excellent example of how problems of law and economics are interrelated, even though the correct policy to follow would seem to be different from that envisioned by Pigou.

Pigou allows one exception to his conclusion that there is a divergence between private and social products in the rabbit example. He adds: ". . . unless . . . the two occupiers stand in the relation of landlord and tenant, so that compensation is given in an adjustment of the rent."[58] This qualification is rather surprising since Pigou's first class of divergence is largely concerned with the difficulties of drawing up satisfactory contracts between landlords and tenants. In fact, all the recent cases on the problem of rabbits cited by Professor Williams involved disputes between landlords and tenants concerning sporting rights.[59] Pigou seems to make a distinction between the case in which no contract is possible (the second class) and that in which the contract is unsatisfactory (the first class). Thus he says that the second class of divergences between private and social net product

cannot, like divergences due to tenancy laws, be mitigated by a modification of the contractual relation between any two contracting parties, because the divergence arises out of a service or disservice rendered to persons other than the contracting parties.[60]

But the reason why some activities are not the subject of contracts is exactly the same as the reason why some contracts are commonly unsatisfactory— it would cost too much to put the matter right. Indeed, the two cases are really the same since the contracts are unsatisfactory because they do not cover certain activities. The exact bearing of the discussion of the first class of divergence on Pigou's main argument is difficult to discover. He shows that in some circumstances contractual relations between landlord and tenant may result in a divergence between private and social products.[61] But he also goes on to show that Government-enforced compensation schemes and rent-controls will also produce divergences.[62] Furthermore, he shows that, when the Government is in a similar position to a private landlord, e.g. when granting a franchise to a public utility, exactly the same difficulties arise as when private individuals are involved.[63] The discussion is interesting but I have been unable to discover what general conclusions about economic policy, if any, Pigou expects us to draw from it.

Indeed, Pigou's treatment of the problems considered in this article is extremely elusive and the discussion of his views raises almost insuperable difficulties of interpretation. Consequently it is impossible to be sure that one has understood what Pigou really meant. Nevertheless, it is difficult to resist the conclusion, extraordinary though this may be in an economist of Pigou's stature, that the main source of this obscurity is that Pigou had not thought his position through.

IX. THE PIGOVIAN TRADITION

It is strange that a doctrine as faulty as that developed by Pigou should have been so influential, although part of its success has probably been due to the lack of clarity in the exposition. Not being clear, it was never clearly wrong. Curiously enough, this obscurity in the source has not prevented the emergence of a fairly well-defined oral tradition. What economists think they learn from Pigou, and what they tell their students, which I term the Pigovian tradition, is reasonably clear. I propose to show the inadequacy of this Pigovian tradition by demonstrating that both the analysis and the policy conclusions which it supports are incorrect.

I do not propose to justify my view as to the prevailing opinion by copious references to the literature. I do this partly because the treatment in the literature is usually so fragmentary, often involving little more than a reference to Pigou plus some explanatory comment, that detailed examination would be inappropriate. But the main reason for this lack of reference is that the doctrine, although based on Pigou, must have been largely the product of an oral tradition. Certainly economists with whom I have discussed these problems have shown a unanimity of opinion which is quite remarkable considering the meagre treatment accorded this subject in the literature. No doubt there are some economists who do not share the usual view but they must represent a small minority of the profession.

The approach to the problems under discussion is through an examination of the value of physical production. The private product is the value of the additional product resulting from a particular activity of a business. The social product equals the private product minus the fall in the value of production elsewhere for which no compensation is paid by the business. Thus, if 10 units of a factor (and no other factors) are used by a business to make a certain product with a value of $105; and the owner of this factor is not compensated for their use, which he is unable to prevent; and these 10 units of the factor would yield products in their best alternative use worth $100; then, the social product is $105 minus $100 or $5. If the business now pays for one unit of the factor and its price equals the value of its marginal product, then the social product rises to $15. If two units are paid for, the social product rises to $25 and so on until it reaches $105 when all units of the factor are paid for. It is not difficult to see why economists have so readily accepted this rather odd procedure. The analysis focusses on the individual business decision and since the use of certain resources is not allowed for in costs, receipts are reduced by the same amount. But, of course, this means that the value of the social product has no social significance whatsoever. It seems to me preferable to use the opportunity cost concept and to approach these problems by comparing the value of the product yielded by factors in alternative uses or by alternative arrangements. The main advantage of a pricing system is that it leads to the employment of factors in places where the value of the product yielded is greatest and does so at less cost than alternative systems (I leave aside that a pricing system also eases the problem of the redistribution of income). But if through some God-given natural harmony factors flowed to the places where the value of the product yielded was greatest without any use of the pricing system and consequently there was no compensation, I would find it a source of surprise rather than a cause for dismay.

The definition of the social product is queer but this does not mean that the conclusions for policy drawn from the analysis are necessarily wrong. However, there are bound to be dangers in an approach which diverts attention from the basic issues and there can be little doubt that it has been responsible for some of the errors in current doctrine. The belief that it is desirable that the business which causes harmful effects should be forced to compensate those who suffer damage (which was exhaustively discussed in section VIII in connection with Pigou's railway sparks example) is undoubtedly the result of not comparing the total product obtainable with alternative social arrangements.

The same fault is to be found in proposals for solving the problem of harmful effects by the use of taxes or bounties. Pigou lays considerable stress on this solution although he is, as usual, lacking in detail and qualified in his support.[64] Modern economists tend to think exclusively in terms of taxes and in a very precise way. The tax should be equal to the damage done and should therefore vary with the amount of the harmful effect. As it is not proposed that the proceeds of the tax should be paid to those suffering the damage, this solution is not the same as that which would force a business to pay compensation to those damaged by its actions, although economists generally do not seem to have noticed this and tend to treat the two solutions as being identical.

Assume that a factory which emits smoke is set up in a district previously free from smoke pollution, causing damage valued at $100 per annum. Assume that the taxation solution is adopted and that the factory owner is taxed $100 per annum as long as the factory emits the smoke. Assume further that a smoke-preventing device costing $90 per annum to run is available. In these circumstances, the smoke-preventing device would be installed. Damage of $100 would have been avoided at an expenditure of $90 and the factory-owner would be better off by $10 per annum. Yet the position achieved may not be optimal. Suppose that those who suffer the damage could avoid it by moving to other locations or by taking various precautions which would cost them, or be equivalent to a loss in income of, $40 per annum. Then there would be a gain in the value of production of $50 if the factory continued to emit its smoke and those now in the district moved elsewhere or made other adjustments to avoid the damage. If the factory owner is to be made to pay a tax equal to the damage caused, it would clearly be desirable to institute a double tax system and to make residents of the district pay an amount equal to the additional cost incurred by the factory owner (or the consumers of his products) in order to avoid the damage. In these conditions, people would not stay in the district or would take other measures to prevent the damage from occurring, when the costs of doing so were less than the costs that would be incurred by the producer to reduce the damage (the producer's object, of course, being not so much to reduce the damage as to reduce the tax payments). A tax system which was confined to a tax on the producer for damage caused would tend to lead to unduly high costs being incurred for the prevention of damage. Of course this could be avoided if it were possible to base the tax, not on the damage caused, but on the fall in the value of production (in its widest sense) resulting from the emission of smoke. But to do so would require a detailed knowledge of individual preferences and I am unable to imagine how the data needed for such a taxation system could be assembled. Indeed, the proposal to solve the smoke-pollution and similar problems by the use of taxes bristles with difficulties: the problem of calculation, the difference between average and marginal damage, the interrelations between the damage suffered on different properties, etc. But it is unnecessary to examine these problems here. It is enough for my purpose to show that, even if the tax is exactly adjusted to equal the damage that would be done to neighboring properties as a result of the emission of each additional puff of smoke, the tax would not necessarily bring about optimal conditions. An increase in the number of people living or of business operating in the vicinity of the smoke-emitting factory will increase the amount of harm produced by a given emission of smoke. The tax that would be imposed would therefore increase with an increase in the number of those in the vicinity. This will tend to lead to a decrease in the value of production of the factors employed by the factory, either because a reduction in production due to the tax will result in factors being used elsewhere in ways which are less valuable, or because factors will be diverted to produce means for reducing the amount of smoke emitted. But people deciding to establish themselves in the vicinity of the factory will not take into account this fall in the value of production which results from their presence. This failure to take into account costs imposed on others is comparable to the action of a factory-owner in not taking into account the harm resulting from his emission of smoke. Without the tax, there may be too much smoke and too few people in the vicinity of the factory; but with the tax there may be too little smoke and too many people in the vicinity of the factory. There is no reason to suppose that one of these results is necessarily preferable.

I need not devote much space to discussing the similar error involved in the suggestion that smoke producing factories should, by means of zoning regulations, be removed from the districts in which the smoke causes harmful effects. When the change in the location of the factory results in a reduction in production, this obviously needs to be taken into account and weighed against the harm which would result from the factory remaining in that location. The aim of such regulation should not be to eliminate smoke pollution but rather to secure the optimum amount of smoke pollution, this being the amount which will maximise the value of production.

X. A CHANGE OF APPROACH

It is my belief that the failure of economists to reach correct conclusions about the treatment of harmful effects cannot be ascribed simply to a few slips in analysis. It stems from basic defects in the current approach to problems of welfare economics. What is needed is a change of approach.

Analysis in terms of divergencies between private and social products concentrates attention on particular deficiencies in the system and tends to nourish the belief that any measure which will remove the deficiency is necessarily desirable. It diverts attention from those other changes in the system which are inevitably associated with the corrective measure, changes which may well produce more harm than the original deficiency. In the preceding sections of this article, we have seen many examples of this. But it is not necessary to approach the problem in this way. Economists who study problems of the firm habitually use an opportunity cost approach and compare the receipts obtained from a given combination of factors with alternative business arrangements. It would seem desirable to use a similar approach when dealing with questions of economic policy and to compare the total product yielded by alternative social arrangements. In this article, the analysis has been confined, as is usual in this part of economics, to comparisons of the value of production, as measured by the market. But it is, of course, desirable that the choice between different social arrangements for the solution of economic problems should be carried out in broader terms than this and that the total effect of these arrangements in all spheres of life should be taken into account. As Frank H. Knight has so often emphasized, problems of welfare economics must ultimately dissolve into a study of aesthetics and morals.

A second feature of the usual treatment of the problems discussed in this article is that the analysis proceeds in terms of a comparison between a state of laissez faire and some kind of ideal world. This approach inevitably leads to a looseness of thought since the nature of the alternatives being compared is never clear. In a state of laissez faire, is there a monetary, a legal or a political system and if so, what are they? In an ideal world, would there be a monetary, a legal or a political system and if so, what would they be? The answers to all these questions are shrouded in mystery and every man is free to draw whatever conclusions he likes. Actually very little analysis is required to show that an ideal world is better than a state of laissez faire, unless the definitions of a state of laissez faire and an ideal world happen to be the same. But the whole discussion is largely irrelevant for questions of economic policy since whatever we may have in mind as our ideal world, it is clear that we have not yet discovered how to get to it from where we are. A better approach would seem to be to start our analysis with a situation approximating that which actually exists, to examine the effects of a proposed policy change and to attempt to decide whether the new situation would be, in total, better or worse than the original one. In this way, conclusions for policy would have some relevance to the actual situation.

A final reason for the failure to develop a theory adequate to handle the problem of harmful effects stems from a faulty concept of a factor of production. This is usually thought of as a physical entity which the businessman acquires and uses (an acre of land, a ton of fertiliser) instead of as a right to perform certain (physical) actions. We may speak of a person owning land and using it as a factor of production but what the land-owner in fact possesses is the right to carry out a circumscribed list of actions. The rights of a land-owner are not unlimited. It is not even always possible for him to remove the land to another place, for instance, by quarrying it. And although it may be possible for him to exclude some people from using "his" land, this may not be true of others. For example, some people may have the right to cross the land. Furthermore, it may or may not be possible to erect certain types of buildings or to grow certain crops or to use particular drainage systems on the land. This does not come about simply because of Government regulation. It would be equally true under the common law. In fact it would be true under any system of law. A system in which the rights of individuals were unlimited would be one in which there were no rights to acquire.

If factors of production are thought of as rights, it becomes easier to understand that the right to do something which has a harmful effect (such as the creation of smoke, noise, smells, etc.) is also a factor of production. Just as we may use a piece of land in such a way as to prevent someone else from crossing it, or parking his car, or building his house upon it, so we may use it in such a way as to deny him a view or quiet or unpolluted air. The cost of exercising a right (of using a factor of production) is always the loss which is suffered elsewhere in consequence of the exercise of that right—the inability to cross land, to park a car, to build a house, to enjoy a view, to have peace and quiet or to breathe clean air.

It would clearly be desirable if the only actions performed were those in which what was gained was worth more than what was lost. But in choosing between social arrangements within the context of which individual decisions are made, we have to bear in mind that a change in the existing system which will lead to an improvement in some decisions may well lead to a worsening of others. Furthermore we have to take into account the costs involved in operating the various social arrangements (whether it be the working of a market or of a government department), as well as the costs involved in moving to a new system. In devising and choosing between social arrangements we should have regard for the total effect. This, above all, is the change in approach which I am advocating.

NOTES

[1] This article, although concerned with a technical problem of economic analysis, arose out of the study of the Political Economy of Broadcasting which I am now conducting. The argument of the present article was implicit in a previous article dealing with the problem of allocating radio and television frequencies (The Federal Communications Commission, 2 J. Law & Econ. [1959]) but comments which I have received seemed to suggest that it would be desirable to deal with the question in a more explicit way and without reference to the original problem for the solution of which the analysis was developed.

[2] Coase, The Federal Communications Commission, 2 J. Law & Econ. 26–27 (1959).

[3] G. J. Stigler, The Theory of Price 105 (1952).

[4] The argument in the text has proceeded on the assumption that the alternative to cultivation of the crop is abandonment of cultivation altogether. But this need not be so.

There may be crops which are less liable to damage by cattle but which would not be as profitable as the crop grown in the absence of damage. Thus, if the cultivation of a new crop would yield a return to the farmer of $1 instead of $2, and the size of the herd which would cause $3 damage with the old crop would cause $1 damage with the new crop, it would be profitable to the cattle-raiser to pay any sum less than $2 to induce the farmer to change his crop (since this would reduce damage liability from $3 to $1) and it would be profitable for the farmer to do so if the amount received was more than $1 (the reduction in his return caused by switching crops). In fact, there would be room for a mutually satisfactory bargain in all cases in which a change of crop would reduce the amount of damage by more than it reduces the value of the crop (excluding damage)—in all cases, that is, in which a change in the crop cultivated would lead to an increase in the value of production.

[5] See Gale on Easements 237–39 (13th ed. M. Bowles 1959).

[6] See Fontainebleu Hotel Corp. v. Forty-Five Twenty-Five, Inc., 114 So. 2d 357 (1959).

[7] 11 Ch. D. 852 (1879).

[8] Auscultation is the act of listening by ear or stethoscope in order to judge by sound the condition of the body.

[9] Note that what is taken into account is the change in income after allowing for alterations in methods of production, location, character of product, etc.

[10] L. R. 5 Eq. 166 (1867–1868).

[11] 4 C.P.D. 172 (1878–1879).

[12] 25 Q.B.D. 481 (1890).

[13] It may be asked why a lost grant could not also be presumed in the case of the confectioner who had operated one mortar for more than 60 years. The answer is that until the doctor built the consulting room at the end of his garden there was no nuisance. So the nuisance had not continued for many years. It is true that the confectioner in his affidavit referred to "an invalid lady who occupied the house upon one occasion, about thirty years before" who "requested him if possible to discontinue the use of the mortars before eight o'clock in the morning" and that there was some evidence that the garden wall had been subjected to vibration. But the court had little difficulty in disposing of this line of argument: ". . . this vibration, even if it existed at all, was so slight, and the complaint, if it can be called a complaint, of the invalid lady . . . was of so trifling a character, that . . . the Defendant's acts would not have given rise to any proceeding either at law or in equity" (11 Ch.D. 863). That is, the confectioner had not committed a nuisance until the doctor built his consulting room.

[14] See Coase, The Nature of the Firm, 4 Economica, New Series, 386 (1937). Reprinted in Readings in Price Theory, 331 (1952).

[15] For reasons explained in my earlier article, see Readings in Price Theory, n. 14 at 337.

[16] See W. L. Prosser, The Law of Torts 398–99, 412 (2d ed. 1955). The quotation about the ancient case concerning candle-making is taken from Sir James Fitzjames Stephen, A General View of the Criminal Law of England 106 (1890). Sir James Stephen gives no reference. He perhaps had in mind Rex. v. Ronkett, included in Seavey, Keeton and Thurston, Cases on Torts 604 (1950). A similar view to that expressed by Prosser is to be found in F. V. Harper and F. James, The Law of Torts 67–74 (1956); Restatement, Torts §§826, 827 and 828.

[17] See Winfield on Torts 541–48 (6th ed. T. E. Lewis 1954); Salmond on the Law of Torts 181–90 (12th ed. R.F.V. Heuston 1957); H. Street, The Law of Torts 221–29 (1959).

[18] Attorney General v. Doughty, 2 Ves. Sen. 453, 28 Eng. Rep. 290 (Ch. 1752). Compare in this connection the statement of an American judge, quoted in Prosser, op. cit. supra n. 16 at 413 n. 54: "Without smoke, Pittsburgh would have remained a very pretty village," Musmanno, J., in Versailles Borough v. McKeesport Coal & Coke Co., 1935, 83 Pitts. Leg. J. 379, 385.

[19] 10 C.B. (N.S.) 268, 142 Eng. Rep. 445 (1861); 13 C.B. (N.S.) 841, 143 Eng. Rep. 332 (1863).

[20] See Gale on Easements 238, n. 6 (13th ed. M. Bowles 1959).

[21] 11 Ch.D. 865 (1879).

[22] Salmond on the Law of Torts 182 (12th ed. R.F.V. Heuston 1957).

[23] C. M. Haar, Land-Use Planning, A Casebook on the Use, Misuse, and Re-use of Urban Land 95 (1959).

[24] See, for example, Rushmer v. Polsue and Alfieri, Ltd. [1906] 1 Ch. 234, which deals with the case of a house in a quiet situation in a noisy district.

[25] [1913] 1 Ch. 269.

[26] [1938] 1 Ch. 1.

[27] See 30 Halsbury, Law of England 690–91 (3d ed. 1960), Article on Public Authorities and Public Officers.

[28] See Prosser, op. cit. supra n. 16 at 421; Harper and James, op. cit. supra n. 16 at 86–87.

[29] Supreme Court of Georgia. 193 Ga. 862, 20 S.E. 2d 245 (1942).

[30] 178 Ga. 514, 173 S.E. 817 (1934).   [31] 116 Ga. 64, 42 S.E. 315 (1902).

[32] 270 Mass. 511, 523, 170 N.E. 385, 390 (1930).

[33] See Sir Alfred Denning, Freedom Under the Law 71 (1949).

[34] M. B. Cairns, The Law of Tort in Local Government 28–32 (1954).

[35] A. C. Pigou, The Economics of Welfare 183 (4th ed. 1932). My references will all be to the fourth edition but the argument and examples examined in this article remained substantially unchanged from the first edition in 1920 to the fourth in 1932. A large part (but not all) of this analysis had appeared previously in Wealth and Welfare (1912).

[36] Id. at xii.

[37] Id. at 127–30.

[38] In Wealth and Welfare, Pigou attributes the "optimism" to Adam Smith himself and not to his followers. He there refers to the "highly optimistic theory of Adam Smith that the national dividend, in given circumstances of demand and supply, tends 'naturally' to a maximum" (p. 104).

[39] Pigou, op. cit. supra n. 35 at 129–30.

[40] Id. at 134.

[41] See 31 Halsbury, Laws of England 474–75 (3d ed. 1960), Article on Railways and Canals, from which this summary of the legal position, and all quotations, are taken.

[42] See 152 H.C. Deb. 2622–63 (1922); 161 H.C. Deb. 2935–55 (1923).

[43] Vaughan v. Taff Vale Railway Co., 3 H. and N. 743 (Ex. 1858) and 5 H. and N. 679 (Ex. 1860).

[44] Sir Dennis Robertson, I Lectures on Economic Principles 162 (1957).

[45] E. J. Mishan, The Meaning of Efficiency in Economics, 189 The Bankers' Magazine 482 (June 1960).

[46] Pigou, op. cit. supra n. 35 at 184.

[47] Id. at 185–86.

[48] Id. at 186 n.1. For similar unqualified statements see Pigou's lecture "Some Aspects of the Housing Problem" in B. S. Rowntree and A. C. Pigou, Lectures on Housing, in 18 Manchester Univ. Lectures (1914).

[49] See G. L. Williams, Liability for Animals—An Account of the Development and Present Law of Tortious Liability for Animals, Distress Damage Feasant and the Duty to Fence,

in Great Britain, Northern Ireland and the Common Law Dominions (1939). Part Four, "The Action of Nuisance, in Relation to Liability for Animals," 236–62, is especially relevant to our discussion. The problem of liability for rabbits is discussed in this part, 238–47. I do not know how far the common law in the United State regarding liability for animals has diverged from that in Britain. In some Western States of the United States, the English common law regarding the duty to fence has not been followed, in part because "the considerable amount of open, uncleared land made it a matter of public policy to allow cattle to run at large" (Williams, *op. cit. supra* 227). This affords a good example of how a different set of circumstances may make it economically desirable to change the legal rule regarding the delimitation of rights.

[50] 5 Coke (Vol. 3) 104 b. 77 Eng. Rep., 216, 217.

[51] See Stearn v. Prentice Bros. Ltd., (1919) 1 K.B., 395, 397.

[52] I have not looked into recent cases. The legal position has also been modified by statutory enactments.

[53] Williams, op. cit. supra n. 49 at 242, 258.

[54] Boulston v. Hardy, Cro. Eliz., 547, 548, 77 Eng. Rep. 216.

[55] Williams, op. cit. supra n. 49 at 243.

[56] 58 Sol.J. 612 (1913–1914).

[57] Williams, op. cit. supra n. 49 at 259.

[58] Pigou, op. cit. supra n. 35 at 185.

[59] Williams, op. cit. supra n. 49 at 244–47.

[60] Pigou, op. cit. supra n. 35 at 192.

[61] *Id.* 174–75.   [62] *Id.* 177–83.   [63] *Id.* 175–77.

[64] *Id.* 192–4, 381 and Public Finance 94–100 (3d ed. 1947).

Toward a Theory of Property Rights

By HAROLD DEMSETZ

When a transaction is concluded in the marketplace, two bundles of property rights are exchanged. A bundle of rights often attaches to a physical commodity or service, but it is the value of the rights that determines the value of what is exchanged. Questions addressed to the emergence and mix of the components of the bundle of rights are prior to those commonly asked by economists. Economists usually take the bundle of property rights as a datum and ask for an explanation of the forces determining the price and the number of units of a good to which these rights attach.

In this paper, I seek to fashion some of the elements of an economic theory of property rights. The paper is organized into three parts. The first part discusses briefly the concept and role of property rights in social systems. The second part offers some guidance for investigating the emergence of property rights. The third part sets forth some principles relevant to the coalescing of property rights into particular bundles and to the determination of the ownership structure that will be associated with these bundles.

THE CONCEPT AND ROLE OF PROPERTY RIGHTS

In the world of Robinson Crusoe property rights play no role. Property rights are an instrument of society and derive their significance from the fact that they help a man form those expectations which he can reasonably hold in his dealings with others. These expectations find expression in the laws, customs, and mores of a society. An owner of property rights possesses the consent of fellowmen to allow him to act in particular ways. An owner expects the community to prevent others from interfering with his actions, provided that these actions are not prohibited in the specifications of his rights.

Reprinted by permission of the publishers and author: Harold Demsetz, "Toward a Theory of Property Rights," *American Economic Review*, 57 (May 1967), pp. 347-359.

It is important to note that property rights convey the right to benefit or harm oneself or others. Harming a competitor by producing superior products may be permitted, while shooting him may not. A man may be permitted to benefit himself by shooting an intruder but be prohibited from selling below a price floor. It is clear, then, that property rights specify how persons may be benefited and harmed, and, therefore, who must pay whom to modify the actions taken by persons. The recognition of this leads easily to the close relationship between property rights and externalities.

Externality is an ambiguous concept. For the purposes of this paper, the concept includes external costs, external benefits, and pecuniary as well as nonpecuniary externalities. No harmful or beneficial effect is external to the world. Some person or persons always suffer or enjoy these effects. What converts a harmful or beneficial effect into an externality is that the cost of bringing the effect to bear on the decisions of one or more of the interacting persons is too high to make it worthwhile, and this is what the term shall mean here. "Internalizing" such effects refers to a process, usually a change in property rights, that enables these effects to bear (in greater degree) on all interacting persons.

A primary function of property rights is that of guiding incentives to achieve a greater internalization of externalities. Every cost and benefit associated with social interdependencies is a potential externality. One condition is necessary to make costs and benefits externalities. The cost of a transaction in the rights between the parties (internalization) must exceed the gains from internalization. In general, transacting cost can be large relative to gains because of "natural" difficulties in trading or they can be large because of legal reasons. In a lawful society the prohibition of voluntary negotiations makes the cost of transacting infinite. Some costs and benefits are not taken into account by users of resources whenever externalities exist, but allowing transactions increases the degree to which internalization takes place. For example, it might be thought that a firm which uses slave labor will not recognize all the costs of its activities, since it can have its slave labor by paying subsistence wages only. This will not be true if negotiations are permitted, for the slaves can offer to the firm a payment for their freedom based on the expected return to them of being free men. The cost of slavery can thus be internalized in the calculations of the firm. The transition from serf to free man in feudal Europe is an example of this process.

Perhaps one of the most significant cases of externalities is the extensive use of the military draft. The taxpayer benefits by not paying the full cost of staffing the armed services. The costs which he escapes are the additional sums that would be needed to acquire men voluntarily for the services or those sums that would be offered as payment by draftees to taxpayers in order to be exempted. With either voluntary recruitment, the "buy-him-in" system, or with a "let-him-buy-his-way-out" system, the full cost of recruitment would be brought to bear on taxpayers. It has always seemed incredible to me that so many economists can recognize an externality when they see smoke but not when they see the draft. The familiar smoke example is one in which negotiation costs may be too high (because of the large number of interacting parties) to make it worthwhile to internalize all the effects of smoke. The draft is an externality caused by forbidding negotiation.

The role of property rights in the internalization of externalities can be made clear within the context of the above examples. A law which establishes the right of a person to his freedom would necessitate a payment on the part of a firm or of the taxpayer sufficient to cover the cost of using that person's labor if his services are to be obtained. The costs of labor thus become internalized in the firm's or taxpayer's decisions. Alternatively, a law which gives the firm or the taxpayer clear title to slave labor would necessitate that the slaveowners take into account the sums that slaves are willing to pay for their freedom. These costs thus become internalized in decisions although wealth is distributed differently in the two cases. All that is needed for internalization in either case is ownership which includes the right of sale. It is the prohibition of a property right adjustment, the prohibition of the establishment of an ownership title that can thenceforth be exchanged, that precludes the internalization of external costs and benefits.

There are two striking implications of this process that are true in a world of zero transaction costs. The output mix that results when the exchange of property rights is allowed is efficient and the mix is independent of who is assigned ownership (except that different wealth distributions may result in different demands).[1] For example, the efficient mix of civilians and military will result from transferable ownership no matter whether taxpayers must hire military volunteers or whether draftees must pay taxpayers to be excused from service. For taxpayers will hire only those military (under the "buy-him-in" property right system) who would not pay to be exempted (under the "let-him-buy-his-way-out" system). The highest bidder under the "let-him-buy-his-way-out" property right system would be precisely the last to volunteer under a "buy-him-in" system.[2]

We will refer back to some of these points later. But for now, enough groundwork has been laid to facilitate the discussion of the next two parts of this paper.

THE EMERGENCE OF PROPERTY RIGHTS

If the main allocative function of property rights is the internalization of beneficial and harmful effects, then the emergence of property rights can be understood best by their association with the emergence of new or different beneficial and harmful effects.

Changes in knowledge result in changes in production functions, market values, and aspirations. New techniques, new ways of doing the same things, and doing new things—all invoke harmful and beneficial effects to which society has not been accustomed. It is my thesis in this part of the paper that the emergence of new property rights takes place in response to the desires of the interacting persons for adjustment to new benefit-cost possibilities.

The thesis can be restated in a slightly different fashion: property rights develop to internalize externalities when the gains of internalization become larger than the cost of internalization. Increased internalization, in the main, results from changes in economic values, changes which stem from the development of new technology and the opening of new markets, changes to which old property rights are poorly attuned. A proper interpretation of this assertion requires that account be taken of a community's preferences for private ownership. Some communities will have less well-developed private ownership systems and more highly developed state ownership systems. But, given a community's tastes in this regard, the emergence of new private or state-owned property rights will be in response to changes in technology and relative prices.

I do not mean to assert or to deny that the adjustments in property rights which take place need be the result of a conscious endeavor to cope with new externality problems. These adjustments have arisen in Western societies largely as a result of gradual changes in social mores and in common law precedents. At each step of this adjustment process, it is unlikely that externalities per se were consciously related to the issue being resolved. These legal and moral experiments may be hit-and-miss procedures to some extent but in a society that weights the achievement of efficiency heavily, their viability in the long run will depend on how well they modify behavior to accommodate to the externalities associated with important changes in technology or market values.

A rigorous test of this assertion will require extensive and detailed empirical work. A broad range of examples can be cited that are consistent with it: the development of air rights, renters' rights, rules for liability in automobile accidents, etc. In this part of the discussion, I shall present one group of such examples in some detail. They deal with the development of private property rights in land among American Indians. These examples are broad ranging and come fairly close to what can be called convincing evidence in the field of anthropology.

The question of private ownership of land among aboriginals has held a fascination for anthropologists. It has been one of the intellectual battlegrounds in the attempt to assess the "true nature" of man unconstrained by the "artificialities" of civilization. In the process of carrying on this debate, information has been uncovered that bears directly on the thesis with which we are now concerned. What appears to be accepted as a classic treatment and a high point of this debate is Eleanor Leacock's memoir on *The Montagnes "Hunting Territory" and the Fur Trade*.[3] Leacock's research followed that of Frank G. Speck[4] who had discovered that the Indians of the Labrador Peninsula had a long-established tradition of property in land. This finding was at odds with what was known about the Indians of the American Southwest and it prompted Leacock's study of the Montagnes who inhabited large regions around Quebec.

Leacock clearly established the fact that a close relationship existed, both historically and geographically, between the development of private rights in land and the development of the commercial fur trade. The factual basis of this correlation has gone unchallenged. However, to my knowledge, no theory relating privacy of land to the fur trade has yet been articulated. The factual material uncovered by Speck and Leacock fits the thesis of this paper well, and in doing so, it reveals clearly the role played by property right adjustments in taking account of what economists have often cited as an example of an externality—the overhunting of game.

Because of the lack of control over hunting by others, it is in no person's interest to invest in increasing or maintaing the stock of game. Overly intensive hunting takes place. Thus a successful hunt is viewed as imposing external costs on subsequent hunters—costs that are not taken into account fully in the determination of the extent of hunting and of animal husbandry.

Before the fur trade became established, hunting was carried on primarily for purposes of food and the relatively few furs that were required for the hunter's family. The externality was clearly present. Hunting could be practiced freely and was carried on without assessing its impact on other hunters. But these external effects were of such small significance that it did not pay for anyone to take them into account. There did not exist anything resembling private ownership in land. And in the *Jesuit Relations,* particularly Le Jeune's record of the winter he spent with the Montagnes in 1633-34 and in the brief account given by Father Druilletes in 1647-48, Leacock finds no evidence of private land holdings. Both accounts indicate a socioeconomic organization in which private rights to land are not well developed.

We may safely surmise that the advent of the fur trade had two immediate consequences. First, the value of furs to the Indians was increased considerably. Second, and as a result, the scale of hunting activity rose sharply. Both consequences must have increased considerably the importance of the externalities associated with free hunting. The property right system began to change, and it changed specifically in the direction required to take account of the economic effects made important by the fur trade. The geographical or distributional evidence collected by Leacock indicates an unmistakable correlation between early centers of fur trade and the oldest and most complete development of the private hunting territory.

By the beginning of the eighteenth century, we begin to have clear evidence that territorial hunting and trapping arrangements by individual families were developing in the area around Quebec. . . . The earliest references to such arrangements in this region indicates a purely temporary allotment of hunting territories. They [Algonkians and Iroquois] divide themselves into several bands in order to hunt more efficiently. It was their custom . . . to appropriate pieces of land about two leagues square for each group to hunt exclusively. Ownership of beaver houses, however, had already become established, and when discovered, they were marked. A starving Indian could kill and eat another's beaver if he left the fur and the tail.[5]

The next step toward the hunting territory was probably a seasonal allotment system. An anonymous account written in 1723 states that the "principle of the Indians is to mark off the hunting ground selected by them by blazing the trees with their crests so that they may never encroach on each other. . . . By the middle of the century these allotted territories were relatively stabilized."[6]

The principle that associates property right changes with the emergence of new and reevaluation of old harmful and beneficial effects suggests in this instance that the fur trade made it economic to encourage the husbanding of fur-bearing animals. Husbanding requires the ability to prevent poaching and this, in turn, suggests that socioeconomic changes in property in hunting land will take place. The chain of reasoning is consistent with the evidence cited above. Is it inconsistent with the absence of similar rights in property among the southwestern Indians?

Two factors suggest that the thesis is consistent with the absence of similar rights among the Indians of the southwestern plains. The first of these is that there were no plains animals of commercial importance comparable to the fur-bearing animals of the forest, at least not until cattle arrived with Europeans. The second factor is that animals of the plains are primarily grazing species whose habit is to wander over wide tracts of land. The value of establishing boundaries to private hunting territories is thus reduced by the relatively high cost of preventing the animals from moving to adjacent parcels. Hence both the value and cost of establishing private hunting lands in the Southwest are such that we would expect little development along these lines. The externality was just not worth taking into account.

The lands of the Labrador Peninsula shelter forest animals whose habits are considerably different from those of the plains. Forest animals confine their territories to relatively small areas, so that the cost of internalizing the effects of husbanding these animals is considerably reduced. This reduced cost, together with the higher commercial value of fur-bearing forest animals, made it productive to establish private hunting lands. Frank G. Speck finds that family proprietorship among the Indians of the Peninsula included retaliation against trespass. Animal resources were husbanded. Sometimes conservation practices were carried on extensively. Family hunting territories were divided into quarters. Each year the family hunted in a different quarter in rotation, leaving a tract in the center as a sort of bank, not to be hunted over unless forced to do so by a shortage in the regular tract.

To conclude our excursion into the phenomenon of private rights in land among the American Indians, we note one further piece of corroborating evidence. Among the Indians of the Northwest, highly developed private family rights to hunting lands had also emerged—rights which went so far as to include inheritance. Here again we find that forest animals predominate and that the West Coast was frequently visited by sailing schooners whose primary purpose was trading in furs.[7]

THE COALESCENCE AND OWNERSHIP OF PROPERTY RIGHTS

I have argued that property rights arise when it becomes economic for those affected by externalities to internalize benefits and costs. But I have not yet examined the forces which will govern the particular form of right ownership. Several idealized forms of ownership must be distinguished at the outset. These are communal ownership, private ownership, and state ownership.

By communal ownership, I shall mean a right which can be exercised by all members of the community. Frequently the rights to till and to hunt the land have been communally owned. The right to walk a city sidewalk is communally owned. Communal ownership means that the community denies to the state or to individual citizens the right to interfere with any person's exercise of communally-owned rights. Private ownership implies that the community recognizes the right of the owner to exclude others from exercising the owner's private rights. State ownership implies that the state may exclude anyone from the use of a right as long as the state follows accepted political procedures for determining who may not use state-owned property. I shall not examine in detail the alternative of state ownership. The object of the analysis which follows is to discern some broad principles governing the development of property rights in communities oriented to private property.

It will be best to begin by considering a particularly useful example that focuses our attention on the problem of land ownership. Suppose that land is communally owned. Every person has the right to hunt, till, or mine the land. This form of ownership fails to concentrate the cost associated with any person's exercise of his communal right on that person. If a person seeks to maximize the value of his communal rights, he will tend to overhunt and overwork the land because some of the costs of his doing so are borne by others. The stock of game and the richness of the soil will be diminished too quickly. It is conceivable that those who own these rights, i.e., every member of the community, can agree to curtail the rate at which they work the lands if negotiating and policing costs are zero. Each can agree to abridge his rights. It is obvious that the costs of reaching such an agreement will not be zero. What is not obvious is just how large these costs may be.

Negotiating costs will be large because it is difficult for many persons to reach a mutually satisfactory agreement, especially when each hold-out has the right to work the land as fast as he pleases. But, even if an agreement among all can be reached, we must yet take account of the costs of policing the agreement, and these may be large, also. After such an agreement is reached, no one will privately own the right to work the land; all can work the land but at an agreed upon shorter workweek. Negotiating costs are increased even further because it is not possible under this system to bring the full expected benefits and expected costs of future generations to bear on current users.

If a single person owns land, he will attempt to maximize its present value by taking into account alternative future time streams of benefits and costs and selecting that one which he believes will maximize the present value of his privately-owned land rights. We all know that this means that he will attempt to take into account the supply and demand conditions that he thinks will exist after his death. It is very difficult to see how the existing communal owners can reach an agreement that takes account of these costs.

In effect, an owner of a private right to use land acts as a broker whose wealth depends on how well he takes into account the competing claims of the present and the future. But with communal rights there is no broker, and the claims of the present generation will be given an uneconomically large weight in determining the intensity with which the land is worked. Future generations might desire to pay present generations enough to change the present intensity of land usage. But they have no living agent to place their claims on the market. Under a communal property system, should a living person pay others to reduce the rate at which they work the land, he would not gain anything of value for his efforts. Communal property means that future generations must speak for themselves. No one has yet estimated the costs of carrying on such a conversation.

The land ownership example confronts us immediately with a great disadvantage of communal property. The effects of a person's activities on his neighbors and on subsequent generations will not be taken into account fully. Communal property results in great externalities. The full costs of the activities of an owner of a communal property right are not borne directly by him, nor can they be called to his attention easily by the willingness of others to pay him an appropriate sum. Communal property rules out a "pay-to-use-the-property" system and high negotiation and policing costs make ineffective a "pay-him-not-to-use-the-property" system.

The state, the courts, or the leaders of the community could attempt to internalize the external costs resulting from communal property by allowing private parcels owned by small groups of person with similar interests. The logical groups in terms of similar interests, are, of course, the family and the individual. Continuing with our use of the land ownership example, let us initially distribute private titles to land randomly among existing individuals and, further, let the extent of land included in each title be randomly determined.

The resulting private ownership of land will internalize many of the external costs associated with communal ownership, for now an owner, by virtue of his power to exclude others, can generally count on realizing the rewards associated with husbanding the game and increasing the fertility of his land. This concentration of benefits and costs on owners creates incentives to utilize resources more efficiently.

But we have yet to contend with externalities. Under the communal property system the maximization of the value of communal property rights will take place without regard to many costs, because the owner of a communal right cannot exclude others from enjoying the fruits of his efforts and because negotiation costs are too high for all to agree jointly on optimal behavior. The development of private rights permits the owner to economize on the use of those resources from which he has the right to exclude others. Much internalization is accomplished in this way. But the owner of private rights to one parcel does not himself own the rights to the parcel of another private sector. Since he cannot exclude others from their private rights to land, he has no direct incentive (in the absence of negotiations) to economize in the use of his land in a way that takes into account the effects he produces on the land rights of others. If he constructs a dam on his land, he has no direct incentive to take into account the lower water levels produced on his neighbor's land.

This is exactly the same kind of externality that we encountered with communal property rights, but it is present to a lesser degree. Whereas no one had an incentive to store water on any land under the communal system, private owners now can take into account directly those benefits and costs to their land that accompany water storage. But the effects on the land of others will not be taken into account directly.

The partial concentration of benefits and costs that accompany private ownership is only part of the advantage this system offers. The other part, and perhaps the most important, has escaped our notice. The cost of negotiating over the remaining externalities will be reduced greatly. Communal property rights allow anyone to use the land. Under this system it becomes necessary for all to reach an agreement on land use. But the externalities that accompany private ownership of property do not affect all owners, and, generally speaking, it will be necessary for only a few to reach an agreement that takes these effects into account. The cost of negotiating an internalization of these effects is thereby reduced considerably. The point is important enough to elucidate.

Suppose an owner of a communal land right, in the process of plowing a parcel of land, observes a second communal owner constructing a dam on adjacent land. The farmer prefers to have the stream as it is, and so he asks the engineer to stop his construction. The engineer says, "Pay me to stop." The farmer replies, "I will be happy to pay you, but what can you guarantee in return?" The engineer answers, "I can guarantee you that I will not continue constructing the dam, but I cannot guarantee that another engineer will not take up the task because this is communal property; I have no right to exclude him." What would be a simple negotiation between two persons under a private property arrangement turns out to be a rather complex negotiation between the farmer and everyone else. This is the basic explanation, I believe, for the preponderance of single rather than multiple owners of property. Indeed, an increase in the number of owners is an increase in the communality of property and leads, generally, to an increase in the cost of internalizing.

The reduction in negotiating cost that accompanies the private right to exclude others allows most externalities to be internalized at rather low cost. Those that are not are associated with activities that generate external effects impinging upon many people. The soot from smoke affects many homeowners, none of whom is willing to pay enough to the factory to get its owner to reduce smoke output. All homeowners together might be willing to pay enough, but the cost of their getting together may be enough to discourage effective market bargaining. The negotiating problem is compounded even more if the smoke comes not from a single smoke stack but from an industrial district. In such cases, it may be too costly to internalize effects through the marketplace.

Returning to our land ownership paradigm, we recall that land was distributed in randomly sized parcels to randomly selected owners. These owners now negotiate among themselves to internalize any remaining externalities. Two market options are open to the negotiators.

The first is simply to try to reach a contractual agreement among owners that directly deals with the external effects at issue. The second option is for some owners to buy out others, thus changing the parcel size owned. Which option is selected will depend on which is cheaper. We have here a standard economic problem of optimal scale. If there exist constant returns to scale in the ownership of different sized parcels, it will be largely a matter of indifference between outright purchase and contractual agreement if only a single, easy-to-police, contractual agreement will internalize the externality. But, if there are several externalities, so that several such contracts will need to be negotiated, or if the contractual agreements should be difficult to police, then outright purchase will be the preferred course of action.

The greater are diseconomies of scale to land ownership the more will contractual arrangement be used by the interacting neighbors to settle these differences. Negotiating and policing costs will be compared to costs that depend on the scale of ownership, and parcels of land will tend to be owned in sizes which minimize the sum of these costs.[8]

The interplay of scale economies, negotiating cost, externalities, and the modification of property rights can be seen in the most notable "exception" to the assertion that ownership tends to be an individual affair: the publicly-held corporation. I assume that significant economies of scale in the operation of large corporations is a fact and, also, that large requirements for equity capital can be satisfied more cheaply by acquiring the capital from many purchasers of equity shares. While economies of scale in operating these enterprises exist, economies of scale in the provision of capital do not. Hence, it becomes desirable for many "owners" to form a joint-stock company.

But if all owners participate in each decision that needs to be made by such a company, the scale economies of operating the company will be overcome quickly by high negotiating cost. Hence a delegation of authority for most decisions takes place and, for most of these, a small management group becomes the *de facto* owners. Effective ownership, i.e., effective control of property, is thus legally concentrated in management's hands. This is the first legal modification, and it takes place in recognition of the high negotiating costs that would otherwise obtain.

The structure of ownership, however, creates some externality difficulties under the law of partnership. If the corporation should fail, partnership law commits each shareholder to meet the debts of the corporation up to the limits of his financial ability. Thus, managerial *de facto* ownership can have considerable external effects on shareholders. Should property rights remain unmodified, this externality would make it exceedingly difficult for entrepreneurs to acquire equity capital from wealthy individuals. (Although these individuals have recourse to reimbursements from other shareholders, litigation costs will be high.) A second legal modification, limited liability, has taken place to reduce the effect of this externality.[9] *De facto* management ownership and limited liability combine to minimize the overall cost of operating large enterprises. Shareholders are essentially lenders of equity capital and not owners, although they do participate in such infrequent decisions as those involving mergers. What shareholders really own are their shares and not the corporation. Ownership in the sense of control again becomes a largely individual affair. The shareholders own their shares, and the president of the corporation and possibly a few other top executives control the corporation.

To further ease the impact of management decisions on shareholders, that is, to minimize the impact of externalities under this ownership form, a further legal modification of rights is required. Unlike partnership law, a shareholder may sell his interest without first obtaining the permission of fellow shareholders or without dissolving the corporation. It thus becomes easy for him to get out if his preferences and those of the management are no longer in harmony. This "escape hatch" is extremely important and has given rise to the organized trading of securities. The increase in harmony between managers and shareholders brought about by exchange and by competing managerial groups helps to minimize the external effects associated with the corporate ownership structure. Finally, limited liability considerably reduces the cost of exchanging shares by making it unnecessary for a purchaser of shares to examine in great detail the liabilities of the corporation and the assets of other shareholders; these liabilities can adversely affect a purchaser only up to the extent of the price per share.

The dual tendencies for ownership to rest with individuals and for the extent of an individual's ownership to accord with the minimization of all costs is clear in the land ownership paradigm. The applicability of this paradigm has been extended to the corporation. But it may not be clear yet how widely applicable this paradigm is. Consider the problems of copyright and patents. If a new idea is freely appropriable by all, if there exist communal rights to new ideas, incentives for developing such ideas will be lacking. The benefits derivable from these ideas will not be concentrated on their originators. If we extend some degree of private rights to the originators, these ideas will come forth at a more rapid pace. But the existence of the private rights does not mean that their effects on the property of others will be directly taken into account. A new idea makes an old one obsolete and another old one more valuable. These effects will not be directly taken into account, but they can be called to the attention of the originator of the new idea through market negotiations. All problems of externalities are closely analogous to those which arise in the land ownership example. The relevant variables are identical.

What I have suggested in this paper is an approach to problems in property rights. But it is more than that. It is also a different way of viewing traditional problems. An elaboration of this approach will, I hope, illuminate a great number of social-economic problems.

NOTES

[1] These implications are derived by R. H. Coase, "The Problem of Social Cost," *J. of Law and Econ.*, Oct., 1960, pp. 1-44.

[2] If the demand for civilian life is unaffected by wealth redistribution, the assertion made is correct as it stands. However, when a change is made from a "buy-him-in" system to a "let-him-buy-his-way-out" system, the resulting redistribution of wealth away from draftees may significantly affect their demand for civilian life; the validity of the assertion then requires a compensating wealth change. A compensating wealth change will not be required in the ordinary case of profit maximizing firms. Consider the farmer-rancher example mentioned by Coase. Society may give the farmer the right to grow corn unmolested by cattle or it may give the rancher the right to allow his cattle to stray. Contrary to the Coase example, let us suppose that if the farmer is given the right, he just breaks even; i.e., with the right to be compensated for corn damage, the farmer's land is marginal. If the right is transferred to the rancher, the farmer, not enjoying any economic rent, will not have the wherewithal to pay the rancher to reduce the number of head of cattle raised. In this case, however, it will be profitable for the rancher to buy the farm, thus merging cattle raising with farming. His self-interest will then lead him to take account of the effect of cattle on corn.

[3] Eleanor Leacock, *American Anthropologist* (American Anthropological Asso.), Vol. 56, No. 5, Part 2, Memoir No. 78.

[4] Cf., Frank G. Speck, "The Basis of American Indian Ownership of Land," *Old Penn Weekly Rev.* (Univ. of Pennsylvania), Jan. 16, 1915, pp. 491-95.

[5] Eleanor Leacock, *op. cit.*, p. 15.

[6] Eleanor Leacock, *op. cit.*, p. 15.

[7] The thesis is consistent with the development of other types of private rights. Among wandering primitive peoples the cost of policing property is relatively low for highly portable objects. The owning family can protect such objects while carrying on its daily activities. If these objects are also very useful, property rights should appear frequently, so as to internalize the benefits and costs of their use. It is generally true among most primitive communities that weapons and household utensils, such as pottery, are regarded as private property. Both types of articles are portable and both require an investment of time to produce. Among agriculturally-oriented peoples, because of the relative fixity of their location, portability has a smaller role to play in the determination of property. The distinction is most clearly seen by comparing property in land among the most primitive of these societies, where crop rotation and simple fertilization techniques are unknown, or where land fertility is extremely poor, with property in land among primitive peoples who are more knowledgeable in these matters or who possess very superior land. Once a crop is grown by the more primitive agricultural societies, it is necessary for them to abandon the land for several years to restore productivity. Property rights in land among such people would require policing cost for several years during which no sizable output is obtained. Since to provide for sustenance these people must move to new land, a property right to be of value to them must be associated with a portable object. Among these people it is common to find property rights to the crops, which, after harvest, are portable, but not to the land. The more advanced agriculturally based primitive societies are able to remain with particular land for longer periods, and here we generally observe property rights to the land as well as to the crops.

Nature of the Firm," *Economica*, New Series, 1937, pp. 386-405.

[9] Henry G. Manne discusses this point in a forthcoming book about the American corporate system.

PART IV
EXTERNALITIES: POLITICAL
ECONOMY AND EXTERNALITIES

Since externalities exist, what should a society do about them? This group of four papers evaluates the basic option of granting to the public sector the responsibility of taking spillovers into account.

J. M. Buchanan's article, "Politics, Policy and the Pigovian Margins," argues that where externalities already exist, other externalities will arise from any attempt to adjust market outcomes. This conclusion is reached by an analysis developed in five interrelated parts. First, a model of society having a simple majority voting rule and universal suffrage is proposed. Buchanan reasons that dominant coalitions will be able to secure net gains at the expense of others and externalities will be present in any voting scheme having a less than unanimity rule. Secondly, assumptions about individual behavior in the simple model are inspected and a collective welfare behavior model is constructed. Outcomes of the two models relative to externalities are appraised.

Third, the relationships of market and nonmarket allocative organizations to assumptions about how individuals choose are investigated. In the fourth section the limited case of purely public goods, or what can be called genuinely collective goods, is considered. Depending upon one's assumption about individual behavior, similar or different externality outcomes emerge. The final section summarizes some conclusions drawn from the preceding parts of the paper and urges further developments in political economy.

Stanislaw Wellisz's paper critically reviews the challenges of several writers to the traditional Pigovian solution to the problem of externalities. The major and general issues are these: Should entire trust be put in the market or is administrative and judicial intervention called for when externalities occur? Should economists recommend specific action to deal with externalities, including the recommendation that externalities be left to the market? Wellisz's detailed analyses leads him to conclude that, in most externality cases, the market fails to reach a social optimum. Workable tax-subsidy systems must be designed or we must resign ourselves to a nonoptimal world. Wellisz maintains much of the recent work on improving understanding about externalities fails because it lacks necessary generality to be of policy importance. Bargaining, he believes, is a limited and costly solution that cannot replace judicial processes.

The Davis-Whinston article claims the analysis of Wellisz is misleading. They go on to offer a new approach which emphasizes information problems created by externalities. In stating the optimization conditions of a firm, marginal externality costs can be separated out. These are the costs, Davis and Whinston argue, that a public authority must know if it is to move effectively to overcome externalities. But prices of input factors and technological changes of varying rates among firms can make "old" taxes set by authorities inappropriate. This is part of the weakness to an authority approach against externalities. But there are also demand side or consumer preferences and information problems facing any authority. The authors proceed into the details of demand and supply side information requirements of authorities seeking to offset externalities. From this analysis they offer a solution which they believe copes better with problems of information and uncertainty. The complete burden of this solution to externalities shifts from the authorities to the guided self-interest of firms that respond to their own market conditions and market-type charges imposed by the authority. The paper concludes by pointing out some limitations that persist in thinking about policy steps related to externalities.

The final paper of this section, "Contracting Costs and Public Policy," is by Harold Demsetz. The author reviews the nature of the efficiency criterion used by economists and explains how voluntary negotiations or contracts between individuals often tend to work toward efficient results. But when individuals find contracting too costly they tend to seek out other solutions, and in particular look to government action. Demsetz points out significant differences between private contracts and outcomes that do not rely on voluntary consent but upon rules such as the law. Insensitivity to different tastes and incomes which have social costs often accompany legal decision making. Moreover, efficiency is liable to be reduced. Explicit cases, such as regulations on automobiles to overcome air pollution externalities, are presented to point out the trade-offs that may result from relying on nonmarket or governmentally structured policies. Demsetz concludes that resource allocation improvements may be achieved either by government policies or from removal of such policies to accomplish lower costs of contracting.

Politics, Policy, and the Pigovian Margins[1]

By JAMES M. BUCHANAN

Since Sidgwick and Marshall, and notably since Pigou's *The Economics of Welfare*, economists have accepted the presence or absence of external effects in production and consumption as a primary criterion of market efficiency. When private decisions exert effects that are external to the decision-maker, " ideal " output is not obtained through the competitive organisation of economic activity even if the remaining conditions necessary for efficiency are satisfied. The market " fails " to the extent that there exist divergencies between marginal private products and marginal social products and/or between marginal private costs and marginal social costs. This basic Pigovian theorem has been theoretically refined and elaborated in numerous works, but its conceptual validity has rarely been challenged.[2] The purpose of this paper is to bring into question a fundamental implication of this aspect of theoretical welfare economics, namely, the implication that externalities are either reduced or eliminated by the shift of an activity from market to political organisation. I shall try to show that this implication will stand up to critical scrutiny only under certain highly restricted assumptions about human behaviour in modern political systems. When these restrictive assumptions are modified, the concept of divergence between marginal " social " product (cost) and marginal private product (cost) loses most of its usefulness.[3]

" Imperfection " and " failure " are descriptive nouns that tell something about the operation of the organism, the activity, or the organisation that is under discussion. These words, and others like them, are meaningful only if the alternative states of " perfection " and " success " are either specifically described or are assumed to be tacitly recognised by participants in the discussion. In the analysis of market organisation, the " perfectly-working " order has been quite carefully defined. The necessary conditions for Paretian optimal-

Reprinted by permission of the publishers and author: James M. Buchanan, "Politics, Policy, and the Pigovian Margins," *Economica*, n.s. 29 (February 1962), pp. 17-28.

ity are now a part of the professional economist's stock-in-trade, and these conditions are known to be satisfied only when all of the relevant costs and benefits resulting from an action are incorporated into the calculus of the decision-maker that selects the action. By contrast with this state of perfection, almost all ordinary or real-world markets are " imperfect ", in greater or lesser degree. Most private decisions exert external effects. So far, so good. If this were the end of it, however, there would be little point in all of the effort. Economists must imply or suggest that the imperfectly-working organisation is, in fact, " perfectible ": that is, they must do so if they are to justify their own professional existence. The analysis of an existing social order must, almost by the nature of science itself, imply that some " improvement " in results can be produced by changes that can be imposed on the variables subject to social control.

Such improvements in the organisation of economic activity have, almost without exception, involved the placing of restrictions on the private behaviour of individuals through the implementation of some *political* action. The various proposals that have been advanced by economists are sufficiently familiar to make a listing at this point unnecessary. They run the gamut from the relatively straightforward tax-subsidy schemes of Marshall to the more sophisticated and highly intricate proposals for multi-part pricing, counter-speculation, collective simulation of ideal market processes, and many other intriguing methods designed to promote and to insure the attainment of economic efficiency. Indeed, economists tend to be so enmeshed with efficiency notions that it seems extremely difficult for them to resist the ever-present temptation to propose yet more complex gimmicks and gadgets for producing greater " efficiency ". In almost every case, and often quite unconsciously, the suggested improvement is assumed to be within the realm of the genuinely attainable. And, if some sceptic dare raise a question on this point, the economist is likely to respond to the effect that his task is not that of the politician, that he does not appropriately concern himself with the political feasibility or workability of his proposals. But if political obstacles to realisation are not, in fact, discussed, the implication is clear that the proposals which are advanced are attainable as a result of some conceivable politically-imposed modifications in the institutional framework within which decisions are made. It seems fully appropriate to charge welfare economists, generally, with an implicit acceptance of this implication of their analyses. If this were not the case, it is difficult to see why, for example, William J. Baumol should have attempted to construct a theory of the state, of collective action, on the basis of the externality argument,[4] why K. W. Kapp should have entitled his work, *The Social Costs of Private Enterprise*,[5] and why Francis Bator should have called his recent summary analysis, " The Anatomy of Market Failure ".[6]

I shall not be concerned here with the analysis of market imperfection or failure, as such. The primary criticism of theoretical welfare economics (and economists) that is advanced in this note is that its failure to include analyses of similar imperfections in realistic and attainable alternative solutions causes the analysis itself to take on implications for institutional change that are, at best, highly misleading. To argue that an existing order is " imperfect " in comparison with an alternative order of affairs that turns out, upon careful inspection, to be unattainable may not be different from arguing that the existing order is " perfect ".[7] The existence of demonstrated imperfection in terms of an unattainable state of affairs should imply nothing at all about the possibility of actual improvement to an existing state. To take this step considerably more is required than the preliminary analysis of " ideal output ". This is not to suggest, of course, that the preliminary analysis is not essential and important.

In what follows I shall try to show that, with consistent assumptions about human behaviour in both market and political institutions, any attempt to replace or to modify an existing market situation, admitted to be characterised by serious externalities, will produce solutions that embody externalities which are different, but precisely analogous, to those previously existing. Indeed, the Pigovian analysis lends itself readily to the analysis of political imperfection.

I

In order to analyse political processes in a manner that is even remotely similar to the methods of economic theory, great simplification and abstraction are required. To the political scientist, accustomed as he is to working with more " realistic " models of human behaviour, the simplified models with which the economist must analyse political institutions can only seem to be grossly inadequate caricatures of the operation of complex organisational structures. This rather sharp methodological gap between the two social sciences incorporated in " political economy " provides an important reason why the political scientist has not filled, and could hardly be expected to fill, the analytical void left open by the incompleteness of welfare economics.

I shall assume the existence of a community composed of separate individuals in which all collective decisions are reached by a voting rule of simple majority with universal suffrage. More complex, and realistic, models introducing representation, political parties, leadership, etc., could be employed but without significantly altering the conclusions reached. Almost any political order described by the term, " democratic ", in the modern Western usage of this term may, for present purposes, be simplified into this extreme model of " pure " democracy. Characteristics of the political structure may modify the majority equivalent in the simple model That is to say, a model of two-thirds or three-fourths majority may be more appropriate to the analysis of some political structures under certain conditions than the simple majority model. However, this quantitative variation in the voting rule equivalent does not affect the conclusions of this paper. Each particular rule, save that of unanimity, leads to conclusions that are identical to those reached in the simple majority model. The magnitude of the distortions produced is, of course, affected by the voting rule. The analysis here is concerned solely with indicating the direction of these effects, not with their magnitude. A distinction among the various " majority equivalents " is not, therefore, necessary.

In the first model, the orthodox assumptions of positive economics will be retained in so far as these concern individual motivation and action. Private individuals are assumed to be sufficiently informed and rational to conduct the required calculus and to reach decisions on the basis of a comparison of private costs and benefits at the relevant margins. No considerations of the " public " or the " social " interest are assumed to enter into this individual calculus within the relationship in question except in so far as this should coincide with individual interest. In determining his voting behaviour on each issue confronted by the group, the individual is assumed, quite simply, to act in that manner which he considers to advance his own interest. The model embodies, therefore, a rather straightforward extension of the behavioural assumptions of orthodox economic theory, as a predictive, explanatory theory, to political choice-making.

If no institutional restrictions are placed on this majority-rule model of the collective choice process, the characteristics of the " solution " should be intuitively clear. The minimum-size effective or dominating coalition of individuals, as determined by the voting rule, will be able to secure net gains at the expense of the other members of the political group. These gains, secured through the political process, will tend to be shared symmetrically (equally) among all members of the dominant coalition. In the simple majority-rule model, this involves, in the limit, fifty plus per cent. of the total membership in the dominating coalition and fifty minus per cent. of the total membership in the losing or minority coalition. That such a solution will, in fact, tend to emerge under the conditions of the model seems hardly subject to question. It is helpful, however, to note that such a solution, and only such, satisfies fully the Von Neumann-Morgenstern requirements for solutions to n-person games which, of course, all political " games " must be.[8]

It is useful to apply the familiar Pigovian calculus to this model of political behaviour. To the individual member of the effective majority, the political process provides a means through which he may secure private gain at the expense of other citizens. In determining the margins to which political activity shall be extended, the individual member of the dominant coalition will include in his calculus a share of the net benefits from public activity that will be larger than the offsetting individualised share or proportion of the net costs of the activity. In the calculus of the individuals effectively making the final collective decision, marginal private benefits will tend to exceed marginal social benefits and/or marginal private costs will tend to fall short of marginal social costs. The distortions produced are, therefore, precisely analogous, in opposing directions, to those present in the market solution characterised by the familiar Pigovian divergencies. In essence, the value of a political vote in this model lies in its potential power to impose external costs on other members of the group. Externalities must be present in any solution reached by the voting process under all less-than-unanimity rules. If the possible " perfectibility " of market organisation is to be determined under these conditions, it is clearly necessary to compare two separate imperfections, in each of which significant divergencies of the Pigovian sort may exist at the individualised margins of decision-making. Since there will be nothing in the collective choice process that will tend to produce the " ideal " solution, as determined by the welfare economist, the presence or absence of a Pigovian marginal divergency in the market solution, even of sufficient seriousness to warrant concern, provides in itself no implication for the desirability of institutional change.[9]

II

This conclusion holds so long as consistency in individual behaviour patterns over market and voting processes is retained, independently of the specific motivation that may be assumed to direct this behaviour. The oversimplified model of Part I may be criticised on the grounds that individuals do not act in the way postulated : that is, they do not follow their own interests when they participate in the formation of social decisions for the community. Several responses might be advanced to such criticism, but it is not the purpose of this note to defend the validity, methodologically or otherwise, of the self-interest assumption about behaviour. The relevant response to the charge of unrealism at this point is surely the frank admission that, of course, individuals do not always act as the model of Part I postulates. A model is a construction that isolates one element of behaviour and, upon this, the analyst may erect conceptually refutable hypotheses. The model of majority rule in the simple pure democracy is not different in this respect from the competitive model of economic theory. Both models isolate that part of human behaviour that does reflect the rational pursuit of private gain by individuals in particular institutional relationships and both models fail to the extent that individuals do not, in fact, behave in this fashion in the relationships under consideration.[10]

Any number of models of individual behaviour can be constructed. The only real limitation lies, ultimately, in the testing of the predictions made. It will not be necessary, however, to develop any large number of additional and complex models to illustrate the central point of this note. One additional extremely simple model will suffice for this purpose. In this second model, I shall drop the assumption that individuals, in both their market and in their political behaviour, act in pursuit of their own narrowly defined self-interest. Instead, I now postulate that individuals act in the other extreme : I assume that each individual, in all aspects of his behaviour, tries to identify himself with the community of which he is a member and to act in accordance with his own view of the overall " public " or " social " interest. Each member of the group tries to act in the genuine interest of the whole group as this is determined for him through the application of some appropriately-chosen Kantian-like rule of action.

The results are again almost intuitively clear. Since each member of the group acts on the basis of identifying his own interest with that of the larger group, no deliberate exploitation of minority by majority can take place through the political process regardless of the voting rule that is applied. Differences that may arise, and which must be resolved by voting, stem solely from differences in individual conceptions of what the group interest on particular issues is. The Pigovian-type marginal divergencies between private and social costs or benefits disappear from the individual calculus in this model of behaviour. It is in application to market, rather than to political, behaviour that this model seems somewhat unorthodox. Under the assumptions of the model, the individual in his market behaviour will also try to identify himself with the group as a whole and to act in accordance with what he considers to be the " public " interest. If his chimney pours out smoke that soils his neighbours' laundry, he will assess these costs as if they were his own in reaching a decision concerning the possible introduction of a smoke-abatement device. The familiar analysis of welfare economics simply does not apply. Each individual decision-maker does, in fact, attempt to balance off " social " benefits against " social " costs at the margin. While, as in the collective sector, differences may arise among members of the group concerning the proper definition of social benefits and social costs, these differences cannot be interpreted in the standard way. The Pigovian divergence between marginal private product and marginal social product disappears in both the market and the political organisation of activity in this universal benevolence model. The policy conclusions are, however, identical with those reached from the use of the extreme self-interest model. If chimneys smoke, or if the majority is observed to impose discriminatory taxes on the minority, these facts carry with them no implications for institutional changes. In this case, they must represent the decision-makers' estimates of genuine community interest. Neither " real " nor " apparent " externalities can, in themselves, provide grounds for suggesting organisational changes.

III

From the analysis of these two extreme and contrasting models of human behaviour, the inference is clear that so long as individuals are assumed to be similarly motivated under market and under political institutions there can be no direct implications drawn about the organisational structure of an activity on the basis of a Pigovian-like analysis of observed externalities. The orthodox implication of Pigovian welfare economics follows only on the assumption that individuals respond to *different* motives when they participate in market and in political activity. The only behavioural model appropriate to the Pigovian analysis is that which has been called " the bifurcated man ". Man must be assumed to shift his psychological and moral gears when he moves from the realm of organised market activity to that of organised political activity and *vice-versa*. Only if there can be demonstrated to be something in the nature of market organisation, as such, that brings out the selfish motives in man, and something in the political organisation, as such, which, in turn, suppresses these motives and brings out the more " noble " ones, can there be assumed to exist any " bridge " between the orthodox externality analysis and practical policy, even apart from problems of specific policy prescription.

The characteristics of the organisational structure within which choices must be made may affect the nature of the value system upon which individual action is based. It seems probable that the individual in his voting behaviour, will tend to choose among alternatives on the basis of a somewhat broader and more inclusive value scale than that which will direct his behaviour in the making of market choices. One reason for this is that, in political behaviour, the individual is made fully conscious of the fact that he is choosing *for* the whole group, that his individual action will exert external effects on other members of the group, that he is acting " socially ". In his market behaviour, on the other hand, the external effects of individual choice are sensed only indirectly by the chooser.[11] But this recognition that the individual value scale may be, to some extent, modified by the institutional structure within which choice is exercised is quite different from accepting the idea that the motivation for individual action is wholly transformed as between two separate structures. While it may be acknowledged as " realistic " to assume that the model of individual choice based on self-interest motivation, the " economic " model, is somewhat more applicable to an analysis of markets than of voting processes, this is far removed from accepting the applicability of the universal benevolence model for the latter. At most, the influence of the different organisational structures, as such, on motivation would seem to be conceptually represented by a reasonably narrow distance on some motivational spectrum. If, at the elementary stages of analysis, a choice must be made between that conception of behaviour that assumes this possible institutionally-generated difference to be absent or negligible (models that I have called consistent) and the conception that assumes wholly different behavioural patterns solely due to the institutional structure, the first alternative seems obviously to be preferred. Yet, as I have shown, it is the second, and clearly extreme, conception of human behaviour that is implicit in much of the discussion of Pigovian welfare economics.

This assumption of behavioural dichotomy, as opposed to behavioural consistency, is most openly expressed in the early literature on socialism, especially that of the Christian and Fabian varieties. The criticism of the market order of affairs was often made by referring to the pursuit of private gain, and the case for socialism was based on the replacement of this pursuit of private gain by that of public good. Although this rather naive conception has perhaps lost some of its appeal since World War II, it continues to be implied in much of the popular discussion. While this is not in itself surprising, it does seem notable that the analytical structure based on this conception of human behaviour should have remained largely unchallenged in the scientific literature.[12]

IV

Up to this point the discussion has been concerned with the most general case in which no limitations are placed on the activities that may be organised through the political process. Can the implications of the Pigovian welfare analytics be rescued by restricting the movement of the political-institutional variables? If collective action can take place only within prescribed limits, which can be assumed to be fixed by constitutional rules, a model may be constructed in which the policy implications of the Pigovian-type of analysis do not run into immediate conflict with reasonable assumptions concerning human motivation. To accomplish this result, however, the range of possible political action must be restricted to such an extent as to make the analysis practically worthless.

Let it be assumed that constitutional rules dictate that all human activity shall be organised privately and voluntarily except that which involves the provision of genuinely collective goods and services. These are defined as those goods and services which, when a unit is made available to one individual member of the group, an equal amount, one unit, is also made available to each other member of the group. These goods and services are completely indivisible. Let it be further assumed that the constitution states that the provision of such goods and services, if politically organised, shall be financed by taxes that are levied on the " marginal benefit principle ". That is to say, each individual shall be required to contribute a " tax-price " that is exactly proportional to his own marginal rate of substitution between the collective good and money (all other goods). This marginal tax will be different for different individuals in the group because, although the good is genuinely collective, the relative marginal utility of it will vary from individual to individual.

If the provision of such a good or service should be organised privately rather than collectively, and if individuals are assumed to be motivated by self-interest considerations, the market solution will be characterised by the presence of significant externalities. The individual, acting privately, will take into account only that share of total marginal benefit or product that he expects to enjoy. By comparison, he will take into account the full amount of the marginal costs which, by hypothesis, he must bear individually. In other words, he cannot exclude other members of the group from the enjoyment of the benefits provided by the good : but there is no way that he may include these other members of the group in the payment of the costs. This market organisation produces, therefore, the familiar result; the private calculus of individuals embodies the Pigovian divergence at the margins of decision. Compared to a Pareto-optimal situation, relatively too few resources will be devoted to the provision of the common good or service.

Under this situation, a shift in organisation from the private or market sector to the collective sector will, under the conditions specified, tend to eliminate the Pigovian divergence, even if the self-interest motivation of individual action is retained. If the individual, in making a political or voting choice concerning the possible marginal extension of the provision of the collective good or service, is required to include in his calculus a share of the total marginal cost of the extension that is proportional to his individualised share of the total marginal benefits provided by the extension, a " solution " will tend to be produced by political choice that will meet all of the necessary conditions for Pareto optimality. If the total marginal costs of extending the activity fall short of the total marginal benefits, individuals will not be in equilibrium and they will, accordingly, vote to extend the activity. At the " solution ", all of the necessary conditions are satisfied, and total incremental benefits equal total marginal costs. No externalities exist.[13]

The reason for this result is not difficult to understand. By imposing the restriction that the individual voter must pay for the marginal unit of the collective good or service in proportion to the marginal benefit enjoyed, it is insured that the individual's private calculus becomes a miniature reflection of the aggregate or " social " calculus that would be made by an omniscient, benevolent despot acting in the interests of all persons in the community. The individual voter cannot, because of the restrictions on the model, impose external costs on others in the group through the political process. In his private voting decision he will recognise that additional units of the collective good will yield benefits to others than himself. But he will, under the self-interest assumption, not be influenced by these spillover benefits at all. There are, however, also spillover marginal costs that the provision of the additional units of the collective good will impose on his fellows, and the neglected external benefits will tend to offset these neglected external costs.

This highly restricted model has several interesting features. First of all, note that the sharp difference in result as between the market and the political solution emerges only if the self-interest assumption about human motivation is consistently adopted and applied. If, by contrast, the universal benevolence assumption is introduced, the market organisation and the political organisation will tend to produce similar results, as in the earlier analyses. Secondly, if the self-interest assumption is adopted, the political result in the restricted model here will tend to be identical under *any* voting rule. Any rule will, under the constitutional restrictions imposed, tend to produce a solution that satisfies all of the necessary conditions for Pareto optimality. The single individual acting as a dictator, the simply majority, and the rule of unanimity: each of these will tend to produce the same results. These separate rules for making political decisions only become important because they reflect differences in the ability of some members of the group to impose costs on other members, an ability that is specifically eliminated by the constitutional restrictions postulated.

It is not, of course, surprising to find that the Pigovian analysis has relevant policy implications only for the provision of genuinely collective (perfectly indivisible) goods and services. Indeed, the statement that externalities exist in any private market solution is one means of stating that genuinely collective elements characterise the activity under consideration. This restricted model indicates clearly, however, that the good must be wholly collective if the implications of the Pigovian analysis are to apply. If an activity is only quasi-collective, that is to say, if it contains elements that are privately divisible as well as collective elements, the political solution must also involve externalities. The restricted model analysed here is perhaps even more useful in pointing up the extremely limited tax scheme that is required for the analysis to apply at all. Even for those goods and services that are wholly collective in nature, the provision of them through the political process will produce Pigovian-like externalities at the margin unless taxes are collected on the basis of marginal benefits. In the real world, very few, if any, goods and services are wholly collective. And even if these few could be isolated, they would not be financed by taxes levied on this principle of incremental benefits enjoyed. Such a principle is not only politically unimaginable in modern democracy: it is also conceptually impossible. Its application would require that the taxing authorities be able to determine, in advance, all individual preference functions. It must be concluded, therefore, that the restricted institutional model in which the implications of the standard externality analysis might apply is nothing but a conceptual toy. In the real world, political results must embody externalities to the extent that individuals follow self-interest in their capacities as collective decision makers: individuals are able, by political means, to impose costs on other individuals.

V

In Part III it was demonstrated that the generalised implications of the Pigovian analysis could be supported only on the adoption of a highly questionable conception of human motivation. In Part IV it was demonstrated that these implications would be drawn from a consistent motivational model only if this model should be so highly restricted as to make the analysis of little practical value. It is much easier, however, to explain the reasons for economists neglecting to examine these aspects of their analysis than it is to justify their neglect. As Knut Wicksell suggested many years ago, most economists are content with assuming the presence of a benevolent despot. In so far as their analysis points toward policy at all, as it must, the improvements in efficiency advanced are assumed to be attainable within the realm of the politically possible. The almost universal neglect of the imperfections that might arise from the political attempts at applying the economists' efficiency criteria represents a serious deficiency in the work of welfare economists and economists generally. To shy away from considerations of the politically feasible has been deemed an admirable trait, but to refuse to examine the politically possible is incomplete scholarship.

NOTES

[1] Although independently developed, this note draws upon and extends certain ideas that have been developed in a larger work undertaken in collaboration with Gordon Tullock. See, *The Calculus of Consent* (forthcoming). I should acknowledge Tullock's indirect as well as his direct influence on the general ideas presented in this paper.

[2] The current work of my colleague, Ronald Coase, should be mentioned as a notable exception. Coase's criticism of the Pigovian analysis concerns the implications of externality for resource allocation. For a preliminary statement of Coase's position see his " The Federal Communications Commission ", *Journal of Law and Economics*, vol. II (1959), especially pp. 26–7. A more complete statement appears in " The Problem of Social Cost ", *Journal of Law and Economics*, vol. III (1960).

[3] It should be noted that I shall not be concerned with the conceptual ability of welfare economists to make specific policy prescriptions, a problem that has been central to much of the modern discussion. It is now widely acknowledged that welfare economics, as such, can provide few guides to positive policy-making in a specific sense. But the analysis continues to be employed for the purposes of demonstrating the existence of market failure. If, as J. de V. Graaff suggests, " *laissez-faire* welfare theory " was " largely concerned with demonstrating the optimal properties of free competition and the unfettered price system ", it is surely equally accurate to suggest that modern welfare theory has been largely concerned with demonstrating that these conclusions are invalid: that is, that competitive markets do not satisfy the necessary conditions for optimality. Graaff's own work is, perhaps, the most elegant example. See his *Theoretical Welfare Economics*, 1957. (Citation from page 170.)

[4] William J. Baumol, *Welfare Economics and the Theory of the State*, 1952.

[5] K. W. Kapp, *The Social Costs of Private Enterprise*, 1950.

[6] Francis Bator, " The Anatomy of Market Failure ", *Quarterly Journal of Economics*, vol. LXXII (1958), pp. 351–79.

[7] Professor Frank Knight's statement that " to call a situation hopeless is equivalent to calling it ideal " may be reversed. To call a situation ideal is merely another means of calling it hopeless: that is, not perfectible.

[8] J. Von Neumann and O. Morgenstern, *Theory of Games and Economic Behavior*, third ed., 1953, p. 264.

[9] I am not suggesting that deliberate exploitation of minority by majority need be the only purpose of collective activity, even in this polar model. The point is rather that, independently of the motivation for collective activity, majority-rule institutions of decision-making create opportunities within which Pigovian-like externalities may arise. There will, of course, arise situations in which the self-interest of the individual dictates the collectivisation of an activity in order that the application of general rules to *all* members of the group can be effected. It is precisely in such cases that, conceptually, unanimity may replace majority rule as the decision device, and the propositions of modern welfare economics become fully appropriate. But so long as majority rule prevails, the " political externalities " are present, whether these be purposeful or ancillary to collective action designed to accomplish other ends,

[10] Care must be taken to distinguish between the self-interest assumption, as the basis for a " logic of choice " and the self-interest assumption as the basis of a predictive, explanatory theory of human action. In the first sense, all action of individuals must be based on self-interest, and it becomes meaningless to discuss alternative models of behaviour. The pure logic of individual choice is not without value, but it should be emphasised that the argument of this paper employs the second version of the self-interest assumption. If conceptually refutable hypotheses are to be developed, the behaviour of choice-making individuals must be externally observable in terms of measurable criteria of choice. In the market relationship,

189

this degree of operational validity is often introduced by stating that the minimal requirement is that individuals, when confronted with choice, choose " more " rather than " less ". But " more " or " less " take on full operational meaning only when they become measurable in something other than subjective utility of the choosers. The " measuring rod of money " must be allowed to enter before the generalised logic of choice can produce even so much as the first law of demand.

[11] For a further discussion on these points see my " Individual Choice in Voting and the Market ", *Journal of Political Economy*, vol. LXII (1954), pp. 334–43.

[12] The behavioural inconsistency here has been, of course, indirectly recognised by many writers. However, the only explicit reference to the private-cost social-cost analysis, to my knowledge, is contained in the paper by William H. Meckling and Armen A. Alchian, " Incentives in the United States ", *American Economic Review*, vol. L (1960), pp. 55–61, and, even here, the reference is only a passing one.

[13] This solution is that which has been rigorously defined by Paul A. Samuelson. See his " The Pure Theory of Public Expenditure ", *Review of Economics and Statistics*, vol. XXXVI (1954), pp. 386–9; " Diagrammatic Exposition of a Theory of Public Expenditure ", *Review of Economics and Statistics*, vol. XXXVII (1955), pp. 350–56.

On External Diseconomies and the Government-Assisted Invisible Hand[1]

By STANISLAW WELLISZ

I. THE MODERN-OLD APPROACH AND ITS LIMITATIONS

The areas of economics in which theory is tailored to the theorist's political beliefs are steadily shrinking. Gone are the days of the " dismal science " and of theories protesting against the " exploitation of man by man ". Even the Keynesian controversies have simmered down.

The gloom which descends upon us with the passing of the colourful era in which theory was pregnant with policies is still occasionally dispelled by welfare economics controversies. Welfare economics, more than any other field, lends itself to wishful theorizing. As Buchanan put it so aptly:

> If, as J. de V. Graaff suggests, " *laissez faire* welfare theory " was " largely concerned with demonstrating the optimal properties of free competition and the unfettered price system," it is surely equally accurate to suggest that modern welfare theory has been largely concerned with demonstrating that these conclusions are invalid; that is, that competitive markets do not satisfy the necessary conditions for optimality.[2]

Much of modern welfare economics is indeed concerned with the problem of market failure, and the analysis of market failure appears to imply the desirability of administrative intervention. Until recently everybody agreed that where there are externalities, market allocation is bound to be non-optimal; the only point of controversy concerned the frequency and the severity of the external effects and the urgency of administrative action.[3]

The apparent unanimity of modern welfare economists has been shattered in the last few years by modern-old welfare economists who launched a vigorous attack on the logic of the modern treatment, and an equally vigorous defence of the old virtues of the market. It now seems that the modern theory is dead and that the modern-old triumphs all along the line.

What is somewhat puzzling in the modern-old vs. modern controversy

Reprinted by permission of the publishers and author: Stanislaw Wellisz, "On External Diseconomies and the Government–Assisted Invisible Hand," *Economica*, n.s. 31 (November 1964), pp. 345-362.

is that all the protagonists apparently agree on the incapacity of theorists to say anything meaningful about welfare problems. J. de V. Graaff, one of the finest exponents of the " modern " school, was widely known for his scepticism concerning the field. Little states that " economic welfare is a subject in which rigour and refinement are probably worse than useless. Rough theory, or good common sense, is, in practice, what we require."[4] Little also voices his preference for intelligent administrative decisions over static analysis.[5] Buchanan, a modern-old theorist, apparently subscribes to the " widely acknowledged " notion " that welfare economics, as such, can provide few guides to policy-making in a specific sense,"[6] while Turvey, in a survey of the recent controversy, buries the administrative interventionist and the economic theorist under a common tombstone: " When negotiation [between the units creating externalities and those suffering from or benefiting from them] is possible, the case for government intervention is one of justice, not of economic efficiency; when it is not, the theorist should be silent and call in the applied economist." [7]

In the face of the prevailing opinions, I would like to consider whether we should put our entire trust in the market or whether administrative and judicial intervention is called for where there are externalities. I shall also discuss whether the economist with theoretical training ought to yield his role to Mr. Little's administrator or to Mr. Turvey's applied economist.

The strongest reason for the theorist's concern with the problem of externalities is that " practical men " work on the dual assumption of the prevalence of externalities and of the necessity of radical steps to improve our imperfect world:

> In a world of rapidly increasing population and of material growth, the problems economists associate with external diseconomies—the inevitable treading on each other's toes—are pushed to the forefront of public controversy. Sooner or later one form or another of external diseconomy becomes recognized as a major social problem and the hands of central or local authorities are forced by the clamour of the public that something be done. Unless economists are prepared to give advice in such cases, initiative will pass into the hands of the " planners," the engineers and the administrators, with results that may well be as irreversible as they are, sometimes, deplorable.[8]

It is painfully clear that administrators and planners frequently avail themselves of the opportunity of interfering with resource alloca-tion. It is possible, of course, that they are the possessors of specialized knowledge which economists do not have. If this is so, their science is hermetic, for it does not appear in any of the writings of the " practical planners ". For the time being it is wise to assume that despite all protestations economists do have a comparative advantage in dealing with economic problems.

Let us now pass to the main question which is whether economists should advocate that specific action be taken to deal with external economies and diseconomies, or whether they should insist that the problem be left to the market mechanism.

The Pigovian tradition, accepted by modern welfare economists, claims that whenever private and social costs diverge, steps should be taken to equalize the two. For instance, if sparks and smoke from a steam railway damage the surrounding land, it is appropriate to impose upon the railway costs equal to the amount of the damage. Unless such action is taken, the railway will disregard the social diseconomy and it will expand beyond the social optimum. Conversely, an activity which yields positive external effects should be encouraged to expand beyond the individual optimum which does not take into account such effects.

The modern-old economists, and especially Coase and Buchanan, challenge the established position: they claim that the private market *can* lead to a Pareto optimum despite externalities since it is possible to establish a market in externalities. Administrative measures, on the other hand, may cause divergences from the optimum.[9] An even stronger case is presented by Davis and Whinston.[10] The two authors consider two types of externalities (to be defined later): in one type, "separable externalities," it is "difficult" to reach an optimum by instituting Pigovian taxes and subsidies, while in the other, more general type, "non-separable externalities," the task is " impossible."[11]

Coase's vigorous and original article provides an excellent starting point for a critical appraisal of the attacks on the Pigovian tradition.

Where Pigou was anxious to compensate the victims of diseconomies, Coase concentrates his attention on the conditions under which the largest social product can be achieved:

> When an economist is comparing alternative social arrangements, the proper procedure is to compare the total social product yielded by those different arrangements. The comparison of private and social costs is neither here nor there.[12]

Coase carries his challenge right into the enemy's camp: he takes up and expands Pigou's example of a railway damaging nearby fields, and unlike Pigou, he concludes that the market is likely to yield the correct allocative solution while judicial and administrative interference is unlikely to achieve the task. The Pigou-Coase example deserves reexamination so that we can see where the strength and the weakness of Coase's argument lie.[13]

According to Coase, " if the railway could make a bargain with everyone having property adjoining the railway line and there were no costs involved in making such bargains, it would not matter whether the railway was liable for damage caused by fires or not."[14] If the damage suffered by the landowners is greater than the benefits reaped by the railway, the landowners will be able to pay a sum sufficient to induce the railway to curtail operations. If the damage is less than the benefit, it would be unwarranted to prevent the railway from operating because total product would thereby be diminished. Coase takes great care to show that if courts award excess damages, they are likely to curtail useful activities in order to protect the interests of the victims of external diseconomies.

The adjustment is, of course, discontinuous where the activity is discrete, but in the case of divisible activities, bargaining will lead to a true Pareto optimum. " In full Pareto equilibrium ... [the] internal benefits measured in terms of some numéraire good, net of costs, must be just equal, at the margin, to the external damage that is imposed on other parties."[15]As long as there is disequilibrium, it pays one of the sides to offer compensation to the other to achieve a modification of the position. By contrast, an administrative imposition of costs will not necessarily produce an adjustment of the level of production leading to the Pareto optimum.

To clarify the reasoning underlying his conclusions in the railway case, Coase constructs the following numerical example. Assume, says Coase, that a railway faces the choice of running one or two trains per day.

> Suppose that the running of one train per day would enable the railway to perform services worth $150 per annum and running two trains a day would enable the railway to perform services worth $250 per annum. Suppose further that the cost of running one train is $50 per annum and two trains $100 per annum. Assuming perfect competition, the cost equals the fall in the value of production elsewhere due to the employment of additional factors of production by the railway. Clearly, the railway would find it profitable to run two trains per day. But suppose that running one train per day would destroy by fire crops worth ... $60 and two trains a day would result in the destruction of crops worth $120. In these circumstances running one train per day would raise the value of total production but the running of a second train would reduce the value of total production.[16]

The second train increases the railway's net return by $50 but causes destruction of $60 worth of crops, hence the total product is diminished by $10. Thus " the conclusion that it would be better if the second train did not run is correct ".[17]

To prevent the second train from being run, Coase says Pigou would make the railway liable for damages. Coase cautions us, however, that if damage liability is imposed, the farmer might intensify production in order to suffer greater damages and collect greater compensation. If he does so, it might not be worthwhile for the railway to run even one train per day. For instance, if the farmer intensifies his production to such an extent that even one train per day causes $110 worth of damage, and two trains per day cause $300 worth of damage, and if the railway has to pay compensation, no trains will be run. Thus if there is no liability, and the market is not permitted to operate, the diseconomy-producing activity is likely to be pushed beyond the Pareto-optimal point, but if there is liability, it will be curtailed below the Pareto-optimal level.[18]

In a no-liability regime the Pareto optimum will be achieved if the farmer(s) enters (enter) into a free bargain with the railway. Since the second train would cause a damage of $60 above and beyond the damage caused by the first train, the farmer(s) will be willing to pay the railway up to $60 for *not* running the second train. Since the railway gains only $50 by running the second train, it will accept any sum above $50 for not running it. Any bargain reached between the limits of $50 and $60 benefits both sides and leads to a Pareto optimum.

To appraise the correctness of reasoning underlying the railway example (and some of the other examples used to illustrate the modern-old approach), it is necessary to specify carefully the market setting within which the bargaining takes place. It is clear that the modern-old bargaining solution does not apply to monopolies, and that the output reached in isolation by a monopolist may be socially preferable to the output level which will pertain after the monopolist strikes a bargain with the units which suffer external diseconomies.[19]To

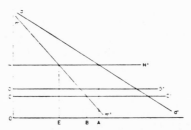

fix a monopolist's output at an optimal level, one must—for better or for worse—attack the problem along Pigovian lines.

To keep within the spirit of the modern-old argument, I shall limit myself from now on to external inter-relations of firms imbedded in the competitive system. Coase's railway, I shall assume, is managed along purely competitive lines, and it faces a perfectly elastic demand curve. This assumption may be difficult to reconcile with reality and also with Coase's own figures,[20]but it is essential for the modern-old argument.

Having specified that the externalities which are under discussion arise among competitive price-takers, let us consider briefly what is meant by an externality in a competitive regime: if the firms make zero profits before external costs are imposed on them, how can they bribe the would-be externality-creating-units to eliminate the externality? Clearly, a brief digression on private and social costs is called for at this point.

In a perfectly competitive industry in which there are no Ricardian rents, external diseconomies result in factor-use changes without creating any social costs. In such a setting, every firm operates at a zero profit level, and all the factors are paid their opportunity cost. If external costs are imposed upon one of the competitive units, that unit will make losses and, in the long run, it will go out of business. As output is curtailed and ultimately abandoned, the displaced factors find employment in alternate uses. In the initial situation the factors were employed at opportunity cost, hence the alternate-use output has the same value as the original output.[21]Thus there is a change in production pattern but no social loss. Moreover, since the unit displaced by the external cost operated initially at zero profit, it has neither the incentive nor the means to bribe the externality-producing unit.

To re-create the modern-old reasoning in a competitive setting, it is necessary to postulate the existence of non-transferable resources giving rise to Ricardian rents. Consider, for instance, a case in which a smokestack is erected next to a farm field, and imagine that the smoke reduces the crops. If all the factors were employed at their opportunity cost, the farmer would move elsewhere, and the land would remain fallow, or it would be put to some alternative use bringing the same rate of return to the land as the initial use. If, however, the land stays under the (now reduced) crop, or if it is put to a use in which it brings a marginal product of lesser value, a reduction of land rent will occur. The external loss caused by the smoke is measured not by the amount of the crop destroyed but by the decline in the difference between the value of the field's product and the opportunity cost of the movable factors, i.e., by the decline in the Ricardian rent. Thus changes in the Ricardian rent measure the external effects of firms imbedded in a competitive setting. The net returns used in Coase's examples can thus be interpreted as net rents.[22]

Let us now return to Coase's railway example and concentrate on the problem of losses to farmers. Coase apparently assumes that the farmers have no foreknowledge of the damage which will be done by the second train. If they had such foreknowledge, they could reduce the damage in most cases—say, by switching to crops which are less affected by smoke or by planting or sowing more sparsely.

Table 1 gives a hypothetical example of net rents accruing to farmers who have three alternative courses of action, A, B and C, with the railway running 0, 1, 2, 3 and 4 trains daily. By stretching our imaginations we can assume that the railway operates in a competitive regime and that its net returns represent net rents. Coase's " net returns " to 1 and 2 trains are thus interpreted in Table 1, and additional numbers are made up for 3, 4 and 5 trains. Column C is consistent with Coase's assumption that no crop-switching will take place (and the figures for the damage caused by 1 and 2 trains are his), while columns A and B show the hypothetical result of crop-switching to reduce the damage:

TABLE I

Number of trains	Net rents to the factors employed by the railway	Net rents to the factors employed by alternative cropping methods		
		A	B	C
	$	$	$	$
0	0	50	100	150
1	100	40	80	90
2	150	30	50	30
3	170	25	20	−30
4	160	10	0	−30
5	0	0	0	−30

If the farmers have no foreknowledge of any damage, they will adopt alternative C, and if two trains are run per day, they will suffer $60 worth of damage (as in Coase's example) and have a net rent of $30, as shown in Table 1. If, however, they know that two trains will be run per day, they will adopt alternative B. This alternative would be less profitable than alternative C if no trains were running, but it is more profitable in a two-train regime because of the lesser damage to crops.

Acting in isolation, the railway would find it profitable to run three trains per day and collect a rent of $170. The farmers would find it best to switch to alternative A, with a net rent of $25 under the three-train regime. Notice, however, that the railway would gain only $20 by running the additional train, and the farmers would lose $25. If bargaining were opened, the railway would reduce the number of trains to 2 if it received compensation larger than $20, and the farmers would be willing to pay up to $25 in exchange for a reduction of train runs from 3 to 2. Thus it is in the interest of all parties concerned to reach a Pareto-optimal solution.

The modern-old solution as presented above is technically unexceptionable, but one may wonder whether it is a mere curiosity or whether it is broadly applicable to externality problems. To obtain the solution it was necessary to assume that (1) bargaining concerns the *marginal* unit and (2) that the bargaining limits are well defined. These assumptions may or may not be satisfied in actual situations.

Consider again the railway example. To obtain the best bargain with the farmers, the railway might threaten to run five trains per day and thus destroy the entire crop. To avoid this possibility and to obtain a reduction in train runs to two a day, the farmers would be willing to pay up to $50. Conversely, if the railway company were seeking permission to run a railway, the farmers would seek to appropriate the entire rent accruing to the railway under the optimal regime, i.e., $150, even though the damage would equal only $100. Thus the bargaining limits are set by the rents accruing to the two parties under the optimal regime, and not by the marginal rents.

It is conceivable, of course, that the modern-old economists think of situations in which large numbers of potential external-diseconomy producers compete for a large number of potential sites so that the bargaining limits are narrowed down through competition to the marginal units. If this is so, the solution is correct, but the assumptions which must be made to achieve the solution are out of harmony with the examples examined by Coase and, what is more serious, have only a faint bearing on reality.[23]

Bargaining for the entire rent accruing to the opposite party does not, in itself, preclude the possibility of reaching a Pareto optimum, for it is to the advantage of both parties to reach a level of joint maximum rent. Moreover, the process opens up magnificent business prospects: any activity can be turned to profit as long as it is sufficiently annoying to someone else. As long as the activity absorbs no resources, i.e., as long as the blackmailers maintain amateur standing, the economist who refrains from social judgment can find no fault with the situation.[24]

A more crucial assumption made by the modern-old school is that the parties to the bargain know how much it pays them to offer in order to induce a change in the output of the other unit. The assumption is reasonable in cases in which unit(s) " 1 " has (have) an external effect on unit(s) " 2," but unit(s) " 2 " does (do) not affect externally the costs of unit(s) " 1." In such situations the unit(s) determines (determine) in isolation the optimal output. The payments are determined by the benefits reaped by the " 2 " unit(s) when " 1 " output changes from the isolation equilibrium level, and the costs to " 1 " of such output changes. If there is a mutual externality between " 1 " unit(s) and " 2 " unit(s), neither the " 1's " nor the " 2's " may be able to achieve an individual optimum; hence it may not be possible to determine the size of payments leading to a joint optimum. As Davis and Whinston have shown, the continuous case corresponds to a two-person, non-zero sum game which, in general, has no saddle point[25] and, therefore, neither simple nor mixed strategies will yield an individual optimum.[26] Thus a bargain may never be reached, and even when it is reached, there will be temptation to improve one's position by violating the agreement.

The bargaining solution also breaks down, as Turvey notes, when the group suffering through (or benefiting from) an externality is too large for the members to " get together ". In such cases, there is " a case for collective action to achieve optimum allocation ".[27] Buchanan also recognizes the case for collective action in the case of goods which are not privately divisible, though he warns us that any political solution involves the imposition of some externalities as long as the goods are not entirely indivisible.[28]

The large-group difficulty lies in that it is to the advantage of any member of the group to refuse to bear any part of the cost of a settlement, while reaping the advantages. If there are n farmers affected by the smoke from a train, it pays any farmer to let the remaining (n-1) bribe the railway and to enjoy cost-free the results of the bargain. Moreover, if the externality does not affect all the firms in a fixed proportion, it pays to form coalitions. For instance, the construction of a higher smokestack might reduce the pollution of nearby fields but increase that of more distant areas. If this be so, one can foresee the formation of separate pressure groups, and the larger the number of possible combinations of interests, the smaller the possibility of Pareto-optimal solutions.[29]

The discussion of conditions under which the modern-old solution is valid leads to the conclusion that far from being a universal panacea, the private bargain solution to external diseconomies applies only to exceptional cases. Such cases are, moreover, of little interest to the policy maker. If a private bargain can be made to everybody's satisfaction, there is no reason for judicial or administrative interference. The policy maker must cope with situations in which " payment cannot be exacted from the benefited parties or compensation enforced on behalf of the injured parties ",[30] that is, with situations where private bargains fail. Moreover, the policy maker cannot be restricted to perfect competition but must also deal with monopolies, and private bargains involving monopolies may, as we have seen, aggravate resource misallocation instead of achieving a social optimum. It is therefore of crucial importance to determine whether it is possible to devise a Pigovian system of taxes and subsidies which will help the market's " invisible hand " in achieving socially optimal results.

II. THE PIGOVIAN SOLUTION TO THE PROBLEM OF EXTERNALITIES

The Pigovian prescription for externalities is: devise a system of taxes and subsidies which will modify the cost function of an externality-creating firm in such a fashion that the firm must produce at the socially optimal level if it wishes to maximize profits.

The Pigovian approach may be attacked on the grounds of practicability: the cost of devising and administering a tax-subsidy scheme may exceed the benefits. Recently Davis and Whinston have attacked the solutions on the grounds of theoretical feasibility, and their conclusions appear to be taken as authoritative by the modern-old economists.[31]

The question whether the Pigovian solutions are practical is one of immense importance, for many a beautiful scheme of economic theorists has failed to pass the test of applicability. Precedence must go, however, to the problem of the theoretical possibility of reaching a solution, for if a solution cannot be found, there is no point in searching for it. If Davis and Whinston are right, the economist has nothing to say where the market fails.[32]

Davis and Whinston make a distinction between " separable " externalities which can, though with " difficulty," be handled through the Pigovian method and completely intractable (except through mergers) " non-separable " externalities. If the output level of unit(s) " 1 " affects the total cost *but not the marginal cost* of unit(s) " 2 " (and/or if there is a linkage of this kind in the reverse direction), the externality is separable. If the output level of unit(s) " 1 " affects the marginal cost of unit(s) " 2 " (and/or there is such a linkage in the reverse direction), the externality is non-separable.[33]

As it turns out, the problem of devising a Pigovian solution for the " separable " case does not arise for, as can be readily demonstrated, the " separable externalities " do not affect the pattern of resource allocation. After showing the irrelevancy of the " separable " case, we shall proceed to construct a Pigovian solution to the " insoluble " problem.

The output level of a firm in a competitive industry is determined by the marginal cost and by the product price which is parametrically given to the firm. As long as the price remains constant and the marginal costs do not change, the optimum output level of the firm will not change. Since " separable " externalities have no effect on marginal cost, they do not alter the firm's optimal output level. As a consequence " separable " externalities have no influence on the allocation of productive resources though they do affect product distribution.[34]

It may seem that " separable " externalities affect resource allocation in the long run, through their effect on the total (produce or shutdown) decisions of the affected firms. A firm's optimal output level may not change as long as the firm remains in production, but as a consequence of the imposition of external costs, the firm may find it most profitable to go out of production altogether. This argument is spurious, however. In considering the total (produce or shutdown) decision, the firm treats *all* the costs as if they were variable, even those costs which are fixed in the short run. The decision to produce or to discontinue production is based on considerations of long-run marginal costs. If an externality modifies the long-run marginal cost of a firm, it must be classified as " non-separable " in the long run.

A different argument purporting to show the impact of " separable " externalities on resource allocation in a competitive setting is based on an apparent analogy with the " prisoner's dilemma."[35] Imagine a residential neighbourhood in which the returns on individual houses are affected by the general condition of other houses. As long as the entire neighbourhood is run down, there is a certain (marginal) return on the improvement of every house. If the general level of maintenance is raised in the neighbourhood as a whole, the rate of return on the improved as well as on the unimproved properties will go up. It is possible for the return on the improved houses and on the (few remaining) unimproved houses to go up by the same amount so that the marginal return from improving an individual property will be the same as before. It is also readily conceivable that as long as the neighbourhood is run down, there will be no incentive to individual improvement but that everybody would benefit from concerted action. We thus have what seems to be a case of separable externalities affecting resource use and calling for a Pigovian tax-subsidy scheme which will benefit all the producers.

The " prisoner's dilemma " argument on which the neighbourhood example is built runs as follows. Imagine there are two individuals accused of committing a joint crime. If neither of them confesses, both will be set free. If one of them confesses, both will be sentenced, but the one who confesses will receive a lighter sentence. Individual behaviour (based on the principle of minimaxing the penalty) calls for confession, but concerted action calls for denial of guilt. It is clearly in the best interest of both prisoners to engage in concerted action. But is it in the interest of society that they should be set free? This somewhat facetious question applies to the neighbourhood example as well as to the prisoners. The fact that the property owners in a given neighbourhood benefit through concerted action does not permit us to conclude that the concerted action benefits the community as a whole. The concerted action is beneficial to the property owners because it increases the demand for their product. This increase in demand can only occur if there is a decrease in demand for property in other neighbourhoods and/or for other goods and services. The *ceteris paribus* assumption underlying partial equilibirum analysis can no longer be made, and the discussion of externalities in a competitive setting (no product variation, price takers' equilibrium) fails to apply.

To remain within the analytical framework of the discussion between the modern-old and the modern welfare economists, we must confine our attention to cases of " non-separable " externalities, that is, to cases where the output of a firm (or firms) affects the marginal cost of another firm (or firms). In such cases it may not be possible for a firm to determine in isolation its optimal output. Davis and Whinston thereby conclude that it is impossible to devise a tax-subsidy scheme which will induce each firm to move to a joint optimum and that the joint optimum objective can be achieved only through merger.[36]

The Davis-Whinston argument appears to be based on the notion that the Pigovian tax-subsidy scheme can only function if the firms involved start from a well-defined equilibrium position. The argument applies to the bargaining solution since it is difficult to strike a bargain unless one knows how much one will gain from it. There is no such requirement for the Pigovian scheme. For the scheme to function it is not necessary to start from any set point; what is required is that there be taxes and subsidies which internalize the external effect. If such taxes and subsidies can be imposed, each firm will move toward the Pareto optimum simply by attempting to equate its marginal costs (including tax) to the price. It will be shown that, contrarily to the Davis-Whinston assertion, such a scheme can be devised where there are " non-separable " externalities.[37]

Consider two perfectly competitive firms, 1 and 2, which seek to maximize their total profits,[38]i.e., to equate marginal costs and marginal revenues:

$$p_1 = \partial C_1 / \partial q_1 \quad ; \quad p_2 = \partial C_2 / \partial q_2$$

where p_1 and p_2 are the prices facing Firm 1 and Firm 2, with q_1, q_2 being their respective outputs and C_1, C_2 their respective cost functions. If the two firms are linked by non-separable external effects, the marginal cost of each firm is a function of the output of the other firm, i.e.,

$$C_1 = f_1(q_1, q_2); \quad C_2 = f_2(q_1, q_2)$$

and

$$\partial^2 C_1 / \partial q_2 \partial q_1 \neq 0; \quad \partial^2 C_2 / \partial q_1 \partial q_2 \neq 0.$$

As a consequence, the individual optimum output of the two firms $\hat{q}_1$ and $\hat{q}_2$ (i.e., the output which yields maximum profit under the given circumstances) is a function of the output level of the other firm:

$$\hat{q}_1 = g_1(q_2) \quad ; \quad \hat{q}_2 = g_2(q_1).$$

The individual optimization process is represented graphically in Figure 1, in which the curve $\hat{q}_1$ represents the optimal output of Firm 1 as a function of q_2, the output of Firm 2, and curve $\hat{q}_2$ shows the optimal output of Firm 2 for various output levels of Firm 1. In the diagram Firm 1 creates external diseconomies to Firm 2, and Firm 2 to Firm 1. As drawn, the equilibrium point given by the intersection of curves $\hat{q}_1$ and $\hat{q}_2$ is unstable (though in some cases it may be stable), and it differs from the socially optimal output E.[39]The purpose of the Pigovian tax-subsidy scheme is so to modify the cost functions faced by the two firms as to induce the two firms to produce at E, i.e., to have a stable equilibrium point at E.

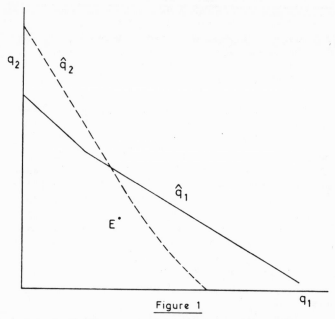

Figure 1

To induce both firms to produce at the social optimum E, it is necessary to make them take into account the social marginal cost, i.e., the sum of the private marginal cost and of the marginal external cost or benefit. At social equilibrium E, each firm must just equate the social marginal cost with the price:

$$\partial C_1/\partial q_1 + \partial C_2/\partial q_1 = p_1 \; ; \; \partial C_2/\partial q_2 + \partial C_1/\partial q_2 = p_2$$

where $\partial C_2/\partial q_1$ represents the marginal cost imposed by 1 upon 2, and $\partial C_1/\partial q_2$ the effect of 2 upon 1.

The Pigovian problem is to impose upon each firm a tax which internalizes the external effects so that each firm will choose the socially optimal output by considering its price and its own marginal costs (including the tax) without taking into account any other factors. Consider, for instance, a Pigovian tax to be imposed upon Firm 1. The new cost function which will include the tax must have the following two properties: (1) the new cost function must equal the sum of internal costs of 1 and of the external costs imposed by 1 on 2, for all values of q_1, and (2) the new cost function must be a single-valued function of q_1. Writing C'_1 for the new cost function of Firm 1, conditions (1) and (2) will be satisfied if:

$$\partial C'_1(q_1)/\partial q_1 \equiv \partial C(q_1 q_2)/\partial q_1$$

where $C(q_1 q_2) = C_1(q_1 q_2) + C_2(q_1 q_2)$.
An analogous condition can be written for the tax to be imposed on Firm 2:

$$\partial C'_2(q_2)/\partial q_2 \equiv \partial C(q_1 q_2)/\partial q_2.$$

Since the new cost function for which we are searching is a function of a single variable it follows that:

$$\partial C'_1/\partial q_1 \equiv dC'_1/dq_1, \text{ and } \partial C'_2/\partial q_2 \equiv dC'_2/dq_2.$$

The problem, then, is to find functions g_1 and g_2 such that $q_2 = g_1(q_1)$ and $q_1 = g_1(q_2)$ where g_1 and g_2 are the solutions to the differential equations

$$\partial C/\partial q_1 = dC_1/dq_1 \text{ and } \partial C/\partial q_2 = dC_2/dq_2.$$

Writing in extenso the above equations we have:

$$\frac{\partial C_1}{\partial q_1} + \frac{\partial C_2}{\partial q_1} = \frac{\partial C_1}{\partial q_1} + \frac{\partial C_1}{\partial q_2}\frac{dq_2}{dq_1}; \text{ and } \frac{\partial C_1}{\partial q_2} + \frac{\partial C_2}{\partial q_2} = \frac{\partial C_2}{\partial q_2} + \frac{\partial C_2}{\partial q_1}\frac{dq_1}{dq_2};$$

and simplifying:

$$\frac{\partial C_2}{\partial q_1} = \frac{\partial C_1}{\partial q_2}\frac{dq_2}{dq_1} \text{ ; and } \frac{\partial C_1}{\partial q_2} = \frac{\partial C_2}{\partial q_1}\frac{dq_1}{dq_2};$$

and by re-arranging terms

$$\frac{dq_2}{dq_1} = \frac{\partial C_2}{\partial q_1} \Big/ \frac{\partial C_1}{\partial q_2} = F_1(q_1 q_2) \text{ ; } \frac{dq_1}{dq_2} = \frac{\partial C_1}{\partial q_2} \Big/ \frac{\partial C_2}{\partial q_1} = F_2(q_1 q_2).$$

The solutions to the last two equations are $q_2 = g_1(q_1)$ and $q_1 = g_2(q_1)$. The solutions exist whenever F_1 and F_2 are continuous functions with continuous partial derivatives $\partial F_1/\partial q_2$ and $\partial F_2/\partial q_1$. The two firms will thus face new cost functions which are respectively $C'_1 = C'_1(q_1, g_1(q_1))$ and $C'_2 = C'_2(q_2, g_2(q_2))$ where g_1 and g_2 are the Pigovian taxes internalizing the external effect.[40]

The formal proof that a Pigovian system of taxes can be designed[41] does not prove that such taxes are easy to design or that their administration is practicable. In some cases it might be preferable to use outright prohibition of certain activities (such as zoning laws) whereas in others it might be less costly to ignore the externalities and let the market function without any interference. The choice of course of action must be dictated by weighing the costs and the benefits of the alternative arrangements.

The Pigovian tax-subsidy scheme, unlike the modern-old bargains, applies to the broad spectrum of externality cases. The scheme is, nevertheless, repugnant to the modern-old economists.

Buchanan's objections to the Pigovian method are based on the observation that any administrative measure is likely to impose externalities of its own.[42] Thus Mr. X might not feel personally threatened by fire (or he lives in an entirely fireproof building); yet he is forced to pay taxes to support the fire department. The objection is valid, alas: there is no way of constructing a non-dictatorial social welfare function,[43] and there is no way of devising an equitable system of payment for public goods.[44] These points are well worth keeping in mind, and one should continuously be reminded of the dangers of administrative meddling in economic affairs. Unfortunately, however, the policy maker must choose between imperfect alternatives, and it might be well worth the economists' while to design the best available system of Pigovian taxes instead of making indignant noises when the policy makers adopt silly measures for want of expert advice.

The cost of administration and the possibility of imposition of excessive burdens on the externality-producing unit cause concern to Coase. It is true, of course, that the cost of regulation may outweigh its benefits, and that governments in general shy away from this kind of cost-benefit analysis. Public welfare would doubtless increase if we dropped the unreasonable expedient of valuing government services at cost, and if we probed into their actual value. Fear of excessive bounties is less warranted. Excessive damages work against the interests of the aggrieved parties as much as against the interests of society. If a socially useful activity is eliminated because damages are too high, no compensation will accrue to the damaged party. Farmers adversely affected by smoke are better off if they receive a steady stream of compensation from a smoke-producing factory, i.e., if they appropriate part of the rent accruing to the factory,[45] than they are if the factory is forced to move away. Thus whether cost allocation is done through bargaining or whether it is done through the judicial-administrative process, it is in the interests of all the parties to reach a social optimum, for at that point the spoils are the greatest. The problem, in either case, is how to divide the spoils; it is always in everybody's interest to make the spoils as large as possible. Unfortunately, in most types of external relations the market does not lead to a social optimum; hence, whether we like it or not, we must try to design a workable Pigovian system of taxes or subsidies, or we must live with the externalities in our non-optimal world.

III. CONCLUSIONS

The critics of the Pigovian tradition have done us a great service by pointing out the ambiguities and the lack of clarity in the orthodox treatment of externalities. They have done well, too, to point out how important it is to reckon the administrative cost of action taken to remedy situations in which there are externalities. Externalities may well be permitted to persist if the administrative action absorbs more resources than are lost through a deviation from a Pareto optimum. This is just common sense, but it is good to put common sense into scientific language every so often. It was also useful to point out (as Kenneth Arrow did before) that any collective action imposes the will of some on others; hence, it too creates externalities of its own.

The mutual bargain solution proposed by the modern-old economists lacks, unfortunately, the necessary generality to be of policy importance. Pigou, as we know, was concerned with externality situations "of such a sort that payment cannot be exacted from the benefited factor or compensation enforced on behalf of the injured factors".[46] To be more precise, he should have also included cases where private bargains cannot be reached, and cases where private bargains are contrary to public interest. In the former category we must include bargains with variable-threat limits, in the latter, bargains in which monopolies are involved.

Even in the rare instances where externalities are a private matter between two parties, the superiority of private bargains over judicial arbitration is hard to accept. Whether it is reached by direct bargaining or by a judicial process, the solution to the conflict is most satisfactory to both sides if the final situation is Pareto optimal. It is clear, moreover, that even if provision is made for judicial recourse, the parties concerned may, if they wish, strike a private bargain. The fact that arbitration and other judicial methods of settling disputes is so prevalent gives proof that it is not always easy, or cheap, to reach a private bargain.

Finally, there is the problem of equity. To be sure, economists abandon their scientific detachment when they start moralizing. It is worth pointing out, however, that while the judicial process, rightly or wrongly, tends to compensate the victim, the bargaining process compensates the threat-making party, and one can hardly claim that threat-making deserves reward.

The attempt to prove the impossibility of devising a Pigovian scheme in cases of " non-separable " externalities was potentially the most dangerous of the attacks on the Pigovian tradition. Luckily for the " modern " welfare economics, the proof demonstrates only that where externalities are " non-separable," it may be impossible to reach a " modern-old " bargain. The Pigovian solution withstood the attack.

The practical problem of devising Pigovian tax-subsidy schemes may be exceedingly complex. Pigou hoped to leave resource allocation to the " invisible hand " and to help guide that hand through taxes and subsidies. He recognized, however, that " when the interrelations of the various private persons affected are highly complex, the Government may find it necessary to exercise some means of authoritative control in addition to providing a bounty ".[4][7]In some cases, too, as the " modern-old " economists remind us, it is best for the government to adopt a hands-off policy.

To sum up, the modern-old counter-attack has left us just about where we were before it was made. Since the counter-attack was thickly hedged with disclaimers concerning the economists' ability to say anything useful about welfare problems, the lack of concrete results cannot come as much of a surprise. Yet this lack of results must be disappointing to those of us who are dissatisfied with the " solutions " to externalities put into effect by " intelligent administrators " and by " applied economists." Perhaps, after all, the welfare economists could do better than the " practical men " if only they were able to apply their skills to the practical problems which cry for solutions.

Columbia University.

NOTES

[1] To all intents and purposes Lester Telser is a co-author of this paper. I also wish to thank Harry Johnson, Harold Demsetz and Merton Miller for their generous help.

[2] J. M. Buchanan, " Policy and the Pigovian Margins ", *Economica*, vol. 29 (1962), p. 17, n. 3.

[3] For a summary of the controversy preceding the modern-old attack, see Francis Bator, " The Anatomy of Market Failure ", *Quarterly Journal of Economics*, vol. 72 (1958).

[4] I. M. D. Little, *A Critique of Welfare Economics*, 2nd ed., 1957, p. 279.

[5] *Ibid.*, p. 184.

[6] Buchanan, *loc. cit.*, p. 17, n. 3.

[7] R. Turvey, " On Divergences between Social Cost and Private Cost ", *Economica*, vol. 30 (1963), p. 313.

[8] E. J. Mishan, " Welfare Criteria for External Effects ," *American Economic Review*, vol. 51 (1961), p. 594.

[9] Buchanan, *loc. cit.*; J. M. Buchanan and W. C. Stubblebine, " Externality ", *Economica*, vol. 29 (1962); R. H. Coase, " The Problem of Social Cost ", *Journal of Law and Economics*, vol. 3 (1960).

[10] O. A. Davis and A. Whinston, " Externalities, Welfare, and the Theory of Games ", *Journal of Political Economy*, vol. 60 (1962).

[11] *Ibid.*, p. 261.

[12] Coase, *loc. cit.*, p. 34.

[13] Coase builds up his case almost exclusively on the basis of diverse court cases concerned with problems of external economies. While this makes for fascinating reading, I shall limit myself to a few examples, and proceed along more theoretical lines, thus sacrificing some realism for the sake of generality of the argument.

[14] Coase, *loc. cit.*, p. 31.

[15] Buchanan and Stubblebine, *loc. cit.*, p. 381.

[16] Coase, *loc. cit.*, p. 32.

[17] *Ibid.*, p. 32.

[18] Coase, *loc. cit.*, pp. 32–3.

[19] Let dd' be the demand curve facing the railway and mm' the marginal revenue curve. As in Coase's example, let us assume that the average cost of running trains is constant, so that CC' represents the average and the marginal cost curve.

Let OG be the marginal cost imposed by the railway on the farmers, and OH be the social marginal cost obtained by summing the railway's marginal cost and the marginal external cost. The Pareto-optimal output OA is determined by the intersection of the social marginal cost with the demand curve. In the absence of bargains with the farmers, the railway's maximum profit output OB is determined by the intersection of the railway's marginal cost with the marginal revenue curve. If the farmers offer the railway compensation in exchange for a reduction in output, the railway will be willing to reduce output to OE, at which point the marginal social cost equals the railway's marginal revenue. In the case shown the output which will obtain in the absence of bargains, i.e., OB, is socially preferable to output OE.

[20] Coase's arithmetic suggests that the railway is a monopolist with constant marginal costs ($50 per train) facing a downward sloping demand curve. Under this interpretation it appears to be useful to run a second train because the marginal social cost of $110 ($50 being the marginal cost to the railway, and $60 being external costs) is less than the average revenue from the two trains ($125). The apparent decrease in the total product under the two-train regime is caused by the neglect of the consumers' surplus. Harold Demsetz disagrees with this interpretation of the railway example and claims that the railway is meant to be a perfectly discriminating monopolist, in which case Coase's one-train solution would be correct. It is a little difficult to accept this interpretation, however, since the perfectly discriminating monopolist violates the Pareto conditions in distribution, since arbitrage among consumers could improve some consumers' welfare without decreasing the welfare of any consumers.

[21] This statement is not strictly true, but in dealing with individual firms in a competitive setting (which is in keeping with the level of discourse of Pigou's critics), it is legitimate to disregard effects of second-order magnitude.

[22] The formal profit-maximization conditions under perfect competiton are not affected, of course, by inclusion of the rent.

[23] When in the absence of zoning, a factory is erected, it is not usual for the factory owner to notify the nearby farmers about the amount of smoke which he intends to produce, so that the bargaining, if any, takes place after the factory is built. It is still more unusual for a number of factories to compete not only for a site but for the privilege of smoking on to nearby fields. The ex-ante bargaining would require rather unusual property relationships which would, in effect, internalize the externality.

[24] Pigou took a rather dim view of the " costless bargaining " assumption: " Of bargaining proper there is little that need be said. It is obvious that intelligence and resources devoted to this purpose, whether on one side or on the other, and whether successful or unsuccessful, yield no product to the community as a whole . . . These

activities are wasted. They contribute to private, but not to social net product."
The Economics of Welfare, 4th ed., 1938, p. 201. Pigou is too harsh in his judgment: insofar as the bargaining process changes the pattern of resource use and provided that it is imbedded in a competitive setting, it does contribute to social product. It is quite possible, however, that just as with public regulation, the absorption of resources may be so great as to nullify the beneficial effects of improved resource use.

[25] Davis and Whinston, *loc. cit.*, p. 259 ff. Curiously enough, the numerical example given by the authors is one in which there is a stable equilibrium which will be reached with each firm acting in isolation. It is very simple, however, to construct plausible cases which do not have such an equilibrium.

[26] For a discussion of the vicissitudes of a bargaining solution in variable threat situations, see R. L. Bishop, " Game-Theoretic Analyses of Bargaining ", *Quarterly Journal of Economics*, vol. 77 (1963).

[27] Turvey, *loc. cit.*, p. 312.

[28] Buchanan, *loc. cit.*, p. 29.

[29] To find a way out of this difficulty, one is tempted to search for a sub-set of units, all of which are willing to co-operate on a voluntary basis. Such a solution has no legitimate place in a purely competitive setting for it is a basic assumption of the theory of perfect competition that all units behave exactly alike. In a large group it is in the interest of every unit to refuse to pay and to let the other units bear the entire cost; in any sub-set of units the same behaviour must pertain.

[30] Pigou, *op cit.*, p. 183.

[31] See especially Turvey, *op. cit.*, p. 312 and *passim*.

[32] As will be shown, the type of externalities which, according to Davis and Whinston, can be handled through the Pigovian method, is of no consequence in resource allocation problems.

[33] Let C_1 and C_2 represent the total cost functions of firms " 1 " and " 2 " respectively, and q_1, q_2 be the respective output levels. If the two firms are externally linked, $C_1 = f_1(q_1, q_2)$ and $C_2 = f_2(q_1, q_2)$ where $\partial C_1/\partial C_2 \neq 0$ and/or $\partial C_2/\partial q_1 \neq 0$. Separability means that $\partial^2 C_1/\partial q_2 \partial q_1 = 0$ and $\partial^2 C_2/\partial q_1 \partial q_2 = 0$, while in cases of non-separability $\partial^2 C_1/\partial q_2 \partial q_1 \neq 0$ and/or $\partial^2 C_2/\partial q_1 \partial q_2 \neq 0$.

[34] As Davis and Whinston rightly observed, the cost functions used in the literature to demonstrate the effect of externalities on the Pareto conditions are invariably of the " separable " type. For instance, J. M. Henderson and R. E. Quandt in their *Microeconomic Theory*, 1958, p. 216, discuss the following cost functions:
$C_1 = 0 \cdot 1 q_1{}^2 + 5q_1 - 0 \cdot 1 q_2{}^2$; $C_2 = 0 \cdot 2 q_2{}^2 + 7q_2 + 0 \cdot 025 q_1{}^2$. The Henderson-Quandt example is especially unfortunate, for the cost functions used by them are incompatible with a long-run competitive equilibrium.

[35] See Davis and Whinston, *loc. cit.*; also the same authors' " Economics of Urban Renewal ", *Law and Contemporary Problems*, Winter 1961, pp. 108–110.

[36] Davis and Whinston, *loc. cit.*, pp. 253–6. The Davis-Whinston assertion also implies that it is impossible to devise a pricing scheme for a divisionalized firm if there are non-separable externalities between the divisions.

[37] I owe this proof to Lester Telser.

[38] The costs are defined here as being net of rent in order to make the analysis consistent with perfectly competitive conditions.

[39] For a discussion of conditions under which the equilibrium point resulting from individual optimization yields a social optimum in spite of external effects, see Buchanan and Stubblebine, *loc. cit.*, p. 375. Such cases are exceptions rather than a rule, however.

[40] The tax on Firm 1 is a function (possibly a highly complicated one) of the output of Firm 1, and similarly for Firm 2. Taxes proportioned to the output will only be appropriate if it is reasonable to give linear approximations of the cost functions in respect to both variables.

[41] For a discussion of the integrability conditions which must be satisfied in the case of more than two units, see H. Wold and L. Juréen, *Demand Analysis*, 1953, pp. 90–94. The proof, developed by Wold for utility analysis, applies to cost analysis as well.

[42] See Buchanan, *loc. cit.*, pp. 25 ff.

[43] On this point see Kenneth J. Arrow, *Social Choice and Individual Values*, 1951.

[44] See J. Wiseman, " The Theory of Public Utility Pricing—An Empty Box ", *Oxford Economic Papers*, vol. IX (1957).

[45] I assume here that the factory collects some Ricardian rent and that it prefers to share the rent with the farmers rather than to move away. If there is no Ricardian

rent accruing to the factory, it is socially indifferent whether the factory moves away or not.

[46]Pigou, *op. cit.*, p. 183.
[47]Pigou, *op. cit.*, p. 194.

On Externalities, Information and the Government-Assisted Invisible Hand[1]

By OTTO A. DAVIS and ANDREW B. WHINSTON

Recently Professor Wellisz [13] critically commented upon some contributions to the " externality problem "[2]. One would welcome such a critical comment were it not for the fact that Wellisz's treatment of the problem is rather misleading. This article attempts to make the issues more clear by (i) pointing out certain errors in Wellisz's article, (ii) indicating where his treatment fails to show an appreciation of one of the main points of these recent contributions, and (iii) briefly sketching a new approach to the problem which has certain advantages over most of the previous proposals. In trying to accomplish these three aims, the problem of information, created by the very existence of externalities, is emphasised.[3]

I. SOME POINTS AT ISSUE

Only a few of the major issues are considered here; and no attempt is made to discuss each of the points where, at least to us, Wellisz seems to misrepresent the positions of the various contributors to the " modern-old vs. modern "[4] controversy on externalities.

First, Wellisz is misleading when he states: " Unfortunately, in most types of external relations the market does not lead to a social optimum; hence, whether we like it or not, we must try to design a workable Pigovian system of taxes or subsidies, or we must live with the externalities in our non-optimal world ".[5] There can be no doubt but that one of the major points of each of the " modern-old " contributors was that the Pigovian tax-subsidy scheme is not a panacea and that it is not the only policy alternative worthy of consideration. Bargaining, which was emphasized by Coase [3] and discussed by Buchanan and Stubblebine [2], is another alternative. Others, sometimes appropriate only under certain circumstances, include merger, re-definition of property rights (and sometimes the establishment of property rights),

Reprinted by permission of the publishers and authors: Otto A. Davis and Andrew B. Whinston, "On Externalities, Information and the Government–Assisted Invisible Hand," *Economica*, n.s. 33 (August 1966), pp. 303-318.

constraints of the zoning type,[6] the establishment of certain " standards ",[7] and, if one is willing to abandon the advantages of a decentralized pricing mechanism, centralized directives. As Turvey [12] emphasized, the policy maker should consider these and other alternatives in attempting to make a choice appropriate to some specific situation. Further, it is worthy of note that Wellisz's objection to the bargaining scheme—that " the process opens up magnificent business prospects: any activity can be turned to profit as long as it is sufficiently annoying to someone else "[8]—can be satisfied by a proper definition of property rights.[9] The point is that economists need not presume that the tax-subsidy scheme is the only available policy in situations characterized by externalities. Much research in this area is needed, not only to discover new policy alternatives, but also to determine the practical and theoretical difficulties associated with known alternatives.

At least a part of the " modern-old " contribution has been aimed at exploring the practical and conceptual difficulties associated with the Pigovian tax-subsidy scheme. It was in this spirit that the distinction between separable and non-separable externalities was introduced in [4] and it was argued that while the difficulties associated with such a scheme in the former instance are great, there are several orders of magnitude larger in the latter instance. We shall return to this point later in our remarks, but for the moment it is important to clear up a misconception concerning the separable case.

Wellisz maintains that ". . . the problem of devising a Pigovian solution for the ' separable ' case does not arise for, as can be readily demonstrated, the ' separable externalities ' do not affect the pattern of resource allocation ".[10] In order to show why Wellisz's assertion is false, we present the following simple example which is based upon the developments in [4]. Consider two firms in a purely competitive industry which are related through their cost functions (externalities on the production side). Assume that the cost functions are

(1)
$$C_1 = C_1(q_1, q_2) = f_1(q_1) + g_1(q_2)$$
$$C_2 = C_2(q_1, q_2) = f_2(q_2) + g_2(q_1),$$

where the sub-scripts refer to the respective firms, C represents costs, and q indicates the output level. Note that these externalities are separable since each cost function can be written as the sum of two functions, both of which involve only one variable as its argument![11] Letting P represent profits and p price, if each firm acts in an individually rational manner and maximizes its own profit without regard to the actions of the other firm, then we have

(2)
$$\max_{q_1} P_1 = pq_1 - f_1(q_1) - g_1(q_2)$$
$$\max_{q_2} P_2 = pq_2 - f_2(q_2) - g_2(q_1)$$

as the maximization problems of the two firms as indicated by the relevant sub-scripts. The necessary conditions are

(3) $$p - df_1/dq_1 = 0 \text{ and } p - df_2/dq_2 = 0,$$

since each firm must maximize profits with respect to the variable under its control. Hence, the first and second firms individually choose values of q_1 and q_2 respectively which equate price with their own marginal costs. Let q'_1 and q'_2 represent these respective quantities. Presuming that the second-order conditions are satisfied, q'_1 and q'_2 represent the profit maximizing outputs of these two firms when neither considers the externality which it imposes upon the other.

It is well known that in a purely competitive market, where p is a parameter, the conditions for the equality of marginal social benefit and marginal social cost can be obtained from the joint maximum problem. Hence consider

(4) $\quad \displaystyle\max_{q_1, q_2} P = pq_1 + pq_2 - f_1(q_1) - g_1(q_2) - f_2(q_2) - g_2(q_1),$

which is this problem. Under the indicated assumptions,

(5)
$$\delta P / \delta q_1 = p - df_1/dq_1 - dg_2/dq_1 = 0$$
$$\delta P / \delta q_2 = p - df_2/dq_2 - dg_1/dq_2 = 0$$

are the necessary conditions for a maximum. Let the values of q_1 and q_2 which satisfy conditions (5) be denoted q^*_1 and q^*_2. Note that $dg_2/dq_1 \neq 0$ and $dg_1/dq_2 \neq 0$ under the presumption that externalities do exist and are relevant. Thus it is obvious that conditions (5) are not the same as conditions (3). It follows that $q^*_1 \neq q'_1$ and $q^*_2 \neq q'_2$. Separable externalities do have an influence upon the allocation of productive resources. It is easily seen from (5) that each firm must select quantities which equate price and marginal social cost (rather than price and their own marginal cost) if the socially optimal outputs q^*_1 and q^*_2 are to be produced.

The above developments make it easy to point out some obvious, but important and often overlooked, difficulties associated with the traditional approach to the tax-subsidy scheme. Let T_1 and T_2 represent (as yet undetermined) per unit taxes or subsidies (depending upon the respective signs). Then the traditional approach is to replace individual problems (2) with the following problems

(6)
$$\max_{q_1} P_1 = pq_1 - f_1(q_1) - g_1(q_2) - T_1 q_1$$
$$\max_{q_2} P_2 = pq_2 - f_2(q_2) - g_2(q_1) - T_2 q_2$$

by introducing the tax-subsidy scheme. The respective (necessary) conditions for a maximum are

(7)
$$dP_1/dq_1 = p - df_1/dq_1 - T_1 = 0$$
$$dP_2/dq_2 = p - df_2 - /dq_2 - T_2 = 0,$$

and it is obvious that conditions (7) are equivalent to conditions (5) if and only if $T_1 = dg_2/dq_1$ when $q_1 = q^*_1$ and $T_2 = dg_1/dq_2$ when $q_2 = q^*_2$.

Consider now the problems of some governmental authority which has been delegated the task of determining the appropriate value for

211

T_1 and T_2. Since, with the exception of Wellisz's contribution which is discussed in the following section, no special approach or computational scheme has been proposed (at least to our knowledge), it would appear that the authority must follow the " natural " procedure. The authority must determine the optimal outputs q^*_1, q^*_2 by some method in order that the " marginal externality costs " dg_2/dq_1 and dg_1/dq_2 can be evaluated at the proper outputs and the per unit taxes or subsidies T_1 and T_2 can be appropriately determined. The " natural " procedure is for the authority to solve problem (4) in order to obtain the optimal outputs q^*_1 and q^*_2. Note that this procedure makes severe demands upon the information-gathering ability of the authority. It must know both cost functions (1). Although it is by no means certain that the authority could obtain this information (at least with our existing state of knowledge), it was shown in [4] that, granted this information, the authority could accomplish its task in a straightforward manner. However, it was also shown that if the externalities were mutual and non-separable, the additional difficulties exist in the sense that the authority must also know the strategic decision rules of both managers in order to predict their reactions. This is an additional difficulty at both the conceptual and practical levels.

However, it is worth pointing out that even in the simple separable case this procedure does not possess the desirable virtues of decentralization. It is easily seen from (5) and (7) that the optimal levels of the taxes or subsidies (T_1 and T_2) depend upon (i) the market price p, (ii) the prices of input factors, and (iii) the technologies of the two firms. If there is a change in any of these variables, then the old taxes and subsidies need not be appropriate and new ones must be computed in order that optimality be attained. Granted the all too obvious difficulties of obtaining the proper information to set up and solve (4) in the first place, the possibility of continually having to seek additional information and recompute does not appear to be a pleasant prospect. Furthermore, it can be pondered, granted that with this procedure the optimal outputs q^*_1 and q^*_2 have to be determined by the authority, whether there is any advantage to computing the proper taxes and subsidies rather than simply dictating that the firms produce the appropriate outputs.

II. DECENTRALIZATION AND THE WELLISZ PROPOSAL

Since the Wellisz proposal for computing the appropriate taxes and subsidies does not follow the natural procedure, it is interesting to determine whether this proposal possesses the advantages of a decentralized scheme. In order to accomplish this, it is convenient to digress briefly upon the centralization-decentralization controversy.

The fundamental proposition of modern welfare economics is that given independent preference orderings for consumers, independent technologies for producers, and certain restrictions on the shapes of these functions, then, if consumers maximize utility subject to given income and price parameters, and if producers maximize profits subject to these price parameters, there exists a set of prices such that a social maximum is achieved where no individual can be made better off without making some other individual worse off.[12]Furthermore, granted other assumptions such as the lack of monopoly power, this Pareto welfare maximum can be achieved via a pricing mechanism and decentralized decisions.

It is well known that with decentralized decisions under a pricing mechanism of the classical type, the informational demands upon the system are minimal. Each consumer needs to know his own preference orderings, income and prices. Each firm needs to know its own technology and prices. Under a perfectly functioning market mechanism, prices have sufficient informational content to lead the system to a co-ordinated, Pareto optimal solution although the decision-making units have only the knowledge indicated above.

On the other hand, it is also well known that in a completely centralized system which seeks to achieve a welfare Pareto optimum, information concerning preference orderings and technologies must not only be known by the various individual units, but must also be communicated to the central group which is in charge of resource allocation. Aside from the various ethical arguments (with which we are not concerned here), the major factor favouring a decentralized system has generally been held to be the difficulty of transmitting such information. How does one obtain information on preference orderings in the absence of a price system? One can imagine conducting experiments on each and every consumer in the economy, but certainly such an activity would be prohibitively expensive. Similarly, how does one obtain knowledge concerning the technologies of individual firms? Is one to conduct an econometric study of each and every firm in the economy? When it is further admitted that in addition to these difficulties one would need to know when technologies and preference orderings changed, it is easy to conclude that to attempt to obtain such information is impractical.

The question arises as to what happens when the various conditions allowing a market mechanism to lead the system to a Pareto optimum are not satisfied.[13]In such situations, various proposals may be made to aid the system to achieve a Pareto optimal solution. Since, at least in principle, and granted that the appropriate information is available to the central group, the proper decisions can be determined under a centralized scheme (although the problem of seeing that these decisions are enacted still remains), it would seem that the (or at least one) relevant basis for judging the various proposals is the strigency of their informational requirements. In the previous section it was argued that the natural approach to the computation of Pigovian taxes and subsidies has approximately the same informational requirements as does the issuing of centralized directives for the firms affecting and affected by externalities. If Pigovian taxes and subsidies are to be recommended on this basis, then it is important to find a computational scheme which has less stringent informational requirements.

It is argued here that the Wellisz proposal, although superficially approaching the externality problem from a decentralized point of view, not only is as demanding as a centralized scheme in terms of needed information, but also that it involves additional difficulties. It is true, of course, that his proposal is not a " proof " (as is claimed) that a truly Pigovian system of taxes and subsidies can be designed. The Pigovian system, by its very nature, requires that the taxes or subsidies be proportional to output. In other words, the taxes or subsidies are stated in per unit terms. Wellisz admits that his scheme need not result in per unit charges (positive or negative).[14] Further, it is hardly necessary to use mathematical analysis to show that a non-linear system of taxes and subsidies is theoretically possible. One may merely observe that, granted the appropriate information, the governmental authority can solve for the proper outputs and then impose an almost infinite tax unless the firms produce these proper outputs. Be this as it may, Wellisz's proposal merits consideration on its own grounds, and it would seem appropriate to judge it in terms of the stringency of its informational requirements and the practical difficulties involved in putting it into operation.

Let $C_1(q_1, q_2)$ and $C_2(q_2, q_1)$ represent the total cost functions of two firms which are interconnected via mutual externalities. Since competitive markets are presumed, at a Pareto optimum each of these firms must equate marginal social cost with price: formally,

(8) $\qquad p_1 = \partial C_1/dq_1 + \partial C_2/dq_1$, and $p_2 = \partial C_2/\partial q_2 + \partial C_1/\partial q_2$,

where p_1 and p_2 represent the prices of the respective goods as indicated by the sub-scripts. Wellisz proposes to find new functions c_1 and c_2 such that (i) these new cost functions equal the sum of internal and external costs, and (ii) they are single-valued functions of each firm's own output. Supposedly, these conditions are satisfied if

(9) $\qquad \dfrac{dc_1}{dq_1} = \dfrac{\partial C_1(q_1, q_2)}{\partial q_1} + \dfrac{\partial C_2(q_2, q_1)}{\partial q_1}$ and $\dfrac{dc_2}{dq_2} = \dfrac{\partial C_1(q_1, q_2)}{\partial q_2} + \dfrac{\partial C_2(q_2, q_1)}{\partial q_2}$.

But it should be noted that there may be some difficulty with these conditions if the mutual externalities are non-separable. In such an instance the terms on the right hand side of the first of the identities (9) are functions of both q_1 and q_2. Thus if dc_1/dq_1 is to be single-valued, it would appear that the domain of q_2 must be restricted. Similar remarks apply to the second of the identities (9). A rationale for these restrictions on the domains is difficult to determine.

Ignoring the above difficulty, the problem is to find functions h_1 and h_2 such that $q_2 = h_1(q_1)$ and $q_1 = h_2(q_2)$, where h_1 and h_2 are the respective solutions to the differential equations

(10) $\qquad \dfrac{\partial C_1}{\partial q_1} + \dfrac{\partial C_2}{\partial q_1} = \dfrac{\partial C_1}{\partial q_1} + \dfrac{\partial C_1}{\partial q_2}\dfrac{dq_2}{dq_1}$ and $\dfrac{\partial C_1}{\partial q_2} + \dfrac{\partial C_2}{\partial q_2} = \dfrac{\partial C_2}{\partial q_2} + \dfrac{\partial C_2}{\partial q_1}\dfrac{dq_1}{dq_2}$.

By simplifying and rearranging the term, the expressions

(11) $\qquad \dfrac{dq_2}{dq_1} = \dfrac{\partial C_2/\partial q_1}{\partial C_1/\partial q_2}$ and $\dfrac{dq_1}{dq_2} = \dfrac{\partial C_1/\partial q_2}{\partial C_2/\partial q_1}$

are obtained, and these may be written

214

(12) $\quad\dfrac{\partial C_1}{\partial q_2}dq_2 - \dfrac{\partial C_2}{\partial q_1}dq_1 = 0 \quad$ and $\dfrac{\partial C_2}{\partial q_1}dq_1 - \dfrac{\partial C_1}{\partial q_2}dq_2 = 0,$

which are the total differentials. Under certain conditions these differentials may be solved (integrated) to obtain expressions of the form

(13) $\qquad G_1(q_1, q_2) = K_1 \quad$ and $\quad G_2(q_1, q_2) = K_2,$

where K_1 and K_2 are the constants of integration. It should be noted, however, that no truly general methods exist for solving expressions such as (12), so further difficulties with the Wellisz proposal are to be expected at this point as a practical matter.

Again under certain conditions, one can obtain from the expressions (13) functional forms

(14) $\qquad q_2 = h_1(q_1) \quad$ and $\quad q_1 = h_2(q_2).$

But note that h_1 and h_2 depend (at least in general) upon the respective constants of integration K_1 and K_2. How are these constants to be selected from the infinity of possible values? Wellisz does not discuss this point, but it appears that just any constants (and, by implication, just any h_1 and h_2 from given families) will not do. After all, or at least according to Wellisz, the h_1 and h_2 indicate the amounts of the taxes or subsidies; and these amounts should make a difference. It appears that in many instances the appropriate values of the constants K_1 and K_2 depend upon the values of the prices p_1 and p_2. Further, it seems that the only way to determine the appropriate values of these constants involves finding the Pareto optimal values of the outputs q^*_1 and q^*_2.

Presuming again that the above difficulties are overcome, one may obtain by substitution

(15) $\qquad c_1 = C_1[q_1, h_1(q_1)] \quad$ and $\quad c_2 = C_2[q_2, h_2(q_2)];$

and these developments constitute the Wellisz proposal.[15] The firms are supposed to use the functions (15) in their decision-making. Since the respective functions (14) which represent the taxes or subsidies are incorporated into these new cost functions (15), it is claimed that the external effects are internalized so that profit maximizing firms will be motivated to select the Pareto optimal outputs q^*_1 and q^*_2.

Wellisz does not discuss the question of who is supposed to determine the functions (15). However, it does not appear to be appropriate to allow the firms themselves to perform the manipulations required to obtain the functions (15) for several reasons. First, the manipulations involve the determination of (usually non-linear) tax or subsidy rates (14) and such a task is usually the domain of a governmental authority or legislature. Second, if firms were left to determine the functions (15), it is easily seen from (9), (10), (11) and (12) that the manipulations require that each firm know the cost function of the other. Such knowledge is not compatible with the assumptions usually employed in competitive price theory. More important, it appears that if such close communication and exchange of knowledge between the two firms is allowed (and is possible), then the situation is conducive to the merger solution, shown in [4] to be beneficial to both firms, so that the need for taxes and subsidies vanishes.

It seems difficult not to conclude that, if the Wellisz proposal is to be taken seriously, some governmental authority must be delegated the task of determining the tax-subsidy functions (14). Of course, this procedure, which seems sensible since some authority must administer the taxes or subsidies in any event, also serves to indicate the informational requirements of the proposal. Note that steps (10), (11) and (12), which are to be completed if the authority is to determine the tax-subsidy functions (14), show that the firms' cost functions are manipulated. Clearly, the authority can accomplish these steps only if it knows these cost functions. Thus the informational requirements of the Wellisz proposal are just as stringent as those of a centralized scheme. Given these informational requirements and the fact that, in general, the authority must find the Pareto optimal outputs q^*_1 and q^*_2 in order to determine the appropriate tax-subsidy functions (14), one may ponder whether there is any advantage in this proposal over having the authority dictate that the firms produce the appropriate outputs.

If the authority does determine the proper tax-subsidy functions (14), then it faces an additional problem. How are the firms to be motivated to use the new functions (15) in their decision-making? The mere introduction of the tax-subsidy functions (14) into the cost functions to produce (15) is not likely to make the firms believe that they are no longer affected by externalities and that their costs are independent of the actions of the other firm.[16] In order to explain this and other difficulties inherent in the Wellisz proposal, the following over simple example is now introduced.

Let the cost functions of the two firms take the following specific form:

(16) $\qquad C_1(q_1, q_2) = q_1 + q_2$ and $C_2(q_1, q_2) = q_1 q_2$.

Presume that a governmental authority is responsible for imposing taxes or subsidies, according to the Wellisz proposal, so that the two firms will produce Pareto optimal outputs. Assume further that, by some means, the authority has acquired a knowledge of the cost curves (16). Then, analogous to (11), the following expressions are obtained:

(17) $\qquad dq_2/dq_1 = q_2$ and $dq_1/dq_2 = 1/q_2$;

and upon solving it is found that

(18) $\qquad q_2 = Ke^{q_1}$ and $q_1 = \log q_2 + \log K,$

where K is a constant of integration.[17] Since the value of K obviously matters, the authority is faced with the problem of determining its appropriate value. This can be accomplished by solving the centralized problem

(19) $\qquad \max_{q_1, q_2} P = p_1 q_1 + p_2 q_2 - (q_1 + q_2) - (q_1 q_2)$

for the welfare optimal outputs q^*_1 and q^*_2. Suppose that the authority determines that the market prices are $p_1 = 3$ and $p_2 = 4$. Then the (necessary) conditions for a maximum to (19) are

(20) $\qquad \partial P/\partial q_1 = 3 - 1 - q_2 = 0$ and $\partial P/\partial q_2 = 4 - 1 - q_1 = 0$

216

so that $q*_1 = 3$ and $q*_2 = 2$. These values serve as the initial conditions to determine the appropriate value of K. Substituting these values into the first of the relations (18) gives $2 = Ke^3$ so that $K = 2/e^3$. When K is made to take on this particular value, then (18) gives the appropriate tax-subsidy functions. Suppose that the authority goes to the two firms and instructs them to use the respective cost functions,

(21) $c_1(q_1) = q_1 + (2/e^3)e^{q_1}$ and $c_2(q_2) = (\log q_2 - \log 2/e^3)q_2$,

in their decision-making.[18] These instructions mean that the two firms now face the following reformulated problems:

$$(22) \qquad \begin{matrix} \max_{q_1} P_1 = 3q_1 - q_1 - (2/e^3)e^{q_1} \\ \max_{q_2} P_2 = 4q_2 - (\log q_2 - \log 2/e^3)q_2. \end{matrix}$$

The necessary conditions are

$$(23) \qquad \begin{matrix} dP_1/dq_1 = 3 - 1 - (2/e^3)e^{q_1} = 0 \\ dP_2/dq_2 = 4 - 1 - \log q_2 + \log 2/e^3 = 0, \end{matrix}$$

and the solutions are $q*_1 = 3$ and $q*_2 = 2$, which agree witn the solution to (19).

It is worth while to make and re-state several points in the context of the above example. First, the authority must know the cost functions (16) in order to perform the necessary steps to obtain general forms of the tax-subsidy functions (18). Thus the informational requirements of the Wellisz proposal are just as stringent as those of a (partially) centralized scheme. Second, in order to obtain the specific tax-subsidy functions, the authority must determine the appropriate value of K. This involves solving the centralized problem (19) for the welfare optimal outputs $q*_1$ and $q*_2$, and these outputs serve as the initial conditions in obtaining the proper value of K. One can suggest that, granted the knowledge of $q*_1$ and $q*_2$, the authority could follow an easier scheme by imposing almost infinite taxes which are collected only if the firms do not produce the outputs $q*_1$ and $q*_2$. This procedure avoids the problem of solving the (generally non-linear) differential equations. Finally, observe that the functions (21) which the authority instructs the firms to use in decision-making, are equivalent to the true cost functions (16) only when the externality producing variables (q_2 for the first firm and q_1 for the second firm) take on appropriate values. Thus, if, for any reason, either of the firms happened to select an inappropriate output, the other firm would experience costs which are not reflected in the new function (21). This suggests that the authority might have difficulty in persuading the firms to use the functions (21) in decision-making.

III. A NEW PROPOSAL

Having shown that the Wellisz proposal, although superficially approaching the externality problem from a decentralized point of view, is not only as demanding as a (partially) centralized scheme in terms of informational requirements but also involves other difficulties, a new proposal is appropriately introduced. This new scheme amounts to a computational procedure for actually determining " Pigou-like" bounties and penalties which are paid from one firm to the other. However, it does have certain advantages over both the "natural" approach and the Wellisz proposal for determining the taxes and subsidies. First, it does not require that information concerning cost functions be communicated to any party (including the government). In this respect it is informationally decentralized. All that is required (aside from requirements that firms know their own cost functions, etc.) is that the existence of externalities be recognised. Second, it provides a method of getting around the problems of uncertainty, which were shown in [4] to exist whenever a truly Pigovian (linear) scheme is used and when the externalities are non-separable and reciprocal. This new proposal does require the creation of an authority (presumably governmental) which acts in a prescribed manner.[19]

Let $C_1(q_1, q_2)$ and $C_2(q_2, q_1)$ represent respectively the total cost functions of two firms, as indicated by the sub-scripts, which suffer under mutual (separable or non-separable) externalities. Similarly, let p_1 and p_2 respectively represent the competitive prices of the outputs. Analogous to (2) above, the individual and unco-ordinated firm problems can be represented by

(24) $\quad \max_{q_1} P_1 = p_1 q_1 - C_1(q_1, q_2)$, and $\max_{q_2} P_2 = p_2 q_2 - C_2(q_2, q_1)$,

which have the following as their respective conditions for individual optima:

(25) $dP_1/dq_1 = p_1 - \partial C_1/\partial q_1 = 0$, and $dP_2/dq_2 = p_2 - \partial C_2/\partial q_2 = 0$.

Similar to (4) above, the joint maximum problem is

(26) $\quad \max_{q_1, q_2} P = p_1 q_1 + p_2 q_2 - C_1(q_1, q_2) - C_2(q_2, q_1)$,

and the necessary conditions are

(27) $\partial P/\partial q_1 = p_1 - \partial C_1/\partial q_1 - \partial C_2/\partial q_1 = 0$, and $\partial P/\partial q_2 = p_2 - \partial C_1/\partial q_2 - \partial C_2/\partial q_2 = 0$.

Let the values of q_1 and q_2 which satisfy (27) be denoted q^*_1 and q^*_2. On the basis of the assumption that the externalities exist and are relevant, $\partial C_2/\partial q_1 \neq 0$ and $\partial C_1/\partial q_2 \neq 0$ so it is obvious that the Pareto optimal outputs (q^*_1 and q^*_2) will not satisfy (25). An iterative procedure of a tatonnement variety for achieving the quantities q^*_1 and q^*_2 is now outlined.

Suppose that a (governmental) co-ordinating authority goes to the first firm and defines a variable x_2 which represents q_2, the output of the second firm. The authority instructs the first firm that it is free to select whatever value of x_2 that it desires. In other words, the first firm is instructed to act as if it could determine the output of the second firm. It will be seen that the simple device removes the ambiguity and uncertainty created by the existence of mutual and non-separable externalities. Thus the first firm has as its profit maximization problem

(28) $\quad \max_{q_1, x_2} P_1 = p_1 q_1 - C_1(q_1, x_2)$,

218

and let $q_1(0)$ and $x_2(0)$ represent the values of q_1 and x_2 respectively which are the solution to this problem. (As will become clear below, the notation indicates that this is the initial step in an iterative solution.)

Similarly, suppose that the authority goes to the second firm, defines a variable x_1 which represents q_1, and instructs the second firm that it is free to select whatever value of x_1 that it desires. The second firm has as its profit maximization problem

$$(29) \qquad \max_{q_2,\, x_1} P_2 = p_2 q_2 - C_2(q_2, x_1),$$

and let $q_2(0)$ and $x_1(0)$ represent the value of q_2 and x_1 respectively which are the solution to this problem.

In general, it is to be expected that $q_1(0) \neq x_1(0)$ and $q_2(0) \neq x_2(0)$. Nevertheless, the authority is searching for a solution where $q_1 = x_1$ and $q_2 = x_2$. The above developments represent the first step in the authority's search. In other words, the authority is seeking a solution to the following maximization problem:

$$(30) \qquad \max_{q_1,\, x_1,\, q_2,\, x_2} P = p_1 q_1 + p_2 q_2 - C_1(q_1, x_2) - C_2(q_2, x_1)$$
$$\text{subject to } q_1 = x_1,\ q_2 = x_2.$$

It is obvious that this problem (30) is equivalent to the above problem (26) in the sense that the solution to (30) is exactly the solution to (26). Thus, if the authority determines the solution to (30), it will have found a Pareto optimal solution.

Note that problem (30) is decomposable into (28) and (29) above if the co-ordinating constraints $q_1 = x_1$ and $q_2 = x_2$ are also admitted. Thus it would appear that the authority has made a good start in its search for a solution to (30).

Presume that $q_1(0) \neq x_1(0)$ and $q_2(0) \neq x_2(0)$ so that the constraints of (30) are not satisfied and a solution is not at hand. The authority now sets per unit charges (positive or negative), which are paid from one firm to the other, on the basis of the following rule:

$$(31) \qquad \lambda_i(0) = \delta_i \{ q_i(0) - x_i(0) \}\ ; i = 1, 2$$

where $\lambda_i(0)$ is the initially proposed per unit charge on the ith commodity and δ_i is a parameter satisfying $0 < \delta_i < 1$. The expression (31) represents an arbitrary rule which merely gives a starting point. Note, however, that it has some desirable properties. If the externality is an external diseconomy, then $q_i(0) - x_i(0) > 0$ is expected. Consequently, $\lambda_1(0) > 0$ and the firm "causing" the externality has positive per unit charges placed on its output. Similarly, the firm "receiving" the externality obtains compensation. Exactly the reverse applies if the externality is an external economy. Of course, it should be observed that since this is a tatonnement type process, no money actually exchanges hands until the iterations are terminated and the solution achieved.

The authority informs the two firms of these (temporary) charges. Thus the first firm has as its maximization problem

219

(32) $$\max_{q_1, x_2} P_1 = p_1 q_1 - C_1(q_1, x_2) - \lambda_1(0)q_1 + \lambda_2(0)x_2$$

so that the payments associated with the externalities are incorporated into its problem as was indicated in the above remarks. Let $q_1(1)$ and $x_2(1)$ represent respectively the values of q_1 and x_2 which are the solution to (32). Similarly, the second firm has the problem

(33) $$\max_{q_2, x_1} P_2 = p_2 q_2 - C_2(q_2, x_1) + \lambda_1(0)x_1 - \lambda_2(0)q_2,$$

and let $q_2(1)$ and $x_1(1)$ represent respectively the values of q_2 and x_1 which are the solution to (33).

If $q_1(1) \neq x_1(1)$ or $q_2(1) \neq x_2(1)$, the authority continues with this iterative process. Suppose that after step $k-1$, $(k > 1)$, the authority determines that either $q_1(k-1) \neq x_1(k-1)$ or $q_2(k-1) \neq x_2(k-1)$ or both. Then the authority alters the per unit charges according to the following rule:

(34) $$\lambda_i(k) = \lambda_i(k-1) + \triangle \lambda_i(k-1); \quad i = 1, 2$$

where $\triangle \lambda_i(k-1)$ is defined as follows:

(35) $$\triangle \lambda_i(k-1) = \alpha_i \{q_i(k-1) - x_i(k-1)\}; \quad i = 1, 2$$

and α_i is a parameter satisfying $0 < \alpha_i < 1$. Note that if one firm desires the other to produce a larger output so that $q_i(k-1) < x_i(k-1)$ obtains, then (35) gives $\triangle \lambda_i(k-1) < 0$ and (34) gives $\lambda_i(k) < \lambda_i(k-1)$. In other words, the per unit payment, which the one firm must make to the other, is reduced accordingly. The developments (36) and (37) below should make clear that in this situation $q_i(k) > q_i(k-1)$ and $x_i(k) < x_i(k-1)$ are expected. Similarly, if one firm desires the other to produce a smaller output so that $q_i(k-1) > x_i(k-1)$ obtains, then $\triangle \lambda_i(k-1) > 0$ and $\lambda_i(k) > \lambda_i(k-1)$. The developments (36) and (37) below indicate that in this situation $q_i(k) < q_i(k-1)$ and $x_i(k) > x_i(k-1)$ are expected. Finally, observe that if one firm desires the other actually to produce the proposed output so that $q_i(k-1) = x_i(k-1)$, then (35) gives $\triangle \lambda_i(k-1) = 0$ and (34) indicates $\lambda_i(k) = \lambda_i(k-1)$.

Granted the authority's computation of the charges $\lambda_i(k)$, the first firm solves the problem

(36) $$\max_{q_1, x_2} P_1 = p_1 q_1 - C_1(q_1, x_2) - \lambda_1(k)q_1 + \lambda_2(k)x_2,$$

and the second firm solves

(37) $$\max_{q_2, x_1} P_2 = p_2 q_2 - C_2(q_2, x_1) + \lambda_1(k)x_1 - \lambda_2(k)q_2;$$

and those solutions are reported to the authority.

This iterative process continues until at some step t, $q_1(t) = x_1(t)$ and $q_2(t) = x_2(t)$. At this point the constraints to (30) are satisfied, a solution to (30) is at hand and, therefore, the solution to (26) is determined with $q_1(t) = q^*_1$ and $q_2(t) = q^*_2$. In other words, the solution is Pareto optimal. The authority now enforces the payments between the firms.

Note now the informational requirements of this proposal. Since the joint maximization problem (30) is decomposable, each firm is required to know only its own cost curve and the price of its output.

Similarly, the governmental authority does not need to have a knowledge of the cost curves of the two firms. It simply adjusts the per unit charges according to the stated rules. It follows that, in terms of the informational requirements, this scheme is a decentralized one. In view of the well known fact that it is difficult to obtain accurate knowledge of cost functions, this appears to be a major advantage for this proposal.

It also should be pointed out again that this proposal provides a method of getting around the problems of uncertainty which are created by non-separable and reciprocal externalities.[20] The simple device of defining the variables x_1 and x_2, and giving the respective firms authority to determine the desired values of these variables, makes it possible for the decision-makers to operate in the realm of certainty rather than uncertainty. It will be recalled that the uncertainty created by non-separable and reciprocal externalities caused additional informational requirements to be placed upon the authority which operated the traditional Pigovian tax-subsidy scheme. Essentially, the uncertainty made it necessary for the authority to know the strategic decision rules of the managers in order to predict how they would react to the imposition of taxes and subsidies. This new proposal avoids the entire problem and removes the informational requirements by eliminating the uncertainty.

Finally, it should be observed that, should this proposal be placed in operation, the passage of time is likely to be accompanied by alterations in the values of such parameters as output and input prices and the technologies of the firms. These alterations are likely to make it desirable to recompute the values of the per unit charges. However, under this proposal the authority is not required to make continual observations to determine when such alterations occur. Instead, the firm "suffering" under the externality should observe that the output of the other firm is not at the desired level. Thus it has a natural incentive to go to the authority and request that the per unit charges be recomputed.

IV. CONCLUDING COMMENTS

It should be obvious, of course, that this new proposal is not offered here as "the solution" to the externality problem. The discussion in Section I indicates that other policy alternatives (such as merger, bargaining or the re-definition of property rights) may be more appropriate in certain situations, and these alternatives should be considered when policy is formulated. It is hoped, however, that this new proposal can be added to the set of existing alternatives as soon as certain questions concerning its operation are answered. Conditions sufficient to insure the convergence of this small-step iterative procedure are well known; however, it is important to know the speed with which convergence takes place under various conditions. While nothing is known about this at present, it is conjectured that convergence is faster if the externalities are separable and not mutual, and slower if they are non-separable and reciprocal. Further, if the convergence of the algorithm is judged to be too slow, then one might consider truncating the process before too much time has elapsed but, hopefully, very near to the optimum. It appears that a computer simulation might be very helpful in throwing light on questions such as these.

Finally, the question of whether the firms have sufficient motivation to give "honest" answers must be faced.[21] It might be argued, for example, that the firms surely know the object of the exercise and have a motivation to "bluff" in hope of obtaining a better solution from their private point of view. This possibility raises a host of complex issues for which completely satisfactory answers are not available. However, in this instance bluffing does not seem to be a likely possibility unless firms are willing to operate in " non-equilibrium" positions.

For the purpose of argument, consider the case in which $\partial C_2/\partial q_1 > 0$ for all q_1 so that we have an external diseconomy. Certainly, at the outset it will be found that $q_1(0) > x_1(0)$ so that a charge $\lambda_1(0) > 0$ results from (31). Now the first firm desires to have the final (equilibrium) charge as small as possible. However, this firm can reduce the charge (or prevent it from increasing as much as it otherwise would) only by proposing to produce at some step k a quantity $\bar{q}_1^{(k)}$ which is smaller than its profit maximizing output $q_1(k)$ which is the solution to (36). Consequently, at any final step the firm must find itself in a nonoptimal position given the computed per unit charge. Similar remarks apply to the second firm and for the case of an external economy. Therefore, firms can engage in successful bluffing only if they are willing to operate in such "non equilibrium" positions.

Next, observe that under conditions of suitable regularity, problem (30) has a unique solution. Consequently, if one of the firms did decide to bluff and departed from rule (36) or (37), then it could obtain a private gain only by imposing a "penalty" on the other firm. Therefore, the latter firm has motivation to challenge the former firm's "good faith" if the institutional arrangements allow such an action. Let the proposal be supplemented by making it illegal for firms to engage in "bluffing", giving participating firms the right of challenge, requiring the authority to conduct an audit of any firm so challenged, and providing severe penalities if the charge of bluffing is substantiated. Such an arrangement would seem to provide firms' motivation to bargain in "good faith" and would call upon the authority to obtain information about the cost functions only in the event of a challenge.

Finally, it merits pointing out that one of the purposes of this article is to emphasize the serious and practical nature of the "modern old counter-attack"[22] on the notion that Pigovian taxes and subsidies are a panacea for externality problems. Perhaps, unlike what is suggested by Wellisz, it is because economists have held to a pat and incomplete answer that administrators, rather than economists, have been the men who attempt to deal with these problems. It seems that much research is needed, with at least one eye looking at the practical aspects of the various possible proposals, before the economist will be competent to give much in the way of serious advice on externality problems.

NOTES

[1] This research was supported both by a grant from Resources for the Future to the Graduate School of Industrial Administration, Carnegie Institute of Technology, and by the Thomas Jefferson Centre for Studies in Political Economy, University of Virginia. The authors are indebted to Professors James M. Buchanan, University of Virginia, W. Craig Stubblebine, University of Delaware, and Charles R. Plott, Purdue University, for helpful comments and constructive criticisms. Only the authors are responsible for errors.

[2] Wellisz is mainly concerned with the following papers: Buchanan and Stubblebine [2], Coase [3], Davis and Whinston [4], and Turvey [12]. References in square brackets are listed on p. 318.

[3] For an excellent survey of most of the recent developments concerning the " externality problem ", see the provocative paper of Mishan [11].

[4] The terminology is that of Wellisz [13], p. 345.

[5] Wellisz [13], p. 361.

[6] See, e.g., Davis and Whinston [5, 6].

[7] For critical discussion of the use of standards when the externalities arise from water pollution, see the excellent book of Kneese [10].

[8] Wellisz [13], p. 353.

[9] See Davis and Whinston [7].

[10] Wellisz [13], p. 355.

[11] A function h is separable if and only if $h(x_1, \ldots, x_n) = h_1(x_1) + \ldots + h_n(x_n)$.

[12] See, e.g., the first essay in Koopmans [9].

[13] See, e.g., Davis and Whinston [8].

[14] See footnote 1 in Wellisz [13], p. 359. It also should be mentioned that the analysis in [4] does not attempt to prove that it is " impossible " (this is the term of Wellisz) to devise a Pigovian scheme; but only that the level of difficulty is much higher, requiring a knowledge of the psychologies of the managers, when reciprocal non-separable externalities are present and the governmental authority uses the natural computational procedure.

[15] Wellisz's development of his proposal is found in [13], pp. 357–359.

[16] We are indebted to Charles Plott for this point.

[17] No subscripts are placed on the K's here since, in this example, both are required to take on the same value for an optimum to be achieved.

[18] These expressions should make clear the earlier remarks concerning the restrictions on the domains if the functions are to be single-valued. Note that expressions (21) are valid if and only if q_1 and q_2 are chosen so that (18) is satisfied.

[19] It is interesting to note, since the footnote, Wellisz [13], p. 357, asserts that the results on non-separable externalities of Davis and Whinston [4] imply the impossibility of devising a transfer pricing scheme for a divisionalised firm, that this scheme originally was developed by one of the authors for divisionalised firms. See Whinston [14, 15] and also Baumol and Fabian [1].

[20] See Davis and Whinston [4].

[21] We are indebted to one of the referees for raising this question. It also is appropriate to note the competitive setting of the proposal. While the scheme can be applied in the case of monopolistic firms, the resulting solutions need not (and in general will not) be Pareto optimal due to unregulated monopoly power.

[22] The terminology is that of Wellisz [13], p. 362.

REFERENCES

[1] Baumol, W. J. and Fabian, T., " Decomposition, Pricing for Decentralization and External Economies ", *Management Science*, September 1964, pp. 1–32.

[2] Buchanan, J. M. and Stubblebine, W. C., " Externality ", *Economica*, November 1962, pp. 371–84.

[3] Coase, R., " The Problem of Social Cost ", *Journal of Law and Economics*, October 1960, pp. 1–44.

[4] Davis, O. A. and Whinston, A. B., " Externalities, Welfare, and the Theory of Games ", *Journal of Political Economy*, June 1962, pp. 241–62.

[5] ——, " The Economics of Complex Systems : The Case of Municipal Zoning ", *Kyklos*, September 1964, pp. 419–46.

[6] ——, " The Economics of Urban Renewal ", *Law and Contemporary Problems*, Winter 1961, pp. 105–17.

[7] ——, " Some Notes on Equating Private and Social Cost ", *Southern Economic Journal*, October 1965, pp. 113–126.

[8] ——, " Welfare Economics and the Theory of Second Best ", *Review of Economic Studies*, January 1965, pp. 1–16.

[9] Koopmans, T. C., *Three Essays on the State of Economic Science*, New York, 1960.

[10] Kneese, A. V., *The Economics of Regional Water Quality Management*, Baltimore, 1964.

[11] Mishan, E. J., " Reflections on Recent Developments in the Concept of External Effects ", *Canadian Journal of Economics and Political Science*, February 1965, pp. 3–34.

[12] Turvey, R., " On Divergencies between Social Cost and Private Cost ", *Economica*, August 1963, pp. 594–613.

[13] Wellisz, S., " On External Diseconomies and the Government-Assisted Invisible Hand ", *Economica*, November 1964, pp. 345–62.

[14] Whinston, A. B., " Price Coordination in Decentralized Systems " (Unpublished Ph.D. dissertation) O.N.R. Research Memorandum No. 99 (Ditto), Carnegie Institute of Technology, Graduate School of Industrial Administration, Pittsburgh, June 1962.

[15] ——, " Price Guides in Decentralized Organization ", in William W. Cooper, Harold J. Leavitt, and Maynard W., Shelly II, eds., *New Perspectives in Organization Research*, New York, 1964.

Contracting Cost and Public Policy

By HAROLD DEMSETZ

Harold Demsetz is Professor of Economics at the Graduate School of Business, University of Chicago.

Like externalities, decreasing costs, and uncertainty, the existence of transaction or contracting costs is a factor to be considered in resolving the question of the efficient mix of private and public sector activities. As Professor Demsetz points out, the primary test for determining whether the market system attains an efficient allocation of resources is whether or not in particular instances it can establish voluntary agreement among parties to an exchange.

Among the prominent costs of contracting are the costs of search and negotiation and the cost of insuring that voluntary agreements are honored. However, while there are significant transaction costs in the private sector, the allocation of resources to the Government also entails costs and inefficiencies. For one thing, allocation by Government substitutes compulsion by law for voluntary consent. Moreover, when the Government allocates resources, the criterion for decisionmaking may well not be consistent with efficiency. Professor Demsetz concludes that "It may be useful to give the Government the responsibility and incentives for allocating resources where contracting cost looms relatively large. But a bigger improvement * * * may be achievable if the Government * * * eliminates many of the legal restrictions and institutional procedures that presently raise the cost of contracting."

Introduction

This essay is related to the larger and more difficult problem of specifying the conditions under which it seems proper to rely on Government to allocate resources, a problem that is difficult for two primary reasons. First, persons who agree on the results that will be produced if either the Government or the market is chosen to resolve the allocation problem may yet disagree on the alternative they prefer because their personal values weigh important outcomes differently; in particular they may place different weights on the value of preserving a style of life in which voluntary agreements play a large role. Secondly, our knowledge of the workings of political systems, and to a much lesser extent of economic systems, is still too meager to produce widespread agreement on just what will be the outcome if either the Government or the market is relied upon to allocate resources.

Reprinted by permission of the author: Harold Demsetz, "Contracting Costs and Public Policy," The Analysis and Evaluation of Public Expenditures: The PPB System, Vol. 1, Joint Committee Print, 91st Congress, 1st Session (Washington, D.C., 1969), pp. 167-174.

We do have a better understanding of this important problem now than 20 or 30 years ago, and I trust that 10 years from now we will be still more confident that we know the answers. But the present state of the analysis is such that the most useful procedure is to discuss a few of the factors that now seem destined to play important roles in resolving the problem of the efficient private-public mix without presuming to know what is the proper resolution. Contracting cost, or as it is sometimes called, transaction cost, one of the more important and neglected of the factors determining this mix, is discussed in this paper.

Much of the discussion by economists of the proper role of Government implicitly accepts the notion that economic efficiency is the tion in which it is possible to exclude one's neighbors from benefiting from the installation of an effective antimissile missile. The cost of excluding nonpurchasers from benefiting is so great that if the purchase of such missiles is left to private individuals all are likely to wait for their neighbors to make the purchase. But if the cost of excluding nonpurchasers is low, the case for allocation by Government is weakened. It may be possible for an additional moviegoer to enjoy viewing a film once that film is being shown to one moviegoer. The viewing of the film is a public good but, because the cost of excluding nonpurchasers is small, this public good can be produced efficiently through markets. All who wish to see the film can be required to pay to view it or forgo the benefits of being admitted to the theater, unlike all who benefit from the installation of a missile. By such exclusion the market can estimate the value, through the sum of the entrance fees collected, of diverting resources from other uses to the production of theaters and films. If the cost of contracting is zero, including the cost of enforcing the contractual agreements, it is possible to collect fees (which may differ from person to person) that give good estimates of the value on the margin of the benefits achievable by expanding the viewing audience and/or the theater.

What allocation of resources is efficient depends in part on underlying contracting cost conditions. One resource allocation, reached through voluntary agreement in the marketplace, will be efficient if contracting costs are zero. A different allocation, reached in the same way, will be efficient if contracting costs are positive, since under this cost condition it no longer is efficient to exploit all exchange opportunities. The gains from exchange that remain unexploited when contracting costs are positive must be of smaller value than the contracting costs or further trading would be undertaken for profit. Thus the reduction in economic value that might be associated with an externality or a monopoly must be less than the cost of contracting; if the loss in economic value were larger, agreements would be made between those involved to reallocate resources so as to reduce the loss in value to the cost of contracting.

If the Government can make some good guesses as to which voluntary exchanges fail to take place because contracting costs are positive, and if it can make these guesses and accomplish the reallocation at lower costs than the contracting costs involved, then it is possible for the Government to improve on the market's allocation of resources. The word "possible" is important in the previous sentence because the incentives provided by the political system may be such that the Government will fail to accomplish the desirable reallocations and may even substitute undesirable reallocations. A Government agency or department usually is made responsible for supplying goods through the Government. These agencies, for political reasons, may put too many or too few resources into the directions that resource reallocation would take if contracting cost were lower. That Government agencies will make the proper decisions does not follow from the fact that governmental reallocation costs are lower than contracting cost.

Little is known about the factors influencing the level of contracting cost. It does not seem to be true that the cost of contracting necessarily rises, per dollar exchanged, as the number of transactions increases. objective sought, where efficiency is interpreted in a much broader sense than the commonly understood engineering concept with the same name. I shall not delve deeply into the technical fine points of the economist's notion of efficiency. For most practical purposes the criterion of efficiency can be defined as the maximization of the total value of economic activity. The components that make up the value of economic activity are not always *recorded* in the market place although they are *measured* through individual decisions in the market place. The distinction between recorded and measured deserves closer examination to show the weight given to the nonpecuniary aspects of life by the efficiency criterion.

An employer sometimes will seek to have some of his employees work overtime. If such work is not a part of the normally understood contractual relationships between the employer and his workers, he will offer an incentive, usually financial, to overcome their reluctance to work overtime. Some of his workers will place small value on the nonpecuniary advantages of enjoying additional leisure time and some will place high value, and, therefore, some will elect to accept the offered financial incentive and others will choose to forego the additional income in order to enjoy more leisure.

Those who choose not to work, place a higher pecuniary value on nonpecuniary leisure than on the financial incentive being offered by their employer. The economic value of the use of their time, as these workers see it, is higher if they reject their employer's offer. The fact that these employees voluntarily have chosen to spend this time at leisure is the only generally accepted standard of evidence that they believe they are better off. This *measurement* of alternatives offered in the market place coupled with voluntary decisions allow one to make deductions about the efficiency of resource allocation.

Can we reach the same conclusion if the problem is viewed from the employer's side? The employer could have secured voluntary consent from this subgroup of workers to work overtime by increasing the financial incentive he offers to them. If he values their overtime labor more than they value their leisure, he would have found it to his advantage to increase sufficiently the financial incentive offered to them to gain their voluntary consent to overtime. The fact that he has not succeeded in negotiating such an agreement is taken to mean that the workers value their leisure more than their employer values their extra work, and hence, that it is efficient for them to stay home even though this may reduce the *recorded* values of their earnings and output.

In the same way, the voluntary acceptance of overtime by the second

227

subgroup of workers allows us to deduce that the value the employer attaches to their extra labor exceeds the value they place on their leisure; in this instance, the recorded value of wages (and output) increases.

In this manner, voluntary negotiations in the market place, whether an exchange is concluded, as with the second subgroup of workers, or is not concluded and not recorded, as with the first subgroup, lead to a maximization of economic value and to efficiency. Nonpecuniary aspects of the alternatives are not ignored but are directly included in this concept of efficiency.

But if the Government seeks to realine resources through compulsion by law, the test of voluntary consent is largely forsaken. Thus, in the marketplace persons can decide on a voluntary basis whether or not they want to purchase automobile safety devices. If, however, a law requiring such devices is adopted, we no longer have the test of voluntary consent to help assure us that many individuals view the extra safety as worth the extra cost. Some persons may have preferred to economize on these safety devices and to divert the savings realized to other uses, many of which might increase safety in other directions, such as buying new automobiles more frequently than will be true if persons are forced to invest large amounts in safety devices. In effect, such a law is a tax levied to promote the purchase of certain types of safety equipment by all new-car drivers.

Precisely because the test of voluntary agreement is lacking it is desirable to undertake special investigations of the cost-benefit variety to help insure against errors. These investigations can provide much useful information to guide such Government decisions. Nonetheless, they still suffer from the absence of the test of voluntary agreement. Suppose that we are interested in determining how much the State should spend on automobile safety devices. To answer this question we can calculate the cost of an additional safety device and compare it to the value of the lives we expect it to save. If we are sophisticated, we can calculate this latter value by multiplying the expected decrease in deaths by the value of a typical live person. The value of a typical live person is frequently taken to depend on the discounted value of that portion of his earnings that an accidental death will eliminate.

Setting aside for the moment problems of externalities, the difficulty with this analysis is that the correct solution will be to equate the additional cost of safety devices to the price that persons are willing to pay for expected reductions in their accident rate. This *price* will be an individual matter. It will depend on a person's demand to live longer, on his income, on the prices of other things, and on his *taste for life*. The latter fact is knowable only to himself in principle and, although it will be revealed through negotiation in the marketplace, it is only approximated by a sophisticated cost-benefit analysis. A poor man may be willing to pay a higher price than a rich man for additional expected years of life, especially if he has a greater fear of hell.

The type of error most likely to filter through cost-benefit analyses is the prescription of too much uniformity. For example, the efficiency of having various kinds of safety devices on automobiles is likely to vary considerably between rural and urban areas and between expressway and local driving. Drivers whose driving circumstances differ will generally find different kinds and quantities of safety devices desirable. The cost-benefit approach could in principle distinguish between many such circumstances, but the finer the distinctions the more expensive will be the analysis and the implementation of its conclusions, and the smaller will be the saving associated with compulsion. It is difficult to see just how nonmarket allocation can be achieved at governmental cost less than contracting cost without relying on a more uniform treatment of individuals than is found in the marketplace. An outstanding example of this is the requirement to install smog-reducing devices in all automobiles. Persons residing away from a few major metropolitan areas are unlikely to benefit significantly from these devices, yet all are required to purchase them with their automobiles.

The second reason that the likelihood of error is increased when nonmarket allocation techniques are selected is that the criterion for decisionmaking brought into play is not necessarily consistent with efficiency. Aside from problems of monopoly in Government or of errors in calculation, in a one-man, one-vote democracy, where votes are not for sale, the polling place will generate information that tends to be based on majoritarian principles rather than on efficiency principles. Thus, suppose some citizens prefer a stronger national defense but that a majority prefer a weaker defense. Left to a vote, the weaker defense will be our chosen policy even though the minority is willing to pay more than the additional cost required to bring defense up to the level they desire (and so, if possible, they may hire private police services). An error in the opposite direction is also possible. The majority of voters may approve of a large space effort even though they would not be able to bid high enough to acquire these resources for space in the absence of forced tax contributions. (Here, however, the minority cannot privately adjust.) It may be that to some extent coalition and logrolling guide majority voting toward more efficient results than would be true with simple majority politics.[1]

The importance of contracting cost in the determination of proper Government policy is revealed by considering the operation of an economic system in which contracting costs are assumed to be zero. Of course, this is an unrealistic assumption just as is the assumption that firms know for a certainty the cost and demand conditions they face. The assumption is useful only because it allows us to grasp the critical role played by contracting cost. That the usual sources of inefficiency fail to exist if contracting costs are zero is described briefly below.*

Externalities.—Persons subjected to harmful effects can, at zero contracting cost, collect payments for bearing these effects and this will lead to an appropriate economizing of the production of these effects. As has been shown by R. H. Coase,[2] divergencies between private and social cost cannot exist in a regime of zero contracting cost. Similarly, those who benefit from what might otherwise be external benefits will pay for such benefits.

In a world of zero contracting cost, the allocation of resources is left unaffected by the assignment of liability for costs. Table 1 shows the costs and returns from operating two enterprises if no damaging interaction is present. Suppose now that some change in the environment, such as a shift in wind, causes the proximity of the two enterprises to result in the suffering of damages equal to $50 by the marginal firm. If the marginal enterprise is left to bear this cost its revenues fall to zero and its inputs shift to other uses where, according to their opportunity costs, they will receive $50. The advent of the damage makes the marginal enterprise submarginal if it must bear the damage cost.

TABLE 1

Marginal enterprise:		Intramarginal enterprise:	
Opportunity cost	$50	Opportunity cost	$100
Revenue	50	Revenue	125

But if the intramarginal enterprise is made liable for the damage the same allocation consequences will follow. Given the $50 damage, if the marginal firm receives full reparation it will still just break even; it will be no better or worse than before the change in environment. Clearly, however, it will be in both parties' interest if the intramarginal enterprise paid some amount less than $50 to the marginal enterprise to induce the marginal enterprise's resources to shift to other work. For example, a payment of $5 certainly reduces the cost to the intramarginal firm and, since the marginal firm's inputs can earn $50 elsewhere, they will gain $5 more than could be made by remaining. Hence, whichever form of liability rule is adopted, the allocation of resources remains unaffected. Of course, this conclusion does not follow necessarily if contracting costs are positive.

Monopoly.—It is well known from the standard treatment of monopoly that output is kept below its efficient level in order to maintain price. But if contracting costs are zero it is possible for both the monopolist and his customers to negotiate to expand output to the efficient level. Since the efficient output level yields the maximum economic value of the resources employed by the monopolist, its production yields the biggest possible pie for all concerned to share. In a regime of zero contracting cost the problem of monopoly is not one of inefficiency but one of equity—what share of this pie is captured by the firm and what share by the customers.

Economies of scale.—The above argument applies equally well to "natural monopoly" situations—situations in which one firm can produce all relevant output rates more cheaply than two or more firms. But, in addition, if contracting costs are zero it is possible to negotiate costlessly with competing bidders for the contract.[3] Even though only one such bidder will win the contract under conditions of scale economies, his monopoly power is eliminated by the competition in bidding. Furthermore, zero contracting cost allows the use of sophisticated pricing techniques, such as multipart tariffs, in the bidding process. These will yield outputs consistent with marginal cost pricing.

Public goods.—If contracts can be costlessly enforced to prevent nonpurchasers from enjoying the benefits of what others have purchased, the implication of private production of public goods is not inefficiency but only that all who derive benefit can do so more cheaply if they contribute to the cost of producing the good. Anyone who does not pay for the good can be excluded from its use and, so, all who benefit will find it in their interest to contribute to its production. A distinction must be made between public goods subject to high contracting cost and those subject to low contracting cost. It is difficult to envision a situa-

There is evidence that the unit cost of contracting falls as the number of transactions increase for certain important goods—those traded on the organized stock and commodity exchanges.[4] In other cases the unit cost of contracting seems to be subject to constant return to scale conditions—retail trading. Where the cost of excluding nonpurchasers from benefiting from the purchases of others is high for technological reasons, such as in the provision of national defense or the establishment of a uniform currency and set of measures and weights, the case for allocation through Government is improved. But often the costs of contracting are high for institutional and legal reasons and not for technological reasons. Usury laws raise the cost of contracting for some loans above the costs associated with the technology of borrowing and lending. Minimum wage laws raise the cost to employers of contracting to employ low-productivity workers. Legal restrictions on entry into occupations and businesses raise the cost to outsiders of contracting with those who would find their services desirable.

Often, property owned by the Government is treated as though it were communal property—all citizens are given a right to use the resourse, say a lake or a road, and no one effectively has the right to exclude others from using the resource. The cost of contracting to prevent congestion and overintensive use of the resource is raised unnecessarily in these instances since a simultaneous decision to reduce usage is required of a large number of prospective users, none of whom can be excluded legally. No one can legally purchase the rights of use from others and, therefore, all are inclined to treat a scarce resource as if it were a free good. A State-owned forest for which the State collects no fee or only a small fee for cutting rights is likely to be cut over too quickly. The same would, of course, be true for a privately owned forest but the private owner's incentives are such that it is unlikely that he will allow much free cutting. *To achieve an efficient allocation of resources, it is necessary for someone,* the Government or private individuals, *to prevent others from using scarce resources as if they were free goods.* This can be accomplished by assessing a proper fee for the use of the resource, but for the cost of contracting to be reduced sufficiently to allow such exclusion to take place it must be possible legally to exclude a nonpurchaser from the use of the resource.

From the viewpoint of efficiency, it may be useful to give the Government the responsibility and incentives for allocating resources where contracting cost looms relatively large. But a bigger improvement in resource allocation may be achievable if the Government reconsiders and eliminates many of the legal restrictions and institutional procedures that presently raise the cost of contracting, sometimes by imposing prohibitions on productive activities.

It should be noted that the decisions made in the market place might be different if wealth were distributed differently, since different distributions of wealth give rise to different demands. In addition, the legal and social norms used by a society will influence the decisions taken in the marketplace. If the law throws bankrupts into jail, a different set of voluntary decisions will be made in incurring debt than will be made if the law merely lets bankrupts bear the mark of poor credit risks. But even if the good wealth distribution and the good social and legal norms are specified, the primary test for efficient allocation remains voluntary agreement.

But what can be concluded if the prospective costs of contracting loom large relative to the prospective gain from such negotiation? All that can be deduced within the framework of the usual criterion for efficiency is that it is inefficient to explore further through market channels these particular exchange opportunities.

The potentiality for beneficially altering the allocation of resources through nonmarket techniques is small the lower is the cost of contracting relative to the gains from trade because such gains are most likely to be exploited through private agreements to voluntarily alter resource allocation. Benefits from the use of nonmarket techniques potentially seem greatest where the cost of contracting is relatively large providing, of course, that the cost of using nonmarket techniques is lower than the contracting cost required by market negotiations.

The cost of contracting can be taken to include the costs of search and negotiation in the market place and the cost of insuring that voluntary agreements are honored. The cost of contracting is the value placed by markets on the resources used to make markets work; it is the cost of utilizing voluntary agreements to resolve the problems that arise from competing claims for scarce resources as this cost is measured in the market place.

Nonmarket allocation devices will, of course, have costs of their own.[*] If taxes are used, there is the cost of collecting and enforcing tax payments. Governmental costs of searching for and administering potentially benefical resource reallocations must be incurred. Nonmarket devices are subject to special errors, as discussed below, and these impose yet more costs on the use of such devices.

Probably the two most important differences between reallocation through the market and through the Government are: (1) The Government need not and does not incur costs to secure the consent of many who will be affected by the resource reallocations; if such costs were incurred, there would be little potentiality for Government reallocation cost to be smaller than contracting cost. (2) There is a greater likelihood of error from the viewpoint of efficiency in reallocating resources through nonmarket techniques. The two sources of this error are the absence of the requirement of voluntary consent on the part of many who are affected and the greater likelihood of a divergence between efficient decisions and politically viable decisions. These two sources of error are briefly discussed below.

The test of voluntary consent, we have seen, is the filter that separates and selects efficient resource allocations from inefficient ones.

NOTES

[1] On this point see James M. Buchanan and Gordon Tullock, *The Calculus of Consent* (The University of Michigan Press, 1962).

[2] R. H. Coase, "The Problem of Social Cast," *The Journal of Law and Economics* (1960), 1–44. Also, H. Demsetz, "The Exchange and Enforcement of Property Rights," *The Journal of Law & Economics* (1964), 11–26.

[*] The reader will find detailed treatment of the traditional sources of inefficiency elsewhere in these essays. This discussion proceeds on the assumption that the reader is familiar with these. See especially the papers in Part I of this volume.

[3] An extended discussion of the absence of a theory of natural monopoly can be found in my paper "Why Regulate Utilities?" *The Journal of Law & Economics* (April 1968), pp. 55–66.

⁴ See, H. Demsetz, "The Cost of Transacting," *The Quarterly Journal of Economics* (February 1968), pp. 33–53.

*For further discussion of this issue, see the paper by Krutilla in this volume.

PART V
EXTERNALITIES: COLLECTIVE
DECISION-MAKING AND POLICY
Section A: The Tax-Subsidy Alternative

One of several policy devices suggested as useful in influencing resource user choices, where these choices induce external costs and benefits, is tax-subsidy schemes. The series of articles in this section is intended to give the reader insights into the following dimensions of these tax-subsidy schemes: legal arrangements, operational problems concerning the requisite information, per-unit tax and Pareto optimality, a tax on outputs or inputs, and market structure differences.

The article "On the Theory of Optimum Externality" by F. Trenery Dolbear, Jr., sets up a series of comments by E. J. Mishan and Mark V. Pauly with a reply from Dolbear. Dolbear's use of indifference curve analysis explicitly reveals that different legal rights do matter as to the amount of externality. Information problems and/or a per-unit tax that will exactly compensate for damages may not in general achieve a Pareto optimum. The comment by E. J. Mishan is a modified treatment of Dolbear's argument and uses marginal curves instead of indifference and transformation curves. Changes in "welfare levels" brought about by distributional effects of a constant excise tax or subsidy are discussed. Mark V. Pauly's comment discusses the assumption of increasing marginal disutility in an externality situation. This assumption is critical in proposing a *constant* tax as a corrective device for an externality that is yielding an *increasing* marginal disutility. Pauly also discusses this assumption in relationship to cases where the externality may be decreased at constant marginal costs. Dolbear's reply to the comments gives further insight into the tax-subsidy scheme and lump-sum transfers so as to achieve a Pareto optimum.

"Externalities and Corrective Taxes," by Charles R. Plott, bears on the aspect of corrective taxes on outputs or inputs. Plott concludes that the traditional corrective tax on output is not a general case and would require explicit assumptions and qualifications, and without these, the traditional prescriptions are in error. Lowell R. Bassett and Thomas E. Borcherding's comment to Plott's argument is that he fails to consider long-run adjustments in the industry which may make the corrective tax on output a more general case than the short-run analysis of the firm would suggest.

Finally, James M. Buchanan deals with another aspect of corrective taxes which traditionally has largely been ignored. The traditional arguments have dealt with externalities in a competitive model, while under a monopolistic model corrective taxes may lead to a reduction in welfare rather than an increase.

The reader will encounter more of the tax-subsidy arguments in subsequent articles; it is hoped that this section will provide a deeper insight into this traditional policy prescription for coping with real world externalities.

On the Theory of Optimum Externality

By F. TRENERY DOLBEAR, JR.

The author, assistant professor of economics at Carnegie Institute of Technology, is at the Graduate School of Business, Stanford University, 1966–67. He would like to acknowledge the helpful comments of William Brainard, Michael Lovell, Morton Kamien and a referee. This research was partially supported by a grant from Resources for the Future, Inc.

Modern welfare economics has established the Pareto optimal properties of a competitive economic system which satisfies such customary requirements as convexity and the absence of externalities. A frequent problem of the welfare economist is: Given all of the *other* requirements for Pareto optimality, how can a situation characterized by the presence of an externality be altered so as to produce a Pareto optimum? In the discussion which follows we will, for convenience, presume an external diseconomy.

Most of the formal analysis on externalities has been concerned with relationships between firms;[1] in this paper the actors will be consumers. As a result our analysis will be derived from the theory of consumer behavior instead of the theory of the firm. Although space limitations prohibit a detailed comparison, some of the results will be sensitive to this distinction since the usual welfare objective of maximizing joint profits subject to price parameters cannot be carried over to consumers without interpersonal comparisons of utility.

The occurrence of an external diseconomy will, in general, lead to a discrepancy between marginal *social* net benefit and cost. It is often presumed that a single device such as a per unit tax or individual negotiations can be used to correct the inequality.[2] While one of these prescriptions may improve the efficiency of the economic system, it will be argued here that it need not, in general, result in a Pareto optimum even if used in the best way.

It is sometimes presumed that the parcelling of legal responsibility[3]

Reprinted by permission of the publishers and author: F. Trenery Dolbear, Jr., "On the Theory of Optimum Externality," *American Economic Review*, 57 (March 1967), pp. 90-103.

does not affect the solution that market-bargaining forces will produce in the presence of an externality.[4] But we will show that where consumers are involved the amount of externality may be very much affected by legal matters.[5] Since changes in legal responsibility will alter the distribution of real income, there may be an "income effect" which will be of some consequence vis-à-vis the amount of externality. Of course, given a specific assessment of legal responsibility there may be a further income effect if the parties involved have opportunities to negotiate along the contract curve.

To illustrate these points we will resort to a highly simplified and somewhat artificial example involving two individuals X and Y. (The results will be extended to a world with m X-type individuals and n Y-type individuals in Section V.) It is hoped that the example will illustrate some difficulties which have been encountered in the analysis of real world problems.

I. A TRIANGULAR EDGEWORTH BOX

Presume two consumers, X and Y, who form a "community" in a large economic society. Both have simple consumption patterns. X lives by bread and heat; Y lives by bread alone. However, Y is so situated that he receives air pollution in the form of smoke produced by X's fire. We presume Y cannot—or at least that it is uneconomical to—move to a location which would escape X's smoke output. Further, X can only reduce the amount of smoke by decreasing heat.[6]

Our analysis will use indifference curves and budget lines. First, X has indifference curves for bread and heat which meet the usual requirements in the theory of consumer choice (Figure 1). On the other hand, Y has indifference curves for varying quantities of bread and smoke. They are also shown in Figure 1 and have the standard characteristic that the more bread and smoke Y has, the more bread he will trade for a given amount of smoke abatement. By construction we establish Y's smoke scale so that it corresponds precisely with X's heat scale.[7] For convenience in developing the argument below, Y's bread axis reads from top to bottom.

Given an X-Y *community* income endowment, the opportunity locus or budget line is shown as FF in Figure 2. The intercepts of budget line FF give the maximum amounts of bread *or* heat (smoke) which the community can purchase, and the slope of FF represents the ratio at which heat can be traded for bread. This price ratio between heat and bread is presumed to reflect society's opportunity cost in terms of bread of producing one unit more of heat (the marginal rate of transformation). We presume that variation in the amounts of bread and heat purchased' by X and Y will not affect this rate of transformation.

The triangle formed in Figure 2 by the two axes and budget line FF may be thought of as a type of Edgeworth box. The standard two-commodity, two-individual, rectangular Edgeworth box has several distinctive features. Any point in the box unambiguously defines quan-

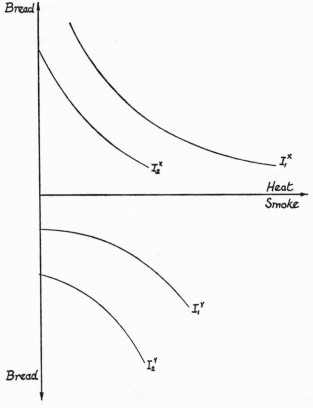

tities of each commodity for both individuals. Thus indifference curves for each individual can be transcribed into the box. The tangencies of these indifference curves provide the locus of efficient allocations, in the Pareto sense, between the two individuals (the contract curve). However, if the total quantities of the two commodities are variable, according to the marginal rate of transformation, the welfare implications of the contract curve do not hold.

In this example, where there is a one-to-one relationship between heat for X and smoke for Y, a construct similar to the Edgeworth box will be developed which in addition incorporates changes in the quantities of the commodities. (A decrease in heat—and thus smoke—means the community will buy more bread. The community's total bread consumption will increase according to the slope of FF.) Since tradeoffs between bread and heat are included, the Pareto welfare implications of the contract curve will be appropriate.

Suppose the consumption of the community is represented by (any) point P in Figure 2. Units of heat and bread for X are determined in the usual manner; thus X receives q units of heat and r units of bread. We require that X and Y exhaust all of their income—community consumption must lie on budget line FF. Y, then, receives q units of smoke and s units of bread. In other words, if we know the amount of bread and heat for X (represented by P), we immediately know the amount

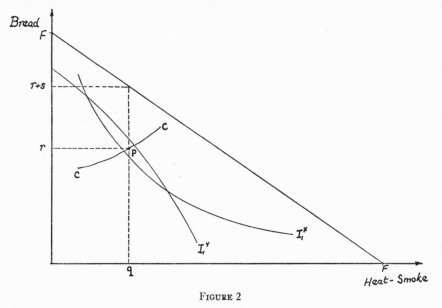

FIGURE 2

of smoke for Y (by reading off the heat-smoke axis) and also the (residual) amount of bread for Y (the vertical distance from point P to the community budget line FF.)

Since we have indicated how to read bread and heat (smoke) consumption for any point P in the triangular Edgeworth box, it is now possible to construct indifference curves in Figure 2 from those shown in Figure 1. First, we transfer X's indifference curves directly into the triangular Edgeworth box of Figure 2. Then, in effect we place Y's bread axis of Figure 1 on the bread axis of Figure 2—the origin is at the intersection of community budget line FF and the bread axis. We "fold-in" the smoke axis of Figure 1 so that it lies on the community budget line FF (again with the origin at the intersection of FF and the bread axis) and "stretch" the smoke axis so that it will correspond to the horizontal scale for heat and smoke for Figure 2. This will, of course, "fold-in" and "stretch" Y's indifference curves also, but they will retain the same general curvature as in Figure 1.

Y's Figure 2 indifference curves will be always steeper than FF since Y requires an increase in bread to compensate for an increase in smoke.

Further, since the more smoke Y has, the more bread Y will trade for a given amount of smoke abatement, the indifference curves must become steeper as Y gets more smoke. Y's indifference curve which has been transferred to Figure 2 may be seen to meet these requirements.

The reader should note that Y's Figure 2 "indifference curves" do not possess the usual property that the slope is the marginal rate of substitution. The algebraic slope of a Y indifference curve in Figure 1 is the negative of the marginal rate of substitution of smoke for bread at a given level of smoke and bread. A Figure 1 indifference curve with zero slope would have a slope in Figure 2 equal to the slope of the FF line, the marginal rate of transformation (MRT). This reflects the requirement that an increase in heat must be offset by a decrease in total community bread consumption. Consequently, the slope of an indifference curve for Y in Figure 2 in general will be $-MRS_{SB}^Y$ *plus MRT.*

Since X's indifference curves are convex to the origin and Y's indifference curves are concave to the origin (in Figure 2), tangencies of X and Y indifference curves will be Pareto optimal as in the standard Edgeworth box. Suppose, for example, that at point P, X is indifferent to trades at a rate of 5 breads for 1 heat; and Y is indifferent to trades at a rate of 2 breads and 1 smoke (heat). If the marginal rate of transformation is 3 breads for 1 heat, the indifference curves of X and Y are tangent since:

$$(1) \qquad MRS_{HB}^X = -MRS_{SB}^Y + MRT$$
$$-5 = -(+2) - 3.$$

It can be seen that no reallocation in consumption or production can make one consumer better off without making the other worse off. Thus P would be a Pareto optimum point.[8] In the triangular Edgeworth box of Figure 2, the contract curve (locus of Pareto optimal points) is labelled as cc.[9]

II. POSSIBLE SOLUTIONS

Now that we have indicated how to interpret the curves in Figure 2, we are ready to impose a distribution of money income between X and Y and consider several legal status quo or starting points which might obtain prior to any "negotiations" to ameliorate the effects of the externality. We will also consider the possible results of such negotiations. (In the next section we will examine government tax schemes designed to ameliorate the external effects.) In Figure 3 budget line GG reveals the distribution of money income between X and Y. X's money income will buy any combination of heat and bread represented by points on the GG line. Y's money income will buy a quantity of bread represented by the vertical distance between FF and GG.

The examples we will consider differ in several ways. First, the legal system might permit X to generate as much smoke as he wishes; at the

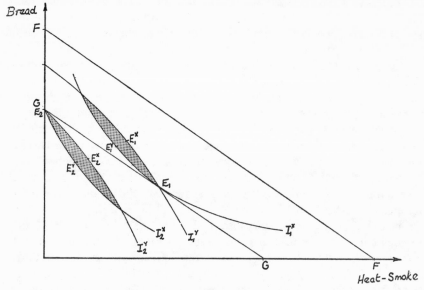

FIGURE 3

other extreme X might be prohibited from generating smoke without Y's permission. Second, given a legal starting point, all of the gains from amelioration of external effects could accrue either to X or to Y. We will consider only "polar" cases; in so doing we will bracket the results which might obtain from intermediate cases.

Initially, we suppose a world in which X has the legal right to generate as much smoke as he wishes. In this case X, who independently maximizes his satisfaction, will be at E_1 on I_1^X (Figure 3). Y will be at E_1 on I_1^Y where he spends all of his money income on bread—the vertical distance between (parallel) budget lines FF and GG—and receives gratuitously smoke from X's fire. Since I_1^X will be tangent to GG while I_1^Y must be everywhere steeper than GG, the two indifference curves cannot be tangent. Thus E_1 will not be Pareto optimal.

The shaded area between I_1^X and I_1^Y is, for the E_1 starting point, the "area of possibilities"; it includes all solutions which will not decrease the satisfaction of either consumer. In this area the contract curve is bounded by E_1^X and E_1^Y where all the gains from amelioration of the externality accrue to X and Y respectively.

Now suppose a world which prohibits X from generating smoke without an agreement with Y. Here X and Y will, in the absence of such an agreement, start on indifference curves I_2^X and I_2^Y at the intersection of budget line GG and the bread axis (E_2). This starting point reflects the prohibition of heat (smoke) production; both X and Y are spending all of their incomes on bread. If I_2^X lies above I_2^Y everywhere but at E_2, then

242

E_2 is a Pareto optimal corner solution. But if $I_2{}^x$ is below $I_2{}^Y$ in the neighborhood of E_2, E_2 will not be Pareto optimal.

For this starting point, the shaded area between $I_2{}^x$ and $I_2{}^Y$ is the area of possibilities. The contract curve in this region is bounded by $E_2{}^x$ and $E_2{}^Y$ where all the gains from amelioration of the externality accrue to X and Y respectively.[10]

We have not determined what point in the triangular Edgeworth box will actually prevail. This is a (largely unresolved) problem in bargaining theory. However, when the legal starting point was altered from E_1 to E_2, nonintersecting areas of possibilities were obtained. Thus legal interpretation may be expected to affect the final allocation of resources; only as a special case would the amount of externality (smoke) be unaltered. Of course if the marginal rates of substitution of heat (or smoke) for bread were independent of the quantity of bread (i.e., indifference curves parallel vertically), then the contract curve would be vertical and the amount of smoke would be independent of the legal starting point.

III. TAXES–1 Y AND 1 X

In this section we will sketch some techniques frequently advanced for "solving" externality problems and briefly examine the properties of these techniques. In the two-person example described above, negotiations (bilateral bargaining) would seem to be the most appropriate method for ameliorating the effects of an externality.[11] However, since economic principles do not determine the outcome of such bargaining, this technique will not be discussed here.

Instead we will consider, in anticipation of our extension to m X-type individuals and n Y-type individuals, the solutions which would result from various tax schemes. We will presume that the individuals do not use their "monopoly power." For example, X does not recognize the effects of his actions on tax rates. He just (blindly) maximizes at the margin. Such behavior will be easier to justify when we think of a community composed of a large number of X's; so that the isolated behavior of one individual has a negligible effect on the total quantity of smoke.[12]

In the real world we frequently encounter externality with the economy in effect operating at E_1 in Figure 4. (Smoke pollution is a possible example.) Suppose a welfare economist suggests that X should, if he wants to continue to produce smoke, be required to pay Y for the damages inflicted. That is, X's bread compensation should be sufficient to keep Y on $I_2{}^Y$ (Figure 4).[13] One technique for achieving this goal, which enjoys the role of the standard solution, is a tax (in bread) on X per unit of smoke. The tax revenue would be given to Y.[14]

This per unit tax has the effect of rotating X's budget line GG around starting point E_2 (The higher the tax rate, the steeper the after-tax budget line.) Then the effective bread price of heat is the market price for heat plus the per unit tax on smoke. The appropriate solution will be obtained if an after-tax budget line is selected which goes through the intersection of $I_2{}^Y$ and X's price-consumption curve, pp (the locus of tangencies of X's indifference curves and after-tax budget lines originating at E_2.) In Figure 4, X and Y will be on $I_3{}^X$ and $I_2{}^Y$ respectively. However, this cannot be Pareto optimal (unless a corner solution at E_2 is appropriate) for $I_2{}^Y$ will intersect the optimum budget ray and $I_3{}^X$ from above, and thus not be tangent to $I_3{}^X$.[15]

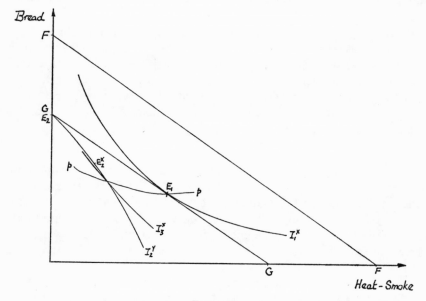

FIGURE 4

This analysis suggests that a per unit tax on X which has the twin objectives of keeping Y on his starting point indifference curve *and* attaining a Pareto optimum is not, in the general case, possible.[16] (The tax rate which leads to a solution at the intersection of the price-consumption curve pp with the contract curve would be Pareto-optimal, but at this tax rate Y would be more than compensated for smoke damages caused by X.) However, a combination of a lump sum *subsidy* and a per unit tax could be used to achieve the Pareto optimal point $E_2{}^X$ on indifference curve $I_2{}^Y$. The appropriate per unit tax could be derived from the slope of an after-tax budget line tangent to $I_2{}^Y$ at $E_2{}^X$; this per unit tax will be higher than the per unit tax derived above. The vertical distance from budget line GG to the intersection of the after-tax budget line with the bread axis represents the lump sum subsidy. Intuitively, since the shape of Y's indifference curves in Figure 2 implies that his smoke damages increase as he encounters more smoke, the appropriate per unit tax is more than enough to pay smoke damages on the infra-marginal units of smoke. The steeper tax rate discourages smoke production appropriately at the margin while the subsidy holds down revenues so that Y is not overcompensated.

IV. A DIGRESSION ON INFORMATION

In the tax example above it was implicitly presumed that an omniscient government or Y had full knowledge of X's indifference curves as well as of $I_2{}^Y$. Thus the appropriate tax could be immediately determined. However, in the real world such knowledge is usually unavailable. To circumvent this information problem the government might use an iterative procedure (similar to a *tatonnement*).[17] In our example the government wishes to permit X to create smoke so long as Y is adequately compensated—kept on $I_2{}^Y$. Suppose the government levies a per unit tax in terms of bread on X's creation of heat (smoke). X responds by selecting that quantity of heat and bread which maximizes his utility. Then if the resulting quantity of smoke and tax revenue (in bread) puts Y to the east (west) of $I_2{}^Y$, the per unit tax should be increased (decreased). The final solution will, of course, be at the intersection of X's price-consumption curve and $I_2{}^Y$.

Suppose, instead, the government seeks to insure the satisfaction of the marginal conditions necessary for Pareto optimality. It can again assume that X will be on an indifference curve tangent to his after-tax budget line. If X's selection puts Y on an indifference curve which cuts the after-tax budget line from above (below), the tax rate should be increased (decreased). A Pareto solution will be achieved at the intersection of the contract curve and X's price-consumption curve.

All of this can be done without knowledge of X's indifference curves (providing X maximizes blindly). However, if Y and not the government is administering this scheme, a Pareto optimum is unlikely. Y can maximize his utility by selecting the tax rate where X's price-consumption line is tangent to a Y indifference curve; this point will not be Pareto optimal. Consequently this *tatonnement* procedure would seem more applicable in situations where Y is not a self-seeking individual but represents a government authority which desires that marginal conditions for Pareto optimality be satisfied. Income redistribution can be achieved (ideally) through some other means such as lump sum transfers.

The above discussion displays techniques for improvements (in the Pareto sense) over the starting point solution when X's indifference curves are not known. However, if this lack of information means the government (or Y) is also ignorant of the starting point, improvements may not be possible. This situation is examined in the remainder of this section.

In some applications of economic theory to externalities, it is presumed that one of the agents takes the initiative in achieving an optimum amount of externality. This (magnanimous) agent presents to the other agent a schedule of damages or benefits which will accrue to him from changes (from the starting point) in the amount of externality. The other agent then is invited to choose that amount of externality (and pay or be paid damages) which maximizes his satisfaction without reducing his "benefactor's" satisfaction below the level achieved at the starting point.[18]

But this "benefactor" technique is not always successful even theoretically. If Y is the benefactor and there are no legal restrictions on smoke production (starting point E_1), a difficulty may result if Y does not know X's indifference curves. Generally, the "magnanimous" agent can derive the starting point from the law and his own preferences.[19] But in this case the starting point E_1 depends on the behavior of X in the absence of any restrictions on smoke production. Perhaps Y will know this behavior historically. But if there is no history or if X's behavior changes over time (because of changes in income for example), Y is faced with a dilemma. If X knows that Y will permit him to move along Y's starting point indifference curve, X can maximize his satisfaction by claiming that his starting point would be an expenditure of *all* of his income on heat (smoke). This would of course put Y on an indifference level below the level of E_1. Y will be understandably reluctant to have his generosity result in such a sacrifice. But Y has no obvious way out of his dilemma. If, on the one hand, he does nothing, the non-Pareto optimal E_1 will obtain. But, on the other hand, if Y takes the initiative in achieving a Pareto optimum, he may be forced to a lower indifference level.[20]

V. TAXES–m   X's AND n Y's

For simplicity and ease of exposition our analysis has thus far been carried out in terms of two individuals X and Y. But the exercise is much more appropriate for applications where there are many individuals such as X and many individuals such as Y. Although the resulting model is still artificial, it is an improvement in an important dimension over the bilateral case.

Suppose there are m bread and heat (smoke-producing) individuals and n individuals who live by bread alone (each must breathe the smoke produced by the m smoke-producing individuals). We need not assume equal incomes or identical tastes for either the X-types or the Y-types. Assuming that a unit of heat for any X-type consumer generates an equal amount of smoke for every Y-type consumer, the condition for a Pareto optimum is:

$$(2) \qquad MRS_{HB}^{X_1} = \cdots = MRS_{HB}^{X_m} = - \sum_{i=1}^{n} MRS_{SB}^{Y_i} + MRT.$$

Following our example of Section III, we consider the starting point where no X is permitted to produce smoke. In the absence of an agreement with the Y community, all of the X's will spend all of their income on bread. Given the income of each X, it is a simple matter to determine the total quantity of bread which would be bought by the X community. If we also know the price ratio between heat and bread, a budget line corresponding to GG can be constructed.

The Y community will spend all of its income on bread also. Given the total income of the Y's, their total bread consumption can be determined. This leads to a budget line corresponding to FF. For each of the Y-type individuals, expenditure of all of his income on bread would put him on a particular starting point indifference curve. A Scitovsky community indifference curve [14] (or a Samuelson minimum-total-requirements contour [13]) corresponding to I_2^Y can be obtained by summing over all Y's the quantity of bread which would be required to keep each Y on his starting point indifference curve at various levels of smoke. The resulting community indifference curve will have the same general shape as I_2^Y (i.e., downward-sloping, concave to the origin); however, it will be steeper.

The intersection of this Y community indifference curve with the X community's aggregate price-consumption curve[21] yields the after-tax budget line which will keep the Y community at their starting point indifference levels. This solution, as in the two-person example, will not be Pareto optimal since all members of the X community will be on indifference curves which are tangent to the after-tax budget line, and the Y community indifference curve will intersect this after-tax budget line from above. Equation (2) will not be satisfied.

Although most of the results obtained in the 1 X and 1 Y example can be carried over to m X's and n Y's, one result cannot. It is well known that the shape of a community indifference curve depends upon the distribution of income.[22] Thus a locus of tangencies between Y community indifference curves and X community indifference curves (the contract curve) cannot be obtained in the absence of information as to how the gains from amelioration of the external effects will be distributed. To be sure, Pareto optimum points exist but the problem of dealing with externality is confounded since the techniques used above for locating such points will not be effective here.

VI. CONCLUSIONS

Although the preceding analysis has been based on a highly simplified model, the following implications for real-world problems involving consumers have been suggested:

1. The amount of externality that will tend to emerge depends on the extent of legal responsibility. The distribution of the "gains from trade" should also have an effect on amount of externality. (Section II).

2. It is not simple to regulate externality with government tax schemes. Some of the standard tax proposals will not generate results

that always satisfy the requirements for Pareto optimality. It is not in general possible to impose a per unit tax which will simultaneously compensate (exactly) for damages and achieve a Pareto optimum. (Sections III and V).

3. With information deficiencies and no legal restriction on pollution (smoke), a government authority set up to offer "bribes" for the reduction of pollution may be unable to make improvements in the Pareto sense. (Section IV).

REFERENCES

1. J. M. BUCHANAN AND W. C. STUBBLEBINE, "Externality," *Economica*, Nov. 1962, *29*, 371–84.
2. R. COASE, "The Problem of Social Cost," *Jour. Law and Econ.*, Oct. 1960, *3*, 1–44.
3. H. J. DAY, F. T. DOLBEAR AND M. KAMIEN, "Regional Water Quality Management—A Pilot Study," *Proceedings of the First Annual Meeting of the American Water Resources Association*, 1965, 283–309.
4. O. A. DAVIS AND A. B. WHINSTON, "Externalities, Welfare, and the Theory of Games," *Jour. Pol. Econ.*, June 1962, *70*, 241–62.
5. ———, "Some Notes on Equating Private and Social Cost," *So. Econ. Jour.*, Oct. 1965, *32*, 113–26.
6. J. DE V. GRAAFF, *Theoretical Welfare Economics*. Cambridge 1957.
7. M. I. KAMIEN, N. L. SCHWARTZ, AND F. T. DOLBEAR, "Asymmetry between Bribes and Charges," *Water Resources Research*, First Quarter 1966, *2*, 147–57.
8. A. V. KNEESE, *The Economics of Regional Water Quality Management*. Baltimore 1964.
9. E. J. MISHAN, "Reflections on Recent Developments in the Concept of External Effects," *Can. Jour. Econ.*, Feb. 1965, *31*, 3–34.
10. A. C. PIGOU, *The Economics of Welfare*, 4th. ed. London 1932.
11. P. A. SAMUELSON, "Diagrammatic Exposition of a Theory of Public Expenditure," *Rev. Econ. Stat.*, Nov. 1955, *37*, 350–56.
12. ———, "The Pure Theory of Public Expenditure," *Rev. Econ. Stat.*, Nov. 1954, *36*, 387–89.
13. ———, "Social Indifference Curves," *Quart. Jour. Econ.*, Feb. 1956, *70*, 1–22.
14. T. SCITOVSKY, "A Reconsideration of the Theory of Tariffs," *Rev. Econ. Stud.*, 1941–2, *9*, 89–110.
15. R. TURVEY, "On Divergencies between Social Cost and Private Cost," *Economica*, Aug. 1963, *30*, 594–613.
16. S. WELLISZ, "On External Diseconomies and the Government-Assisted Invisible Hand," *Economica*, Nov. 1964, *31*, 345–62.

NOTES

[1] For example, Davis and Whinston [4], Wellisz [16], Coase [2], Kneese [8], and Kamien, Schwartz and Dolbear [7].

[2] For some qualifications on the use of these devices see Coase [2], Buchanan and Stubblebine [1], Davis and Whinston [4, 5], Turvey [15], Wellisz [16], and Mishan [9].

[3] It is not for an economist *qua* economist to assess legal responsibility for an externality. For example, suppose my neighbor has a coal furnace and I find the smoke from his chimney noxious. Most people (I know) would hold my neighbor responsible. Now, suppose my neighbor paints his house gray and I find gray a depressing color. Here most people would hesitate to blame my neighbor. Determination of responsibility for externalities seems to have more to do with private property rights than with economics—which makes it a matter for the courts or for a legislative body. Of course, the law might permit a certain amount of externality as the "status quo" (starting point); i.e., the law does not always stipulate a polar solution (see Davis and Whinston [5]). Pigou [10], who is most frequently footnoted as the precursor of externality discussions, did not explicitly recognize this indeterminacy. To my knowledge the point was articulated first by Coase [2].

[4] Coase [2] and Kneese [8] obtain this result for externalities among firms.

[5] This point has been made (but not demonstrated) by Buchanan and Stubblebine [1].

[6] Buchanan and Stubblebine [1] analyze a comparable problem (for a fence and a numeraire good). Their construction, using "marginal evaluation curves," is similar in content to the one presented here; however, income effects cannot be analyzed directly because costs (for the fence) are handled by modification of the marginal evaluation curves. Also their example is restricted to two individuals.

[7] We have no conventional measure for units of smoke (nor of heat). For our purposes it is sufficient that units of smoke be a multiplicative function of units of heat.

[8] Readers who are familiar with Samuelson [11, 12] will recognize the condition expressed in (1). Samuelson suggested that Pareto optimality for a public good requires the sum (over consumers) of the marginal rates of substitution of the public good for the private good to equal the marginal rate of transformation. The same condition is used for this example—which could be called a public "bad" (social evil) for consumers other than X.

[9] We assume that heat (for X), smoke abatement (for Y) and bread (for both) are not inferior goods. Consequently, the contract curve must have a slope which is greater algebraically than that of the budget line. When Y moves to a lower indifference level along the contract curve, he must obtain more smoke and less bread. X, who will be moving to a higher indifference curve, must receive more heat, but since the total amount of bread decreases, we cannot be sure he will receive more bread.

[10] The possible legal starting points need not be restricted to E_1 and E_2. If restrictions on smoke output could be varied continuously from no restriction to total restriction, the area of possibilities could include all points lying between I_1^Y and I_2^X.

[11] Most of the recent literature has discussed the possibilities for negotiations, e.g., Coase [2], Buchanan and Stubblebine [1], Turvey [15], Davis and Whinston [5].

[12] For some suggestions as to how to use taxes when many individuals are involved in the example of water pollution, see Kneese [8] and Day, Dolbear and Kamien [3].

[13] The following analysis could be carried out for other sets of assumptions. For example, X might be permitted to produce at E_1, and Y required to compensate X for any reduction in smoke output. Such analysis is not included here since it would be mostly repetitious.

[14] It is important that the tax revenue be given to Y; the argument that Y is on indifference curve I_2^Y depends upon this transfer.

[15] Another solution which might be considered is a tax achieving a lump sum bread transfer from X to Y for damages. In this case X will move from E_1 to a tangency with a lower "after-tax" budget line parallel to GG; the appropriate transfer can be determined from the intersection of I_2^X and X's income-consumption curve (the locus of tangencies between X indifference curves and budget lines parallel to GG.) The vertical distance from the lower budget line to GG represents the lump sum bread transfer. Since I_2^Y must be everywhere steeper than the after-tax budget lines, a tangency solution will not result and the lump sum tax will not be Pareto optimal.

[16] I have been unable to find any welfare economists who recommend a complete set of goals and techniques for internalizing an externality. However, per unit taxes, compensation, and Pareto optimality are not uncommon classroom presumptions and they can be found individually, if not *in toto*, in the modern literature.

[17] Such a procedure was suggested by Davis and Whinston [5].

[18] For example, such a system is implicit in Kneese [8]. A (magnanimous) water authority is the counterpart of Y and a polluting firm is the counterpart of X.

[19] If the law indicates prohibition, Y or X (as a benefactor) can determine his starting point indifference curve. And if the law indicates no smoke restrictions, X can determine what he (as a benefactor) would do, i.e., he can locate E_1 and indifference curve I_1^X.

[20] A similar problem is analyzed in a paper by Kamien, Schwartz, and Dolbear [7]. In that article a profit-maximizing firm (X) finds it advantageous to create "uneconomic" pollution in order to convince the (magnanimous) water authority (Y) of a false starting point which works to the advantage of the firm in terms of income distribution. But since the increase in the profits of the firm is less than the decrease of profits of the authority (increase and decrease are measured as deviations from the result which would obtain using the "true" starting point), the solution is not Pareto optimal.

[21] This price-consumption curve is the sum of the price-consumption curves of all of the X-type individuals. Each after-tax budget line leads to a point on each individual's price-consumption curve. Quantities of heat and bread are summed and these numbers generate a point on the aggregate price-consumption curve. The aggregate curve will have the same general curvature as pp in Figure 4.

[22] For an expanded discussion of community indifference curves, see J. de V. Graaff [6, pp. 45–58].

On the Theory of
Optimum Externality: Comment

By E. J. MISHAN
The author is reader in economics at the London School of Economics and Political Science.
He is indebted to F. T. Dolbear, Jr. for useful criticisms of a first draft.

While acknowledging the ingenuity of Dolbear's diagrammatic construction [1], a "general" model of a two-person economy that produces in effect one good and one "bad" in fixed proportions appears to yield no conclusion that could not be drawn more simply from a partial analysis—at least, one wherein we permit ourselves the convenience of using money as a yardstick and wherein we use a Figure having marginal curves instead of indifference and transformation curves. The treatment presented here enables us to elaborate in a more familiar way the arguments leading to his first conclusion: (1) that the optimal output produced will depend upon the extent of legal responsibility. In addition, it simplifies the critical examina-

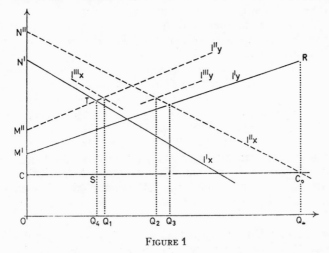

FIGURE 1

tion of three other conclusions (in my order); (2) that it is not in general possible to impose a constant per unit tax that both achieves an optimal out-

Reprinted by permission of the publishers and author: E. J. Mishan, "On the Theory of Optimum Externality: Comment," *American Economic Review*, 58 (June 1968), pp. 523-527.

put and compensates exactly for damages; (3) that some of the standard tax proposals will not in general establish an optimal output; and (4) that it is not simple "to regulate externality" with tax schemes.

Along the horizontal axis of Figure 1 we measure units of heat and smoke, these being produced in fixed proportions.[1] Along the vertical axis we measure for X (assumed provisionally to be affected only by heat) the marginal value of successive units of heat and, for Y (assumed provisionally to be affected only by smoke), the marginal value of compensation required for

	England	Portugal
Cloth (equal quantity)	90 man-years	60 man-years
Wine (equal quantity)	120 man-years	80 man-years

Portugal clearly has the higher per worker real income. It is equally clear that there is no basis for trade between the two nations.

successive units of smoke. OC measures the constant per unit cost of heat. Any point along X's marginal indifference curve[2] $N'-I'_x$ is consistent with X's welfare prior to any heat being available at all. Thus, X would pay a maximum of ON' for a first unit of heat, the vertical height of the $N'-I'_x$ curve indicating the maximum payments X would make for successive units of heat which, if paid, make him no better off than he is without heat. If, however, X were permitted to buy heat freely at cost OC, he would make a consumer's surplus of CN' on the first unit, an addition to his welfare that would raise his marginal indifference curve—assuming a positive welfare effect—and would, therefore, raise the maximum amounts he would pay for all successive units. A consumer's surplus on his second unit would further raise his welfare and therefore his marginal indifference curve, and so on for all successive units until he was in equilibrium buying OQ_0 units of heat, at which point his final marginal indifference curve $N''-I''_x$ would cut the CC_0 line.[3] In the absence of an anti-smoke law, and prior to any agreement between X and Y, OQ_0 is the output of heat, and smoke, produced.

At the welfare level remaining to Y when Q_0 units of smoke are produced the maximum he will pay to rid himself of the first unit is given by C_0R. If he paid the maximum for each unit of smoke successively withdrawn his welfare would remain unchanged and the marginal indifference curve traced would be that in the Figure shown by $M'-I'_y$.[4] If, however, an anti-smoke law were in effect, his welfare would be higher, and the minimum sum that would induce him to bear with a first unit of smoke would be measured by CM''. If he were paid the minimum acceptable to him for all successive units of smoke the sums would trace the marginal indifference curve $M''-I''_y$.

I

We now consider Dolbear's conclusion (1), that the optimal output of smoke production depends on legal responsibility, by reference to this construct. Obviously if an anti-smoke law exists there is initially no smoke, and if there is no such law the initial smoke output is OQ_0. If we ignore all costs of decision-taking—which, in practice, might prevent any movement from either of these extremes—and allow negotiation, the optimal output of smoke (and heat) will vary with the law. If in the first place an anti-smoke law prevailed which, however, could be waived in particular instances by voluntary agreement between the affected parties, Y could be exactly compensated by X with a payment of CM'' for the first unit of smoke suffered by Y, successive units borne by Y being compensated according to the height of the $M''-I''_y$ curve measured from the CC_0 line. The optimal smoke output would be at Q_1 at which point some marginal indifference curve for X, $I''\,'_x$, $(I'_x<I'\,''_x<I''_x)$ cuts the I''_y curve. For, as a result of X's making compensatory payments to Y that are less than X's initially maximum payments (as indicated by his I'_x curve), X's welfare continues to rise until the optimal output is reached and, along with it, his marginal indifference curve.

If, on the other hand, the law were permissive with respect to smoke, we begin at output OQ_0 with Y taking the initiative in offering compensation to X for foregoing heat. If Y paid exact compensation to X, payments per unit would follow the difference between CC_0 and the $N''-I''_x$ line moving leftward. Since these payments are smaller than the maximum that Y could offer to rid himself of successive units of smoke (while maintaining his welfare at the OQ_0 smoke level), Y's welfare increases as compared with his situation when OQ_0 units of smoke are produced, and his corresponding marginal indifference curve rises from I'_y to $I''\,'_y$ $(I'_y<I'\,''_y<I''_y)$ at which level it cuts the $N''-I''_x$ curve. The optimal amount of smoke is now at Q_2, which amount is necessarily larger than the amount Q_1 reached from the anti-smoke law.

The conclusion that—assuming always positive welfare effects—the optimal amount of "social damage" will always be smaller if the law is initially anti-"social damage" (regardless of decision costs) is not altered, indeed it is strengthened, if either side pays more than the required minimum compensation. Beginning from an anti-smoke law, for example, if X paid to Y more than is indicated by Y's $M''-I''_y$ curve, X's resulting $I''\,'_x$ curve would be lower than that indicated in the Figure while the relevant marginal indifference curve for Y would be above $M''-I''_y$. The resulting optimal output would therefore be still less than Q_1. Similar reasoning beginning with a permissive smoke law would reveal an optimal output greater than Q_2. For "normal," or positive, welfare effects it therefore follows that if more than exact compensation is paid the difference in optimal outputs arising from a difference in the law is greater.

II

Let us now take the analysis a stage further by considering the opportunities for tax-induced optima. In the absence of an anti-smoke law the welfares of X and Y *before agreement* are those associated with $M'-I'_y$ and $N''-I''_x$. As distinct from the realized output under these conditions, Q_0, the optimal smoke output consistent with these particular levels of welfare is that given by Q_3 at the intersection of the two curves in question. Regardless of what the government does with the tax proceeds, it is just not possible to reach Q_3 by imposing any kind of excise tax on heat alone—unless the excise tax paid by X is exactly offset by a direct subsidy to him—simply because the effect of such a tax is to reduce X's welfare and place him on a marginal indifference curve below that of $N''-I''_x$. However, in qualification of conclusion (2), Q_3 could be realized if, instead, the government offered X an excise subsidy for reducing his consumption of heat from Q_0 to Q_3 by reference to X's $N''-I''_x$ curve while at the same time levying an excise tax on Y for the removal of successive units of smoke from Q_0 to Q_3 by reference to Y's $M'-I'_y$ curve.

Similarly, if, instead, an anti-smoke law prevailed in the first instance, the relevant welfares would be those associated with I'_x and I''_y for which levels of welfare the optimal output is OQ_4. This optimal output could be realized on removing the smoke prohibition only by imposing an excise tax on X according to his $N'-I'_x$ curve while offering an excise subsidy to Y according to his $M''-I''_y$ curve up to output Q_4. In this case also, since the welfare levels of X and Y remain unchanged, the government will be left with some net revenue. In contrast, if instead X and Y negotiated their way to some optimal output (which could not be Q_4 or Q_3) the government would gain nothing but the welfare levels of one or both parties would be raised.

What is not generally possible, however, is to impose only a *constant* excise tax on heat and reach exactly either Q_4 or Q_3 (where initial welfare gains or losses are exactly compensated) since such a tax must alter X's initial welfare as indicated either by I'_x or I''_x. Even if one is constrained to constant excise taxes, however, this distributional effect need not worry one since the government can always influence the distribution of welfare through transfer payments while promoting optimal outputs by excise taxes.

Conclusion (3) also needs qualifying, if not correcting. If we do decide to introduce an excise tax on each successive unit of heat produced by X then, prior to any heat production, the initial marginal indifference curves are $N'-I'_x$ and $M''-I''_y$, with optimal output OQ_4 corresponding to these respective levels of welfare. The excise tax suggested by the diagram is equal to TS. But the levying of constant excise tax on heat of exactly TS may not result in an optimal output—assuming the government does not use any of the tax proceeds to compensate Y.[5] This is because the constant excise tax, TS, being initially below the maxima that X would pay for successive units of heat, raises X's welfare and also, therefore, his marginal indifference curve above $N'-I'_x$. For Y, on the other hand, the introduction of successive units of smoke serves only to reduce his marginal indifference curve below $M''-I''_y$. Thus, the tax TS may prove too high or too low to coincide with the intersection of the resultant marginal indifference curves for X and Y, and if so it would not be an optimal tax. However, if the tax TS turns out to be above the intersection of the resultant marginal indifference curves it is clearly too high and must be revised downward. Conversely, if it turns out to be below this intersection, it is too low and must be revised upward. Allowing for continuity, there is always some constant excise tax which is consistent with the resulting intersection of the marginal indifference curves for X and Y and, therefore, is consistent with an optimal output.

III

These results are not surprising. Levels of welfare for X and Y corresponding to an initial nonoptimal output—either to that of a smoke-permitting law or that of an anti-smoke law—cannot be maintained if, in establishing optimal outputs, excise taxes or subsidies are such as to alter these welfare levels. If it *is* important that such welfare levels be maintained it may be achieved as indicated, either by a system of excise taxes and subsidies that follow the path of each of the relevant marginal indifference curves, or else by constant excise taxes plus lump sum transfers. In the absence of such special measures, however, it must be accepted that government tax intervention, in particular a constant excise tax or subsidy, will have distributive effects on welfare. If an exact optimal output is established—and in principle it may always be established by some constant excise tax—it will not in general be consistent with the initial levels of welfare. However, any desired distribution of welfare can be established in the first instance by lump sum transfers and to any such welfare distribution there corresponds an optimal output, one that could be realized, if necessary, by either of the tax devices indicated above.

And this brings us to the last of Dolbear's conclusions considered here (4), that it is not simple to "regulate externality" with a tax system. This is a practical matter. An exact rate of excise tax, though conceptually determinate for some optimal output, would obviously be difficult to calculate. But such a difficulty is not peculiar to external effects. It is general to the calculation of any excise tax aimed to produce an exact optimal output, an exact amount of tax revenue, or an exact reduction in output. For in all such cases the distribution of welfare is to some extent affected and consequently the relevant marginal indifference curves are shifted. Thus, even if statistical estimates of the demand and supply schedules were perfect, and were deemed to be absolutely reliable over the future, we could not calculate an exact result without having, also, perfectly accurate information about welfare-induced shifts of the marginal indifference curves.

Does this matter? Hardly. Provided the welfare effects involved are small, the deviation from some exactly defined output is likely to be small. In a science of human behavior, where a ten per cent error of prediction over a several-year period is more an occasion for rejoicing than dismay, such difficulties cannot be taken seriously. If by excise taxes and/or subsidies the government can bring the economy as a whole closer to overall optimality—while correcting, if necessary, unwanted distributional effects through direct transfers—it need not feel inhibited by the practically insurmountable difficulties of exact calculations.[6]

REFERENCE

1. F. T. DOLBEAR, JR. "On the Theory of Optimum Externality," *Am. Econ. Rev.*, March 1967, *57*, 90–103.

NOTES

[1] I adopt Dolbear's assumption of fixed proportions which is not, however, essential in the treatment proposed here. Whatever the amounts of smoke associated with successive units of heat production, they entail compensatory payments that have to be subtracted from the marginal valuation of heat.

[2] The *marginal* indifference curve is the curve of the first derivative of the corresponding indifference curve.

[3] Thus, the marginal indifference curve $N''-I''_x$ is the first derivative of the highest indifference curve reached when (OQ_0) units of heat are bought at price OC. Any point along $N''-I''_x$ reveals the maximum payment X is willing to make for the corresponding unit when his welfare remains unchanged at the level associated with the $N''-I''_x$ curve.

[4] This upward-sloping curve has the normal shape, in that paying for a "bad" to be removed is akin to buying a good, and is downward-sloping when moving from *right to left*. On the other hand, the $M''-I''_y$ curve is to be regarded as moving from left to right, in the usual way, since Y's acceptance of successive units of smoke, a "bad," is akin to surrender of successive units of a good for which he requires increasing amounts of compensation.

[5] If the government exactly compensates Y, his original $M''-I''_y$ curve is maintained, the required tax exceeds TS, and the optimal output to be reached is still greater than OQ_4. If however, the government more than fully compensates Y, the required tax is greater still, but the optimal output could be anywhere in the neighbourhood of OQ_4.

[6] As an addendum to the above, it may be remarked that the introduction of many buyers of heat and many smoke victims, which requires that individual marginal indifference curves be added, the aggregate marginal indifference curves will, in general, be different for each different initial distribution of welfare. This implication, plus the possibility that some individuals will both buy heat and suffer smoke, poses no special conceptual problems. Optimal positions are multiplied, but, as in the two-person case, they are all exactly determinate. The actual calculation of exact optimal positions, however, will always be impracticable.

On the Theory of
Optimum Externality: Comment

By MARK V. PAULY

The author is assistant professor of economics at Northwestern University. He wishes to thank Roger Sherman and Thomas Willett for helpful comments.

One of the major points in a recent article by F. T. Dolbear, Jr., which appeared in this *Review* [1], was the demonstration that "it is not in general possible to impose a per-unit tax [on someone generating external diseconomies] which will simultaneously compensate (exactly) for damages and achieve a Pareto optimum" [1, p. 102]. If this is so, it obviously has serious consequences for public authorities who desire to eliminate the inefficiencies associated with marginal external diseconomies of various types. This note will show, however, that Dolbear's conclusion is really less general than it appears. There will always be some "per-unit tax" which will exactly compensate for damages and attain a Pareto optimum, if it is possible to attain a Pareto optimum at all.

A brief summarization of Dolbear's reasoning will help to illustrate this point. He considers a two-person model in which one person in producing heat for himself also generates smoke, which adversely affects the other person. He further makes the assumption, which turns out to be critical, that the damaged individual suffers in increasing marginal disutility from smoke (or experiences decreasing marginal utility from fresh air). Presumably, as this individual approaches asphyxiation, each increment of smoke imposes larger and larger amounts of disutility on him, so that he is willing to pay more and more to avoid or remove additional smoke. This implies that the cost, in terms of subjective utility loss, which smoke imposes on the damaged person is not constant for each unit of heat-smoke, but rather increases as more and more units of smoke are consumed.

When this assumption about the shapes of indifference curves is translated into a statement about subjective costs, Dolbear's conclusion does not appear surprising. It is no wonder that a tax imposed at a constant rate per unit of heat-smoke will not exactly compensate an individual who experiences costs which increase per unit of smoke.

Reprinted by permission of the publishers and author: Mark V. Pauly, "On the Theory of Optimum Externality: Comment," *American Economic Review,* 58 (June 1968), pp. 528-529.

What kind of tax would exactly and optimally compensate is also clear from this analysis. It would be a per-unit tax, because its base would be the number of physical units of smoke (or heat), but it would be an *increasing,* rather than a constant per-unit tax. Such a tax would imply an after-tax budget line which is not straight, but rather is concave to the origin. In Dolbear's Figure 4, this line would be tangent to the damaged party's "starting point" indifference curve. This tax would allow the damaged individual to be exactly compensated and at the same time would lead to a Pareto optimum.[1]

This conclusion is not without some practical significance. It suggests, for instance, that in situations in which Dolbear's assumption of increasing marginal disutility of dirty air is appropriate, decision-makers who desire to compensate exactly should consider, not constant per-unit taxes, but ones which increase per unit output of the externality-generating good.[2]

More generally, and perhaps more importantly, it suggests that qualitative characteristics of an optimal tax should be tailored to those of the cost being imposed. It might well be the case that consumers experience *decreasing* marginal disutility from pollution. For instance, once pollution makes a lake unfit for swimming and drinking purposes, additional increments of pollution, which serve only to make it more odiferous, might produce smaller and smaller reduction in consumers' utilities. In such a case, optimality could be achieved by a per-unit tax which *decreased* per unit of output.[3]

Another and probably quite common situation would be one in which consumers experience *constant* costs of pollution. For instance, by the operation of some kind of mechanical device, consumers might well be able to remove pollution at a constant marginal cost of pollution removed.[4] It would then be irrelevant whether they get decreasing marginal utility from clean air or not, so long as the global optimality conditions were not violated (i.e., so long as the total cost of removing the pollutant did not exceed the total benefits from cleaner air to the damaged individuals). In his analysis, Dolbear ignored the possibility, which may be fairly general, that the damaged individual could be returned to his starting-point indifference curve by methods other than compensation for damages suffered. If this possibility is considered, it appears that a constant per-unit tax may exactly and optimally compensate damaged individuals in a great number of cases. A per-unit tax, even a constant one, will lead to a Pareto optimum more often than Dolbear suggests.

REFERENCE

F. T. DOLBEAR, JR., "On the Theory of Optimum Externality," *Am. Econ. Rev.,* March 1967, 90–103.

NOTES

[1] Dolbear's suggestion of a lump-sum *subsidy* plus a per-unit tax on the source of pollution amounts to an increasing per-unit tax when averaged over all units of output. See [1, p. 99].

[2] This analysis assumes, as does Dolbear's, that there is a one-to-one relationship between output of the externality-generating good and that of the externality.

On the Theory of
Optimum Externality: Reply

By F. TRENERY DOLBEAR, JR.

The author is a Brookings Economic Policy Fellow at the U.S. Bureau of the Budget.

It was not my intention to suggest that taxes (or subsidies) cannot play a major role in mitigating the effects of externalities. Rather, I wished to indicate, using conventional assumptions of price theory, that some *qualifications* to the usual classroom externality prescription are necessary. Such qualifications notwithstanding, I have considerable sympathy for Pigovian tax-subsidy policies.

Pauly's comment is directed toward my conclusion that "it is not in general possible to impose a per-unit tax which will simultaneously compensate (exactly) for damages and achieve a Pareto optimum." He promises to show the desired result *can* be achieved with a "per-unit tax." However, it turns out that he has in mind an "increasing per-unit tax"; the average as well as the total tax depends on quantity consumed.[1] In general of course, the necessary marginal conditions can be satisfied with a constant per-unit tax which equates marginal social and private cost, and the distribution of income can be changed through lump sum transfers. Pauly accomplishes the same end—through variable inframarginal tax rates. His method is similar to variable rates often advanced for optimal pricing of public utilities.

Pauly also shows that increasing, constant, or decreasing per-unit taxes would be appropriate where the marginal disutility of smoke was increasing, constant, or decreasing (respectively). I agree. However, as I pointed out in section V, there are difficulties in applying these tax rules to situations involving many polluters. In these cases, Pauly's suggestions—to move along the damaged party's indifference curve—will not work. To be sure, it will still be possible in theory to achieve a Pareto optimum with exact compensation for damages. But the exact compensation tax rates which should be presented to the individual polluters cannot be simply derived from the curvature of the starting point indifference curve. Damage (and thus exact compensation) depends on aggregate pollution; consequently, information on the preferences of

Reprinted by permission of the publishers and author: F. Trenery Dolbear, Jr., "On the Theory of Optimum Externality: Reply," *American Economic Review*, 58 (June 1968), pp. 529-531.

the polluters is required to derive taxes on individuals which will yield appropriate aggregate payments. Moreover, Pauly's increasing per-unit tax will not, in the general case, be sufficient. If individual polluters are spread over the range of output, a constant marginal rate will be necessary (to satisfy the marginal conditions) and lump sum transfers will be required.

Turning to Mishan's comments, I find his restatement of the problem interesting though I must confess I do not find marginal evaluation curves easy to work with. They are particularly troublesome in analyzing income effects, an important ingredient in the problem at hand. This difficulty is (at first blush) avoided where, in internalizing the externality, Mishan holds constant the welfare levels of *both* parties. However, as Mishan realizes, this is an illusion because income is generated for a third party (government) whose preferences are not represented in the model. This of course is what makes it a "partial analysis." Mishan's construct is especially ill suited for handling cases which involve constant per-unit taxes since not only will the income of the government be affected but also the level of welfare of the two parties. Although Mishan does consider this latter effect on optimal output, the analysis is awkward. It is an unfortunate feature of the model that changes in income cannot be treated systematically but require *ad hoc* shifting of curves.

I have several specific comments. First, Mishan's extensions of my results are easily exhibited in my "triangular Edgeworth box." For example, optimum solution Q_3, holding welfare levels in the absence of an anti-smoke law constant, can be located in my Figure 3 (p. 95) where the slopes of indifference curves I_1^X and I_1^Y are equal. The income (bread) which the government receives is represented by the vertical distance between the two curves. A similar correspondence can be found between solution Q_4 and curves I_2^X and I_2^Y.

Second, Mishan's use of taxes and subsidies as *incentives* to internalize externality is not clear. In section II, he employs variable taxes or subsidies to transform the opportunity locus of X and Y onto the appropriate marginal evaluation curve. However, this will not, contrary to Mishan's expectation, induce either to select the intersection of the curves over other (equally desirable) points along the appropriate marginal evaluation curve. Since neither is being made better off, neither has an incentive to maximize. The intersection could be induced through lump sum transfers combined with a per-unit tax (or subsidy) on X.

Finally, Mishan considers whether it will be simple to regulate externality with a tax system. I agree that it is a practical matter. He suggests the problem is likely to be small because the welfare effects of the internalizing technique will be small. However, in some real world cases that come to mind (e.g., Pauly's example of water pollution), compensation at marginal damage rates leads to considerable deviation from exact compensation.

NOTES

[1] From an informal poll of my colleagues, I feel reinforced that most economists think a per-unit tax involves a *constant* rate per unit. However, as the discussion below will indicate, I feel the problem is more than semantics.

[3] Alternatively, optimality could be attained by a per-unit tax and a lump-sum tax levied on the source of pollution.

[4] In such a case, knowledge of the costs of reducing damage from pollution may also be much easier to obtain than in the cases Dolbear [1, pp. 99-101] considers.

Externalities and Corrective Taxes [1]

By CHARLES R. PLOTT

Consider a factory which produces some unspecified product called X. The process of producing X involves the creation of an external diseconomy for a nearby business. It is generally recognized that this diseconomy may be the result of some resource used in the production of X such as smoke created from a burning process. However, the participants in the recent discussion of externalities, as well as Pigou, have assumed either by means of their examples,[2] or explicitly,[3] that in such cases the corrective tax should be placed on the production of X. This procedure, except under rather restrictive conditions, is fundamentally incorrect. If a corrective tax exists, it must be placed either on the smoke output or, under certain conditions, on the resource input from which the smoke is generated.

That the tax should be placed on the correct thing seems a sufficiently simple point. However, in practice the actual identification of the proper variable may not be so easy (as is made evident by the examples and the vagueness of the literature). The point becomes even more important when it is realized that a tax on X, the traditional candidate for taxation, may make the situation worse rather than better. As an example of such an extreme case, the following may be considered.

Assume the producer of X has the production function $X = X(a, b)$ where a is some factor input such as labour and the other factor, b, is a burning process.[4] A laundry next door has the production function $L = L(l, b)$ where l is a labour input and b is the burning activity connected with the production of X[5]. The production function of X is shown by Figure 1. Each isoquant represents an additional unit of X, i.e., X_{10} represents 10 units of X per unit of time, etc. The budget constraints represent the ratio of prices of the resource inputs a and b. The marginal cost of producing X is represented by the distances between the budget constraints. That is, the marginal cost of the tenth unit of X in terms of b is AB. If the price of X is AB, the equilibrium output of X is 10 units and the equilibrium level of resource inputs are a_1 and b_1.

Reprinted by permission of the publishers and author: Charles R. Plott, "Externalities and Corrective Taxes," *Economica,* n.s. 129 (February 1966), pp. 84-87.

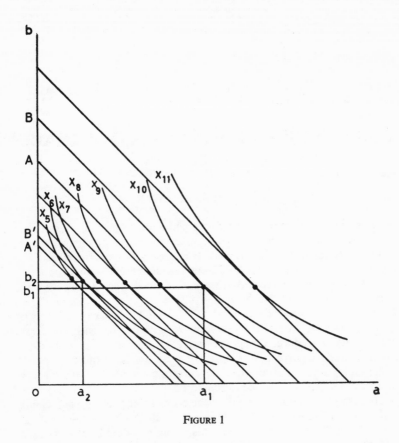

FIGURE 1

It is known, by hypothesis, that external diseconomies are involved in the production of X. The traditional prescription is that some tax should be placed on X, thus lowering the price faced by the producer. Assume the price of X after the tax is $(AB-\text{tax})=A'B'$. On the figure, the equilibrium level of X at the lower price would be X_6. Less X would be produced at the lower price. However, at this new output level of X, the amount of burning and, hence, the amount of undesirable smoke is even greater. This result will hold for any positive tax placed on X.[6]

It is often said that when external diseconomies are involved in the production of X, we are assured that there exists an over-production of X. If the externality is due to some resource input, however, this position does not hold. It would be a simple matter to give an example where the proper correction of the externality by means of a tax involves an increase in the production of X rather than a decrease.

When the problem is correctly formulated, the shortcomings of the traditional prescriptions can easily be seen. The problem is one of joint production. The firm produces two products X and S where S is the smoke that actually does the damage. As above, it is assumed that

262

X is produced by burning b and some other resources a, while S is produced only by burning. The firm attempts to maximize

(1)
$$\pi_x = P_x X + P_s S - P_b b - P_a a$$
$$= P_x X(a, b) + P_s S(b) - P_a a - P_b b$$

where $X = X(a, b)$, $S = S(b)$, $P_i =$ market price of $i = X, S, a, b$. The usual market failure example is where $P_s = 0$.

The laundry producer's production function is $L = L[l, S(b)]$.[7] And he attempts to maximize

(2)
$$\pi_L = P_L L[l, S(b)] - P_1 l - P_s S(b).$$

In the absence of a bribe, tax or subsidy, $P_s = 0$.

The Pareto optimal outputs are represented by

(3) max $P_x X(a, b) + P_s S(b) + P_L L[l, S(b)] - P_a a - P_b b - P_1 l - P_s S(b)$.

Notice that $P_s S(b)$ cancels. This shows that an output to one is an input to the other, or that a subsidy on one must be a tax on the other. The first order maximum conditions are:

(4)
$$P_x \frac{\partial X(a, b)}{\partial a} = P_a$$

(5)
$$P_L \frac{\partial L[l, S(b)]}{\partial l} = P_1$$

(6)
$$P_x \frac{\partial X(a, b)}{\partial b} + P_L \frac{\partial L[l, S(b)]}{\partial S(b)} \frac{\partial S(b)}{\partial b} = P_b.$$

Conditions (4) and (5) are the usual Pareto conditions that the value of the marginal product equals price. Condition (6) is that the sum of the values of the marginal product be equal to the price. This is the usual condition for collective goods.

Condition (6) rearranged is

(6)
$$P_x \frac{\partial X(a, b)}{\partial b} = P_b - P_L \frac{\partial L[l, S(b)]}{\partial S(b)} \frac{\partial S(b)}{\partial b}.$$

Thus, the producer of X must pay a tax on the use of b equal to $P_1 \dfrac{\partial L(l, S)(b))}{\partial b}$. Notice that the tax must be placed on b.[8] If the tax is placed on X such that condition (6) is satisfied, condition (4) would be violated. And, in general, it is impossible to place a tax on X that will assure optimality. Such a tax will always violate the input conditions when more than one resource is used.

The analysis that has been developed in the literature is generally correct if the proper assumptions are made and the proper qualifications are placed on the examples. Without these qualifications, however, the traditional prescriptions are not only misleading but are, in fact, completely wrong. And, if the proper qualifications are to be made, the first problem, that of determining just exactly what variable should be taxed, becomes just as difficult as the second problem, that of determining what the optimum tax should be.

Purdue University, Lafayette, Indiana.

NOTES

[1] I am indebted to Professor J. M. Buchanan and Professor A. Whinston of the University of Virginia for their helpful suggestions.

[2] J. E. Meade, "External Economies and Diseconomies in a Competitive Situation", *Economic Journal*, vol. LXII (1952), pp. 54–67; O. A. Davis and A. Whinston, "Externalities, Welfare and the Theory of Games", *Journal of Political Economy*, vol. LX (1962), pp. 241–62; J. M. Buchanan and W. C. Stubblebine, "Externality", *Economica*, vol. XXIX (1962), pp. 371–84; S. Wellisz, "On External Diseconomies and the Government Assisted Invisible Hand", *Economica*, vol. XXXI (1964), pp. 345–62; A. C. Pigou, *The Economics of Welfare*, 4th ed., 1932, p. 192. It should be noted that not all of the participants in the discussion have been so careless. See R. H. Coase, "The Problem of Social Cost", *Journal of Law and Economics*, vol. III (1960), p. 1.

[3] E. J. Mishan, "Reflections on Recent Developments in the Concepts of Externalities", *Canadian Journal of Economics and Political Science*, vol. XXI (1965), pp. 21–22; Pigou, p. 224.

[4] To make the example more realistic one should say that $X=X'(a, h)$ where h is heat used and is a function $h=h(b)$ of the level of the burning process. The production function is then $X=X'[a, h(b)]=X(a, b)$, as above.

[5] Generally, the laundry production function should be $L=L'(l, S)$ where S is the actual smoke that does damage, and where $S=S(b)$ showing that the damaging smoke is some function of the burning process. The production function would then be $L=L'[l, S(b)]$ or $L=L(l, b)$ which the production function in the text above is assumed to represent.

[6] This paper was written before the publication of an article by D. V. T. Bear, in which he also points out the possible existence of inferior factors of production. Those interested in further implications of such possibilities should read his "Inferior Inputs and the Theory of the Firm", *Journal of Political Economy*, vol. lxxiii, (1965), pp. 287–9.

[7] As above, the problem could be reformulated as $L=L[l, S(b)]=L'(l, b)$. The former is a formulation of "joint supply" whereas the latter is the traditional formulation of "externality". I wish to thank J. M. Buchanan for pointing out this relationship between the two concepts.

[8] Of course the tax could be placed on S thus giving S a negative price for the producers of X and L. Even though this procedure would reduce ultimately to a tax on b, very complicated adjustments can be avoided by placing the tax on S. For example, optimal adjustments may take place by a change in the form of the function $S(b)$, i.e. a change in the smoke-preventing device. These problems are ignored above in order to simplify the point that a tax on X is necessarily non-optimal.

Externalities and Output Taxes[*]

By LOWELL R. BASSETT and THOMAS E. BORCHERDING

In a recent paper Charles Plott purports to establish the theorem that a tax on a competitive firm's output will actually lead to an increase in the production of an undesirable externality when that externality results from the employment by the firm of an inferior or regressive[1] input.

While this analysis is correct in the short run for the individual firm considered in isolation, the results are not valid when the analysis is generalized to incorporate the long-run adjustment of the industry. As will be shown below, a careful distinction must be drawn between the short-run and the long-run equilibrium adjustments of the firm and industry to the tax as well as between the short-run and the long-run effects of these adjustments on the production of the externality both by the firm and by the industry. Plott's failure to make these distinctions can lead one to draw incorrect inferences from his paper.

It is our purpose to demonstrate that under widely-used assumptions a tax on output will always cause a long-run reduction in the amount of the externality supplied by the industry, whether the input producing the externality is inferior or normal to the firm. Further, we extend the analysis of an output tax to a general model, namely an n-input, competitive-market model with imperfectly elastic factor supply functions facing the taxed industry. In this case comparative statics results are not necessarily determinate; however, this ambiguity does not arise because of the presence of an inferior factor but because of the general problem of complementarity.

Consider a competitive industry in long-run equilibrium that in the process of supplying an output, X, to consumers also supplies the surrounding community with an external diseconomy, S, where S is that non-appropriable[2] portion of the service flow of the regressive input, b. If, as commonly assumed in economic analysis, factor supply functions are taken to be perfectly elastic over the range of demand, the long-run supply, or entry-exit, curve of the industry is necessarily perfectly elastic.[3]

Now impose a tax on X. In the short run this tax reduces the effective price facing each firm within the industry causing each of them to reduce its rate of

*We are indebted to John Floyd and J. Allan Hynes of the University of Washington for their helpful suggestions.

Reprinted by permission of the authors: Lowell R. Bassett, and Thomas E. Borcherding, "Externalities and Output Taxes," *Southern Economic Journal,* 37 (April 1970), pp. 462-464.

production of X and increase its employment of b and its production of S, since b is assumed to be inferior over this range. The aggregate *short-run* effect is an expansion of the industry's output of S.

In the long run, however, some firms must necessarily leave the industry because the full opportunity cost of the inputs employed exceeds revenues net of taxes. Since input prices remain constant, the marginal and average cost functions of each firm are unaltered and the effective price to the remaining producers must rise by the full amount of the tax, leaving the new equilibrium price and firm output the same as before the tax. Thus, whether or not inputs employed by existing firms are inferior, an output tax occasions only an exit of some of the firms from the industry. Clearly under these conditions the quantity of all factors employed by the industry declines and, as a result, the supplied quantity of S declines.

The example just analyzed is a particular instance of the case where the supply elasticity of each factor employed is identical. If all factor-supply elasticities to the *industry* are equal, relative factor prices remain constant and the output associated with the firm's minimum long-run average costs is unaltered by changes in industry output. As long as industry output declines after imposition of an output tax, the employment of all factors must decline. Of course, if factor supplies are all perfectly inelastic, industry output remains constant and factor prices fall proportionately without any change in the externality.

Now let factor supplies of a and b have different non-negative elasticities and restrict the production function to two factors. The usual assumption that the same production function is available to all firms in a competitive industry implies an aggregate linear homogeneous production function for the industry. The fall in industry output occasioned by the tax shifts the industry factor-demand schedules and, hence, causes relative prices of factors to change. Since output falls, the industry obviously will use less of at least one of the factors; we will show it must use less of both factors.

The argument can easily be illustrated on an industry isoquant diagram. Original industry equilibrium occurs on isoquant y_1, at point A where quantities

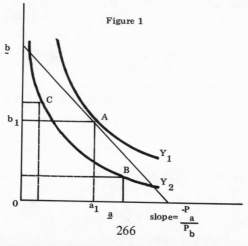

Figure 1

a_1 and b_1 of the inputs are used. The tax reduces industry output to y_2. The new equilibrium may occur along y_2 inside rectangle ob_1Aa_1, or along y_2 outside that rectangle. Suppose it occurs outside at a point such as C. In this case more b is being employed than previously and less a. Since we have upward sloping factor supplies to the industry the price ratio Pa/Pb must fall. However, this contradicts the fact that C is the new equilibrium. With a linear homogeneous production function the slope of isoquants depends only on factor ratios and the lower ratio of a/b at C requires a steeper price line or thus P_a/P_b would have had to rise rather than fall. A similar argument can be used to show that the new equilibrium could not occur at a point such as B. Thus the new equilibrium must occur inside rectangle Ob_1Aa_1 where less of both factors is used. Given a two-input model, we conclude an output tax necessarily reduces the quantity of the undesirable activity independently of its source.[4]

The above analysis holds as well in the n-input case ($n > 2$) only if the supply elasticities of all n factors are equal. In the case where all n factor-supply functions are non-negatively sloped and do not possess the same elasticities the results are different. An output tax will certainly lead to a reduction in some factors, but not necessarily in all.[5] If one of the factors whose quantity increases is b, the peccant input, Plott's conclusions hold, but for reasons having nothing to do with b's inferiority in the firm's production function. On the contrary, b might well be a normal input to the firm and its quantity will rise as an output tax is levied on the industry.

Whether this case where input complementarity exists (and where the relevant cross partial derivatives have sufficient negativity) is enough to establish the importance of a perverse reaction to an output tax is a matter for empirical investigation. If such a case is unusual, one might argue for an output tax over an input tax on "second best" grounds. The administrative capacity to attach the *correct* taxes to input prices may be extremely difficult, particularly since the source of the externality may be the nonappropriable flow not of a single input but of several inputs whose negative joint-service flow varies with both the quantities and the proportions of the contributing inputs. In a world where information is not costless an output tax may, therefore, be desirable.

NOTES

1. An input is said to be inferior or regressive when its use is inversely related to the firm's output. This point was first discussed by Hicks [3, 93] and more recently has received some elaboration by Bear [2, 287-289].

2. That part of the service flow of a factor that escapes the economic calculation of the several parties contracting for the purchase and sale of the services of the input.

3. This statement implies, as is well known, that all firms have the same minimum average cost which requires a perfectly elastic supply of entrepreneurial skills. As a typical example of the general acceptance of this assumption see Stigler [5, 174], "The distribution of entrepreneurial aptitudes is fairly continuous and ... there are relatively many entrepreneurs with almost every combination of entropreneurial skills." If we assume that the entrepreneur is the embodiment of the production function it naturally follows that an industry able to attract additional inputs and entrepreneurs (firms) at no additional cost than price of the inframarginal units will be one of constant cost.

4. Under monopoly the results are quite different. An output tax always decreases the

firm's output and therefore increases its use of inferior factors while decreasing its use of normal factors.

5. It is relatively easy if tedious to verify this assertion. Take the expressions found in Allen [1, 508], for the factor elasticities of demand and by suitable choice of values for the cross partial derivatives of the aggregate linear homogeneous production function one can obtain a larger percentage increase in a factor whose price does not fall relatively the most. For instance consider a production function $y = f(a, b, c)$. Let a fall relatively the most in price, with b complementary and c competitive with a. Now choose $f_{ab} > 0$, $F_{ac} > 0$ and $f_{bc} < 0$. With this sign configuration it is possible to pick values consistent with homogeneity and cost minimization such that the percentage increase in the employment of b is greater than that of a. The decrease in the use of c increases the marginal product of b and decreases the marginal product of a, which thus favors the use of b over a although a's price has fallen relative to all other prices. A necessary condition for this result is a negative cross partial derivative of the production function. Economic theory does not rule out such a case; therefore, it is clearly possible that after the tax the use of some factor complementary with a will be greater than before the tax.

REFERENCES

1. Allen, R. G. D. *Mathematical Analysis for Economists.* New York: Macmillan, 1960.
2. Bear, D. V. T., "Inferior Inputs and the Theory of the Firm," *Journal of Political Economy,* June 1965, 287-289.
3. Hicks, J. R. *Value and Capital.* Oxford: Clarendon Press, 1946.
4. Plott, Charles R., "Externalities and Corrective Taxes," *Economica,* February 1966, 84-87.
5. Stigler, George J. *The Theory of Price* (rev. ed.). New York: Macmillan, 1952.

External Diseconomies, Corrective Taxes, and Market Structure

By JAMES M. BUCHANAN*

This note is presented as a contribution to the continuing dismantling of the Pigovian tradition in applied economics, defined here as the emphasis on internalizing externalities through the imposition of corrective taxes and subsidies. My central point is much more elementary than those advanced by some of the other contributors to the recent discussion. R. H. Coase [1] demonstrated the inherently bilateral aspects of any externality relationship, and he showed that applying the Pigovian policy norms in neglect of the two-sidedness of the account may reduce rather than increase efficiency. Davis and Whinston [2] concentrated on the impossibility of determining the size of a corrective tax that would lead to an efficient outcome under conditions of reciprocal externalities when production functions are nonseparably related. Plott [3] called attention to the necessity of identifying properly the aspect of the production process that generates the externality. I shall demonstrate that (1) even if the directional gains-from-trade are such that an orthodox corrective tax would increase efficiency, and (2) even if production functions are separable, and (3) even if no changes in the input mix are technically possible, the imposition of a corrective tax (under external diseconomy) will often reduce rather than increase welfare in the Pareto-efficiency sense. Only when the industry generating the external diseconomy is competitively organized can the corrective tax be unambiguously hailed as welfare-improving, even in the presence of all of the other required conditions. Under monopolistic organization, the corrective tax may well lead to a reduction in welfare rather than an increase.

My criticism is aimed more at the "Pigovian tradition" than at Pigou himself. His whole analytics, and that of Marshall, was implicitly based on the assumption of competitive structures, as, indeed, some of the contributors to the

*The author is professor of economics at the University of California, Los Angeles.

Reprinted by permission of the publishers and author: James M. Buchanan, "External Diseconomies, Corrective Taxes, and Market Structure," *American Economic Review*, 59 (March 1969), pp. 174-177.

externality literature seem to have recognized.[1] It is necessary to distinguish, however, between the relevance of market structure for the emergence of externality and the relevance of market structure for the application of the Pigovian policy norms. For example, Ellis and Fellner state that "the 'atomistic' character of one producer's output under competition, frequently thought to be crucial in the external economies-diseconomies context, is not decisive of itself" [5, p. 262]. Ellis and Fellner were referring here to the potential for the emergence of externalities, but it is relatively easy to see how this statement could be taken to imply that market structure also has little relevance to the application of the standard externality-correcting devices. And we know that the levy of corrective taxes under diseconomies and the provision of corrective subsidies under economies have been widely discussed without reference to market organization. This attitude is surely characteristic of modern treatments of pollution control. If, as I shall demonstrate, it is necessary to limit the Pigovian correctives on the tax side to situations of competition much of the current discussion on these problems requires substantial revision. As we recognize, most of the problems falling under "congestion" as a general category involve external diseconomies.

My argument can be presented geometrically in the simplest of models, one in which constant cost is assumed. More complex models are not needed. An industry demand curve is shown as D in Figure 1, with the cost curve shown by $MC(AC)$. If the industry is competitively organized, equilibrium output is Q_c, and price is P_c. Let us now assume that a "bad" is suddenly discovered to be inherent in the output of this industry, an external diseconomy that is directly related to the number of units produced and not to any particulars of the input mix or to the rate of output for any other industry. This external diseconomy

Figure 1

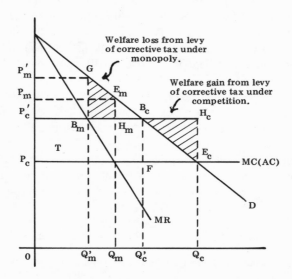

270

does affect the production functions of all firms in a second industry, also assumed to be competitively organized. The firms in the second industry have no legal claims to compensation for damages. Furthermore, for purposes of simplification, we assume that the costs of organizing firms in the second industry for the purpose of bribing firms in the first industry are prohibitive.

Given these restrictions, it is possible to indicate the size of a per unit tax to be imposed on the firms in the externality-generating industry. The orthodox Pigovian analysis suggests that the levy of this tax will induce behavioral changes that will move the economy to the efficiency locus. Let us suppose that the external diseconomy per unit is $P'cPc$, generating the unit tax T in Figure 1. Price will rise to $P'c$, and industry output will fall to $Q'c$. How can the subsequent increase in welfare be measured? The rectangle $PcP'cBcF$ represents a true "cost" that was previously treated as if it were consumers' surplus by the buyers of the first industry's product. If the proceeds of the tax are transferred to firms in the damaged industry, this now becomes consumers' surplus to the buyers of the product of this industry. If the proceeds are generally expended in the economy, these become diffused among all persons. Welfare gains and losses occur only with respect to the change in relative industry outputs. The buyers' evaluation of the quantity that was produced before the tax in the externality-generating industry but which quantity is eliminated by the tax is shown by the area under the demand curve over the range $Q'cQc$, or by the area, $Q'cBcEcQc$. The "cost" of this quantity to the community is indicated by the rectangle $Q'cBcHcQc$. Hence, the welfare gain is shown by the shaded triangle, $BcHcEc$.[2]

To this point, no problems are encountered given the restrictions initially placed on the model. However, let us now assume that the industry that generates the external diseconomy is organized as a monopoly, with a single profit-maximizing firm. Before the levy of any corrective tax, monopoly output is Qm and price is Pm. As in the competitive case, Pigovian analysis suggests the levy of a corrective tax of T per unit of output. Monopoly output falls to $Q'm$ and price increases to $P'm$.

It is easy to show that, under the conditions as shown in Figure 1, welfare has *decreased*, not increased as a result of the levy of the corrective tax. The cost of the change in quantity is measured as before, by the rectangle $Q'mBmHmQm$. The evaluation of the quantity is measured as before, by the area under the demand curve, or by $Q'mGEmQm$. Since the latter area clearly exceeds the former, welfare has been reduced as indicated by the shaded area. The geometry makes clear that, in this simple case, this result must hold so long as the corrective tax, which we assume to have been estimated properly, is less than the difference between price and marginal revenue at the initial monopoly output.

As I have indicated, the point is a very elementary one. It is a particularly clear example of the theory of second-best. The monopolist simultaneously imposes two external diseconomies, at least in a general sense. He "pollutes" and hence increases costs of firms in the damaged industry. Also, however, he holds down output and hence increases costs of his product to buyers. So long as the second diseconomy is more highly valued than the former, any levy of a per unit

271

tax on the ·monopolist's output will decrease total welfare. There are gains-from-trade here in two opposing directions, and there is no means of determining a priori which set of "trades" is potentially the more efficient. Conceptually, and ignoring costs of organizing, the firms in the damaged industry could bribe the monopolist to reduce output and thereby to reduce "pollution." At the same time, again ignoring the costs of organizing, the buyers of the monopolist's product could bribe the monopolist to increase output. In some costless three-way negotiation process, the ultimate outcome under conditions such as those depicted in Figure 1 is the corrected equilibrium output at $Q'c$.

As the construction as well as the discussion indicates, there is an important asymmetry between external diseconomies and external economies with respect to the possible offsetting welfare effects of market structure. With external economies, the provision of corrective subsidies reinforces the directional change in output that reforms in market structure would indicate to be desirable. In this case, buyers of the monopolist's own product could join forces with firms in an externally benefitted industry to bribe the monopolist to increase output.

As Coase has correctly emphasized, the whole approach of the Pigovian tradition is responsible for many confusions in applied economics that are slowly coming to be clarified. This approach involves an undue concentration on the decision-calculus of the firm or individual that is observed to be generating the external effects. Even if we disregard all problems of measurement, making the marginal private cost as faced by the decision-taking unit equal to marginal social cost does not provide the Aladdin's Lamp for the applied welfare theorist, and the sooner he recognizes this the better.

NOTES

1. R.H. Coase, "The Problem of Social Cost," *Jour. Law and Econ.*, Oct. 1960, 3, 1-44.

2. O. A. Davis and Andrew Whinston, "Externalities, Welfare, and the Theory of Games," *Jour. Pol. Econ.*, June 1962, 70, 241-62.

3. Charles Plott, "Externalites and Corrective Taxes," *Economica*, Feb., 1966, 33, 84-87.

4. J. E. Meade, "External Economies and Diseconomies in a Competitive Situation," *Econ. Jour.*, March 1952, 62, 54-67.

5. H. S. Ellis and William Fellner, "External Economies and Diseconomies," *Am. Econ. Rev.*, Sept. 1943, 33, 493-511, reprinted in G. J. Stigler and K. E. Boulding, ed., *Readings in Price Theory*, Homewood, Ill. 1952, pp. 242-63.

Section B:
Externalities in Welfare Economics and Collective Decision Situations

Each of the papers of this section extends the definition of the externality concept; all point to policy implications; but the main concern remains theoretical. These works might be viewed as extensions of welfare economics; at the same time, the policy implications run directly into an area that can be called modern political economy or public finance.

Many arguments developed in these articles are, as the writers point out, interrelated. Ralph Turvey, for example, declares his article is an attempt to synthesize some major insights worked up by Coase, by Buchanan and Stubblebine, and by Davis and Whinston.

The first paper in this section, "Externality," by James M. Buchanan and William Craig Stubblebine, presents readers with a clear and perhaps classic definition of an externality. Definitional distinctions are made with respect to a "marginal externality" and an "inframarginal externality."

The authors of "Externality" set up marginal conditions for defining a Pareto-relevant externality where gains from trade are possible. At the same time it is possible to have marginal externalities in a Pareto equilibrium position (e.g., where gains from trade are not possible).

One of the important implications of Buchanan and Stubblebine's analysis is that unilaterally imposed taxes and subsidies will not attain a full Pareto-equilibrium position. Moreover, if a tax-subsidy method is to be introduced rather than "trade," it should involve bilateral taxes (subsidies). Finally, as the authors point out, they have discussed only a single kind of (nonreciprocal) externality. For discussions of reciprocal externalities, see James M. Buchanan and Milton Z. Kafoglis, "A Note on Public Goods Supply," *American Economic Review* (June 1963), and James M. Buchanan and Gordon Tullock, "Public and Private Interaction under Reciprocal Externality," J. Margolis, editor, in *The Public Economy of Urban Communities*, Baltimore, 1965. Space limitations did not allow these papers to be included here.

Otto Davis and Andrew Whinston in "Externalities, Welfare and Theory of Games" emphasize production or supply side externalities. They point up analytical differences between separable and nonseparable cases by stating in a game theoretic mode the different marginal cost and pricing relationships of firms. In both cases maximum social welfare may not occur from strategies followed by the firms, and the question of desirable policy alternatives to improve outcomes is raised. Mergers may be one solution. Governmental taxes and subsidies are another. As complex and information-demanding as a government policy of tax-subsidy may be, it appears possibly effective only in the case of firms with separable externalities. When externalities are nonseparable and the strategies of firms are unpredictable, the output outcomes induced by tax-subsidy policies are indeterminate. In conclusion, Davis and Whinston review how governments might adapt the game payoff matrix approach to policy.

The third article in this section, by Ralph Turvey, is called "On Divergencies Between Social Cost and Private Cost." In it Turvey neatly pulls together key elements of a series of papers on the externality issue and emphasizes policy-making implications.

A simple smoke emission externality case is used to look at conditions of costs, gains, and efficiency implications of various policies. The physical production characteristics and costs of production of the party causing an externality—and the conditions relating to preference functions of parties affected by an externality—must be considered if policy steps aimed at reaching optimal outcomes are to be made. Governments must be able to understand the actual conditions operative, and be able to enforce moves by the parties involved, to achieve the desired optimum. Moreover, the cost of accomplishing this must be less than the gains achieved. Going further, the necessity of making these government moves with no unfavorable effects on income distribution is noted.

Simplistic solutions, such as a tax, may not lead to optimal outcomes; indeed, Turvey concludes that "any general prescription of a tax to deal with external diseconomies is useless."

Just as Davis and Whinston explore the externality concept through insights made possible by game theory, James Buchanan probes the gray area between purely private and purely public goods through a model of club ownership (supply) and membership (demand). Buchanan makes a statement of the marginal rates of substitutions and marginal costs of producing and consuming goods, allowing for the numbers of persons who are to join in this production or consumption. He goes on to describe conditions where individuals will, as club members, have available the optimal quantity of some good, and will be sharing this quantity optimally with other members. Preference maps are used to point up relationships between costs and benefits, and numbers of club members and amounts of output.

From a public policy standpoint, a more fully developed theory of clubs could provide meaningful insights into the cost and benefit conditions that exist for many goods that have a mix of direct as well as spill-over costs or benefits.

The fifth article of this section is by E. J. Mishan, titled "The Relationship Between Joint Products, Collective Goods, and External Effects." Mishan analyzes the marginal cost-pricing conditions for private and collective goods, with and without externalities, and jointly produced private and collective goods, with and without externalities. Marginal social cost pricing of collective goods when costs are fixed (short run) and variable (long run) are also discussed. The analysis sheds light on investment or planning decisions with respect to provision of collective goods. Finally, Mishan makes a distinction between an indirect effect, usually considered a synonym for externality, and the incidental or unintentional character of external effects. While operational difficulties may confront a policy of marginal social cost pricing, especially with respect to the provision of collective goods, it is one policy alternative that has commanded a great deal of attention in the literature.[1].

Mishan not only covers large amounts of ground by elaborating upon various theoretical aspects involved in the externality concept; he also points out a series of practical cases where these elaborations come into play. Examples are smoke pollution, traffic congestion, and flood control projects.

NOTES

1. The reader is referred to the following two articles for a further discussion of marginal cost pricing of public goods: Jora R. Minasian, "Television Pricing and the Theory of Public Goods," *The Journal of Law and Economics* (October 1964), and Paul A. Samuelson, "Public Goods and Subscription TV: Correction of the Record," *The Journal of Law and Economics* (October 1964).

For a whole menu of policies concerning solutions to externalities, see Otto A. Davis and Morton I. Kamien, "Externalities, Information and Alternative Collective Action," Joint Committee Print (The Analysis and Evaluation of Public Expenditures: The PPB System), Joint Economic Committee, 91st Congress, 1st Session, Vol. 1, 1969.

Externality

By JAMES M. BUCHANAN and WILLIAM CRAIG STUBBLEBINE

Externality has been, and is, central to the neo-classical critique of market organisation. In its various forms—external economies and diseconomies, divergencies between marginal social and marginal private cost or product, spillover and neighbourhood effects, collective or public goods—externality dominates theoretical welfare economics, and, in one sense, the theory of economic policy generally. Despite this importance and emphasis, rigorous definitions of the concept itself are not readily available in the literature. As Scitovosky has noted, " definitions of external economies are few and unsatisfactory ".[1] The following seems typical:

> External effects exist in consumption whenever the shape or position of a man's indifference curve depends on the consumption of other men.
> [External effects] are present whenever a firm's production function depends in some way on the amounts of the inputs or outputs of another firm.[2]

It seems clear that operational and usable definitions are required.

In this paper, we propose to clarify the notion of externality by defining it rigorously and precisely. When this is done, several important, and often overlooked, conceptual distinctions follow more or less automatically. Specifically, we shall distinguish marginal and inframarginal externalities, potentially relevant and irrelevant externalities, and Pareto-relevant and Pareto-irrelevant externalities. These distinctions are formally developed in Section I. As we shall demonstrate, the term, " externality ", as generally used by economists, corresponds only to our definition of Pareto-relevant externality. There follows, in Section II, an illustration of the basic points described in terms of a simple descriptive example. In Section III, some of the implications of our approach are discussed.

It is useful to limit the scope of the analysis at the outset. Much of the discussion in the literature has been concerned with the distinction between *technological* and *pecuniary* external effects. We do not propose

Reprinted by permission of the publishers and authors: James M. Buchanan and William Craig Stubblebine, "Externality," *Economica*, n.s. 29 (November 1962), pp. 371-384.

to enter this discussion since it is not relevant for our purposes. We note only that, if desired, the whole analysis can be taken to apply only to technological externalities. Secondly, we shall find no cause for discussing production and consumption externalities separately. Essentially the same analysis applies in either case. In what follows, " firms " may be substituted for " individuals " and " production functions " for " utility functions " without modifying the central conclusions. For expositional simplicity only, we limit the explicit discussion to consumption externalities.

I

We define an external effect, *an externality*, to be present when,

(1) $u^A = u^A (X_1, X_2, \ldots, X_m, Y_1)$.

This states that the utility of an individual, A, is dependent upon the " activities ", $(X_1, X_2, \ldots, X_m)$, that are exclusively under his own control or authority, but also upon another single activity, Y_1, which is, by definition, under the control of a second individual, B, who is presumed to be a member of the same social group. We define an *activity* here as any distinguishable human action that may be measured, such as eating bread, drinking milk, spewing smoke into the air, dumping litter on the highways, giving to the poor, etc. Note that A's utility may, and will in the normal case, depend on other activities of B in addition to Y_1, and also upon the activities of other parties. That is, A's utility function may, in more general terms, include such variables as $(Y_2, Y_3, \ldots, Y_m; Z_1, Z_2, \ldots, Z_m)$. For analytical simplicity, however, we shall confine our attention to the effects of one particular activity, Y_1, as it affects the utility of A.

We assume that A will behave so as to maximise utility in the ordinary way, subject to the externally determined values for Y_1, and that he will modify the values for the X's, as Y_1 changes, so as to maintain a state of " equilibrium ".

A marginal externality exists when,

(2) $u^A_{Y_1} \neq 0$.

Here, small u's are employed to represent the " partial derivatives " of the utility function of the individual designated by the super-script with respect to the variables designated by the subscript. Hence, $u^A_{Y_1} = \partial u^A / \partial Y_1$, assuming that the variation in Y_1 is evaluated with respect to a set of " equilibrium " values for the X's, adjusted to the given value for Y_1.

An infra-marginal externality holds at those points where,

(3) $u^A_{Y_1} = 0$,

and (1) holds.

These classifications can be broken down into economies and diseconomies: a marginal external economy existing when,

(2A) $u^A_{Y_1} > 0$,

that is, a small change in the activity undertaken by B will change the utility of A in the same direction; a marginal external diseconomy existing when,

(2B) $u_{Y_1}^A < 0$.

An infra-marginal external economy exists when for any given set of values for $(X_1, X_2, \ldots, X_m)$, say, $(C_1, C_2, \ldots, C_m)$,

(3A) $u_{Y_1}^A = 0$, and $\int_0^{Y_1} u_{Y_1}^A \, d_{Y_1} > 0$.

This condition states that, while incremental changes in the extent of B's activity, Y_1, have no affect on A's utility, the total effect of B's action has increased A's utility. An infra-marginal diseconomy exists when (1) holds, and, for any given set of values for $(X_1, X_2, \ldots, X_m)$, say, $(C_1, C_2, \ldots, C_m)$, then,

(3B) $u_{Y_1}^A = 0$, and $\int_0^{Y_1} u_{Y_1}^A \, d_{Y_1} < 0$.

Thus, small changes in B's activity do not change A's level of satisfaction, but the total effect of B's undertaking the activity in question is harmful to A.

We are able to classify the effects of B's action, or potential action, on A's utility by evaluating the " partial derivative " of A's utility function with respect to Y_1 over all possible values for Y_1. In order to introduce the further distinctions between *relevant* and *irrelevant* externalities, however, it is necessary to go beyond consideration of A's utility function. Whether or not a relevant externality exists depends upon the extent to which the activity involving the externality is carried out by the person empowered to take action, to make decisions. Since we wish to consider a single externality in isolation, we shall assume that B's utility function includes only variables (activities) that are within his control, including Y_1. Hence, B's utility function takes the form,

(4) $u^B = u^B (Y_1, Y_2, \ldots, Y_m)$.

Necessary conditions for utility maximisation by B are,

(5) $u_{Y_1}^B / u_{Y_j}^B = f_{Y_1}^B / f_{Y_j}^B$,

where Y_j is used to designate the activity of B in consuming or utilising some numeraire commodity or service which is, by hypothesis, available on equal terms to A. The right-hand term represents the marginal rate of substitution in " production " or " exchange " confronted by B, the party taking action on Y_1, his production function being defined as,

(6) $f^B = f^B(Y_1, Y_2, \ldots, Y_m)$,

where inputs are included as activities along with outputs. In other words, the right-hand term represents the marginal cost of the activity, Y_1, to B. The equilibrium values for the Y_i's will be designated as Y_i's.

An externality is defined as *potentially relevant* when the activity, to the extent that it is actually performed, generates *any* desire on the part of the externally benefited (damaged) party (A) to modify the behaviour of the party empowered to take action (B) through trade, persuasion, compromise, agreement, convention, collective action, etc. An externality which, to the extent that it is performed, exerts no such influence is defined as *irrelevant*. Note that, so long as (1) holds, an externality remains; utility functions remain interdependent.

A potentially relevant marginal externality exists when,

$$(7) \quad u^A_{Y_1}\Big|_{Y_1=\overline{Y}_1} \neq 0.$$

This is a potentially relevant marginal external economy when (7) is greater than zero, a diseconomy when (7) is less than zero. In either case, A is motivated, by B's performance of the activity, to make some effort to modify this performance, to increase the resources devoted to the activity when (7) is positive, to decrease the quantity of resources devoted to the activity when (7) is negative.

Infra-marginal externalities are, by definition, irrelevant for small changes in the scope of B's activity, Y_1. However, when large or discrete changes are considered, A is motivated to change B's behaviour with respect to Y_1 in all cases *except* that for which,

$$(8) \quad u^A_{Y_1}\Big|_{Y_1=\overline{Y}_1} = 0, \text{ and}$$
$$u^A (C_1, C_2, \ldots, C_m, \overline{Y}_1) \geqq u^A (C_1, C_2, \ldots, C_m, Y_1), \text{ for all } Y_1 \neq \overline{Y}_1.$$

When (8) holds, A has achieved an absolute maximum of utility with respect to changes over Y_1, given any set of values for the X's. In more prosaic terms, A is satiated with respect to Y_1.[3] In all other cases, where infra-marginal external economies or diseconomies exist, A will have some desire to modify B's performance; the externality is potentially relevant. Whether or not this motivation will lead A to seek an expansion or contraction in the extent of B's performance of the activity will depend on the location of the infra-marginal region relative to the absolute maximum for any given values of the X's.[4]

Pareto relevance and irrelevance may now be introduced. The existence of a simple desire to modify the behaviour of another, defined as potential relevance, need not imply the ability to implement this desire. An externality is defined to be Pareto-relevant when the extent of the activity may be modified in such a way that the externally affected party, A, can be made better off without the acting party, B, being made worse off. That is to say, " gains from trade " characterise the Pareto-relevant externality, trade that takes the form of some change in the activity of B as his part of the bargain.

A marginal externality is Pareto-relevant when[5]

$$(9) \quad (-) \; u^A_{Y_1}/u^A_{Xj} > [u^B_{Y_1}/u^B_{Yj} - f^B_{Y_1}/f^B_{Yj}]_{Y_1=\overline{Y}_1} \text{ and when } u^A_{Y_1}/u^A_{Xj} < 0, \text{ and}$$
$$u^A_{Y_1}/u^A_{Xj} > (-) \; [u^B_{Y_1}/u^B_{Yj} - f^B_{Y_1}/f^B_{Yj}]_{Y_1=\overline{Y}_1} \text{ when } u^A_{Y_1}/u^A_{Xj} > 0.$$

In (9), X_j and Y_j are used to designate, respectively, the activities of A and B in consuming or in utilising some numeraire commodity or service that, by hypothesis, is available on identical terms to each of them. As is indicated by the transposition of signs in (9), the conditions for Pareto relevance differ as between external diseconomies and economies. This is because the " direction " of change desired by A on the part of B is different in the two cases. In stating the conditions for Pareto relevance under ordinary two-person trade, this point is of no significance since trade in one good flows only in one direction. Hence, absolute values can be used.

The condition, (9), states that A's marginal rate of substitution between the activity, Y_1, and the numeraire activity must be greater than the " net " marginal rate of substitution between the activity and the numeraire activity for B. Otherwise, " gains from trade " would not exist between A and B.

Note, however, that when B has achieved utility-maximising equilibrium,

$$(10) \quad u^B_{Y_1}/u^B_{Y_j} = f^B_{Y_1}/f^B_{Y_j}.$$

That is to say, the marginal rate of substitution in consumption or utilisation is equated to the marginal rate of substitution in production or exchange, i.e., to marginal cost. When (10) holds, the terms in the brackets in (9) mutually cancel. Thus, potentially relevant marginal externalities are also Pareto-relevant when B is in utility-maximising equilibrium. Some trade is possible.

Pareto equilibrium is defined to be present when,

$$(11) \quad (-)u^A_{Y_1}/u^A_{X_j} = [u^B_{Y_1}/u^B_{Y_j} - f^B_{Y_1}/f^B_{Y_j}], \text{ and when } u^A_{Y_1}/u^A_{X_j} < 0, \text{ and}$$
$$u^A_{Y_1}/u^A_{X_j} = (-)[u^B_{Y_1}/u^B_{Y_j} - f^B_{Y_1}/f^B_{Y_j}] \text{ when } u^A_{Y_1}/u^A_{X_j} > 0.$$

Condition (11) demonstrates that marginal externalities may continue to exist, even in Pareto equilibrium, as here defined. This point may be shown by reference to the special case in which the activity in question may be undertaken at zero costs. Here Pareto equilibrium is attained when the marginal rates of substitution in consumption or utilisation for the two persons are precisely offsetting, that is, where their interests are strictly opposed, and *not* where the left-hand term vanishes.

What vanishes in Pareto equilibrium are the Pareto-relevant externalities. It seems clear that, normally, economists have been referring only to what we have here called Pareto-relevant externalities when they have, implicitly or explicitly, stated that external effects are not present when a position on the Pareto optimality surface is attained.[6]

For completeness, we must also consider those potentially relevant infra-marginal externalities. Refer to the discussion of these as summarised in (8) above. The question is now to determine whether or not, A, the externally affected party, can reach some mutually satisfactory agreement with B, the acting party, that will involve some discrete (non-marginal) change in the scope of the activity, Y_1. If, over some range, any range, of the activity, which we shall designate by $\triangle Y_1$, the rate of substitution between Y_1 and X_j for A exceeds the " net " rate of substitution for B, the externality is Pareto-relevant. The associated changes in the utilisation of the numeraire commodity must be equal for the two parties. Thus, for external economies, we have

$$(12) \quad \frac{\triangle u^A}{\triangle Y_1} \bigg/ \frac{\triangle u^A}{\triangle X_j} > (-) \left[\frac{\triangle u^B}{\triangle Y_1} \bigg/ \frac{\triangle u^B}{\triangle Y_j} - \frac{\triangle f^B}{\triangle Y_1} \bigg/ \frac{\triangle f^B}{\triangle Y_j} \right]_{Y_1 = \bar{Y}_1}, \quad \text{and the}$$

same with the sign in parenthesis transposed for external diseconomies. The difference to be noted between (12) and (9) is that, with infra-marginal externalities, potential relevance need not imply Pareto relevance. The bracketed terms in (12) need not sum to zero when B is in his private utility-maximising equilibrium.

We have remained in a two-person world, with one person affected by the single activity of a second. However, the analysis can readily be modified to incorporate the effects of this activity on a multi-person group. That is to say, B's activity, Y_1, may be allowed to affect several parties simultaneously, several A's, so to speak. In each case, the activity can then be evaluated in terms of its effects on the utility of each person. Nothing in the construction need be changed. The only stage in the analysis requiring modification explicitly to take account of the possibilities of multi-person groups being externally affected is that which involves the condition for Pareto relevance and Pareto equilibrium.

For a multi-person group $(A_1, A_2, \ldots, A_n)$, any one or all of whom may be externally affected by the activity, Y_1, of the single person, B, the condition for Pareto relevance is,

$$(9\text{A}) \quad (-) \sum_{i=1}^{n} u_{Y_1}^{Ai}/u_{Xj}^{Ai} > [u_{Y_1}^{B}/u_{Y_j}^{B} - f_{Y_1}^{B}/f_{Y_j}^{B}]_{Y_1 = \bar{Y}_1} \quad \text{when } u_{Y_1}^{Ai}/u_{Xj}^{Ai} < 0, \text{ and,}$$

$$\sum_{i=1}^{n} u_{Y_1}^{Ai}/u_{Xj}^{Ai} > (-)[u_{Y_1}^{B}/u_{Y_j}^{B} - f_{Y_1}^{B}/f_{Y_j}^{B}]_{Y_1 = \bar{Y}_1} \quad \text{when } u_{Y_1}^{Ai}/u_{Xj}^{Ai} > 0.$$

That is, the summed marginal rates of substitution over the members of the externally affected group exceed the offsetting " net " marginal evaluation of the activity by B. Again, in private equilibrium for B, marginal externalities are Pareto-relevant, provided that we neglect the important element involved in the costs of organising group decisions. In the real world, these costs of organising group decisions (together with uncertainty and ignorance) will prevent realisation of some " gains from trade "—just as they do in organised markets. This is as true for two-person groups as it is for larger groups. But this does not invalidate the point that potential " gains from trade " are available. The condition for Pareto equilibrium and for the infra-marginal case summarised in (11) and (12) for the two-person model can readily be modified to allow for the externally affected multi-person group.

II

The distinctions developed formally in Section I may be illustrated diagrammatically and discussed in terms of a simple descriptive example. Consider two persons, A and B, who own adjoining units of residential property. Within limits to be noted, each person values privacy, which may be measured quantitatively in terms of a single criterion, the height of a fence that can be constructed along the common boundary line. We shall assume that B's desire for privacy holds over rather wide limits. His utility increases with the height of the fence up to a reasonably high level. Up to a certain minimum height, A's utility also is increased as the fence is made higher. Once this minimum height is attained, however, A's desire for privacy is assumed to be fully satiated. Thus, over a second range, A's total utility does not change with a change in the height of the fence. However, beyond a certain limit, A's view of a mountain behind B's property is progressively obscured as the fence goes higher. Over this third range, therefore, A's utility is reduced as the fence is constructed to higher levels. Finally, A will once again become wholly indifferent to marginal changes in the fence's height when his view is totally blocked out.

We specify that B possesses the sole authority, the only legal right, to construct the fence between the two properties.

The preference patterns for A and for B are shown in Figure 1, which is drawn in the form of an Edgeworth-like box diagram. Note, however,

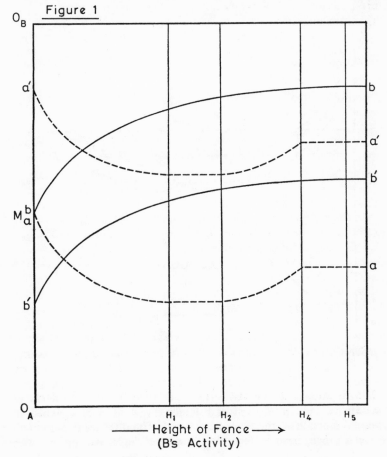

Figure 1

Height of Fence ⟶
(B's Activity)

283

that the origin for B is shown at the upper left rather than the upper right corner of the diagram as in the more normal usage. This modification is necessary here because only the numeraire good, measured along the ordinate, is strictly divisible between A and B. Both must adjust to the same height of fence, that is, to the same level of the activity creating the externality.

As described above, the indifference contours for A take the general shape shown by the curves aa, $a'a'$, while those for B assume the shapes, bb, $b'b'$. Note that these contours reflect the relative evaluations, for A and B, between money and the activity, Y_1. Since the costs of undertaking the activity, for B, are not incorporated in the diagram, the "contract locus" that might be derived from tangency points will have little relevance except in the special case where the activity can be undertaken at zero costs.

Figure 2 depicts the marginal evaluation curves for A and B, as derived from the preference fields shown in Figure 1, along with some

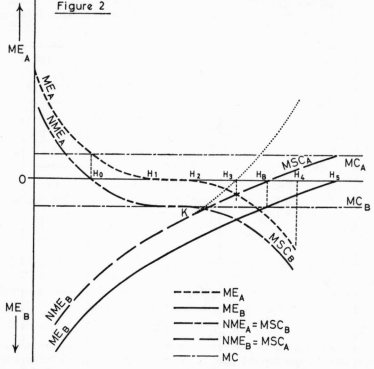

Figure 2

incorporation of costs. These curves are derived as follows: Assume an initial distribution of "money" between A and B, say, that shown at M on Figure 1. The marginal evaluation of the activity for A is then derived by plotting the negatives (i.e., the mirror image) of the slopes of successive indifference curves attained by A as B is assumed to increase the height of the fence from zero. These values remain positive for a range, become zero over a second range, become negative

284

for a third, and, finally, return to zero again.[7]

B's curves of marginal evaluation are measured downward from the upper horizontal axis or base line, for reasons that will become apparent. The derivation of B's marginal evaluation curve is somewhat more complex than that for A. This is because B, who is the person authorised to undertake the action, in this case the building of the fence, must also bear the full costs. Thus, as B increases the scope of the activity, his real income, measured in terms of his remaining goods and services, is reduced. This change in the amount of remaining goods and services will, of course, affect his marginal evaluation of the activity in question. Thus, the marginal cost of building the fence will determine, to some degree, the marginal evaluation of the fence. This necessary interdependence between marginal evaluation and marginal cost complicates the use of simple diagrammatic models in finding or locating a solution. It need not, however, deter us from presenting the solution diagrammatically, if we postulate that the marginal evaluation curve, as drawn, is based on a single presumed cost relationship. This done, we may plot B's marginal evaluation of the activity from the negatives of the slopes of his indifference contours attained as he constructs the fence to higher and higher levels. B's marginal evaluation, shown in Figure 2, remains positive throughout the range to the point H_5, where it becomes zero.

The distinctions noted in Section I are easily related to the construction in Figure 2. To A, the party externally affected, B's potential activity in constructing the fence can be assessed independently of any prediction of B's actual behaviour. Thus, the activity of B would,

(1) exert marginal external economies which are potentially relevant over the range OH_1;

(2) exert infra-marginal external economies over the range H_1H_2, which are clearly irrelevant since no change in B's behaviour with respect to the extent of the activity would increase A's utility;

(3) exert marginal external diseconomies over the range H_2H_4 which are potentially relevant to A; and,

(4) exert infra-marginal external economies or diseconomies beyond H_4, the direction of the effect being dependent on the ratio between the total utility derived from privacy and the total reduction in utility derived from the obstructed view. In any case, the externality is potentially relevant.

To determine Pareto relevance, the extent of B's predicted performance must be determined. The necessary condition for B's attainment of " private " utility-maximising equilibrium is that marginal costs, which he must incur, be equal to his own marginal evaluation. For simplicity in Figure 2, we assume that marginal costs are constant, as shown by the curve, MC. Thus, B's position of equilibrium is shown at H_B, within the range of marginal external diseconomies for A. Here the externality imposed by B's behaviour is clearly Pareto-relevant: A can surely work out some means of compensating B in exchange for

B's agreement to reduce the scope of the activity—in this example, to reduce the height of the fence between the two properties. Diagrammatically, the position of Pareto equilibrium is shown at H_3 where the marginal evaluation of A is equal in absolute value, but negatively, to the "net" marginal evaluation of B, drawn as the curve NME_B. Only in this position are the conditions specified in (11), above, satisfied. [8]

III

Aside from the general classification of externalities that is developed, the approach here allows certain implications to be drawn, implications that have not, perhaps, been sufficiently recognised by some welfare economists.

The analysis makes it quite clear that externalities, external effects, may remain even in full Pareto equilibrium. That is to say, a position may be classified as Pareto-optimal or efficient despite the fact that, at the marginal, the activity of one individual externally affects the utility of another individual. Figure 2 demonstrates this point clearly. Pareto equilibrium is attained at H_3, yet B is imposing marginal external diseconomies on A.

This point has significant policy implications for it suggests that the observation of external effects, taken alone, cannot provide a basis for judgment concerning the desirability of some modification in an existing state of affairs. There is not a *prima facie* case for intervention in all cases where an externality is observed to exist. [9] The internal benefits from carrying out the activity, net of costs, may be greater than the external damage that is imposed on other parties.

In full Pareto equilibrium, of course, these internal benefits, measured in terms of some numeraire good, net of costs, must be just equal, at the margin, to the external damage that is imposed on other parties. This equilibrium will always be characterised by the strict opposition of interests of the two parties, one of which may be a multi-person group.

In the general case, we may say that, at full Pareto equilibrium, the presence of a marginal external diseconomy implies an offsetting marginal *internal* economy, whereas the presence of a marginal external economy implies an offsetting marginal *internal* diseconomy. In "private" equilibrium, as opposed to Pareto equilibrium, these net internal economies and diseconomies would, of course, be eliminated by the utility-maximising acting party. In Pareto equilibrium, these remain because the acting party is being compensated for "suffering" internal economies and diseconomies, that is, divergencies between "private" marginal costs and benefits, *measured in the absence of compensation*.

As a second point, it is useful to relate the whole analysis here to the more familiar Pigovian discussion concerning the divergence between marginal social cost (product) and marginal private cost (product). By saying that such a divergence exists, we are, in the terms of this paper, saying that a marginal externality exists. The Pigovian terminology tends to be misleading, however, in that it deals with the acting party to the exclusion of the externally affected party. It fails to take into account the fact that there are always two parties involved in a single externality relationship.[10] As we have suggested, a marginal externality is Pareto-relevant except in the position of Pareto equilibrium; gains from trade can arise. But there must be two parties to any trading arrangement. The externally affected party must compensate the acting party for modifying his behaviour. The Pigovian terminology, through its concentration on the decision-making of the acting party alone, tends to obscure the two-sidedness of the bargain that must be made.

To illustrate this point, assume that A, the externally affected party in our model, successfully secures, through the auspices of the " state ", the levy of a marginal tax on B's performance of the activity, Y_1. Assume further that A is able to secure this change without cost to himself. The tax will increase the marginal cost of performing the activity for B, and, hence, will reduce the extent of the activity attained in B's " private " equilibrium. Let us now presume that this marginal tax is levied " correctly " on the basis of a Pigovian calculus; the rate of tax at the margin is made equal to the negative marginal evaluation of the activity to A. Under these modified conditions, the effective marginal cost, as confronted by B, may be shown by the curve designated as MSC_B in Figure 2. A new " private " equilibrium for B is shown at the quantity, H_3, the same level designated as Pareto equilibrium in our earlier discussion, if we neglect the disturbing interdependence between marginal evaluation and marginal costs. Attention solely to the decision calculus of B here would suggest, perhaps, that this position remains Pareto-optimal under these revised circumstances, and that it continues to qualify as a position of Pareto equilibrium. There is no divergence between marginal private cost and marginal social cost in the usual sense. However, the position, if attained in this manner, is clearly neither one of Pareto optimality, nor one that may be classified as Pareto equilibrium.

In this new " private " equilibrium for B,

(13) $\quad u^B_{Y_1}/u^B_{Y_j} = f^B_{Y_1}/f^B_{Y_j} - u^A_{Y_1}/u^A_{X_j}$,

where $u^A_{Y_1}/u^A_{X_j}$ represents the marginal tax imposed on B as he performs the activity, Y_1. Recall the necessary condition for Pareto relevance defined in (9) above, which can now be modified to read,

(9B) $\quad (-) u^A_{Y_1}/u^A_{X_j} > [u^B_{Y_1}/u^B_{Y_j} - f^B_{Y_1}/f^B_{Y_j} + u^A_{Y_1}/u^A_{X_j}]_{Y_1 = \overline{\overline{Y}}_1}$, when $u^A_{Y_1}/u^A_{X_j} < 0$,

and $u^A_{Y_1}/u^A_{X_j} > (-)[u^B_{Y_1}/u^B_{Y_j} - f^B_{Y_1}/f^B_{Y_j} + u^A_{Y_1}/u^A_{X_j}]_{Y_1 = \overline{\overline{Y}}_1}$, when $u^A_{Y_1}/u^A_{X_j} > 0$.

In (9B), $\overline{\overline{Y}}_1$ represents the " private " equilibrium value for Y_1, determined by B, after the ideal Pigovian tax is imposed. As before, the bracketed terms represent the " net " marginal evaluation of the activity for the acting party, B, and these sum to zero when equilibrium is reached. So long as the left-hand term in the inequality remains non-zero, a Pareto-relevant marginal externality remains, despite the fact that the full " Pigovian solution " is attained.

The apparent paradox here is not difficult to explain. Since, as postulated, A is not incurring any cost in securing the change in B's behaviour, and, since there remains, by hypothesis, a marginal diseconomy, further " trade " can be worked out between the two parties. Specifically, Pareto equilibrium is reached when,

$$(11A) \quad (-)u^A_{Y_1}/u^A_{X_j} = [u^B_{Y_1}/u^B_{Y_j} - f^B_{Y_1}/f^B_{Y_j} + u^A_{Y_1}/u^A_{X_j}] \text{ when } u^A_{Y_1}/u^A_{X_j} < 0, \text{ and}$$
$$u^A_{Y_1}/u^A_{X_j} = (-)[u^B_{Y_1}/u^B_{Y_j} - f^B_{Y_1}/f^B_{Y_j} + u^A_{Y_1}/u^A_{X_j}] \text{ when } u^A_{Y_1}/u^A_{X_j} > 0.$$

Diagrammatically, this point may be made with reference to Figure 2. If a unilaterally imposed tax, corresponding to the marginal evaluation of A, is placed on B's performance of the activity, the new position of Pareto equilibrium may be shown by first subtracting the new marginal cost curve, drawn as MSC_B, from B's marginal evaluation curve. Where this new " net " marginal evaluation curve, shown as the dotted curve between points H_3 and K, cuts the marginal evaluation curve for A, a new position of Pareto equilibrium falling between H_2 and H_3 is located, neglecting the qualifying point discussed in Footnote 1, page 380.

The important implication to be drawn is that full Pareto equilibrium can never be attained via the imposition of unilaterally imposed taxes and subsidies until all marginal externalities are eliminated. If a tax-subsidy method, rather than " trade ", is to be introduced, it should involve bi-lateral taxes (subsidies). Not only must B's behaviour be modified so as to insure that he will take the costs externally imposed on A into account, but A's behaviour must be modified so as to insure that he will take the costs " internally " imposed on B into account. In such a double tax-subsidy scheme, the necessary Pareto conditions would be readily satisfied.[11]

In summary, Pareto equilibrium in the case of marginal externalities cannot be attained so long as marginal externalities remain, until and unless those benefiting from changes are required to pay some " price " for securing the benefits.

A third point worthy of brief note is that our analysis allows the whole treatment of externalities to encompass the consideration of purely collective goods. As students of public finance theory will have recognised, the Pareto equilibrium solution discussed in this paper is similar, indeed is identical, with that which was presented by Paul Samuelson in his theory of public expenditures.[12] The summed marginal rates of substitution (marginal evaluation) must be equal to marginal costs. Note, however, that marginal costs may include the negative marginal evaluation of other parties, if viewed in one way. Note, also, that there is nothing in the analysis which suggests its limitations to purely collective goods or even to goods that are characterised by significant externalities in their use.

Our analysis also lends itself to the more explicit point developed in Coase's recent paper.[13] He argues that the same " solution " will tend to emerge out of any externality relationship, regardless of the structure of property rights, provided only that the market process works smoothly. Strictly speaking, Coase's analysis is applicable only to inter-firm externality relationships, and the identical solution emerges only because firms adjust to prices that are competitively determined. In our terms of reference, this identity of solution cannot apply because of the incomparability of utility functions. It remains true, however, that the basic characteristics of the Pareto equilibrium position remain unchanged regardless of the authority undertaking the action. This point can be readily demonstrated, again with reference to Figure 2. Let us assume that Figure 2 is now redrawn on the basis of a different legal relationship in which A now possesses full authority to construct the fence, whereas B can no longer take any action in this respect. A will, under these conditions, " privately " construct a fence only to the height H_0, where the activity clearly exerts a Pareto-relevant marginal external economy on B. Pareto equilibrium will be reached, as before, at H_3, determined, in this case, by the intersection of the " net " marginal evaluation curve for A (which is identical to the previously defined marginal social cost curve, MSC, when B is the acting party) and the marginal evaluation curve for B.[14] Note that, in this model, A will allow himself to suffer an internal marginal diseconomy, at equilibrium, provided that he is compensated by B, who continues, in Pareto equilibrium, to enjoy a marginal *external* economy.

Throughout this paper, we have deliberately chosen to introduce and to discuss only a single externality. Much of the confusion in the literature seems to have arisen because two or more externalities have been handled simultaneously. The standard example is that in which the output of one firm affects the production function of the second firm while, at the same time, the output of the second firm affects the production function of the first. Clearly, there are two externalities to be analysed in such cases. In many instances, these can be treated as separate and handled independently. In other situations, this step cannot be taken and additional tools become necessary.[15]

REFERENCES

[1] Tibor Scitovosky, " Two Concepts of External Economies ", *Journal of Political Economy*, vol. LXII (1954), p. 143.

[2] J. de V. Graaf, *Theoretical Welfare Economics*, Cambridge, 1957, p. 43 and p. 18.

[3] Note that, $u_{Y_1}^A \big|_{Y_1 = \bar{Y}_1} = 0$, is a necessary, but not a sufficient, condition for irrelevance.

[4] In this analysis of the relevance of externalities, we have assumed that B will act in such a manner as to maximise his own utility subject to the constraints within which he must operate. If, for any reason, B does not attain the equilibrium position defined in (5) above, the classification of his activity for A may, of course, be modified. A potentially relevant externality may become irrelevant and *vice versa*.

[5] We are indebted to Mr. M. McManus of the University of Birmingham for pointing out to us an error in an earlier formulation of this and the following similar conditions.

[6] This applies to the authors of this paper. For recent discussion of external effects when we have clearly intended only what we here designate as Pareto-relevant, see James M. Buchanan, " Politics, Policy, and the Pigovian Margins ", *Economica*, vol. XXVIX (1962), pp. 17–28, and, also, James M. Buchanan and Gordon Tullock, *The Calculus of Consent*, Ann Arbor, 1962.

[7] For an early use of marginal evaluation curves, see J. R. Hicks, " The Four

Consumer's Surpluses ", *Review of Economic Studies,* vol. xi (1943), pp. 31–41.

[8] This diagrammatic analysis is necessarily oversimplified in the sense that the Pareto equilibrium position is represented as a unique point. Over the range between the " private " equilibrium for *B* and the point of Pareto equilibrium, the sort of bargains struck between *A* and *B* will affect the marginal evaluation curves of both individuals within this range. Thus, the more accurate analysis would suggest a " contract locus " of, equilibrium points. At Pareto equilibrium, however, the condition shown in the diagrammatic presentation holds, and the demonstration of this fact rather than the location of the solution is the aim of this diagrammatics.

[9] Cf. Paul A. Samuelson, *Foundations of Economic Analysis,* Cambridge, Mass., 1948, p. 208, for a discussion of the views of various writers.

[10] This criticism of the Pigovian analysis has recently been developed by R. H. Coase; see his " The Problem of Social Cost ", *Journal of Law and Economics,* vol. iii (1960), pp. 1–44.

[11] Although developed in rather different terminology, this seems to be closely in accord with Coase's analysis. Cf. R. H. Coase, *loc. cit.*

[12] Paul A. Samuelson, " The Pure Theory of Public Expenditure ", *Review of Economics and Statistics,* vol. xxxvi (1954), pp. 386–9.

[13] R. H. Coase, *loc. cit.*

[14] The H_3 position, in this presumably redrawn figure, should not be precisely compared with the same position in the other model. We are using here the same diagram for two models, and, especially over wide ranges, the dependence of the marginal evaluation curves on income effects cannot be left out of account.

[15] For a treatment of the dual externality problem that clearly shows the important difference between the separable and the non-separable cases, see Otto Davis and Andrew Whinston, " Externalities, Welfare, and the Theory of Games ", *Journal of Political Economy,* vol. lxx (1962), pp. 241–62. As the title suggests, Davis and Whinston utilise the tools of game theory for the inseparable case.

Externalities, Welfare, and the Theory of Games[1]

By OTTO A. DAVIS and ANDREW WHINSTON

I. INTRODUCTION

It has traditionally been argued that, if firms create external economies and diseconomies, the proper role of a welfare-maximizing government is to constrain the behavior of firms by arranging rates of taxes and subsidies in order to equate private with social benefit. We attempt to establish both the conditions under which this classical policy prescription might work and is needed, and those under which it cannot be expected to work.

First, we argue that motivation exists for firms themselves to try to eliminate externalities in production through merger. Second, we attempt to show that technological externalities can be divided neatly into two cases, which we label "separable" and "non-separable," respectively. Third, if merger has not eliminated the externalities, we argue that the classical scheme of per unit taxes and subsidies can be clearly successful in equating private with social benefit only in the separable cases. Fourth, if the externality is non-separable, we argue that it is not clear that the classical prescription can work even at the conceptual level, since problems of uncertainty and the non-existence of equilibrium arise. Finally, we note that this latter possibility poses some difficult problems for policy-makers, and we attempt to outline and explore briefly alternative policy approaches.

The analytic approach which we shall employ involves the consideration of two firms in a competitive industry. The traditional or classical approach, on the other hand, often involves an analysis of externality between competitive industries. We choose to depart from this traditional approach for several reasons. First, the firm is an entity which fits more easily into the framework of our analysis. Second, and more fundamental, it is individual decision units—firms—which react to externalities so that it seems more "natural" to conduct the analysis at that level.[2] Furthermore, concentration upon the industry (as op-

Reprinted by permission of the publishers and authors: Otto A. Davis and Andrew Whinston, "Externalities, Welfare, and the Theory of Games," *Journal of Political Economy,* 70 (June 1962), pp. 241-262.

posed to the firm) requires a certain amount of aggregation which tends to mask some of the more important and interesting points at issue. This aggregation is especially misleading with respect to public policy regulation, where the problem is made to appear much more simple than it actually is. Finally, utilization of the firm as the basic analytic unit gives a level of generality which is greater than can be obtained through the traditional approach. The reason for this is that no two firms in an industry may be affected identically by an externality, or some firms in an industry may impose (different "amounts" of) an externality upon other production units, while the remaining firms in the industry may not create externalities. And it should be emphasized at the outset that our concern with firms within the same industry is only a device to simplify the analysis. A more elaborate use of subscripts would allow the firms under consideration to be in different industries.

Yet another result of our approach will be a demonstration that externality problems involve *many aspects of duopoly problems*. This will be particularly striking in the case which we consider—reciprocal externality between two firms—but, peculiarly enough, these duopoly-like problems remain even if the number of firms under consideration is expanded to n. We shall not attempt such an expansion here, however, since all relevant aspects of the problem seem to be contained in the two-firm case, so that a sufficient level of generality can be achieved without resort to additional complications.

II. MOTIVATION AND MERGER

Consider two firms in a purely competitive industry which are related through their cost functions (external economies and diseconomies on the production side),[3] Assume that the cost functions are

$$C_1 = C_1(q_1, q_2)$$
$$C_2 = C_2(q_1, q_2),$$
(1)

where the subscripts refer to the respective firms, C represents cost, and q indicates the output level.[4] If each firm maximizes profit, we have the relationships

$$p = \frac{\partial C_1}{\partial q_1} \quad \text{and} \quad p = \frac{\partial C_2}{\partial q_2},$$
(2)

where p represents price.[5] Each firm must maximize its profit with respect to the variable under its control, although the level of its profit depends by assumption upon the output level of the other firm.

It is well known that the welfare associated with the production of the commodity can be measured by the difference between social benefit and social cost, and that in a competitive market the social benefit can be measured by the firms' total revenue, $p(q_1 + q_2)$, while social costs can be measured by the firms' total costs, $C_1(q_1, q_2) + C_2(q_1, q_2)$. It follows that, in order to maximize welfare, the joint profits of the firms must be maximized. In other words, using

292

P to represent profits, let

$$P = P_1 + P_2 = p(q_1 + q_2)$$
$$-C_1(q_1, q_2) - C_2(q_1, q_2)$$

(3)

represent the total profits of these two firms as indicated by the relevant subscripts. A necessary condition for maximization under the indicated assumptions is

$$\frac{\partial P}{\partial q_1} = p - \frac{\partial C_1}{\partial q_1} - \frac{\partial C_2}{\partial q_1} = 0$$

$$\frac{\partial P}{\partial q_2} = p - \frac{\partial C_1}{\partial q_2} - \frac{\partial C_2}{\partial q_2} = 0,$$

(4)

and a sufficient condition is

$$\frac{\partial^2 P}{\partial q_1^2} < 0, \qquad \frac{\partial^2 P}{\partial q_2^2} < 0$$

$$\frac{\partial^2 P}{\partial q_1^2} \frac{\partial^2 P}{\partial q_2^2} > \left(\frac{\partial^2 P}{\partial q_1 \partial q_2} \right)^2$$

(5)

Attention will now be focused on the first-order (necessary) conditions as given in (4). Note that if either $(\partial C_2)/(\partial q_1) \neq 0$ or $(\partial C_1)/(\partial q_2) \neq 0$, then conditions (2) and (4) will not coincide. Due to the technological externalities, profit maximization by the individual firms will not give the greatest social benefit that is possible.[6]

Marshall and Pigou, considering the case of a negatively sloped supply curve, suggested the possible use of taxes and subsidies as one way to handle this type of difficulty. Meade has effected a modern statement of this classical solution.[7] In particular, Meade argues that a tax-subsidy solution is sufficient to achieve the desired welfare-maximizing solution. We shall argue at a later point in this paper that a tax-subsidy approach is not sufficient to guarantee the attainment of a welfare maximum and, furthermore, that in some cases it is not even clear that it will lead to an improvement in social welfare. We shall attempt now to show that this scheme is not necessary for the optimal welfare solution.

In contrast to the above authors, we do not take the firms as given. Rather, we shall argue that there is a "natural unit" for decision-making and that this unit is responsive to market forces. A "natural unit" is defined as one which results after sufficient mergers have taken place to produce a certain "minimal" set of interrelationships with other units in society. In the context of this discussion, these "interrelationships" may be thought of as external economies and diseconomies.

As might be expected, the formation of natural units poses certain problems. These range from the question of how a competitive market structure is maintained in the face of mergers to the question of the terms on which such mergers may be arranged. For the moment, however, let these problems be waived. Then if either or both

$$\frac{\partial C_2}{\partial q_1} \neq 0, \qquad \frac{\partial C_1}{\partial q_2} \neq 0 \tag{6}$$

obtains, it seems clear that either (a) there would be some price at which one firm would be willing to acquire the other or (b), more generally, gains to both firms can be secured by effecting a merger. These two cases are lumped into one here simply to argue that a tendency toward such mergers is consistent with, if not implied by, the idea of profit maximization. Consequently, there would be a tendency for such mergers to occur, for production externalities to be internalized, and for joint profits (hence social welfare, if competition is maintained) to be maximized. Insofar as this occurs, a natural unit for decision-making would be realized and, assuming competition, welfare maximized without the use of externally imposed subventions or penalties.[8]

We do not claim, of course, that the natural unit will always be achieved. Instead, we are content to point out that motivation exists for the formation of natural units, and we argue that there should be a tendency toward such mergers. However, realism compels us to recognize that such problems as might be associated with decentralized administration within the merged entity might prevent the achievement of the natural unit in some instances. In addition, from the standpoint of social policy, some mergers might result in a change of market structure and, therefore, be deemed socially undesirable. Hence, it seems appropriate to analyze the externality question further in order to determine whether there exist workable schemes for welfare maxima when the natural unit has not been realized.

III. SEPARABILITY AND DOMINANCE

Since we shall argue that the classical tax-subsidy prescription will not achieve the optimal welfare solution in all cases, it seems desirable to try to determine the conditions under which the scheme can or cannot be expected to work. In this regard it is convenient, in order to make clear the distinction between what at a later point we call the "separable" and the "non-separable" types of externalities, to introduce the following definition. A function, $f(x_1, x_2)$, is said to be "separable"[9] if and only if

$$f(x_1, x_2) = f_1(x_1) + f_2(x_2). \tag{7}$$

In other words, separability means that it must be possible to express the function, $f(x_1, x_2)$, as a sum of two functions each of which involves only one variable in its argument.[10]

As a case in point, we may consider a specific example of two interrelated, but separable, cost functions:

$$C_1(q_1, q_2) = A_1 q_1^n + B_1 q_2^m$$
$$C_2(q_1, q_2) = A_2 q_2^r - B_2 q_1^s. \tag{8}$$

The profit maximization condition (2) then gives

$$p = \frac{\partial C_1}{\partial q_1} = n A_1 q_1^{n-1}$$
$$p = \frac{\partial C_2}{\partial q_2} = r A_2 q_2^{r-1}. \tag{9}$$

Note in particular that the marginal cost of each firm is given entirely in terms of its own output variable.

The typical cases with which the classical analysis has been concerned have, infact, assumed the condition of separability.[11] When this assumption is dropped, there is inevitably introduced an element of uncertainty which becomes rather difficult to deal with in terms of traditional tools and concepts. We shall also attempt to show at a later point that the absence of this condition complicates policy choices and, in particular, renders the tax-subsidy scheme practically useless.

For the moment, however, let us continue our analysis under the traditional assumption of separability. Consider the rule "price equals marginal cost" for each firm as represented in (9). Evidently, each firm may calculate its marginal cost unambiguously at every output, and, therefore, it can also determine its output unambiguously in accordance with the stipulated rule.

To bring out the importance of this consequence of separability, it is desirable to reformulate the problem in terms of a two-person non-zero sum continuous game.[12] To accomplish this reformulation we note that by definition

$$P_1 = P_1(q_1, q_2) = p q_1 - C_1(q_1, q_2)$$
$$P_2 = P_2(q_1, q_2) = p q_2 - C_2(q_1, q_2), \tag{10}$$

where p is taken as given by the market. The game aspect of this problem is the fact that the profit level of each firm depends upon the output (strategy) selected by the other firm. Consonant with the assumptions of classical analysis, it is assumed that the game is non-cooperative. Neither firm communicates with or consults the other while making its choice of output. Then the rule of profit maximization gives "price equals marginal cost" for each firm. But since the marginal cost of each firm as stated in (9) is defined entirely in terms of its own output, this rule means that whatever the output chosen by firm 2, there is a unique output which maximizes firm 1's profit. Similarly, for firm 2 there exists a unique output at which, whatever the output of firm 1, its profits are maximal. In the context of game theory, this is the Von Neumann-Morgenstern concept of dominance.

We shall shortly state this result in terms of mathematical theorems and explore more fully its implications within the relatively simpler context of discrete games. Before leaving the continuous case, however, it seems appropriate to describe what separability means in terms of the familiar graphical approach. In the particular case which we are examining, the total cost of each firm is a function of two variables, its own output and the output of the other firm, and can be represented on a two-dimensional graph by a family of curves relating the firm's costs to its own ouput for various given levels of the other firm's output. "Separability" means that a change in the other firm's output simply shifts the cost curve of the firm vertically upward or downward.

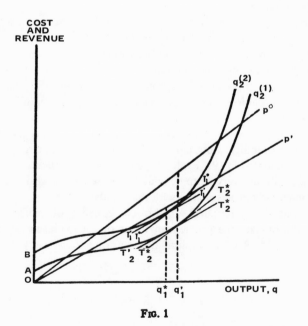

FIG. 1

296

This case is depicted in Figure 1. Here two functions are drawn $-Aq_2{}^1$ and $Bq_2{}^2$. If the externality is an external economy, then $q_2{}^1 > q_2{}^2$; and if the externality is an external diseconomy, then the inequality is reversed. As we have shown, separability means in the context of this discussion that externalities do not affect marginal cost. Hence, the cost functions differ from each other by the value of a constant (the value of the externality) since the slopes of the tangent lines (marginal cost) of all possible total cost functions at any specified level of output must be equal to each other. Thus, given some specified price and total revenue curve—say Op'—an alteration in the value of the externality, q_2, will not change the optimal output q_1^* of the firm.[13] The effect of separable externalities is strictly intra-marginal. They affect the over-all profit position of the firm but do not alter marginal cost and, hence, do not alter the optimal output choice of the firm.

We are now able to state precisely the major results obtained thus far:

Theorem I: The presence of separable externalities in a firm's cost function implies, under the usual convexity assumption, that the firm must follow the "marginal cost equals price" rule in order to maximize profits. Conversely, an operational "marginal cost equals price" rule for profit maximization implies that any technological externality must be separable.[14]

Our previous discussion has dealt extensively with the first part of this theorem; we content ourselves with two further observations. First, note that as long as the firm remains in operation, the value of the externality is irrelevant to the firm's attempt to maximize profits because (*a*) by assumption the possibilities of merger, collusion, or co-operation are not admitted here and (*b*) the firm by definition cannot exercise control over the externality in the absence of these possibilities. Second, we note that by definition separability means, in this context, that marginal cost is defined in terms of the firm's own output variable. Consequently, if

$$\frac{\partial C_1}{\partial q_1} \neq p,$$

profits are not maximal and are made so, by well-known theorems, only when this equality is established.

The second part of the theorem has not been explicitly considered. Again we choose to proceed along intuitively appealing routes rather than with nothing but mathematical rigor. Accordingly, we again turn our attention to Figure 1. We wish to show that, if the firm can follow operationally the "marginal cost equals price" rule, then the externality must be separable.

First, for the "price equals marginal cost" rule to be operational, the firm must be able to equate marginal cost to price over all relevant ranges of price variation. Accordingly, we have drawn two total revenue curves, Op' and Op^*, corresponding to the two prices which we wish explicitly to consider. Let us consider now the price represented by the slope of Op'. Call this price p'. If the firm follows the "marginal cost equals price" rule, then it must equate the tangent to its cost curve, say $Aq_2{}^1$, with price p'. Therefore, the firm would choose output q_1^* since the slope of $T'_2 T'_2$ equals the slope of Op' at this point.

But for the marginal cost curve to be uniquely defined, any other cost curve (caused by a change in the value of the externality), say $Bq_2{}^2$ must have a tangent $T'_1 T'_1$ with the same slope at q_1^*. This means that the total cost curves differ from one another by some constant amount at q_1^*

Now let us consider any other price, p^*, which is represented by the slope of Op^*. The same argument applies here as was used above. The firm must equate the slope of the tangent to its cost curve, say $T_2^* T_2^*$, to price p^*. Therefore, output q'_1 is chosen. But in order for the marginal cost curve to be unambiguously defined,[15] the tangents to all other total cost curves—$T_1 T_1^*$, for example—must have the same slope at q'^*_1 as $T_2^* T_2^*$. Therefore, the total cost curves differ from each other by some constant amount at q'^*_1.

Since, as long as the firm remains in operation, the above argument applies for all prices, it follows that the total cost curves differ from each other only by some constant amount. This can only be the case if the externalities are separable.

Theorem II: Separable externalities imply the game theoretic concept of dominance.

We have shown that separable externalities imply the "price equals marginal cost" rule for profit maximization. But this means, as long as the firm remains in operation, that the same output is optimal for the firm no matter what value the externality takes on. This means that one firm's output decision is independent of the other firm's decision and this is, by definition, the game-theoretic concept of dominance in the context of our approach.

Let us now turn our attention to discrete cases in order that we may explore the welfare implications of separable externalities with the analytical tools of game theory without having to resort to the mathematical complications of continuous games. It can be argued, of course, that most firms will not know their marginal cost functions exactly. But it is usually assumed that to a satisfactory degree of approximation they can at least determine noticeable stepped increments in cost for discrete variations in production. And if this argument is accepted, then the discrete formulation is entirely appropriate. We prefer the discrete formulation, however, for additional reasons. First, it entails no real loss of generality and avoids resort to more complicated mathematics. Second, the theory of discrete games is easily available and widely known.[16]

Before proceeding to the discrete game formulation, however, it is necessary to digress briefly on the meaning of the "price equals marginal cost" rule for discrete cases.

We first note that, under the usual convexity assumptions, the "marginal cost pricing" rule is derived from a maximization problem. This fact is the essence of our argument for the discrete case. Each firm is assumed to attempt to pick that (discrete) output for which its profits are maximal. What is required is that we formalize this condition—the analogue of the marginal-cost-pricing rule—for the discrete case.

Let us consider first the simpler problem where externalities are not present. Suppose that the cost function $C(q)$ of a firm is defined for only certain values of q. In other words, this firm produces only at discrete levels of output. We now define a set Q

$$Q = [q \mid C(q) \text{ defined}] . \tag{11}$$

In other words, the set Q is composed of all the values of q which the firm could choose. Still using P to represent profits and p price, we note that the firm would desire to maximize

$$P(q) = pq - C(q) \tag{12}$$

over the set Q. Suppose that q^* is that feasible output for which (12) is maximal. Then it is obvious that

$$P(q^* + \Delta q) - P(q^*) \leqslant 0 \tag{13}$$

must hold for all admissible choices for Δq since otherwise q^* could not be the most profitable output as was assumed. Now we may use the profit function (12) in order to rewrite (13) in the following form:

$$p(q^* + \Delta q) - C(q^* + \Delta q) \tag{14}$$
$$- pq^* + C(q^*) \leqslant 0.$$

From (14) we can obtain

$$p \Delta q \leqslant C(q^* + \Delta q) - C(q^*). \tag{15}$$

And from this the formal statement for the discrete analogue for the "marginal cost equals price" rule becomes rather obvious.

$$p \leq \frac{C(q^* + \Delta q) - C(q^*)}{\Delta q} \qquad p \geq \frac{C(q^* + \Delta q) - C(q^*)}{\Delta q} \tag{16}$$
$$\text{for } \Delta q > 0 \qquad\qquad \text{for } \Delta q < 0.$$

In other words, the optimal output q^* must satisfy the condition that if output were to be increased by any admissible amount Δq, then price would be less than the slope of the line segment joining the two points $C(q^* + \Delta q)$ and $C(q^*)$. Conversely, if output were to be decreased by any admissible amount Δq, then price would be greater than the slope of the line segment joining these two points.

Let us now examine this discrete problem when externalities are present. Suppose that the cost function $C(q_1, q_2)$ of the firm under consideration is separable, so that

$$C(q_1, q_2) = \bar{c}(q_1) + \hat{c}(q_2). \tag{17}$$

Since this firm is assumed to produce only certain (discrete) outputs, $C(q_1, q_2)$ is defined only for these values of q_1. Let a set Q_1, composed of all values of q_1

which can be chosen, be defined as in (11). Note that the firm would desire to maximize a profit function

$$P(q_1, q_2) = pq_1 - C(q_1, q_2) \qquad (18)$$

over the set Q_1. Assuming that q_1^* is a feasible output for which (18) is maximal, given any particular value of q_2, then it follows that

$$P(q_1^* + \Delta q_1, q_2) - P(q_1^*, q_2) \leq 0 \qquad (19)$$

must hold for all admissible choices of Δq_1. As was done for the previous example, we may substitute the profit function into the above in order to obtain

$$\begin{aligned} p(q_1^* + \Delta q_1) &- \bar{c}(q_1^* + \Delta q_1) \\ &- \hat{c}(q_2) - pq_1^* + \bar{c}(q_1^*) \\ &+ \hat{c}(q_2) \leq 0 . \end{aligned} \qquad (20)$$

Collecting terms gives

$$p\Delta q_1 \leq \bar{c}(q_1^* + \Delta q_1) - \bar{c}(q_1^*), \qquad (21)$$

from which it follows that

$$p \leq \frac{\bar{c}(q_1^* + \Delta q_1) - \bar{c}(q_1^*)}{\Delta q_1} \quad \text{for } \Delta q_1 > 0 \qquad p \geq \frac{\bar{c}(q_1^* + \Delta q_1) - \bar{c}(q_1^*)}{\Delta q_1} \quad \text{for } \Delta q_1 < 0. \qquad (22)$$

These are, of course, the discrete analogue of the "marginal cost equals price" rule for the case with separable externalities, and, as was expected, there is a similarity between (22) and (16). Note that the externality, $\hat{c}(q_2)$, does not appear in (22). Evidently, in the case of separable externalities, discreteness does not affect the results which were obtained for the continuous case. The firm may calculate the cost associated with each discrete change in output and, therefore, it can determine its output unambiguously in accordance with the stipulated rule (22). In particular, it is interesting to note that no matter what value the externality takes on, the firm will still select, as long as it remains in operation, the output q_1^*.

It should be obvious that both Theorem I and Theorem II apply for the discrete case with appropriate modifications in wording. In other words, Theorem I can be restated as follows: the presence of separable externalities in a firm's discrete cost function implies that the firm must follow the discrete analogue (22) to the "marginal cost equals price" rule in order to maximize profits. Conversely, the discrete analogue to the "marginal cost equals price" rule for profit maximization implies that any technological externality must be separable. Theorem II is applicable as it stands. No rewording is needed.

Since the proofs for the discrete case follow the same form as those for the continuous case, we choose to omit them here. The theorems are intuitively obvious in any event.

We are now able to formulate this problem in terms of a discrete, two-person, non-zero sum game in order to explore the welfare implications of separable externalities. Thus let us represent the various combinations of outputs (strategies) of the two firms by the following game matrix:

$$\begin{matrix} & \text{Firm 2} \\ & j = 1, \ldots, m \\ i = 1 \\ \text{Firm 1} \quad \begin{array}{c} \cdot \\ \cdot \\ n \end{array} \left[\quad (a_{ij}, b_{ij}) \quad \right] \end{matrix} \quad (23)$$

The profit accruing to firm 1 when it chooses the output associated with row i, and firm 2 chooses the output associated with column j a_{ij}. Similarly, b_{ij} represents the profit accruing to firm 2 when the indicated output choices are made.[17]

Consonant with the assumptions of classical analysis and with our assumptions of this section, it is assumed that the game is non-co-operative. Then, since we assume separability and a competitive market, Theorem I tells us that the supposition of profit maximization gives "price equals marginal cost" for each firm. But, since separability requires that the marginal cost of each firm be given entirely in terms of its own output, this rule means that for firm 1 there exists a row for which, given any particular output of firm 2, its profits are maximal. Similarly, for firm 2 there exists a column for which, given any particular output of firm 1, its profits are greater than at any other output level. These results are apparent from the discussion concerning Theorem I where it was shown that the value of the externality (or the output decision of the other firm) was irrelevant for the optimal output decision by either of the firms under consideration. Theorem II tells us that this is the Von Neumann-Morgenstern concept of dominance.

It is true, of course, that individual maxima need not—indeed, in general will not—be equal to the maxima for both firms considered together as a coordinated unit. This is apparent from (18) and was the cause of our concern in section 2 when we attempted to show that, under competition, joint maximization is a necessary condition for a welfare optimum. A simple example, attributed to A. W. Tucker and developed in an entirely different context, may be helpful here.[18]

Assume that the payoff (profit) matrix for the two "interrelated" firms is as follows:

$$\begin{matrix} & & \text{Firm 2} \\ & & Q_1 & \quad Q_2 \\ \text{Firm 1} & \begin{matrix} R_1 \\ R_2 \end{matrix} & \left[\begin{matrix} (0.9, 0.9) & (0, 1) \\ (1, 0) & (0.1, 0.1) \end{matrix} \right] \end{matrix} \quad (24)$$

Clearly, row R_2 is dominant for firm 1 since $1 > 0.9$ and $0.1 > 0$. Column Q_2 is dominant for firm 2 since $1 > 0.9$ and $0.1 > 0$. Hence, the non-co-operative solution is R_2, Q_2, which yields a profit of 0.1 to each firm.[19]

Since a competitive market structure is assumed here, the appropriate welfare solution is the joint maximum R_1, Q_1, with an individual profit to each firm of 0.9. The problem of social policy is how to bring about this solution.

IV. SOME POSSIBLE APPROACHES

Let us now discuss possible ways in which the desired welfare solution could be accomplished. First, the government could adopt a "planning" approach and impose direct constraints so that the appropriate outputs—R_1, Q_1 for the previous example—would be chosen. While we shall postpone a detailed discussion of this "constrained-game" formulation until a later point in the paper, it is appropriate that we point out here some of the difficulties associated with this approach. In a more complicated situation than that represented by our simple example (24), such as the more general cases conceptualized in the matrix (23) or the continuous game formulation, the governmental policy-maker must possess some knowledge of the cost functions of the individual firms, or at least some knowledge of the entries in the payoff matrix, in order to accomplish this solution. Since many firms and multitudes of externalities may be present in the real world, the problem of gaining adequate information appears to be very great.[20]

Second, the welfare solution could be achieved by imposing a tax-subsidy arrangement that brought the appropriate output decisions—for example, R_1, Q_1 in (24)—into a position of dominance. Although it might appear a simple task for the policy-maker to accomplish this result in the simple example (24), since an exact knowledge of the costs and profits of each firm would not be required, but only sufficiently large tax-subsidy arrangements to reverse the indicated dominance, the general cases are more complicated and demanding. Therefore, it seems entirely appropriate to consider the conditions which the tax or subsidy would have to meet in order to accomplish the desired solution.

Let us consider, first, the continuous case. The policy-maker must be able to determine (at least approximately) appropriate outputs for each firm in order that proper taxes and subsidies can be levied. This could be accomplished in our two-firm examples by solving equations (4) simultaneously in order to obtain the $q1$ and q_2 that achieve joint maximization. Designate these welfare-optimal outputs q_1^* and q_2^*. Then, using t to represent both taxes and subsidies (a positive t indicates a subsidy and a negative t a tax), the proper subvention or penalty would be given by

$$p + t_1 = \frac{\partial C_1(q_1, q_2)}{\partial q_1} \bigg| q_1^* \qquad p + t_2 = \frac{\partial C_2(q_1, q_2)}{\partial q_2} \bigg| q_2^* . \qquad (25)$$

Of course, p is easily available. But the partial derivatives which have to be evaluated here (and available for a solution to [4]) may not be so readily obtainable. To say the least, the policy-maker would have to make an intensive study in order to obtain the desired information.

We now turn our attention to the discrete case. Here, too, the policy-maker must be able to determine appropriate welfare outputs—perhaps by simultaneously solving discrete equations for a joint maxima—in order to determine proper taxes and subsidies. Designate a welfare optimal output for firm 1 byq_1^*.[21] Since the firm is free to choose any output q_1 which it pleases, it is obvious that, if the welfare optimal output q_1^* is to be chosen, the per unit tax or subsidy must be such that (19) is satisfied. If t is used as it was in the previous discussion, then $p + t_1$ *can be used instead of* p in the derivation (equations [20] and [21]) of condition (22) with the result that

$$p + t_1 \leqslant \frac{\bar{c}(\overset{*}{q}_1 + \Delta q_1) - \bar{c}(\overset{*}{q}_1)}{\Delta q_1} \qquad p + t_1 \geqslant \frac{\bar{c}(q_1^* + \Delta q_1) - \bar{c}(q_1^*)}{\Delta q_1} \qquad (26)$$
$$\text{for } \Delta q_1 > 0 \qquad\qquad\qquad \text{for } \Delta q_1 < 0$$

must obtain. Once again, p is easily available for the policy-maker, but the slopes of the line segments joining $c(q_1^* \quad Yq_1)$ and $c(q_1^*)$ may not be so readily obtainable although, of course, an evaluation may be possible. The interesting point concerning the discrete case, however, is that taxes and subsidies are not necessarily determined uniquely. Instead, there may be limits, which depend upon the relative slopes of the line segments, between which the taxes and subsidies can vary.[22]

It is almost trivial to point out, however, that in both the discrete and continuous cases the tax-subsidy solution does not possess one of the most important characteristics of a perfectly functioning market mechanism. Each time there is a technological change which affects the firms under consideration, there would have to be a recomputation and adjustment of the taxes and subsidies. A perfectly functioning market, on the other hand, automatically adjusts for these changes (at least from the point of view of comparative statics).

As a final policy approach, we note that, provided that the market structure can remain competitive, forces may exist within the price system that will tend to produce the optimal solution even with no action by the government. For merger might be mutually beneficial to both firms and could be expected to occur if either the rules of society or possible internal problems of decentralized administration within the merged entity did not prevent such action.[23]

It is interesting to note that Meade, who produced the modern restatement of the classical tax-subsidy prescription for the externality problem, does not even consider the possibility of the merger solution in his "unpaid factors case."[24] In fact, in the particular example that Meade uses, this solution appears possible. The example involves apple growers and honey producers. The nectar from apple blossoms is a scarce commodity which, it is postulated, cannot be priced. (Later in his analysis Meade also assumes that the bees help to pollinate the apples, thus creating a mutual externality.) Thus Meade advocates the classical solution of taxes and subsidies. If, however, there exists a spatial distribution of apple growers and honey producers such that after merger one firm's bees would not be expected to wander over into some other firm's apple orchard, the externality would be internalized and, if competition could be maintained, the optimal solution would result.

V. NON-SEPARABLE COST FUNCTIONS

Let us now consider the non-separable type of externality where it is not clear that the usual solution of taxes and subsidies will work, even at the conceptual level. The difference between the separable and the non-separable cases lies in the fact that externality enters the cost function in a "multiplicative" manner rather than in a manner which is strictly "additive." In other words, the separability condition (7) is not satisfied.

Once again, it is necessary for us to discuss both continuous and discrete cases. We consider the continuous case first. And it also seems completely appropriate, because of the greater clarity achieved, to proceed by assuming specific cost functions:

$$C_1(q_1, q_2) = A_1 q_1^n + B_1 q_1 q_2^m$$

$$C_2(q_1, q_2) = A_2 q_2^r - B_2 q_2^t q_1^s .$$

(27)

Profit maximization by each individual firm implies the following relationships:

$$p = \frac{\partial C_1}{\partial q_1} = n A_1 q_1^{n-1} + B_1 q_2^m$$

$$p = \frac{\partial C_2}{\partial q_2} = r A_2 q_2^{r-1} - t B_2 q_2^{t-1} q_1^s .$$

(28)

Now note that, from the individual firm's standpoint, marginal cost is defined not only in terms of the variable which it can control—its own output—but also in terms of the variable which it cannot control—the other firm's output. Both q_1 and q_2 enter into each equation. How, then, can the firm choose an output which will maximize its profit when its own marginal cost depends upon the decision of the other firm?

Let us now compare and contrast the continuous cases of separable and non-separable externalities in order to bring out the effects of non-separability. It will be recalled from Figure 1 that a change in the value of a separable externality had the effect of vertically shifting the total cost curve upward or downward. The curves differ from one another only by the value of a constant. Thus at any given output the slopes of the tangent curves—that is, marginal cost—were not affected by alterations in the value of the externality. The non-separable case does not have this property. While alterations in the value of the externality cause the total cost curve to shift upward and downward, there is no reason to expect that this shift will be a simple vertical displacement. In general, total cost curves generated by changes in the value of a non-separable externality will not simply differ from each other by the value of a constant. Rotation or some other type of alteration is likely to take place when the externality changes in value. This fact is, of course, obvious from the fact that the separability condition (7) is not satisfied. It can also be seen from observation of the marginal cost curves (28) of our special example.

It is now obvious that the "marginal cost equals price" rule is affected by non-separable externalities. For whereas separable externalities had a strictly intramarginal effect, non-separable externalities affect the margin. In (28) the externality enters into the definition of marginal cost. Since by definition the firm cannot control the value of the externality, it clearly follows that the firm will find it difficult *operationally* to follow the "marginal cost equals price" rule of profit maximization. The fact is that, for the non-separable case, marginal cost is ambiguously defined in terms of the firm's own output.

From the game-theoretic standpoint, this type of externality suggests the absence of dominance. This point, too, is obvious from the separability condition (7) and from the marginal cost curves (28) of our example. For, supposing that the firm desires to maximize profits, it must alter its output with every change in the value of the externality in order to attempt to equate marginal costs with price. This means that the optimal output (strategy) of one firm depends upon the output (strategy) selected by the other firm. Such interdependence is the essence of non-dominance.

Now let us examine the discrete case, in order to utilize the analytical tools of the theory of games in exploring the welfare implications of non-separable externalities. It is necessary, of course, that we state the discrete analogue for the "marginal cost equals price" rule for the non-separable case. Then, assuming that $C(q_1, q_2)$ is a non-separable cost function which is defined for a set Q_1 of discrete outputs, we may derive

$$p \leqslant \frac{C(q_1^* + \Delta q_1, q_2) - C(q_1^*, q_2)}{\Delta q_1} \qquad p \geqslant \frac{C(q_1^* + \Delta q_1, q_2) - C(q_1^*, q_2)}{\Delta q_1} \qquad (29)$$

$$\text{for } \Delta q_1 > 0 \qquad\qquad\qquad \text{for } \Delta q_1 < 0$$

as the desired rule.[25] But note that, since $C(q_1, q_2)$ is non-separable, the terms involving the externality cannot be canceled out and that condition (29), unlike its separable counterpart (22), involves q_2. Thus q_2 affects the discrete analogue to marginal cost. This means that the output q_1^{**} which satisfies (29) must depend, in general, upon the value which it assumes. Therefore, in the discrete as in the continuous case, non-separable externalities introduce an interdependence in decision-making.

From the standpoint of discrete games, the presence of non-separable externalities suggests that there is no row-column dominance. In other words, in a matrix representation such as (23), for firm 1 there does *not* exist a row in which, for *every output* of firm 2, its profits are maximal. Similarly, for firm 2 there does *not* exist a column in which, for *every output* of firm 1, its profits are greater than at any other output level.[26] Non-dominance is evident, of course, from the fact that the externality enters the discrete analogue to marginal cost.

It seems clear that in both the continuous and discrete cases non-separable externalities introduce an interdependence between decision-making units. We have here, even in what is usually considered the certain world of competitive price theory, an example in which decisions must be made under uncertainty. It is this aspect of the externality problem which is roughly analogous to duopoly theory.[27] How can a firm determine its profit-maximizing output in this situation? One possible approach would be for each firm to attach subjective probability to its set of possible outputs and select that output which would maximize its expected profits.[28] A max-min approach might be another possibility. Or one can make various other assumptions concerning how the

305

firms might act and react. But there seems to be *no a priori method* for determining the outputs (strategies) selected. Non-separable externalities raise the possibility of the non-existence of equilibrium.

The important point here, as in the separable case, is that there is no reason to expect the output which maximizes social benefit (meaning the solution which maximizes joint profits in the assumed competitive market) to be chosen. Again it seems desirable from the standpoint of society that either the game be constrained, the scores altered, or other changes be affected so that the appropriate welfare solution will emerge. But whereas the separable case raised only the problem of the misallocation of resources, the non-separable case raises both the problem of the misallocation of resources and the problem of mal-coordination of decision-making because of the interdependence between marginal cost curves.

VI. POLICY APPROACHES AND
EQUILIBRIUM

We now discuss possible ways in which the welfare objective might be accomplished in the case of non-separable externalities. The first possibility is the proposed merger solution. With no action by the government and provided that the market can remain competitive, forces may exist within the price system which will tend to produce the optimal welfare solution, since merger might be mutually beneficial to firms operating under the postulated types of externalities. It merits repeating here that, if problems such as might be associated with decentralized administration do not prevent merger, firms are motivated to merge until the postulated externalities which can be "internalized" are eliminated; that is, until the "natural unit" for decision-making is reached.[29]

Second, the government could try the classic prescription of levying special taxes and subsidies. This solution, however, appears even less feasible in this case, and this point can be seen clearly by a comparison with the separable externality example. In the latter case a dominant solution existed. The governmental policy-maker, if he knew the relevant cost functions, could levy excise taxes and give subsidies on output as a constant function for each firm according to rules (25) and (26) so that profit maximizing firms would be induced to choose the optimal welfare outputs. However, in the non-separable externality case, even assuming that the governmental policy-maker knows the relevant cost functions and desires to maximize welfare, there seems to be no dominant solution to aim at. It is well known that there does not exist a known, unique equilibrium solution in pure strategies for this type of game (which is not to say that the firms will not make a decision on each play, but only that the decisions cannot be predicted). Thus it seems improbable that the governmental policy-maker would know the strategies which the individual firms would play since, as was pointed out above, there is no a priori method for determining the outputs which might be selected. In fact, for the policy-maker to be able to determine the strategy which individual firms might be playing, it would seem necessary, in the absence of a priori methods, to obtain information concerning the psychologies of the managers, their "taste" for risk, and so on. Of course, this knowledge is not readily available; and if the policy-maker did not know these strategies, he could not possibly predict the reaction of the firms if he tried to rotate the total revenue curve (or, what is analytically the same, shift the price line; shift the marginal cost functions; or, in game-theoretical terms, alter the payoffs) through the tax-subsidy method. Thus, even if the policy-maker determined what might be considered "appropriate" subventions or penalties by methods analogous to those suggested by (25) and (26) for the separable case, there is no assurance—and even little likelihood—that the firms would voluntarily choose the welfare optimal outputs. Non-separable externalities affect firms' marginal costs and thus create interaction between the decision-making efforts of individual firms.[30]

It follows from the above analysis that the classical tax-subsidy solution, originally stated by Marshall and Pigou and recently restated by Meade, breaks down for the case of this non-separable type of externality.[31]

Meade's analysis, although it is carefully developed and illuminating, is especially interesting in this respect. Like most of the other writers on this subject, he uses for much of his analysis a general functional notation which makes it impossible to determine accurately whether the externalities are separable or non-separable.[32] But, perhaps because he deals more thoroughly with the problem than other writers, Meade introduces in his "Atmosphere Case"[33] the production functions

$$x_1 = H_1(l_1, c_1) A_1(x_2)$$
$$x_2 = H_2(l_2, c_2) A_2(x_1),$$

which necessarily contain externalities of the non-separable type because of the "multiplicative" terms $A_1(x_2)$ and $A_2(x_1)$. It is true, of course, that Meade is dealing with industries rather than firms and that he (at least implicitly) assumes that the firms in each of these industries takes the output of the other industry as a parametric constant. On the basis of this assumption it might be argued that a tax-subsidy scheme could work in principle, although it would require elaborate computations which would have to be repeated each time a price alteration, or a technological change occurred. However, the major objective of our game-theoretic analysis of non-separable externalities has been to show that this type of interdependence creates uncertainties which, in turn, make such an assumption arbitrary and unwarranted. And our analysis, which has been developed for two firms but which certainly can be extended to cover any number of firms, shows that in the non-dominance case a stable equilibrium is unlikely to be achieved. There seems to be no a priori method for determining what strategies (output choices) firms will select in the presence of non-separable externalities.

Since our discussion of the non-dominance case has been based upon a game-theoretical analysis, an approach which we feel is to be preferred to the approach used by Meade and others, it might be argued that our conclusions that there is no *obvious* equilibrium solution in pure strategies are based solely upon our choice of tools of analysis and that the "usual" tools do logically show that an equilibrium must be achieved. The usual tools involve the solution of a set of simultaneous equations. We shall show that an analysis with these usual tools need not imply the existence of an equilibrium solution. Our main point will be that the assumptions needed for an equilibrium solution are not consistent with the other assumptions of the model.

Let us consider the simple example upon which we based much of our analysis of the non-separable case. The usual method would be to solve the following equations:

$$\frac{\partial P_1}{\partial q_1} = p - nA_1 q_1^{n-1} - B_1 q_2^m = 0$$

$$(30)$$

$$\frac{\partial P_2}{\partial q_2} = p - rA_2^{r-1} + tB_2 q_2^{t-1} q_1^s = 0.$$

Let q_1^* d q_2^* be the "equilibrium" solutions to these two equations: if both firms happened to select the outputs q_1^* and q_2^*, neither firm would have any desire to change its output plans upon hearing the output plans of the other firm. We assume that these solutions are unique and non-negative. Suppose that, for some reason, some other outputs q_1' and q_2' were chosen. Then each firm would desire to alter its output in order to adjust for the externality in its efforts to maximize profits. But when the new outputs were chosen, say q_1'' and q_2'', $q_1'' \neq q_1^{**}$, $q_2'' \neq q_2^*$, then it would be desirable to alter outputs again and so on ad infinitum.

We now distinguish two sets of assumptions that might lead one to infer that the process of "an infinite progression" of mutual adjustments and readjustments would lead to an "equilibrium" solution.

First, the firms might be assumed to communicate with each other, announcing tentative outputs but not producing until the "equilibrium" outputs q_1^* and q_2^* are announced. But if the firms are allowed to communicate, it seems unlikely that they would just exchange output data. Why would they not also exchange data about cost functions? But if they exchange data about cost functions (or even if they just communicate), why would they not make the most of the ability to communicate by exchanging information that would lead to a *joint maximization,* since both would stand to gain thereby Thus, on the basis of the simple communication assumption it would seem that they would exchange such information as would make them act *as if* they were merged instead of trying to seek the so-called "equilibrium" solution.

Under the other set of assumptions, the firms strive to reach "equilibrium outputs in the long run." Since one firm cannot be assumed to know the other firm's cost function, there is little reason to suspect that in the initial period the "equilibrium" outputs would be chosen. Each period each firm observes the other's behavior, which it desires to take into account in its own decisions. Thus each firm would be led to try to predict, on the basis of past data, the other firm's output for the next period. The firms observe, predict, make their decisions accordingly, and produce. This process goes on period after period. As we saw earlier, unless the equilibrium values are chosen, both outputs will change. A (somewhat naive) application of Muth's "Rational Expectations Hypothesis"[34] suggests that the one hypothesis that the firms would *not* be expected to use would be that the other firm would not change its output in the next period. Change would be expected. Thus, under this hypothesis, even if the two firms do happen to reach the unique "equilibrium" outputs after "an infinite progression" of periods of adjustment, each firm would expect the other to alter output in the following period; this expectation would be taken into account in making decisions for that next period, and equilibrium would not be maintained. For it is only at one unique point that the equations in the model predict no change for the next period, and this point is unknown to the firms.

It follows from the above line of reasoning that the only way in which the firms would reach and maintain the equilibrium solution would be by one firm assuming that the other firm would not change its output from period to period even though observations revealed otherwise.

However, the game-theoretic formulation shows clearly that there is unlikely to be a unique equilibrium solution (the case of non-dominance) for this type of externality.[35] In order to know how the firms would react to the possible taxes and subsidies, the policy-maker would have to know, as has been pointed out, not only the exact nature of the cost functions, but also the psychological characteristics of the decision-makers within the firm or at least the general qualitative properties of their preference-satisfaction functions to be able to predict the strategies which might be chosen by the players.

Finally, the governmental policy-maker might adopt the method of the constrained game approach. While this approach is subject to the difficulties of gaining adequate information that were pointed out previously, it does seem to offer hope for some type of solution either where merger will not work because of the impossibility of "internalizing" the externalities, or where it will result in the creation of monopoly.

The government could try, of course, to "strictly constrain" the game by dictating appropriate outputs to the firms. However, granted our ethical bias against such direct planning, we assume that decentralized (non-governmental) decision-making is desirable wherever it is possible. Thus we propose to discuss now some cases where it may be possible to employ a combination of various constraints and the pricing mechanism in order to obtain an approximation to the appropriate welfare solution.

Let us consider a simple case where there is "almost" row-column dominance:

Firm 2

$$
\text{Firm 1}\quad
\begin{array}{c}
R_1 \\ R_2 \\ R_3 \\ R_4
\end{array}
\begin{bmatrix}
(10,\ 10) & (\ 4,\ 17) & (2,\ 12) & (\ 6,\ 4) \\
(12,\ 3) & (15,\ 8) & (3,\ 6) & (\ 8,\ 9) \\
(\ 3,\ 4) & (\ 4,\ 15) & (2,\ 10) & (\ 9,\ 7) \\
(13,\ 8) & (\ 7,\ 3) & (5,\ 14) & (11,\ 11)
\end{bmatrix}
\qquad (31)
$$

with columns $Q_1\ \ Q_2\ \ Q_3\ \ Q_4$.

Row R_2 dominates row R_1 *and column* Q_3 dominates column Q_1. The remaining rows and columns introduce a non-dominance situation. If the governmental policy-maker imposes regulations so as to constrain behavior to rows R_1 and R_2 and columns Q_1 and Q_3, then the row-column dominance case is achieved. Once choices are so constrained, the use of the price mechanism will result in strategies R_2, Q_3 being chosen. It would now be possible to use taxes and subsidies in order too cause the "optimal" strategies R_1, Q_1 to be achieved.[36] In other examples, of course, the simple imposition of the direct constraints might result in an optimal, dominant solution.

The phenomenon of municipal zoning seems to afford a practical example of a case where "partial constraints" are used. The existence of height, area, and use restrictions may be viewed as evidence of the fact that these property features impose externalities upon certain types of other property.[37] As a very simple illustration, let us consider two entrepreneurs who own adjacent lots and who are trying to decide what types of plant they should erect upon their lots. Assume that for some reasons (noise, smoke, vibrations) the payoff to each entrepreneur depends upon the decision of the other entrepreneur. The game situation is evident. Assume, as seems reasonable in this instance, that the expected payoff associated with the operation of each type of plant at its individually optimal output level is similar to that represented in (31), where the subscripts now refer to the two entrepreneurs; but here entrepreneurs, instead of firms, make choices and the R's and the Q's represent types of plants rather than output levels. Obviously, from the viewpoint of social policy it is desirable that this game be constrained, and a method actually used in modern municipal zoning is to place use restrictions upon an area so that certain property uses (plants in this example) are excluded. In this illustration, uses R_3, R_4, Q_2, and Q_4 would certainly be forbidden in the area by any rational zoning ordinance. Granted these restrictions, the price mechanism would be allowed to operate, and each entrepreneur would be able to pick the most profitable type of plant not excluded by the restrictions. Of course, in this particular example, the unhappy choice R_2, Q_3 would result; so regulations might exclude these possibilities also. In other examples the simple elimination of rows and columns which cause non-dominance might produce a more desirable result; but this particular example does have the merit of suggesting the possibility of using taxes and subsidies in order to rely more on the pricing mechanism and less on direct constraints in municipal zoning.[38]

VII. CONCLUDING REMARKS

Throughout much of the analysis of this paper we have assumed that the market structure remains competitive even after a sufficient number of mergers have occurred for the natural unit for decision-making to be achieved. This assumption has been necessary, of course, to permit welfare statements to be made. We do not propose to debate here the question of whether or not markets in the "real world" are competitive. Yet, since it might be inferred that a logical implication of our argument is that the natural unit for decision-making will be so large that the market structure will change, it must be pointed out that this implication is not necessarily true. The importance and extent (or "scope") of externalities is an empirical fact of the real world, and we have as yet no systematic evidence about this. A priori, it does seem plausible that in some instances the natural unit for decision-making will be so large that a competitive market structure will not exist, but this is not a novel conclusion. It has long been recognized that natural monopolies exist, and it is equally well known that some competitive markets exist.

The main point of our argument has been that the "classical" tax-subsidy solution to the problem of externalities on the production side would be difficult to achieve in the dominance case and impossible in the non-dominance case even if the government could be assumed to be trying to maximize welfare. We have argued that a much easier solution may exist in the case of competitive markets (and it is in this context that the problem has been analyzed by Meade and others) simply by allowing mergers to take place until the "natural unit" for decision-making has been achieved. Of course, mergers may not always be technically best. An implication of our argument is that it is less likely that the government will need to be concerned about externalities on the production side than is often thought, as long as the market is and remains competitive.

The difficult problem for the policy-maker when there are externalities on the production side arises when the market is not competitive, or when possible mergers which would "truly internalize" the externalities would result in a change in the market structure. Here some measures must be devised to indicate the possible welfare gains from merger and the welfare loss that would result from the divergence from the competitive situation.

Let us now consider briefly some possible methods of estimating the effects of externalities. Admittedly, the problems here are very difficult, and this is precisely the point which we have tried to emphasize in our previous discussion of possible solutions. It is not easy for the governmental policy-maker to obtain needed information on the nature of the cost functions and thus the entries in the payoff matrix. But, presumably, after study of each particular instance of externalities, some estimates could be made. So let us assume discreteness and consider the problems the policy-maker would face in the case of separable externalities when a possible merger which would truly internalize external effects might change the market structure from competitive to non-competitive. The policy-maker could use the estimated payoff matrix to determine the difference in total profits between the dominant solution and the maximum-

311

profit solution. This difference in profits could be used as a crude measure of the change in welfare which is associated with a change from a situation of competitive markets and externalities to a situation of competitive markets and no externalities. Assuming merger is feasible, one must subtract from this difference a sum which would reflect the welfare loss associated with the alteration of the market to a situation of no externalities and a non-competitive market structure. One approach toward the estimation of this latter magnitude might be to consider this part of the welfare change as some function of the change in output and price that would result from the change in market structure.[39]

The policy-maker must also compare with this estimated net gain the net welfare gains that might result from direct regulation, inequality constraints, and other alternatives. These gains could be estimated by deducting from the estimate of the welfare gain calculated from the payoff matrix an estimate of the costs of the constraints themselves.

With an externality of the non-separable type the measurement problem is even more difficult. Cruder methods of approximation are necessary. Again assuming discreteness, statistical analysis of variance suggests one such possibility. Since, if there are no externalities present, the payoff matrix is composed of constant elements, a variance analysis would give a zero value here. Thus a variance analysis of the payoff matrix which gave a non-zero value could be taken as an approximation to the welfare value of the change from a situation of externalities and competition to a situation of no externalities and a competitive market. Thus the policy-maker might be able to make the appropriate comparisons as in the previous case. In situations where externalities exist and the market structure is non-competitive to begin with, the measurement problem is even more difficult. Yet, our a priori judgment is that this may be the more important area for policy choice by a welfare-maximizing government.

This paper has been limited largely to externalities on the *production side*. Other important externality problems associated with, for example, interrelated utility functions have not been treated here, although the game-theoretic approach does seem promising for future research in these areas.

NOTES

1. This paper was written as part of the project "The Planning and Control of Industrial Operations" under a grant from the Office of Naval Research and the Bureau of Ships at the Graduate School of Industrial Administration, Carnegie Institute of Technology. The authors would like to express their appreciation to Professors W. W. Cooper and J. F. Muth, both of Carnegie Institute of Technology, Dr. R. R. Nelson, Council of Economic Advisers, and Professor James M. Buchanan, University of Virginia, for their very helpful comments and criticisms.

2. Interestingly enough, J. de V. Graaff also considers that externalities are a phenomenon which relates to the firm rather than the industry, and, furthermore, he seems to think this point quite important (see his *Theoretical Welfare Economics* [Cambridge: Cambridge University Press, 1957], p. 19).

3. The analysis in this paper is conducted within the context of a competitive industry, although some of our results are applicable even if the market structure is not

312

competitive. We have made the competitive assumptions simply because of a desire to make welfare statements which require such a framework.

4. It should be emphasized that we consider only technological externalities in this paper. We are not concerned with possible problems associated with pecuniary externalities. The usual convexity conditions are assumed whenever appropriate.

5. Although we assume the two firms to be in the same industry, this assumption is not necessary either here or in the remainder of the paper. All that is required for the general case is to assume two prices, p_1 and p_2, instead of the single price p.

6. The usual discussion of technological externalities deals in terms of production functions. We work with cost functions merely for convenience. Identical results are achieved when production functions are considered. For example, consider a single firm in a competitive industry, with the production function

$$q_1 = f(L, q_2), \qquad \text{(a)}$$

where q_1 represents the output of firm 1, L represents an input of labor, and q_2 is an output of firm 2 which affects the production of q_1; q_2 is a non-priced and uncontrolled "input" of firm 1. By assumption the firm desires to maximize the following profit function, where P represents profits, p the price of output, and w the wage rate.

$$P = pq_1 - wL . \qquad \text{(b)}$$

Note that q_2 does not enter "directly" into *(b)*, but it does affect *(b)* since we can write

$$P = pf(L, q_2) - wL \qquad \text{(c)}$$

by making a simple substitution.

In its attempt to maximize profits the firm would hire labor up to the point where

$$\frac{\partial P}{\partial L} = p\frac{\partial f}{\partial L} - w = 0 . \qquad \text{(d)}$$

However, by the externality assumptions, firm 1 does not control the output q_2 of firm 2. Therefore if

$$\frac{\partial P}{\partial q_2} = p\frac{\partial f}{\partial q_2} \neq 0, \qquad \text{(e)}$$

firm 1 would not be able to achieve its over-all profit maximum. This means, under the assumed conditions, that welfare is not maximal.

7. James E. Meade, "External Economies and Diseconomies in a Competitive Situation," *Economic Journal*, LXII (March, 1952), 54-67. See also chap. x of his *Trade and Welfare* (London: Oxford University Press, 1955).

8. The idea of natural units is not original with us. George J. Stigler, commenting on the production theory of Alfred Marshall, observed that when production functions are technically related there may exist motivation for combination and merger *Production and Distribution Theories* [New York: Macmillan Co., 1946], p. 75).

9. See A. Charnes and C. E. Lemke, "Minimization of Non-linear Separable Convex Functionals," *Naval Research Logistics Quarterly*, Vol. II (June, 1954).

10. Note that transformations of the kind discussed in A. Charnes and W. W. Cooper, "Non-linear Power of Adjacent Extreme Point Methods in Linear Programming," *Econometrica*, Vol. XXV (January, 1957), are also admitted.

11. It may seem presumptuous of us to assert that the typical cases in the classical analysis implicitly have assumed separability. After all, if the discussion is verbal, then it is difficult to determine the implicit assumptions underlying the analysis; and if the discussion is mathematical but utilizes only general functional notation, then implicit assumptions are equally obscure. Both these cases have been the rule in the literature. Witness, for example, P. A. Samuelson, *Foundations of Economic Analysis* (Cambridge, Mass.: Harvard University Press, 1947); W. J. Baumol, *Welfare Economics and the Theory*

of the State (Cambridge, Mass.: Harvard University Press, 1952); and J. de V. Graaff, *op. cit.* However, as will become clear from our later discussion, the conclusions of these analyses necessarily require the separability assumption if one presumes that they are correct. However, it is only fair to point out that K. J. Arrow, while discussing consumption externalities, expressed some doubts about the classical tax-subsidy scheme. He observed, "The general feeling is that in these cases, optimal allocation can be achieved by a price system, accompanied by a system of taxes and bounties. However, the problem has been only discussed in simple cases and no system has been shown to have, in the general case, the important property possessed by the price system" ("An Extension of the Basic Theorems of Classical Welfare Economics," *Second Berkeley Symposium on Mathematical Statistics and Probability,* ed. J. Neyman [Berkeley: University of California Press, 1951], pp. 528-29).

12. For a brief discussion of continuous games, see I. L. Glicksberg, "A Further Generalization of the Kakutani Fixed Point Theorem with Application to Nash Equilibrium Points," *Proceedings of the American Mathematical Society,* III (1952), 170-74.

13. This assumes, of course, that average variable costs are covered.

14. We use the term "operational" in a special sense here. Our usage requires that the firm be able to know its own marginal cost curve in the absence of knowledge of the other firm's output decisions.

15. The terms "uniquely defined" and "unambiguously defined" are used in a special manner here. We mean that the marginal cost curve is defined if one firm does not know the output of the other firm.

16. For an especially clear and understandable exposition on discrete games, see R. Duncan Luce and Howard Raiffia, *Games and Decisions* (New York: John Wiley & Sons, 1957), esp. chap. v.

17. It is assumed that b_{ij}, $a_{ij} \geqslant 0$ for all relevant i, j choices so that there is no problem of covering average variable cost.

18. This example, known as the "Prisoner's Dilemma," is adopted from Luce and Raiffa, *op. cit.* pp. 94-102.

19. Some empirical data confirm the hypothesis that, if communication does not take place, players continually choose the *individual rational* strategy. In terms of the above example, this choice would mean R_2 and Q_2. For the results of the laboratory experiments, see A. Scodel, J. S. Minas, P. Ratoosh, and M. Lipetz, "Some Descriptive Aspects of Two-Person Non-Zero Sum Games," *Journal of Conflict Resolution,* III (1959), 114-19.

20. Throughout this paper we assume that the government desires to maximize welfare, an assumption which may not always be completely appropriate.

21. We use "a welfare optimal output" here because with discreteness it is likely that more than one optimum output exists. Also note that we use q_1^* (and q_2^*) here and in the previous discussion of the continuous case as welfare-optimal outputs which are determined by the policy-maker. Since these become optimal outputs for the individual firms *only after* proper taxes and subsidies have been levied, they are not to be confused with the firm maximal outputs of the previous section which were designated by the same symbols.

22. Many of our externality problems appear to fit into the discrete case. For example, problems associated with plant location, municipal zoning, or even minimum building codes can be viewed as discrete (see Tjalling C. Koopmans and Martin Beckmann "Assignment Problems and the Location of Economic Activities," *Econometrica,* XXXIV [January 1957], 53-76; and Otto A. Davis and Andrew B. Whinston, "The Economics of Complex Systems; The Case of Municipal Zoning" [O.N.R. Research Memorandum, Graduate School of Industrial Administration, Carnegie Institute of Technology. Unfortunately, it appears as if many of these externalities are not separable.

23. A further problem for research would be to determine the "fair" terms under which the merger would take place, with reference to the division of the gains among the individual stockholders in the two firms. While this is not the appropriate place to go into this problem, it appears that a possible method of analysis would be along the lines outlined by L. S. Shapley, "A Value for *n*-Person Games," *Annals of Mathematics,* Study No. 24 (Princeton, N.J.: Princeton University Press).

24. Meade, *op. cit.,* pp. 56-61.

25. We present this derivation in a footnote since it is similar to that used for the separable case. The firm desires to maximize the profit function

$$\dot{P}(q_1, q_2) = pq_1 - C(q_1, q_2) \tag{a}$$

over the set Q_1 of possible outputs. By assumption the firm cannot control the value of the externality q_2. But for some given q_2 it is obvious that any profit maximizing output q_1^* must satisfy

$$P(q_1^* + \Delta q_1, q_2) - P(q_1^*, q_2) \leqslant 0 \tag{b}$$

for all admissible choices Δq_1. Substituting the actual profit function *(a)* into *(b)* we obtain

$$p(q_1^* + \Delta q_1) - C(q_1^* + \Delta q_1, q_2)$$
$$- pq_1^* + C(q_1^*, q_2) \leqslant 0. \tag{c}$$

Since $C(q_1, q_2)$ is non-separable, collecting terms gives

$$p \Delta q_1 \leqslant C(q_1^* + \Delta q_1, q_2)$$
$$-C(q_1^*, q_2) \tag{d}$$

from which (29) follows directly.

26. A very simple example of non-dominance is the following:

Firm 2

$$\text{Firm 1} \begin{array}{c} R_1 \\ R_2 \end{array} \begin{array}{cc} Q_1 & Q_2 \\ \left[\begin{array}{cc} (.9, 0) & (.1, .9) \\ (0, 1) & (1, .1) \end{array} \right] \end{array}$$

It is not clear whether firm 1 will choose strategy (output) R_1 where $.9 > 0$ or strategy R_2 where $1 > .1$. Similarly, it is not clear whether firm 2 will choose strategy (output) Q_2 where $.9 > 0$ or Q_1 where $1 > .1$.

27. It is to be emphasized, however, that this resemblance to duopoly theory is somewhat superficial. Although we have developed our analysis in terms of two firms, this approach has been used only for expository convenience. It is obvious that, with non-separable externalities, interdependence between decision-making units is the source of the difficulty, and this interdependence exists if the number of firms is two, three, or n, where n can be an indeterminately large number.

28. Such an approach would be similar to that of L. J. Savage, *The Foundations of Statistics* (New York: John Wiley & Sons, 1954). On the other hand, Von Neumann and Morgenstern assert that the difficulties inherent in situations in which neither participant controls the relevant variables cannot be obviated by recourse to statistical assumptions and analysis *(The Theory of Games and Economic Behavior* [Princeton, N.J.: Princeton University Press, 1947], p. 11).

29. The notion of a natural unit can be taken as roughly corresponding to the concept of a stable coalition in n- person game theory. In this respect it might be noted that throughout this analysis we have chosen to ignore the possible instabilities which might be associated with entry into the industry.

30. It might be suggested that the tax-subsidy scheme could be made appropriate even in this case by having the policy-maker simply solve for the optimal outputs and offer a subsidy conditional upon firms producing those specified outputs. But this would entail abandoning the advantages of a decentralized market system, since the policy-maker must actually specify acceptable outputs. Also note that if acceptable outputs are specified in policy, then there would seem to be little reason to offer conditional subsidies. Why not simply dictate to the firms that certain outputs must be produced? This, however, weakens the case for private ownership of the facilities under consideration.

31. Our results here hold for the case of reciprocal, non-separable externalities. If the externalities are not reciprocal in any sense—that is, if firm 1 imposes a non-separable externality upon firm 2 but not vice versa, and if there are no other externality-creating firms which are relevant—then our analysis does not hold. For a given output of firm 1, firm 2's marginal cost curve will be precisely determined so that, at least conceptually, the policy-maker can compute the appropriate rate of the tax or subsidy; but, of course, this rate will have to be recomputed each time firm 1 alters its output. If the situation is more complex (as for example, firm 1 imposing a non-separable externality upon firm 2, firm 2 imposing one upon firm 3, and firm 3 upon firm 1), then the anylisis does hold. It is the necessity of "simultaneous" decision-making in the presence of this type of interdependence that creates the uncertainty and difficulty here.

32. Meade makes the usual assumption of linear homogeneous production functions. It can be shown, however, that this assumption does not rule out the possibility of non-separable externalities.

33. Meade, *op. cit.*, pp. 61-66.

34. John F. Muth, "Rational Expectations and the Theory of Price Movements," *Econometrica*, XXIX, No. 3 (July, 1961), 315-35.

35. The simultaneous solutions q_1^*, q_2^* to the set of equations (30) correspond to a Nash equilibrium point in a two-person, non-zero-sum game. Since we do not assume that one player knows the payoffs to the other player, expectations are all important for the attainment of an equilibrium. In this respect, a comment by Luce and Raiffa on the Nash equilibrium seems especially relevant here. "These strategies will be in equilibrium provided that no player finds it is to his advantage to change to a different strategy *so long as he believes that the other players will not change*" (*op. cit.*, pp. 170-71). (Our italics.) For a discussion of further difficulties associated with this type of equilibrium notion see *ibid.*, 171-73.

36. The R_1, Q_1 solution is not the over-all optimum, which is, of course, R_2, Q_2. This latter solution, however, would be impossible to achieve unless there was "complete" regulation.

37. See Otto A. Davis, "The Economics of Municipal Zoning" (unpublished Ph.D. dissertation, University of Virginia, 1959), for a more complete analysis of the zoning phenomenon which is not in game theoretic terms. See also Davis and Whinston, *op. cit.*, for a discussion which utilizes game theory and programming. It also might be pointed out that the phenomenon of urban renewal involves externalities and that a "preventative" solution can be obtained throughout a constrained game approach (see Davis and Whinston, "The Economics of Urban Renewal," *Law and Contemporary Problems*, Vol. XXVI [Winter, 1961]).

38. Koopmans and Beckmann have shown, in a theoretical analysis of plant location, that in the absence of interaction a pricing mechanism will be given an optimal solution; but if interdependencies via transportation costs on "intermediate commodities" exist, no optimal equilibrium solution can be expected (see Tjalling C. Koopmans and Martin Beckmann, "Assignment Problems and the Location of Economic Activities," *Econometrica*, XXIV [January, 1957], 53-76).

39. Franco Modigliani has suggested methods for predicting the change in output and price which accompany change in market structure ("New Developments on the Oligopoly Front," *Journal of Political Economy*, LXVI [June, 1958], 215-32).

On Divergences between Social Cost and Private Cost*

By RALPH TURVEY

The notion that the resource-allocation effects of divergences between marginal social and private costs can be dealt with by imposing a tax or granting a subsidy equal to the difference now seems too simple a notion. Three recent articles have shown us this. First came Professor Coase's "The Problem of Social Cost", then Davis and Whinston's "Externalities, Welfare and the Theory of Games" appeared, and, finally, Buchanan and Stubblebine have published their paper "Externality".[1] These articles have an aggregate length of eighty pages and are by no means easy to read. The following attempt to synthesise and summarise the main ideas may therefore be useful. It is couched in terms of external diseconomies, i.e. an excess of social over private costs, and the reader is left to inver the analysis himself should he be interested in external economies.

The scope of the following argument can usefully be indicated by starting with a brief statement of its main conclusions. The first is that if the party imposing external diseconomies and the party suffering them are able and willing to negotiate to their mutual advantage, state intervention is unnecessary to secure optimum resource allocation. The second is that the imposition of a tax upon the party imposing external diseconomies can be a very complicated matter, even in principle, so that the *a priori* prescription of such a tax is unwise.

To develop these and other points, let us begin by calling A the person, firm or group (of persons or firms) which imposes a diseconomy, and B the person, firm or group which suffers it. How much B suffers will in many cases depend not only upon the *scale* of A's diseconomy-creating activity, but also upon the precise *nature* of A's activity and upon B's *reaction* to it. If A emits smoke, for example, B's loss will depend not only upon the quantity emitted but also upon the height of A's chimney and upon the cost to B of installing air-conditioning, indoor clothes-dryers or other means of reducing the effect of the smoke. Thus to ascertain the optimum resource allocation will frequently require an investigation of the nature and costs both of alternative activities open to A and *of the devices by which B* can reduce the impact of each activity. The optimum

*I am indebted to Professor Buchanan, Professor Coase, Mr. Klappholz, Dr. Mishan and Mr. Peston for helpful comments on an earlier draft.

Reprinted by permission of the publishers and author: Ralph Turvey, "On Divergences Between Social Cost and Private Cost," *Economica*, n.s. 119 (August 1963), pp. 309-313.

involves that kind and scale of A's activity and that adjustment to it by B which maximises the algebraic sum of A's gain and B's loss as against the situation where A pursues no diseconomy-creating activity. Note that the optimum will frequently involve B suffering a loss, both in total and at the margin.[1]

If A and B are firms, gain and loss can be measured in money terms as profit differences. (In considering a social optimum, allowance has of course to be made for market imperfections.) Now assuming that they both seek to maximise profits, that they know about the available alternatives and adjustments and that they are able and willing to negotiate, they will achieve the optimum without any government interference. They will internalize the externality by merger[2], or they will make an agreement whereby B pays A to modify the nature or scale of its activity.[3] Alternatively,[4] if the law gives B rights against A, A will pay B to accept the optimal amount of loss imposed by A.

If A and B are people, their gain and loss must be measured as the amount of money they respectively would pay to indulge in and prevent A's activity. It could also be measured as the amount of money they respectively would require to refrain from and to endure A's activity, which will be different unless the marginal utility of income is constant. We shall assume that it is constant for both A and B, which is reasonable when the payments do not bulk large in relation to their incomes.[5] Under this assumption, it makes no difference whether B pays A or, if the law gives B rights against A, A compensates B.

Whether A and B are persons or firms, to levy a tax on A which is *not* received as damages or compensation by B may prevent optimal resource allocation from being achieved—still assuming that they can and do negotiate.[6] The reason is that the resource allocation which maximises A's *gain less B's loss* may differ from that which maximises A's *gain less A's tax less B's* loss.

The points made so far can usefully be presented diagrammatically (Figure 1). We assume that A has only two alternative activities, I and II, and that their scales and B's losses are all continuously variable. Let us temporarily disregard the dotted curve in the right-hand part of the diagram. The area under A's curves then gives the total gain to A. The area under B's curves gives the total loss to B after he has made the best adjustment possible to A's activity. This is thus the direct loss as reduced by adjustment, plus the cost of making that adjustment.

If A and B could not negotiate and if A were unhampered by restrictions of any sort, A would choose activity I at a scale of OR. A scale of OS would obviously give a larger social product, but the optimum is clearly activity II at scale OJ, since area 2 is greater than area 1. Now B will be prepared to pay up to $(1a + 1\ t\text{-}2a)$ to secure this result, while A will be prepared to accept down to $(1 + 1a\ 2 - 2a)$ to assure it. The difference is $(1b - 1 + 2)$, the maximum gain to shared between them, and this is clearly positive.

If A is liable to compensate B for actual damages caused by either activity I or II, he will choose activity II at scale OJ (i.e. the optimum allocation), pay $2a$ to B and retain a net gain of 2. The result is the same as when there is no such liability, though the distribution of the gain is very different: B will pay A up to $(1a + 1b - 2a)$ to secure this result. Hence whether or not we should advocate the imposition of a liability on A for damages caused is a matter of fairness, not of resource allocation. Our judgment will presumably depend on such factors as who got there first, whether one of them is a non-conforming user (e.g. an establishment for the breeding of maggots on putrescible vegetable matter in a residential district), who is richer, and so on. Efficient resource allocation requires the imposition of a liability upon A only if we can show that inertia, obstinacy, etc. inhibit A and B from reaching a voluntary agreement.[7]

We can now make the point implicit in Buchanan-Stubblebine's argument, namely that there is a necessity for any impost levied on A to be paid to B when A and B are able to negotiate. Suppose that A is charged an amount equal to the loss he imposes on B; subtracting this from his marginal gain curve in the right-hand part of the diagram gives us the dotted line as his marginal net gain. If A moves to point J it will then pay B to induce him to move back to position K (which is sub-optimal) as it is this position maximises the *joint* net gain to A and B together.

There is a final point to be made about the case where A and B can negotiate. This is that if the external diseconomies are reciprocal, so that each imposes a loss upon the other, the problem is still more complicated.[8]

We now turn to the case where A and B cannot negotiate, which in most cases will result from A and/or B being too large a group for the members to get together. Here there are certain benefits to be had from resource re-allocation which are not privately appropriable. Just as with collective goods,[9] therefore, there is thus a case for collective action to achieve optimum allocation. But all this means is that *if* the state can ascertain and enforce a move to the optimum position at a cost less than the gain to be had, and *if* it can do this in a way which does not have unfavourable effects upon income distribution, then it should take action.

These two "ifs" are very important. The second is obvious and requires no elaboration. The first, however, deserves a few words. In order to ascertain the optimum type and scale of A's activity, the authorities must estimate all of the curves in the diagrams. They must, in other words, list and evaluate all the alternatives open to A and examine their effects upon B and the adjustments B could make to reduce the loss suffered. When this is done, if it can be done, it is necessary to consider how to reach the optimum. Now, where the nature as well as the scale of A's activity is variable, it may be necessary to control both, and this may require two controls, not one. Suppose, for instance, that in the diagram, both activities are the emission of smoke: I from a low chimney and II from a tall chimney. To induce A to shift from emitting OR smoke from the low chimney to emitting OJ smoke from the tall chimney, it will not suffice to levy a tax of PJ per unit of smoke.[10] If this alone were done, A would continue to use a low chimney, emitting slightly less than OR smoke. It will also be necessary to regulate chimney heights. A tax would do the trick alone only if it were proportioned to losses imposed rather than to smoke emitted, and that would be very difficult.

These complications show that in many cases the cost of achieving optimum resource allocation may outweigh the gain. If this is the case, a second-best solution may be appropriate. Thus a prohibition of all smoke emission would be better than *OR* smoke from a low chimney (since 1 is less than 1*b*) and a requirement that all chimneys be tall would be better still (giving a net gain of 2 less 2*b*). Whether these requirements should be imposed on existing chimney-owners as well as on new ones then introduces further complications relating to the short run and the long run.

There is no need to carry the example any further. It is now abundantly clear that any general prescription of a tax to deal with external diseconomies is useless. Each case must be considered on its own and there is no *a priori* reason to suppose that the imposition of a tax is better than alternative measures or indeed, that any measures at all are desirable unless we assume that information and administration are both costless.[11]

To sum up, then: when negotiation is possible, the case for government intervention is one of justice not of economic efficiency; when it is not, the theorist should be silent and call in the applied economist.

NOTES

1. *Journal of Law and Economics,* Vol. III, October, 1960, *Journal of Political Economy,* June, 1962, and *Economica,* November, 1962, respectively.

1. Buchanan-Stubblebine, pp. 380-1.

2. Davis-Whinston, pp. 244, 252, 256; Coase, pp. 16-17.

3. Coase, p. 6; Buchanan-Stubblebine agree, p. 383.

4. See previous references.

5. Dr. Mishan has examined the welfare criterion for the case where the only variable is the scale of A's activity, but where neither A nor B has a constant marginal utility of income; Cf. his paper "Welfare Criteria for External Effects", *American Economic Review,* September, 1961.

6. Buchanan-Stubblebine, pp. 381-3.

7. Cf. the comparable argument on pp. 94-8 of my *The Economics of Real Property,* 1957, about the external economy to landlords of tenants' improvements.

8. Davis-Whinston devote several pages of game theory to this problem.

9. Buchanan-Stubblebine, p. 383.

10. Note how different *PJ* is from *RT*, the initial observable marginal external diseconomy.

11. Coase, pp. 18, 44.

An Economic Theory of Clubs[1]

By JAMES M. BUCHANAN

The implied institutional setting for neo-classical economic theory, including theoretical welfare economics, is a régime of private property, in which all goods and services are privately (individually) utilized or consumed. Only within the last two decades have serious attempts been made to extend the formal theoretical structure to include communal or collective ownership-consumption arrangements.[2] The " pure theory of public goods " remains in its infancy, and the few models that have been most rigorously developed apply only to polar or extreme cases. For example, in the fundamental papers by Paul A. Samuelson, a sharp conceptual distinction is made between those goods and services that are " purely private " and those that are " purely public ".[3] No general theory has been developed which covers the whole spectrum of ownership-consumption possibilities, ranging from the purely private or individualized activity on the one hand to purely public or col-lectivized activity on the other. One of the missing links here is " a theory of clubs ", a theory of co-operative membership, a theory that will include as a variable to be determined the extension of ownership-consumption rights over differing numbers of persons.

Everyday experience reveals that there exists some most preferred or " optimal " membership for almost any activity in which we engage, and that this membership varies in some relation to economic factors. European hotels have more communally shared bathrooms than their American counterparts. Middle and low income communities organize swimming-bathing facilities; high income communities are observed to enjoy privately owned swimming pools.

In this paper I shall develop a general theory of clubs, or consumption ownership-membership arrangements. This construction allows us to move one step forward in closing the awesome Samuelson gap between the purely private and the purely public good. For the former, the optimal sharing arrangement, the preferred club membership, is clearly one person (or one family unit), whereas the optimal sharing group

Reprinted by permission of the publishers and author: James M. Buchanan, "An Economic Theory of Clubs," *Economica*, n.s. 32 (February 1965), pp. 1-14.

for the purely public good, as defined in the polar sense, includes an infinitely large number of members. That is to say, for any genuinely collective good defined in the Samuelson way, a club that has an infinitely large membership is preferred to all arrangements of finite size. While it is evident that some goods and services may be reasonably classified as purely private, even in the extreme sense, it is clear that few, if any, goods satisfy the conditions of extreme collectiveness. The interesting cases are those goods and services, the consumption of which involves some " publicness ", where the optimal sharing group is more than one person or family but smaller than an infinitely large number. The range of " publicness " is finite. The central question in a theory of clubs is that of determining the membership margin, so to speak, the size of the most desirable cost and consumption sharing arrangement.[4]

I

In traditional neo-classical models that assume the existence of purely private goods and services only, the utility function of an individual is written,

(1) $U^i = U^i (X_1^i, X_2^i, \ldots, X_n^i),$

where each of the X's represents the amount of a purely private good available during a specified time period, to the reference individual designated by the superscript.

Samuelson extended this function to include purely collective or public goods, which he denoted by the subscripts, $n+1, \ldots, n+m,$ so that (1) is changed to read,

(2) $U_i = U^i (X_1^i, X_2^i, \ldots, X_n^i; X_{n+1}^i, X_{n+2}^i, \ldots X_{n+m}^i).$

This approach requires that all goods be initially classified into the two sets, private and public. Private goods, defined to be wholly divisible among the persons, $i = 1, 2, \ldots, s,$ satisfy the relation

$$X_j = \sum_{i=1}^{s} X_j^i,$$

while public goods, defined to be wholly indivisible as among persons, satisfy the relation,

$$X_{n+j} = X_{n+j}^i.$$

I propose to drop any attempt at an initial classification or differentiation of goods into fully divisible and fully indivisible sets, and to incorporate in the utility function goods falling between these two extremes. What the theory of clubs provides is, in one sense, a " theory of classification ", but this emerges as an output of the analysis. The first step is that of modifying the utility function.

Note that, in neither (1) nor (2) is it necessary to make a distinction between " goods available to the ownership unit of which the reference individual is a member " and " goods finally available to the individual for consumption ". With purely private goods, consumption by one individual automatically reduces potential consumption of other individuals by an equal amount. With purely public goods, consumption by any one individual implies equal consumption by all others. For goods falling between such extremes, such a distinction must be made. This is because for such goods there is no unique translation possible between the " goods available to the membership unit " and " goods finally consumed ". In the construction which follows, therefore, the " goods " entering the individual's utility function, the X_j's, should be interpreted as " goods available for consumption to the whole membership unit of which the reference individual is a member ".

Arguments that represent the size of the sharing group must be included in the utility function along with arguments representing goods and services. For any good or service, regardless of its ultimate place along the conceptual public-private spectrum, the utility that an individual receives from its consumption depends upon *the number of other persons with whom he must share its benefits.* This is obvious, but its acceptance does require breaking out of the private property straitjacket within which most of economic theory has developed. As an extreme example, take a good normally considered to be purely private, say, a pair of shoes. Clearly your own utility from a single pair of shoes, per unit of time, depends on the number of other persons who share them with you. Simultaneous physical sharing may not, of course, be possible; only one person can wear the shoes at each particular moment. However, for any finite period of time, sharing is possible, even for such evidently private goods. For pure services that are consumed in the moment of acquisition the extension is somewhat more difficult, but it can be made none the less. Sharing here simply means that the individual receives a smaller quantity of the service. Sharing a " haircut per month " with a second person is the same as consuming " one-half haircut per month ". Given any quantity of final good, as defined in terms of the physical units of some standard quality, the utility that the individual receives from this quantity will be related functionally to the number of others with whom he shares.[5]

Variables for club size are not normally included in the utility function of an individual since, in the private-goods world, the optimal club size is unity. However, for our purposes, these variables must be explicitly included, and, for completeness, a club-size variable should be included for each and every good. Alongside each X_j there must be placed an N_j, which we define as the number of persons who are to participate as " members " in the sharing of good, X_j, including the ith person whose utility function is examined. That is to say, the club-size variable, N_j, measures the number of persons who are to join in the consumption-utilization arrangements for good, X_j, over the relevant time period. The sharing arrangements may or may not call for equal consumption on the part of each member, and the peculiar manner of sharing will clearly affect the way in which the variable enters the utility function. For simplicity we may assume equal sharing, although this is not necessary for the analysis. The rewritten utility function now becomes,

(3) $U^i = U^i[(X_1^i, N_1^i), (X_2^i, N_2^i), \ldots, (X_{n+m}^i, N_{n+m}^i)].$[6]

323

We may designate a numeraire good, X_r, which can simply be thought of as money, possessing value only as a medium of exchange. By employing the convention whereby the lower case u's represent the partial derivatives, we get u_j^i/u_r^i, defined as the marginal rate of substitution in consumption between X_j and X_r for the ith individual. Since, in our construction, the size of the group is also a variable, we must also examine, u_{Nj}^i/u_r^i, defined as the marginal rate of substitution " in consumption " between the size of the sharing group and the numeraire. That is to say, this ratio represents the rate (which may be negative) at which the individual is willing to give up (accept) money in exchange for additional members in the sharing group.

We now define a cost or production function as this confronts the individual, and this will include the same set of variables,

(4) $\quad F = F^i[(X_1^i, N_1^i), (X_2^i, N_2^i), \ldots, (X_{n+m}^i, N_{n+m}^i)].$

Why do the club-size variables, the N_j's, appear in this cost function ? The addition of members to a sharing group may, and normally will, affect the cost of the good to any one member. The larger is the membership of the golf club the lower the dues to any single member, given a specific quantity of club facilities available per unit time.

It now becomes possible to derive, from the utility and cost functions, statements for the necessary marginal conditions for Pareto optimality in respect to consumption of each good. In the usual manner we get,

(5) $\quad u_j^i/u_r^i = f_j^i/f_r^i.$

Condition (5) states that, for the ith individual, the marginal rate of substitution between goods X_j and X_r, in consumption, must be equal to the marginal rate of substitution between these same two goods in " production " or exchange. To this acknowledged necessary condition, we now add,

(6) $\quad u_{Nj}^i/u_r^i = f_{Nj}^i/f_r^i.$

Condition (6) is not normally stated, since the variables relating to club size are not normally included in utility functions. Implicitly, the size for sharing arrangements is assumed to be determined exogenously to individual choices. Club size is presumed to be a part of the environment. Condition (6) states that the marginal rate of substitution " in consumption " between the size of the group sharing in the use of good X_j, and the numeraire good, X_r, must be equal to the marginal rate of substitution " in production ". In other words, the individual attains full equilibrium in club size only when the marginal benefits that he secures from having an additional member (which may, and probably will normally be, negative) are just equal to the marginal costs that he incurs from adding a member (which will also normally be negative).

Combining (5) and (6) we get,

(7) $\quad u_j^i/f_j^i = u_r^i/f_r^i = u_{Nj}^i/f_{Nj}^i.$

Only when (7) is satisfied will the necessary marginal conditions with respect to the consumption-utilization of X_j be met. The individual will have available to his membership unit an optimal quantity of X_j, measured in physical units and, also, he will be sharing this quantity "optimally" over a group of determined size.

The necessary condition for club size may not, of course, be met. Since for many goods there is a major change in utility between the one-person and the two-person club, and since discrete changes in membership may be all that is possible, we may get,

$$(7A) \quad \frac{u_j^i}{f_j^i} = \frac{u_r^i}{f_r^i} > \frac{u_{Nj}^i}{f_{Nj}^i}\bigg|_{Nj=1} \quad ; \quad \frac{u_j^i}{f_j^i} = \frac{u_r^i}{f_r^i} < \frac{u_{Nj}^i}{f_{Nj}^i}\bigg|_{Nj=2}$$

which incorporates the recognition that, with a club size of unity, the right-hand term may be relatively too small, whereas, with a club size of two, it may be too large. If partial sharing arrangements can be worked out, this qualification need not, of course, be made.

If, on the other hand, the size of a co-operative or collective sharing group is exogenously determined, we may get,

$$(7B) \quad \frac{u_j^i}{f_j^i} = \frac{u_r^i}{f_r^i} > \frac{u_{Nj}^i}{f_{Nj}^i}\bigg|_{Nj=k}$$

Note that (7B) actually characterizes the situation of an individual with respect to the consumption of any purely public good of the type defined in the Samuelson polar model. Any group of finite size, k, is smaller than optimal here, and the full set of necessary marginal conditions cannot possibly be met. Since additional persons can, by definition, be added to the group without in any way reducing the availability of the good to other members, and since additional members could they be found, would presumably place some positive value on the good and hence be willing to share in its costs, the group always remains below optimal size. The all-inclusive club remains too small.

Consider, now, the relation between the set of necessary marginal conditions defined in (7) and those presented by Samuelson in application to goods that were exogenously defined to be purely public. In the latter case, these conditions are,

$$(8) \quad \sum_{i=1}^{s}(u_{n+j}^i/u_r^i) = f_{n+j}/f_r,$$

where the marginal rates of substitution in consumption between the purely public good, X_{n+j}, and the numeraire good, X_r, summed over all individuals in the group of determined size, s, equals the marginal cost of X_{n+j} also defined in terms of units of X_r. Note that when (7) is satisfied, (8) is necessarily satisfied, provided only that the collectivity is making neither profit nor loss on providing the marginal unit of the public good. That is to say, provided that,

$$(9) \quad f_{n+j}/f_r = \sum_{i=1}^{s}(f_{n+j}^i/f_r^i).$$

The reverse does not necessarily hold, however, since the satisfaction of (8) does not require that each and every individual in the group be in a position where his own marginal benefits are equal to his marginal costs (taxes).[7] And, of course, (8) says nothing at all about group size.

The necessary marginal conditions in (7) allow us to classify all goods only after the solution is attained. Whether or not a particular good is purely private, purely public, or somewhere between these extremes is determined only after the equilibrium values for the N_j's are known. A good for which the equilibrium value for N_j is large can be classified as containing much " publicness ". By contrast, a good for which the equilibrium value of N_j is small can be classified as largely private.

II

The formal statement of the theory of clubs presented in Section I can be supplemented and clarified by geometrical analysis, although the nature of the construction implies somewhat more restrictive models.

Consider a good that is known to contain, under some conditions, a degree of " publicness ". For simplicity, think of a swimming pool. We want to examine the choice calculus of a single person, and we shall assume that other persons about him, with whom he may or may not choose to join in some club-like arrangement, are identical in all respects with him. As a first step, take a facility of one-unit size, which we define in terms of physical output supplied.

On the ordinate of Fig. 1, we measure total cost and total benefit per person, the latter derived from the individual's own evaluation of the facility in terms of the numeraire, dollars. On the abscissa, we measure the number of persons in possible sharing arrangements. Define the full cost of the one-unit facility to be Y_1, and the reference individual's

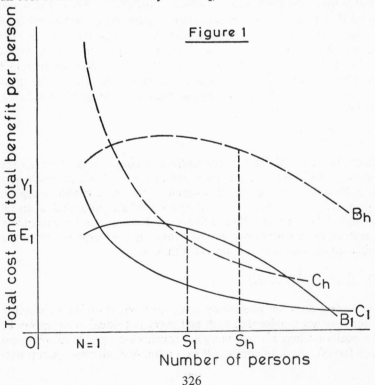

Figure 1

evaluation of this facility as a purely private consumption good to be E_1. As is clear from the construction as drawn, he will not choose to purchase the good. If the single person is required to meet the full cost, he will not be able to enjoy the benefits of the good. Any enjoyment of the facility requires the organization of some co-operative-collective sharing arrangement. [8]

Two functions may now be traced in Fig. 1, remaining within the one-unit restriction on the size of the facility. A total benefit function and a total cost function confronting the single individual may be derived. As more persons are allowed to share in the enjoyment of the facility, of given size, the benefit evaluation that the individual places on the good will, after some point, decline. There may, of course, be both an increasing and a constant range of the total benefit function, but at some point congestion will set in, and his evaluation of the good will fall. There seems little doubt that the total benefit curve, shown as B_1, will exhibit the concavity property as drawn for goods that involve some commonality in consumption. [9]

The bringing of additional members into the club also serves to reduce the cost that the single person will face. Since, by our initial simplifying assumption, all persons here are identical, symmetrical cost sharing is suggested. In any case, the total cost per person will fall as additional persons join the group, under any cost-sharing scheme. As drawn in Fig. 1, symmetrical sharing is assumed and the curve, C_1, traces the total cost function, given the one-unit restriction on the size of the facility. [10]

For the given size of the facility, there will exist some optimal size of club. This is determined at the point where the derivatives of the total cost and total benefit functions are equal, shown as S_1 in Fig. 1, for the one-unit facility. Consider now an increase in the size of the facility. As before, a total cost curve and a total benefit curve may be derived, and an optimal club size determined. One other such optimum is shown at S_h, for a quantity of goods upon which the curves C_h and B_h are based. Similar constructions can be carried out for every possible size of facility; that is, for each possible quantity of good.

A similar construction may be used to determine optimal goods quantity for each possible size of club; this is illustrated in Fig. 2. On the ordinate, we measure here total costs and total benefits confronting the individual, as in Fig. 1. On the abscissa, we measure physical size of the facility, quantity of good, and for each assumed size of club membership we may trace total cost and total benefit functions. If we first examine the single-member club, we may well find that the optimal goods quantity is zero; the total cost function may increase more rapidly than the total benefit function from the outset. However, as more persons are added, the total costs to the single person fall; under our symmetrical sharing assumption, they will fall proportionately. The total benefit functions here will slope upward to the right but after some initial range they will be concave downward and at some point will reach a maximum. As club size is increased, benefit

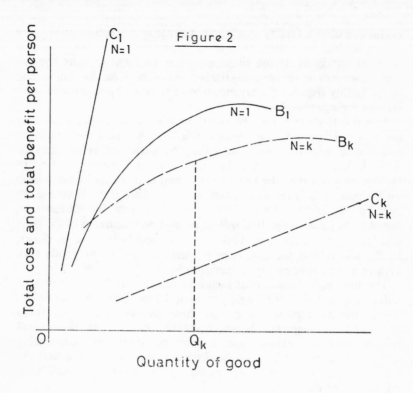

Figure 2

Total cost and total benefit per person

C_1
N=1

N=1 B_1

N=k B_k

C_k
N=k

O

Q_k

Quantity of good

functions will shift generally downward beyond the initial non-congestion range, and the point of maximum benefit will move to the right. The construction of Fig. 2 allows us to derive an optimal goods quantity for each size of club; Q_k is one such quantity for club size $N=K$.

The results derived from Figs. 1 and 2 are combined in Fig. 3. Here the two variables to be chosen, goods quantity and club size, are measured on the ordinate and the abscissa respectively. The values for optimal club size for each goods quantity, derived from Fig. 1, allow us to plot the curve, N_{opt}, in Fig. 3. Similarly, the values for optimal goods quantity, for each club size, derived from Fig. 2, allow us to plot the curve, Q_{opt}.

The intersection of these two curves, N_{opt} and Q_{opt}, determines the position of full equilibrium, G. The individual is in equilibrium both with respect to goods quantity and to group size, for the good under consideration. Suppose, for example, that the sharing group is limited to size, N_k. The attainment of equilibrium with respect to goods quantity, shown by Q_k, would still leave the individual desirous of shifting the size of the membership so as to attain position L. However, once the group increases to this size, the individual prefers a larger quantity of the good, and so on, until G is attained.

Fig. 3 may be interpreted as a standard preference map depicting the tastes of the individual for the two components, goods quantity

Figure 3

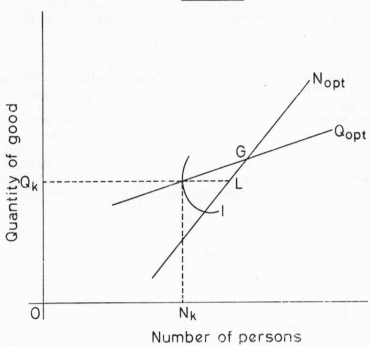

and club size for the sharing of that good. The curves, N_{opt} and Q_{opt}, are lines of optima, and G is the highest attainable level for the individual, the top of his ordinal utility mountain. Since these curves are lines of optima within an individual preference system, successive choices must converge in G.

It should be noted that income-price constraints have already been incorporated in the preference map through the specific sharing assumptions that are made. The tastes of the individual depicted in Fig. 3 reflect the post-payment or net relative evaluations of the two components of consumption at all levels. Unless additional constraints are imposed on the model, he must move to the satiety point in this construction.

It seems clear that under normal conditions both of the curves in Fig. 3 will slope upward to the right, and that they will lie in approxim-ately the relation to each other as therein depicted. This reflects the fact that, normally for the type of good considered in this example, there will exist a complementary rather than a substitute relationship between increasing the quantity of the good and increasing the size of the sharing group.

This geometrical model can be extended to cover goods falling at any point along the private-public spectrum. Take the purely public good as the first extreme case. Since, by definition, congestion does not occur, each total benefit curve, in Fig. 1, becomes horizontal. Thus, optimal club size, regardless of goods quantity is infinite. Hence, full equilibrium is impossible of attainment; equilibrium only with respect to goods quantity can be reached, defined with respect to the all-inclusive finite group. In the construction of Fig. 3, the N curve cannot be drawn. A more realistic model may be that in which, at goods quantity equilibrium, the limitations on group size impose an inequality. For example, in Fig. 3, suppose that the all-inclusive group is of size, N_k. Congestion is indicated as being possible over small sizes of facility, but, if an equilibrium quantity is provided, there is no congestion, and, in fact, there remain economies to scale in club size. The situation at the most favourable attainable position is, therefore, in all respects equivalent to that confronted in the case of the good that is purely public under the more restricted definition.

Figure 4

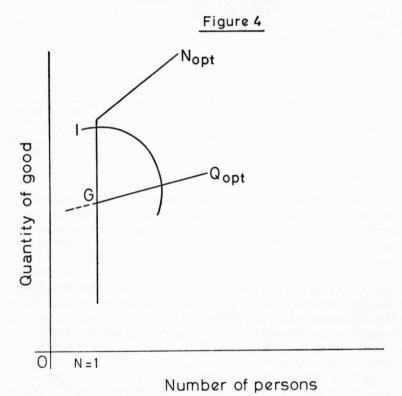

Consider now the purely private good. The appropriate curves here may be shown in Fig. 4. The individual, with his income-price constraints is able to attain the peak of his ordinal preference mountain without the necessity of calling upon his fellows to join him in sharing arrangements. Also, the benefits that he receives from the good may be so exclusively his own that these would largely disappear if others were brought in to share them. Hence, the full equilibrium position, G, lies along the vertical from the $N=1$ member point. Any attempt to expand the club beyond this point will reduce the utility of the individual.[11]

III

The geometrical construction implies that the necessary marginal conditions are satisfied at unique equilibrium values for both goods quantity and club size. This involves an oversimplification that is made possible only through the assumptions of specific cost-sharing schemes and identity among individuals. In order to generalize the results, these restrictions must be dropped. We know that, given any group of individuals who are able to evaluate both consumption shares and the costs of congestion, there exists some set of marginal prices, goods quantity, and club size that will satisfy (7) above. However, the quantity of the good, the size of the club sharing in its consumption, and the cost-sharing arrangements must be determined simultaneously. And, since there are always " gains from trade " to be realized in moving from non-optimal to optimal positions, distributional considerations must be introduced. Once these are allowed to be present, the final " solution " can be located at any one of a sub-infinity of points on the Pareto welfare surface. Only through some quite arbitrarily chosen conventions can standard geometrical constructions be made to apply.

The approach used above has been to impose at the outset a set of marginal prices (tax-prices, if the good is supplied publicly), translated here into shares or potential shares in the costs of providing separate quantities of a specific good for groups of varying sizes. Hence, the individual confronts a predictable set of marginal prices for each quantity of the good at every possible club size, independently of his own choices on these variables. With this convention, and the world-of-equals assumption, the geometrical solution becomes one that is relevant for any individual in the group. If we drop the world-of-equals assumption, the construction continues to hold without change for the choice calculus of any particular individual in the group. The results cannot, of course, be generalized for the group in this case, since different individuals will evaluate any given result differently. The model remains helpful even here, however, in that it suggests the process through which individual decisions may be made, and it tends to clarify some of the implicit content in the more formal statements of the necessary marginal conditions for optimality.[12]

IV

The theory of clubs developed in this paper applies in the strict sense only to the organization of membership or sharing arrangements where " exclusion " is possible. In so far as non-exclusion is a characteristic of public goods supply, as Musgrave has suggested,[13] the theory of clubs is of limited relevance. Nevertheless, some implications of

331

the theory for the whole excludability question may be indicated. If the structure of property rights is variable, there would seem to be few goods the services of which are non-excludable, solely due to some physical attributes. Hence, the theory of clubs is, in one sense, a theory of optimal exclusion, as well as one of inclusion. Consider the classic lighthouse case. Variations in property rights, broadly conceived, could prohibit boat operators without " light licenses " from approaching the channel guarded by the light. Physical exclusion is possible, given sufficient flexibility in property law, in almost all imaginable cases, including those in which the interdependence lies in the act of consuming itself. Take the single person who gets an inoculation, providing immunization against a communicable disease. In so far as this action exerts external benefits on his fellows, the person taking the action could be authorized to collect charges from all beneficiaries under sanction of the collectivity.

This is not, of course, to suggest that property rights will, in practice, always be adjusted to allow for optimal exclusion. If they are not, the " free rider " problem arises. This prospect suggests one issue of major importance that the analysis of this paper has neglected, the question of costs that may be involved in securing agreements among members of sharing groups. If individuals think that exclusion will not be fully possible, that they can expect to secure benefits as free riders without really becoming full-fledged contributing members of the club, they may be reluctant to enter voluntarily into cost-sharing arrangements. This suggests that one important means of reducing the costs of securing voluntary co-operative agreements is that of allowing for more flexible property arrangements and for introducing excluding devices. If the owner of a hunting preserve is allowed to prosecute poachers, then prospective poachers are much more likely to be willing to pay for the hunting permits in advance.

NOTES

[1] I am indebted to graduate students and colleagues for many helpful suggestions. Specific acknowledgement should be made for the critical assistance of Emilio Giardina of the University of Catania and W. Craig Stubblebine of the University of Delaware.

[2] It is interesting that none of the theories of Socialist economic organization seems to be based on explicit co-operation among individuals. These theories have conceived the economy either in the Lange-Lerner sense as an analogue to a purely private, individually oriented social order or, alternatively, as one that is centrally directed.

[3] See Paul A. Samuelson, " The Pure Theory of Public Expenditure ", Review of Economics and Statistics, vol. xxxvi (1954), pp. 387–89; " Diagrammatic Exposition of a Theory of Public Expenditure ", Review of Economics and Statistics, vol. xxxvii (1955), pp. 350–55.

[4] Note that an economic theory of clubs can strictly apply only to the extent that the motivation for joining in sharing arrangements is itself economic; that is, only if choices are made on the basis of costs and benefits of particular goods and services as these are confronted by the individual. In so far as individuals join clubs for camaraderie, as such, the theory does not apply.

⁵ Physical attributes of a good or service may, of course, affect the structure of the sharing arrangements that are preferred. Although the analysis below assumes symmetrical sharing, this assumption is not necessary, and the analysis in its general form can be extended to cover all possible schemes.

⁶ Note that this construction of the individual's utility function differs from that introduced in an earlier paper, where " activities " rather than " goods " were included as the basic arguments. (See James M. Buchanan and Wm. Craig Stubblebine, " Externality," *Economica*, vol. XXXI (1962), pp. 371–84.) In the alternative construction, the " activities " of other persons enter directly into the utility function of the reference individual with respect to the consumption of all other than purely private goods. The construction here incorporates the same interdependence through the inclusion of the N_j's although in a more general manner.

⁷ In Samuelson's diagrammatic presentation, these individual marginal conditions are satisfied, but the diagrammatic construction is more restricted than that contained in his earlier more general model.

⁸ The sharing arrangement need not be either co-operative or governmental in form. Since profit opportunities exist in all such situations, the emergence of profit-seeking firms can be predicted in those settings where legal structures permit, and where this organizational form possesses relative advantages. (Cf. R. H. Coase, " The Nature of the Firm ", *Economica*, vol. IV (1937), pp. 386–405.) For purposes of this paper, such firms are one form of club organization, with co-operatives and public arrangements representing other forms. Generally speaking, of course, the choice among these forms should be largely determined by efficiency considerations.

⁹ The geometrical model here applies only to such goods. Essentially the same analysis may, however, be extended to apply to cases where " congestion ", as such, does not appear. For example, goods that are produced at decreasing costs, even if their consumption is purely private, may be shown to require some sharing arrangements in an equilibrium or optimal organization.

¹⁰ For simplicity, we assume that an additional " membership " in the club involves the addition of one separate person. The model applies equally well, however, for those cases where cost shares are allocated proportionately with predicted usage. In this extension, an additional " membership " would really amount to an additional consumption unit. Membership in the swimming club could, for example, be defined as the right to visit the pool one time each week. Hence, the person who plans to make two visits per week would, in this modification, hold two memberships. This qualification is not, of course, relevant under the strict world-of-equals assumption, but it indicates that the theory need not be so restrictive as it might appear.

¹¹ The construction suggests clearly that the optimal club size, for any quantity of good, will tend to become smaller as the real income of an individual is increased. Goods that exhibit some " publicness " at low income levels will, therefore, tend to become " private " as income levels advance. This suggests that the number of activities that are organized optimally under co-operative collective sharing arrangements will tend to be somewhat larger in low-income communities than in high-income communities, other things equal. There is, of course, ample empirical support for this rather obvious conclusion drawn from the model. For example, in American agricultural communities thirty years ago heavy equipment was communally shared among many farms, normally on some single owner-lease-rental arrangement. Today, substantially the same equipment will be found on each farm, even though it remains idle for much of its potential working time.

The implication of the analysis for the size of governmental units is perhaps less evident. In so far as governments are organized to provide communal facilities, the size of such units measured by the number of citizens, should decline as income increases. Thus, in the affluent society, the local school district may, optimally, be smaller than in the poor society.

¹² A note concerning one implicit assumption of the whole analysis is in order at this point. The possibility for the individual to choose among the various scales of consumption sharing arrangements has been incorporated into an orthodox model of individual behaviour. The procedure implies that the individual remains indifferent as to which of his neighbours or fellow citizens join him in such arrangements. In other words, no attempt has been made to allow for personal selectivity or discrimination in the models. To incorporate this element, which is no doubt important in many instances, would introduce a wholly new dimension into the analysis, and additional tools to those employed here would be required.

¹³ See R. A. Musgrave, *The Theory of Public Finance*, New York, 1959.

The Relationship between Joint Products, Collective Goods, and External Effects

By E. J. MISHAN

I propose in this paper to introduce a scheme that will enable us to display the relationships and distinctions among the optimal conditions applicable to single private goods, jointly produced private goods, collective goods, and external effects. In the course of elaborating the scheme, occasions present themselves for re-examining the definitions of collective goods and of external effects, and for relating our findings to existing concepts.

I. THE MODEL

Let a typical activity produce a maximum of m goods, positive or negative,[1] the purchases of which, by each member of the community, enter into the utility functions of each of the s individuals. The proportions in which the m goods are produced may or may not be independent of the scale of the activity and may or may not be independent of the relative prices of the m goods; the optimal conditions for the several cases treated below remain unaltered.

In addition to the typical activity k, there is a numeraire activity that produces only one good x_r, which, when used as money, enables us to give the necessary optimal conditions for the kth activity in value terms.

The more general term v_{kh}^{ij} (which is interpreted as the increment of value to person j [positive, zero, or negative] arising from person i's marginal purchase or use of the hth good of activity k) can always be used if a person's response to the activity of another depends generally upon the identity of the actor and, also, if we do not need to distinguish between *tangible* external effects, or spillovers, and *psychic* external effects usually associated with the term "interdependent utilities" (Duesenberry, 1949, pp. 97–101). Indeed the term v_{kh}^{ij} can include either or both of these effects.

Reprinted by permission of the publishers and author: E. J. Mishan, "The Relationship Between Joint Products, Collective Goods, and External Effects," *Journal of Political Economy*, 77, No. 3 (May/June 1969), pp. 329-348.

Here I wish to ignore these psychic externalities—except for a brief treatment in the "Note on Derivation of Optimal Conditions" which follows the paper. They play no part in economic policy and are ignored in all cost-benefit studies. More important, however, the close relationship between collective goods and external effects is brought out most clearly in the absence of these psychic effects. Nonetheless, I might add in parentheses that the reader who craves for complete generality can satisfy himself by attaching to each of the equated expressions to the left of c_k (the marginal cost of activity k) in equation (3) a term

$$\sum_{h=1}^{g} \sum_{j=1}^{s} v_{kh}^{ij} \; (i = 1, 2, \ldots, j, \ldots, s)$$

to include the psychic external effects on the rest of the community arising from any ith person's marginal consumption of each of, say, g private goods produced by activity k.

Turning to the tangible external effects, or spillovers, treated in this paper, we can use a notation to emphasize their distinctness by recourse to the common assumption that the response of any one person to the marginal unit of spillover is the same irrespective of which person is responsible for it. Thus, v_{kh}^{ij} is the same for *any* ith person. To remind us of this, we shall write $v_{kh}^{01}, v_{kh}^{02}, \ldots, v_{kh}^{0s}$, respectively, for the effect on persons $1, 2, \ldots, s$, of the marginal unit of spillover h, irrespective of which person produced it. (The same notation is also used to indicate the effects on persons $1, 2, \ldots, s$, of a marginal unit of an unavoidable collective good.) Let $v_{kh}^{01} + v_{kh}^{02} + \ldots + v_{kh}^{0s} \equiv v_{kh}^{0j}$. This last term indicates that the sum of the effects on *all* s persons of a marginal unit of spillover h will be the same irrespective of how it is produced.

It will simplify the exposition if (unless otherwise stated) we assume (i) that each of the s persons in the community takes some of each of the goods and (ii) that there is sufficient divisibility of all of the goods to enable us to avoid inequality signs.

II. PRIVATE GOODS WITHOUT EXTERNAL EFFECTS

A "private" good can be defined as a good that is not collective, but, since we defer discussion of collective goods to the following section, we may provisionally conceive of private goods as those goods which the individual does not share with others. Each unit of a private good enters into some particular individual's utility function but not into those of any others.

Since we are supposing, in general, that—apart from the numeraire activity r—any kth activity produces up to m joint goods, some of each of such goods being taken by every person in the community, the necessary optimal conditions for the private goods case are given by the equation

$$\sum_{h=1}^{m} v_{kh}^{11} = \sum_{h=1}^{m} v_{kh}^{22} = \ldots = \sum_{h=1}^{m} v_{kh}^{ss} = c_k \ldots,^2 \qquad (1)$$

where the jj superscripts act as a reminder that the effects of any jth person's use of the m goods fall on the jth person alone.[3]

Equation (1) states the simple requirement that the sum of the marginal valuations of all the m jointly produced goods of the kth activity to the first person be equal to that for each of the other s persons in the community, and equal also to the marginal cost of producing the m goods of the kth activity. If, for example, given the scale of production in the kth activity, the unit activity consists of one pound of bread, one ounce of bran, and one quarter of straw, the necessary optimal condition requires that the *sum* of the marginal valuations of these three joint products be equal for each of the s consumers, and equal also to the marginal cost of their joint production.

This condition is achieved if the kth industry is perfectly competitive, which, in that case, requires a perfect market for each of the m jointly produced goods. Since a single price will rule for each of those goods, the exchange optimum is also met, the goods rate of substitution for each pair of the m goods being the same for each of the s persons.

In the private goods case (without external effects), the necessary optimal condition clearly implies also that the quantity of any one good taken by each of the individuals should add to the total produced; that is, $x_h^1 + x_h^2 + \ldots + x_h^s = x_h$, where x_h^i is the quantity of h taken by any ith person and x_h is the total quantity of h produced.

The more familiar case of a single private good is derived simply by stripping equation (1) of the summation signs, that is, by assuming the kth activity to produce one good only:

$$v_k^{11} = v_k^{22} = \ldots = v_k^{ss} = c_k \ldots. \qquad (1')$$

Equation (1') is translated as requiring simply that the marginal valuation of the kth good for each person be equal to the marginal cost of producing the kth good.

III. COLLECTIVE GOODS WITHOUT EXTERNAL EFFECTS

The necessary optimal conditions for collective goods, when generalized from the more familiar case of a single collective good to that of m joint collective goods of the kth activity, will appear for *optional* collective goods—those for which each person is free to choose the amount he wishes—as in the equation:

$$\sum_{h=1}^{m} v_{kh}^{11} + \sum_{h=1}^{m} v_{kh}^{22} + \ldots + \sum_{h=1}^{m} v_{kh}^{ss} = c_k \ldots. \qquad (2a)$$

Equation (2a) states, as do equations (2b) and (2c) below, the optimal requirement that the sum of the marginal valuations of each of the m jointly produced collective goods to person 1, plus the sum of their marginal valuations to person 2, plus their sum to person 3, and so on to include those of each of the s persons in the community, should in total equal the marginal cost of producing these m joint collective goods.

An example of two jointly produced collective services of this optimal kind would arise in the case of a dam which both produced street lighting for a town and supplied its public fountains. Each person is free to choose the time spent in availing himself both of the street lighting and of the view of the public fountains, and does so (in the provisional absence of external effects) without depriving any one else of these services.

The degree to which each person avails himself of each of these collective services, however, differs from one service to another and differs also from one person to another, though obviously, the maximum a person takes cannot exceed the total amount of the service provided. In symbols, for collective goods $h = 1, 2, \ldots, m$, $x_1^i \gtreqqless x_2^i \gtreqqless \ldots \gtreqqless x_m^i$ for any ith person. For persons $i = 1, 2, \ldots, s$, $x_h^1 \gtreqqless x_h^2 \gtreqqless \ldots \gtreqqless x_h^s$ for any hth good. And for all i and all h, $x_h^i \leq x_h$.

However, for jointly produced collective goods that are *non-optional*—those for which each person has no choice but is constrained to absorb the whole of the collective good provided—the necessary optimal condition appears, instead, as:

$$\sum_{h=1}^{m} v_{kh}^{01} + \sum_{h=1}^{m} v_{kh}^{02} + \ldots + \sum_{h=1}^{m} v_{kh}^{0s} = c_k. \ldots \quad (2b)$$

By seeding the clouds over some area of farmland, both increased rain and increased sunshine may be induced. But no person within the area can choose how much of each to take; he is compelled to accept the same rainfall and sunshine as everyone else. For this case, then, $x_h^i = x_h$ for all i and for all h. It follows that any person's benefit from the marginal unit of any one or more of these jointly produced collective goods may be negative, notwithstanding which, equation (2b) requires that the total amount of these goods be adjusted so that the algebraic sum of all persons' joint marginal valuations of the m collective goods be positive and equal to their joint marginal cost.

The mixed case in which both optional and non-optional collective goods are jointly produced can be regarded as the general case. If, say, g goods out of the m jointly produced collective goods are optional, and the remainder non-optional, the necessary optional condition is written as:

$$\left(\sum_{h=1}^{g} v_{kh}^{11} + \sum_{g+1}^{m} v_{kh}^{01} \right) + \left(\sum_{h=1}^{g} v_{kh}^{22} + \sum_{g+1}^{m} v_{kh}^{02} \right) + \ldots$$

$$+ \left(\sum_{h=1}^{g} v_{kh}^{ss} + \sum_{g+1}^{m} v_{kh}^{0s} \right) = c_k. \ldots \quad (2c)$$

A simple two-good example in this connection would be that of a dam constructed both for flood control (a non-optional collective good) and for providing street lighting (an optional collective good).

It is clearly possible to simplify these expressions by assuming that the kth activity produces only one good, thus enabling us to drop the summation signs. A single optional collective good requires the condition

$$v_k^{11} + v_k^{22} + \ldots + v_k^{ss} = c_k \ldots \tag{2a'}$$

For a single non-optional collective good, the necessary optimal condition is

$$v_k^{01} + v_k^{02} + \ldots + v_k^{0s} = c_k \ldots \tag{2b'}$$

Just as the familiar equation (1') corresponds to Samuelson's equation (1) in his well-known paper on public goods (Samuelson, 1954), so does the above equation (2a') correspond to his equation (2). But it is important to notice that this latter equation (in which the marginal cost of the collective good is required to equal the sum of the individual marginal valuations) can be extended so as to yield a comprehensive optimal condition which covers both collective and private goods.

To illustrate in the case of private goods, if instead of equating all the terms to the right of c_k in equation (1), we sum them together and extend the increment of cost on the left-hand side to cover the production of the s final units of the kth activity (instead of just the one unit), the partial second-order stability conditions require

$$\sum_{h=1}^{m} v_{kh}^{11} + \sum_{h=1}^{m} v_{kh}^{22} + \ldots + \sum_{h=1}^{m} v_{kh}^{ss} \geqq \Delta c_k \ldots, \tag{1s}$$

where Δc_k indicates the incremental cost of the final s units of k, which incremental cost must not exceed the sum of the left-hand terms—the sum, that is, of the marginal valuations of all the m jointly produced private goods by the first person, plus their sum by the second person, plus those of all the remaining persons. Needless to remark, the analogous equation for the single good may be derived from (1s) by removing the summation signs.

It follows that equation (2a'), taken by itself, does not disclose the distinguishing characteristic of a single collective good, since it can be extended, as indicated, to cover private goods also. Equation (1'), however, does reveal the distinguishing characteristic of a single private good. We therefore have a single optional collective good if equation (2a'), and *only* equation (2a'), can be applied to it.

IV. DEFINITION OF A COLLECTIVE GOOD

According to Samuelson, the distinction between a private good and a collective good resides in the latter's being a good "which all enjoy in common in the sense that each individual's consumption of such a good leads to no subtraction from any other individual's consumption of that good" (Samuelson, 1954, p. 387) and that such goods "*simultaneously* enter into many persons' indifference curves" (Samuelson, 1958, p. 334). This is not altogether satisfactory, as Margolis pointed out (1955), simply because it does not appear to be true of such common examples of collective goods as, for instance, education, hospitals, highways, courts of law, and police. In such cases it is not true that the use of the good by person A does not involve any costs to person B. There are capacity limitations, congestion, and rationing in connection with the public's use of these sorts of goods.

In reply, Samuelson appeared to think that this was only a question of going beyond "the polar cases of (1) pure private goods and (2) pure public goods to (3) some kind of mixed model which takes account of all external, indirect, joint-consumption effects" (Samuelson, 1958, p. 335). This third case, however, was not formally elaborated, and we are left with the problem of reconciling ourselves to a neat definition of collective goods that is apparently inapplicable to nearly all the familiar instances of collective goods.

The problem is resolved, however, by recognizing that any inference from equation (2) of a zero marginal cost of sharing the collective good is not warranted. Indeed, it is readily admitted that, whether the costs in question are factor costs or social costs, they will tend to rise with the increase in the number of beneficiaries. If they are the former, then, in the long period at least, when the size and cost of the collective project depend upon the number of persons it is designed to serve, the cost of providing for a larger number of people is, with few exceptions, larger than that of providing for a smaller number. In this sense, the marginal cost of sharing is likely to be positive. If, on the other hand, we consider a shorter period during which the capacity of the project cannot be extended, the use of a collective good by a larger number of people than that anticipated can cause spillover effects such as congestion. Such external effects, however, can apply in the production or consumption of both private and collective goods. It is advisable, therefore, to make a distinction between private and collective goods in a context in which all external effects are omitted.

The need for a formulation such as that given by equation (2a) arises from the fact that the factor costs incurred in providing any unit of the collective service cannot be divided among the given number of beneficiaries on any economic principle. We can, of course, employ optimal conditions to determine the number of beneficiaries (implying that the marginal cost of sharing benefits is positive), but, whatever this number is, each one of them partakes jointly of the benefits of any unit of the collective service. The value placed on any particular unit of the collective service will in general differ from one person to another, and the optimal condition states that, irrespective of the differences in the valuations of the marginal benefits of the various persons, the sum of these valuations must equal the marginal cost of the collective service.

In contrast, a private good is one in which (in the absence of external effects) the whole of the benefit of the unit of good provided is appropriated by one person. The value of his benefit alone must therefore not be smaller than the cost of the additional factors required to supply it. If the units of the good in question are large, each person buying only a few, the optimal output may indeed be consistent with a difference in the marginal valuation as between one person and another. But the assumption of perfect divisibility of the output of the good offers us the convenience of the equation (1) formulation of the optimal condition, for it implies a large enough quantity bought by each person as to allow him to adjust his total purchase in order to equate his marginal valuation to the price which itself is to be set to the marginal cost of the optimal output. A number of services provided by such conventional collective goods as hospitals, clinics, and public utilities fall into the category of private goods inasmuch as their optimal outputs, granted divisibility, are to be determined by equation (1).

V. MARGINAL COSTS AND PRICING OF COLLECTIVE GOODS

As observed above, equation (2a) is quite consistent with the concept of positive marginal costs incurred in increasing the number of beneficiaries of a collective good, for there will generally be some costs associated with extending the capacity of a collective good in order to provide the service(s) to additional persons. But the search for an optimal number of persons to be served by a collective good, through equating the marginal value generated by an additional person to the marginal cost incurred in providing the necessary addition to capital capacity, does not take us to equation (1). What has to be done is to compare equations of type (2) with and without the extra person. Suppose, for example, that equation (2a) is met for an existing s number of persons who enjoy some optimal amount and quality of a collective service. Now the question of an extension in the number of beneficiaries by one person arises. We proceed by forming a second equation (2a) with the marginal valuations of $s + 1$ persons on the left-hand side. On the right-hand side, we calculate the long-period marginal cost of extending the same collective service to $s + 1$ persons. We can subtract the first equation from the second and compare the differences on each side. But we need not do so, for if the sum of $s + 1$ marginal valuations on the left-hand side of the new equation exceeds the marginal cost on the right-hand side, we can proceed in the same way to consider extending capital capacity to another person until the optimal number of beneficiaries for the given collective service is reached.[4] It should be apparent, moreover, that equation (2a) is entailed for an optimal position with respect to any one feature and, indeed, for an optimal position reached simultaneously with respect to membership and to all other features of the collective good which are fully variable in the long period.

There are, however, one or two types of collective goods such as street lighting or television broadcasting, often thought of as collective goods par excellence, for which the term "capacity costs of extending membership" may be ambiguous. For example, once street lighting is introduced into a town, there is nothing to prevent additional people coming into the town to enjoy the illumination. If a television transmitter covers a radius of fifty miles, any number of people can change their residence so as to be within the required area and enjoy the programs without in the least reducing the reception of the original viewers. The marginal cost of extending membership is therefore zero insofar as additional people move into a locality in order to avail themselves of an existing collective service. But it is not zero if instead the service is extended to others by moving or installing additional facilities into other localities. If additional streets are illuminated, or a television station is installed in a new area, the marginal costs of increasing the number of beneficiaries are positive.[5]

For shorter periods the number of variable factors are fewer, and therefore, for some range of outputs, the marginal variable costs of a collective service are lower. Once a highway is constructed, total variable costs—those of maintenance and administration—may be very low and increase only slightly with the increase in traffic. Once a park is laid out, maintenance costs may vary little with the use of the park by the given number of people in the community, while the maintenance costs of a bridge or tunnel may be zero, irrespective of the frequency of its use.[6] In the shortest possible period in which all costs are overheads, the variable costs of the output produced being zero, the question of rules for an optimal output does not arise. The only relevant question is that of pricing the preempted output so as to clear the market.

Last, having determined the optimal amount of the collective good by reference, say, to equation (2a), it remains only to set prices that will insure the purchase of this optimal amount.[7] Clearly, if a tax is imposed on each person, he willingly takes all that is offered to him so long as his marginal value of the collective service is not negative. If, instead, he is allowed to choose freely at a price, the price to be set can vary from person to person—for "ideally" the price to be set for each person must equal his marginal valuation (always provided this is non-negative) of the optimal amount of the particular collective service being provided. If prices are set lower than this ideal set of prices, a sense of frustration will arise, although the optimal amount of the collective service will continue to be taken by everyone. If, however, the prices are higher than this ideal set of prices, potential benefits are forgone by some persons who choose to take less than the amount provided. If, therefore, a uniform price above zero is to be set, the optimal amount is taken by every person only if this uniform price is set no higher than the lowest of the marginal valuations placed by some person on the optimal amount of the service. In the event finally of case (2b), of the production of non-optional collective goods where people are constrained to absorb the full amount of the collective service—as they would be in the case of flood control or artificial rain—it should be obvious that the price set can make no difference to the amount taken.[8]

VI. PRIVATE GOODS WITH EXTERNAL EFFECTS

We have been deliberately evading the problem of external effects in the preceding sections so as to deal with them more systematically in the present section. It will clarify the exposition if, initially, we conceive of external effects as additions to or subtractions from the valuation side (rather than as subtractions from or additions to the cost side).

In considering private goods jointly produced, it is required that some of the m goods of the kth activity be external effects or spillovers. For example, our bread-making industry of Section II might be regarded as producing not only joint private and, therefore, marketable goods—bread, bran, and straw—but also collective disservices such as smoke and noise. If there were but a single person in the community, he could be allowed to choose an amount of the kth activity that would equate the sum of the marginal valuations of each of its jointly produced goods and disservices to the marginal cost of the kth activity. For in this special case, the one person takes account of the value of all the effects arising from the amount of the kth activity he causes to be produced. Once there are a number of people in the community, however, the disservices associated with the production of activity k fall on everyone irrespective of their valuation of the disservices. Smoke, for example, is not only a disservice or negative good; it cannot be appropriated and exchanged. Consequently a market, say, for smoke-absorbing services cannot be established, and a common price for such a service cannot emerge—hence, the crucial feature of an external effect in an allocative context: the quanta of it absorbed by people cannot be apportioned among them according to willingness to receive at a price. The nature of the process is such that an external diseconomy is, in effect, a non-optional (or unavoidable) collective "bad," in every way symmetrical with a non-optional collective good save in respect of intention. In considering, therefore, the optimal amount of the kth activity, we must bear in mind that whereas, say, the qth unit of bread provides a benefit only to a particular purchaser, the qth unit of smoke causes discomfort not only to the buyer of the qth loaf but also—though in varying degrees—to each of the s persons in the community.

In general, the optimal amount of the kth activity producing several private goods, numbered, say, 1 to g, and several external effects, numbered $g + 1$ to m, is that which, by permitting each of the s persons to choose amounts of any of the jointly produced private goods by reference to the prices of such goods, sets the combined prices of these jointly produced goods at a level that realizes the condition

$$\sum_{h=1}^{g} v_{kh}^{11} + \sum_{g+1}^{m} v_{kh}^{0j} = \sum_{h=1}^{g} v_{kh}^{22} + \sum_{g+1}^{m} v_{kh}^{0j} = \ldots$$

$$= \sum_{h=1}^{g} v_{kh}^{ss} + \sum_{g+1}^{m} v_{kh}^{0j} = c_k. \ldots \tag{3}$$

If there are no external effects, the second-summation-sign terms vanish from each equation and we are left, in effect, with equation (1), which applies to private goods alone. If we now introduce a single external diseconomy, such as smoke, the sum of the marginal effects falling on each of the s persons of the smoke incurred in producing the total amount of the kth activity has to be added algebraically to the joint marginal valuations of the private goods of the kth activity taken by each person. The same occurs for any other external effect, say, noise, incurred in producing the kth activity. The effect, in general, is to add to the $\sum v_{kh}^{jj}$ terms of equation (1)—each equated to one another and to c_k for joint private goods numbered 1 to g—a sum of terms exactly comparable to those on the left-hand side of equation (2b), except that some or all of these non-optional goods (here numbered $g + 1$ to m) can now be negative.

Moreover, the same equation (3) applies to instances in which the external effects arise, not in the actual production of the goods of the kth activity, but directly from the consumption or use of any of the k goods. An obvious example is the private automobile, which produces, when operated, such unavoidable collective "bads" as noise, air pollution, visual distraction, and—above a certain number—traffic congestion. The marginal valuation of the services of the private car must include, therefore, not only the marginal benefit enjoyed alone by the operator of the car, but also the marginal losses imposed in respect of each spillover on every member of the community, the owner included. If the service enjoyed by the jth car operator is numbered 1, and the four collective "bads" are numbered 2, 3, 4, and 5, then for the private good 1 the term v_{k1}^{jj} is positive. For collective "bad" 2, however, all the terms of v_{k2}^{0j} are negative. The same applies to each of the three remaining "bads."

Finally, for the special case of a single spillover effect, whether external economy or diseconomy, the production of at least one private good is required in order that a non-optional collective good or "bad" be generated.[9] The optimal output of a private good, bread, each additional unit of which generates additional smoke that affects each of the inhabitants of an area, is given by equation (3'), which differs from equation (3) only in having two goods, one positive and one negative, instead of m.

344

If the private good, bread, is numbered 1, and the collective "bad" is numbered 2, then with respect to private good 1, it is required that

$$v_{k1}^{11} + v_{k2}^{0j} = v_{k1}^{22} + v_{k2}^{0j} = \ldots = v_{k1}^{ss} + v_{k2}^{0j} = c_k. \tag{3'}$$

The necessary optimal condition thus implies the production and consumption of an amount of bread such that the marginal cost of bread is equal to its price (and, therefore, to the marginal valuation for any jth person) *after* subtracting therefrom the sum of the marginal losses suffered by each of the s persons in the community as a result of the smoke generated in its production.

VII. COLLECTIVE GOODS WITH EXTERNAL EFFECTS

The external effects that arise in the production or consumption of collective goods present no difficulty, since they may be regarded in this context as non-optional goods or "bads." If the jointly produced collective goods (none of which are external effects) are all non-optional, the introduction of external effects is covered by equation (2b), always bearing in mind that one or more of the non-optional collective "goods" which are external diseconomies will be negative. If, on the other hand, some of the jointly produced collective goods that are not external effects are optional collective goods, the introduction of external effects, regarded as non-optional collective goods or "bads," is covered by equation (2c), which again may be regarded as the general case.

A simple example of the latter case would be that of a dam system which provides two collective goods for an area—flood control (non-optional) and electric power (optional)—and one external diseconomy or collective "bad"—the disappearance of fish from the river. Of course, not every person who benefits from flood control or electric power stands to lose as a result of the destruction of fishing facilities. But this presents no difficulty, as we can extend the set of s persons to cover each person who either benefits or loses, respectively, from any non-optional collective good or "bad." Equations (2b) and (2c), therefore, apply as well to the case of

TABLE 1

	WITHOUT EXTERNAL EFFECTS	WITH EXTERNAL EFFECTS
Jointly produced private goods	$\sum\limits_{h=1}^{m} v_{kh}^{11} =$	$\left(\sum\limits_{h=1}^{g} v_{kh}^{11} + \sum\limits_{h=g+1}^{m} v_{kh}^{0j} \right) =$
Jointly produced collective goods	$\left(\sum\limits_{h=1}^{g} v_{kh}^{11} + \sum\limits_{g+1}^{m} v_{kh}^{01} \right) +$	$\left(\sum\limits_{h=1}^{g} v_{kh}^{11} + \sum\limits_{g+1}^{m} v_{kh}^{01} \right) +$

external effects produced along with joint collective goods as they do to the case of joint collective goods without external effects.[10]

345

Accepting joint production as the more general condition, we can, finally, juxtapose the relationships between the four cases dealt with by summarizing their optimal equations in Table 1. In each case, the expression for person 1 alone is given. An equal sign following an expression indicates that the analogous expression of each of the other s persons is equal to it and equal also to c_k. A plus sign following the expression indicates that the analogous expressions for all other s persons are added to it and the sum set equal to c_k. In the interests of brevity, only the expression for the more general case of optional and non-optional collective goods, as given by equation (2c), is used.

VIII. FURTHER REMARKS ON EXTERNAL EFFECTS

The Concept of Marginal Social Cost and Equation (3)

Of the m joint products of the kth activity, let the first g be private goods and the remaining $(m - g)$ be external economies or diseconomies arising from the consumption or production of the g private goods. The optimal output of k, as determined by equation (3), requires that the sum of the prices of the joint *private* goods be set above the marginal cost of the kth activity in the case where the community's joint marginal valuation of all external effects—as given by the component

$$\sum_{h=g+1}^{m} v_{kh}^{0j}$$

in equation (3)—is, on balance, positive (indicating a predominance of external economies over external diseconomies) and below this marginal cost if, on balance, the value of this component is negative. Whether positive or negative, however, this component can be subtracted from each of the equated expressions of (3) so as to yield the alternative form

$$\sum_{h=1}^{g} v_{kh}^{11} = \sum_{h=1}^{g} v_{kh}^{22} = \ldots = \sum_{h=1}^{g} v_{kh}^{ss} = c_k - \sum_{h=g+1}^{m} v_{kh}^{0j} \ldots \quad (3^*)$$

Marginal (private) cost c_k *less* the double summation term is clearly the marginal *social* cost of the kth activity. If this double summation term, representing the net marginal effect of the $(m - g)$ spillovers on all s persons, is *positive*, then marginal social cost is *below* marginal private cost. Conversely, if this double summation term is negative, the marginal social cost is above the marginal private cost. The equated expressions to the left of this marginal social cost represent the equality of marginal valuations for each individual's consumption of the jointly produced g private goods—exactly comparable to the left-hand side of equation (1)—which is realized by setting the sum of the prices of the g jointly produced private goods equal to the marginal social cost of the kth activity.

When the optimal condition is left as it is in equation (3), it is to be interpreted as marginal *social* valuation for each person equals marginal *private* cost. If, on the other hand, the value of the positive or negative sum, arising from the g external effects on s persons, is transferred to the marginal cost side, the optimal equation takes shape as (3*) and is interpreted as marginal *private* valuation for each person equals marginal *social* cost.[11]

Definition of an External Effect

In developing the scheme presented here, a definition of external effects emerges that accords with the common conception but differs somewhat from other definitions in which external effects turn on (*a*) welfare or production effects that are wholly or partially unpriced,[12] or (*b*) the dependence of a production function or a consumption function on the activities of others,[13] or (*c*) the inability of the firm to control the factor.[14]

The essence of the common conception of an external effect, one that is consistent with the usage in this paper, turns on its *incidental* character. The effect on others' welfare, though direct—and not an indirect effect, which is what is involved in any alteration of the set of product and factor prices consequent upon any change in tastes or in supply conditions—is always an *unintentional* product of some otherwise legitimate employment. It therefore does not cease to exist when the external economy or diseconomy is properly priced so as to insure than an optimal output is attained. And it does not necessarily exist when the production function of a firm or the consumption function of a person is altered by the activities of others. If I deliberately, and with malice aforethought, pour hydrochloric acid into the pure waters of a stream used by a whiskey distillery, or if I gradually poison my mother-in-law, I certainly affect the production function of the former and the consumption function of the latter. But neither activity accords with the popular notion of an external or spillover effect. Nor will the deliberate sabotage of a works by a gang of neo-Luddites do so, notwithstanding that their activities are outside the control of the firm.

Note on Derivation of Optimal Conditions

I

Maximize $W = W(U^1, U^2, \ldots, U^i, U^j, \ldots, U^s)$, where $U^i = U^i(x_{k1}^1, x_{k1}^2, \ldots, x_{k1}^s; \ldots; x_{km}^1, x_{km}^2, \ldots, x_{km}^s; x_r^i)$ $(i = 1, 2, \ldots, s, k = 1, 2, \ldots, n)$, subject to $F(y_1, y_2, \ldots, y_n; y_r) = 0$, where $y_k = y_k(x_{k1}, x_{k2}, \ldots, x_{km})$ $(k = 1, 2, \ldots, n)$ and $y_r = y_r(x_r)$.

Therefore, maximize $W^* = W + \lambda F$ by setting

$$
\begin{cases}
0 = \dfrac{\partial W^*}{\partial x_{k1}^j} = W_1 \dfrac{\partial U^1}{\partial x_{k1}^j} + W_2 \dfrac{\partial U^2}{\partial x_{k1}^j} + \ldots + W_s \dfrac{\partial U^s}{\partial x_{k1}^j} + \lambda F_k \dfrac{\partial y_k}{\partial x_{k1}^j} \\
\quad \vdots \qquad\quad \vdots \qquad\quad \vdots \qquad\qquad \vdots \qquad\qquad \vdots \\
0 = \dfrac{\partial W^*}{\partial x_{km}^j} = W_1 \dfrac{\partial U^1}{\partial x_{km}^j} + W_2 \dfrac{\partial U^2}{\partial x_{km}^j} + \ldots + W_s \dfrac{\partial U^s}{\partial x_{km}^j} + \lambda F_k \dfrac{\partial y_k}{\partial x_{km}^j}
\end{cases}
$$

$$(j = 1, 2, \ldots, s)$$
$$(k = 1, 2, \ldots, n)$$

$$0 = \frac{\partial W^*}{\partial x_r^j} = W_j \frac{\partial U^j}{\partial x_r^j} \qquad\qquad\qquad + \lambda F_r \frac{\partial y_r}{\partial x_r^j}$$

$$(j = 1, 2, \ldots, s)$$

$$0 = \frac{\partial W^*}{\partial \lambda} = F(y_1, y_2, \ldots, y_n; y_r).$$

A. Private Goods with External Effects

By making assumption A, that $x_{kh}^1 + x_{kh}^2 + \ldots + x_{kh}^s = x_{kh}$, for goods $h = 1, 2, \ldots, m$, for any kth activity, where x_{kh}^i is the quantity of the khth good received by the ith person and x_{kh} is the total quantity of it produced, we can show

$$\frac{\partial y_k}{\partial x_{k1}^1} = \frac{\partial y_k}{\partial x_{k1}^2} = \ldots = \frac{\partial y_k}{\partial x_{k1}^s} = \frac{\partial y_k}{\partial x_{k1}}$$

$$\therefore \sum_{j=1}^{s} W_j \frac{\partial U^j}{\partial x_{kh}^1} = \sum_{j=1}^{s} W_j \frac{\partial U^j}{\partial x_{kh}^2} = \ldots = \sum_{j=1}^{s} W_j \frac{\partial U^j}{\partial x_{kh}^s} = -\lambda F_k \frac{\partial y_k}{\partial x_{k1}} \ldots \quad (4)$$

$$(h = 1, 2, \ldots, m)$$

In order to reduce these expressions to value terms by reference to the numeraire good x_r, use the same A assumption, $x_r^1 + x_r^2 + \ldots + x_r^s = x_r$, to show that

$$W_1 \frac{\partial U^1}{\partial x_r^1} = W_2 \frac{\partial U^2}{\partial x_r^2} = \ldots = W_s \frac{\partial U^s}{\partial x_r^s} = -\lambda F_r \frac{\partial y_r}{\partial x_r} \ldots \quad (5)$$

Since we can divide each of the terms in any of the summated expressions in (4) by each of the corresponding equated terms in (5), we obtain:

$$\sum_{j=1}^{s} \frac{W_j \frac{\partial U^j}{\partial x_{kh}^1}}{W_j \frac{\partial U^j}{\partial x_r}} = \sum_{j=1}^{s} \frac{W_j \frac{\partial U^j}{\partial x_{kh}^2}}{W_j \frac{\partial U^j}{\partial x_r}} = \ldots = \sum_{j=1}^{s} \frac{W_j \frac{\partial U^j}{\partial x_{kh}^s}}{W_j \frac{\partial U^j}{\partial x_r}} = \frac{F_k \frac{\partial y_k}{\partial x_{kh}}}{F_r \frac{\partial y_r}{\partial x_r}},$$

$$(h = 1, 2, \ldots, m),$$

rewritten as

$$\sum_{j=1}^{s} v_{kh}^{1j} = \sum_{j=1}^{s} v_{kh}^{2j} = \ldots = \sum_{j=1}^{s} v_{kh}^{sj} = c_{kh} \ldots \quad (6)$$

$$(h = 1, 2, \ldots, m),$$

where v_{kh}^{ij} is interpreted as the effect of person i's marginal quantity of the hth good of the kth activity on person j's marginal valuation (in terms of numeraire).

Finally, to obtain necessary optimal conditions for joint production, that is, for activity y_k, where $y_k = y_k(x_{k1}, x_{k2}, \ldots, x_{km})$, since

$$\frac{\dfrac{\partial F}{\partial y_k}}{\dfrac{\partial F}{\partial x_r}} = \frac{F_k \dfrac{\partial y_k}{\partial x_{k1}}}{F_r \dfrac{\partial y_r}{\partial x_r}} + \frac{F_k \dfrac{\partial y_k}{\partial x_{k2}}}{F_r \dfrac{\partial y_r}{\partial x_r}} + \ldots + \frac{F_k \dfrac{\partial y_k}{\partial x_{km}}}{F_r \dfrac{\partial y_r}{\partial x_r}},$$

or

$$c_k = c_{k1} + c_{k2} + \ldots + c_{km}.$$

We can add together equations (4) to m in (6) to obtain:

$$\sum_{h=1}^{m} \sum_{j=1}^{s} v_{kh}^{1j} = \sum_{h=1}^{m} \sum_{j=1}^{s} v_{kh}^{2j} = \ldots = \sum_{h=1}^{m} \sum_{j=1}^{s} v_{kh}^{sj} = c_k. \ldots \tag{7}$$

Note, in the special "independent" case in which all v_{kh}^{ij} terms $= 0$ ($i \neq j$), equation (7) reduces to

$$\sum_{h=1}^{m} v_{kh}^{11} = \sum_{h=1}^{m} v_{kh}^{22} = \ldots = \sum_{h=1}^{m} v_{kh}^{ss} = c_k. \ldots \tag{7'}$$

B. Collective Goods with External Effects

Instead of the A assumption we now introduce assumption B, that $x_{kh}^1 = x_{kh}^2 = \ldots = x_{kh}^s = x_{kh}$ ($h = 1, 2, \ldots, m$). Since the quantity x_{kh} is simultaneously available for each person $1, 2, \ldots, s$, the marginal cost c_{kh} makes the marginal unit of x_{kh} simultaneously available to each of the s persons. Therefore, all the s-equated terms to the left of c_{kh} in equation (6) are added to give:

$$\sum_{j=1}^{s} v_{kh}^{1j} + \sum_{j=1}^{s} v_{kh}^{2j} + \ldots + \sum_{j=1}^{s} v_{kh}^{sj} = c_{kh} \ldots \tag{8}$$

while, for the activity y_k, the condition is

$$\sum_{h=1}^{m} \sum_{j=1}^{s} v_{kh}^{1j} = \sum_{h=1}^{m} \sum_{j=1}^{s} v_{kh}^{2j} + \ldots + \sum_{h=1}^{m} \sum_{j=1}^{s} v_{kh}^{sj} = c_k. \ldots \tag{9}$$

Note, in the special "independent" case in which all $v_{kh}^{ij} = 0$ ($i \neq j$), equation (9) reduces to

$$\sum_{h=1}^{m} v_{kh}^{11} + \sum_{h=1}^{m} v_{kh}^{22} + \ldots + \sum_{h=1}^{m} v_{kh}^{ss} = c_k. \ldots \tag{9'}$$

C. Summary of Results

The results obtained so far for the joint output of m goods produced by any kth activity can be summarized in a matrix in which the terms $\sum_{h=1}^{m} v_{kh}^{ij}$ are abbreviated to $\sum v^{ij}$.

$$\begin{bmatrix} \sum v^{11} & \sum v^{12} & \cdots & \sum v^{1s} \\ \sum v^{21} & \sum v^{22} & \cdots & \sum v^{2s} \\ \vdots & \vdots & & \vdots \\ \sum v^{s1} & \sum v^{s2} & \cdots & \sum v^{ss} \end{bmatrix}$$

The necessary optimum conditions for: (1) private goods without externalities require that we *equate* all the diagonal terms to one another and to c_k; (2) collective goods without externalities require we *add* all the diagonal terms together and equate to c_k; (3) private goods with externalities require that we *equate* the row sums to one another and to c_k; and (4) collective goods with externalities require that we *add* the row sums together and equate to c_k.

II

D. Alternative Treatment of External Effects

Though formally indistinguishable using the above notation, *psychic* externalities should, for policy purposes, be separated from *tangible* externalities such as spillover effects on the environment. With the above notation, if person i suffers from the spillover generated by his new automobile, the term v_{kh}^{ii} would be interpreted as person i's net marginal valuation after subtracting the spillover from his car. The term v_{kh}^{ij}, the effect of i's new automobile on person j, might then include two effects, the tangible spillover effect (suffered also by person i) and the psychic effect, say, envy of person i.

We can use the terms v_{kh}^{ij} ($i \neq j$), where in general $v_{kh}^{1j} \neq v_{kh}^{2j} \neq \ldots \neq v_{kh}^{sj}$, to denote only the psychic terms, should we wish to use them. However, we disregard them in the text. The tangible spillover effects, on the other hand, will be treated as *non-optional* collective goods, or bads, that are produced incidentally (at zero cost), though unavoidably, along with the other goods of the activity that are deliberately produced—whether the latter are private goods or collective goods.

Thus, if we rewrite equation (7′), the optimal condition for jointly produced private goods *without* (psychic) externalities for only $(m - 1)$ goods, we can treat the remaining good as a jointly produced spillover. Any ith person's purchase of the $(m - 1)$ jointly produced outputs inflicts, say, an adverse spillover on each of the s persons, himself included. This spillover can be regarded as a zero-cost non-optional bad—$c_{km} = 0$. The marginal cost of producing a marginal unit of the kth activity for any ith person must now equal the sum of each person's negative marginal valuation of the spillover along with the sum of the ith person's marginal valuation of the $(m - 1)$ goods.

Since this is true for any person's incurring the marginal unit of the kth activity, we write the optimal condition for this single spillover case as:

$$\sum_{h=1}^{m-1} v_{kh}^{11} + \sum_{j=1}^{s} v_{km}^{1j} = \sum_{h=1}^{m-1} v_{kh}^{22} + \sum_{j=1}^{s} v_{km}^{2j} = \dots$$

$$= \sum_{h=1}^{m-1} v_{kh}^{ss} + \sum_{j=1}^{s} v_{km}^{sj} = c_k. \dots \quad (10)$$

If we now assume that the response of any given jth person to a marginal unit of this spillover is the same irrespective of the person responsible for it, that is, $v^{1j} = v^{2j} = \dots = v^{sj}$, for any jth person, it follows that:

$$\sum_{j=1}^{s} v_{km}^{1j} = \sum_{j=1}^{s} v_{km}^{2j} = \dots = \sum_{j=1}^{s} v_{km}^{sj} =, \text{ say, } v_{km}^{0j},$$

which is to say that the sum of the responses to the marginal unit of spill-over by all persons has the same value, which we denote by v_{km}^{0j}, irrespective of the person responsible for the marginal unit. Using this latter term we can rewrite equation (10) as:

$$\sum_{h=1}^{m-1} v_{kh}^{11} + v_{km}^{0j} = \sum_{h=1}^{m-1} v_{kh}^{22} + v_{km}^{0j} = \dots = \sum_{h=1}^{m-1} v_{kh}^{ss} + v_{km}^{0j} = c_k. \dots \quad (10a)$$

For the more general case of $(m - g)$ spillovers, we write:

$$\sum_{h=1}^{g} v_{kh}^{11} + \sum_{h=g+1}^{m} v_{kh}^{0j} = \sum_{h=1}^{g} v_{kh}^{22} + \sum_{h=g+1}^{m} v_{kh}^{0j} = \dots$$

$$= \sum_{h=1}^{g} v_{kh}^{ss} + \sum_{h=g+1}^{m} v_{kh}^{0j} = c_k. \dots \quad (11)$$

E. Notation for Collective Goods

Once a spillover is treated as a non-optional zero-cost collective good or bad, the optimal condition for a *single* non-optional collective good itself—one in which $x_{kh}^1 = x_{kh}^2 = \dots = x_{kh}^s = x_{kh}$—has to be written as $v_{kh}^{01} + v_{kh}^{02} + \dots + v_{kh}^{0s} = c_{kh}$, and for m non-optional collective goods as

$$\sum_{h=1}^{m} v_{kh}^{01} + \sum_{h+1}^{m} v_{kh}^{02} + \dots + \sum_{h=1}^{m} v_{kh}^{0s} = c_k. \dots \quad (12)$$

The *optional* collective good, in contrast, is one for which the amount taken by each person can differ from the total provided; that is,

$$\begin{cases} x_{kh}^i \gtreqless x_{kh}^j \\ x_{kh}^i \leq x_{kh} \end{cases} \quad \text{(for any } h \text{ and for any } i; j; i \neq j\text{).}$$

The optimal condition for a *single* optional collective good is written

$$v_{kh}^{11} + v_{kh}^{22} + \dots + v_{kh}^{ss} = c_{kh}.$$

For the general case of m optional collective goods, we write:

$$\sum_{h=1}^{m} v_{kh}^{11} + \sum_{h=1}^{m} v_{kh}^{22} + \dots + \sum_{h=1}^{m} v_{kh}^{ss} = c_k. \dots \quad (13)$$

Further Note on the v_{kh}^{0j} Term*

The term v_{kh}^{0j} has been used as a shorthand for $v_{kh}^{01} + v_{kh}^{02} + \ldots + v_{kh}^{0s}$, the zero superscript to indicate that the response of each ith person experiencing the spillover is unaffected by the identity of the person causing the spillover. The use of this term in the text is correct for any spillovers arising in the *production* of a good inasmuch as —in a community of more than a few people—the individual does not link the spillover he causes in having the good produced with his purchase of it. Since he equates only the direct utility of the good with its price, the spillover effects to be added cover all s members, himself included.

* Added in proof.

In the case of spillovers arising from the act of *consuming*, or *using*, the good, however, the user of the good is generally assumed to associate the spillover he causes with his own use of the good. It therefore does enter directly into his valuation of the good. And the spillovers to be added to his own valuation term now cover only the $(s - 1)$ remaining persons. Strictly speaking, then, the spillover term for any ith person is

$$\sum_{j=1}^{s} v_{k2}^{ij} \quad (j \neq i)$$

for a spillover numbered 2 arising in connection with the use of good 1. The spillover generated by each user and experienced by the remaining $(s - 1)$ persons therefore must differ as between one user and another by the exclusion of the particular user. Nonetheless, as the number of persons, s, increases, the differences between the

$$\sum_{j=1}^{s} v_{k2}^{ij} \quad (j \neq i)$$

terms for different people become negligible as does the difference between that term and the sum

$$\sum_{j=1}^{s} v_{k2}^{ij} \quad (j = i),$$

which can therefore be assumed to equal v_{k2}^{0j}.

NOTES

[1] Since m is the maximum number of goods that can be produced jointly by any one activity, the outputs of up to $(m - 1)$ goods of any activity can be zero.

[2] The derivation of all the optimal conditions are in the *Note* following the text.

[3] This total value to person j is a measure of his compensating variation—the amount of money he must pay or receive to be as well off as before, following the consumption of the marginal units of these m goods by person i.

[4] In his economic theory of clubs, Buchanan (1965) arrives at the optimal number of people sharing a given size of collective, or club, facility, under the simplifying assumption of identical tastes, by comparing the eventual rising marginal cost of the diseconomies to existing members (of bearing with an additional member) with the value of the benefit of membership to the candidate. In contrast to the treatment above, Buchanan concentrates on the left-hand terms of equation (2) in the first part of his paper, the optimal membership depending upon the external diseconomies of an increasing membership. The treatment of external diseconomies in the present paper is, however, left to Section VI. Marginal sharing costs in the text refer only to factor costs.

[5] Since television programs are not homogeneous units of a collective service, there is the additional problem of selecting over a period of time the optimal combination of programs. However, no single program should be transmitted unless the sum of the expected valuations of all viewers exceeds the additional cost of the program. Once the decision to transmit a program is irrevocable, the price, ideally, should be

set at zero, as—within this shortest period—the variable costs of providing the service to additional viewers is zero. See Samuelson (1958, p. 335) and Davis and Whinston (1967).

[6] If the output in any period is variable at zero cost, equation (2a), (2b), or (2c) requires that we expand output until the combined sum of all persons' marginal valuations is equal to zero. This would necessarily imply a marginal valuation of zero for each person only for equation (2a), referring to an optional collective good of which people could choose—as, say, in television viewing—to absorb less than the optimal amount of the collective good that is provided. If, on the other hand, equation (2b) applies and each person is constrained to absorb the full amount of the collective good—as, say, in flood control or artificial rainfall—the marginal valuations of some people may be negative, the sum of their negative marginal valuations being offset by the sum of the positive marginal valuations of others.

[7] It is assumed in all these cases that the total conditions are always met: the sum of the s persons' total valuations exceeding total costs in the provision of the optimal amount of any single or joint collective services.

[8] Given discretion in the means of raising revenues, it need hardly be added that any of these collective goods can, in principle, be operated at ideal outputs under either private or public ownership. If the number of the beneficiaries is roughly coterminous with the size of the community, if the costs of collecting revenues through taxes is lower than by other methods, if the service is regarded as a social priority and justifies some effective subsidy of the service for some people as a way of redistributing income, the case for public ownership and operation is strong. In general, the choice of placing the enterprise in question under public or under private management has to be decided by pragmatic considerations of this sort.

[9] In the case of "imaginary" external effects, in which the things enjoyed by other people, or their real income, has psychological effects on a person's welfare—the case familiarly classed under "interdependent utilities"—one may be disinclined to separate an attribute, say, envy, from the functional attributes of the good. One may prefer formally to introduce the expression

$$\sum_{j=1}^{s} v_{kh}^{ij}$$

for any hth good, so attributing to each of the s persons a marginal valuation, positive or negative, arising from person i's consumption of the good and requiring that the sum of these responses be equal to the marginal cost of producing the good.

[10] For completeness we might want to include the omnibus case of an activity k that jointly produces private goods, collective goods, and external effects. If the collective goods are all non-optional, the necessary optimal condition is given by equation (3), with goods $g + 1$ to m including both collective goods and external effects. If, however, some of the collective goods were optional goods, say, those from $g + 1$ to l, this number would have to be summed separately from the remaining $(m - l)$ non-optional collective goods, positive and negative (which, therefore, include external economies and diseconomies). The expression for person 1 is then equal to

$$\sum_{h=1}^{g} v_{kh}^{11} + \sum_{j=1}^{s} \sum_{h=g+1}^{l} v_{kh}^{jj} + \sum_{h=l+1}^{m} v_{kh}^{0j},$$

which must be set equal to the analogous expressions for each of the other persons and equal to c_k.

[11] An expression occasionally met with, to the effect that marginal *social* benefit should be equated to marginal *social* cost, is obviously erroneous.

[12] In a previous paper (Mishan, 1965), I suggested that external effects be said to arise "when relevant effects on production or welfare go wholly or partially unpriced." This definition accords with Pigou's notion of uncompensated services and disservices.

[13] Graaff states that an external effect arises when a firm's production function depends upon the amounts of inputs or outputs of another firm (1957, p. 18), or

353

whenever the shape or position of a man's indifference curves depends upon the activities of other men (1957, p. 43). Buchanan and Stubblebine (1962) argue that an external effect is present whenever A's welfare depends upon the activity of another person B.

[14] Bohm (1964, p. 14) asserts that external factors of production are factors which the firm is not able to control.

REFERENCES

Bohm, Peter. *External Economies in Production.* Stockholm: Almquist & Wiksells, 1964.

Buchanan, J. M. "An Economic Theory of Clubs," *Economica*, XXXII (February, 1965).

Buchanan, J. M., and Stubblebine, W. C. "Externality," *Economica*, XXIX (November, 1962).

Davis, O. A., and Whinston, A. B. "On the Distinction between Public and Private Goods," *A.E.R.*, LVII (May, 1967).

Duesenberry, J. *Income, Saving and the Theory of Consumer Behaviour.* Cambridge, Mass.: Harvard Univ. Press, 1949.

Graaff, J. de V. *Theoretical Welfare Economics.* Cambridge: Cambridge Univ. Press, 1957.

Margolis, J. "A Comment on the Pure Theory of Public Expenditure," *Rev. Econ. and Statis.*, XXXVII (November, 1955).

Mishan, E. J. "Reflections on Recent Developments in the Concept of External Effects," *Canadian J. Econ. and Polit. Sci.*, XXXI (February, 1965).

Samuelson, P. A. "The Pure Theory of Public Expenditure," *Rev. Econ. and Statis.*, XXXVI (November, 1954).

———. "Aspects of Public Expenditure Theories," *Rev. Econ. and Statis.*, XL (November, 1958).